Ethiopia
a country study

Federal Research Division
Library of Congress
Edited by
Thomas P. Ofcansky
and LaVerle Berry
Research Completed
July 1991

On the cover: Largest of the standing obelisks at Aksum, capital of the ancient Aksumite state

Fourth Edition, First Printing, 1993.

Library of Congress Cataloging-in-Publication Data

Ethiopia : a country study / Federal Research Division, Library of
   Congress ; edited by Thomas P. Ofcansky and LaVerle Berry. —
4th ed.
        p.   cm. — (Area handbook series, ISSN 1057-5294)
   (DA pam ; 550-28)
   "Supersedes the 1981 edition of Ethiopia: a country study,
edited by Harold D. Nelson and Irving Kaplan"—T.p. verso.
   "Research completed July 1991."
   Includes bibliographical references (pp. 347-376) and index.
   ISBN 0-8444-0739-9
   1. Ethiopia.   I. Ofcansky, Thomas P., 1947-   . II. Berry,
LaVerle, 1942-   .   III. Library of Congress. Federal Research
Division. IV. Area handbook for Ethiopia. V. Series. VI. Series:
DA pam ; 550-28.
DT373.E83   1993   92-507
963—dc20   CIP

Headquarters, Department of the Army
DA Pam 550-28

For sale by the Superintendent of Documents, U.S. Government Printing Office
Washington, D.C. 20402

Foreword

This volume is one in a continuing series of books prepared by the Federal Research Division of the Library of Congress under the Country Studies/Area Handbook Program sponsored by the Department of the Army. The last page of this book lists the other published studies.

Most books in the series deal with a particular foreign country, describing and analyzing its political, economic, social, and national security systems and institutions, and examining the interrelationships of those systems and the ways they are shaped by cultural factors. Each study is written by a multidisciplinary team of social scientists. The authors seek to provide a basic understanding of the observed society, striving for a dynamic rather than a static portrayal. Particular attention is devoted to the people who make up the society, their origins, dominant beliefs and values, their common interests and the issues on which they are divided, the nature and extent of their involvement with national institutions, and their attitudes toward each other and toward their social system and political order.

The books represent the analysis of the authors and should not be construed as an expression of an official United States government position, policy, or decision. The authors have sought to adhere to accepted standards of scholarly objectivity. Corrections, additions, and suggestions for changes from readers will be welcomed for use in future editions.

Louis R. Mortimer
Chief
Federal Research Division
Library of Congress
Washington, D.C. 20540

Acknowledgments

The authors wish to acknowledge their use and adaptation of information in the 1981 edition of *Ethiopia: A Country Study,* edited by Harold D. Nelson and Irving Kaplan. The authors are also grateful to numerous individuals in various government agencies and private institutions who generously shared their time, expertise, and knowledge about Ethiopia. These people include Paul B. Henze, The Rand Corporation; Thomas L. Kane, Department of Defense; Thomas Collelo, Department of Defense; Carol Boger, Department of Defense; Major Dale R. Endreson, United States Army; and Ralph K. Benesch, who oversees the Country Studies/Area Handbook Program for the Department of the Army. None of these individuals is in any way responsible for the work of the authors, however.

The authors also wish to thank those who contributed directly to the preparation of the manuscript. These include Sandra W. Meditz, who reviewed all textual and graphic materials and served as liaison with the sponsoring agency; Marilyn Majeska, who managed the editing; Vincent Ercolano, who edited the chapters; Joshua Sinai, who helped prepare the manuscript for prepublication review; and Barbara Edgerton, Janie L. Gilchrist, and Izella Watson, who did the word processing. Andrea T. Merrill performed the final prepublication editorial review and managed production. Joan C. Cook compiled the index. Malinda B. Neale of the Library of Congress Printing and Processing Section performed the phototypesetting, under the supervision of Peggy Pixley.

David P. Cabitto provided invaluable graphics support. Harriett R. Blood and Greenhorne and O'Mara prepared the maps, which were drafted by Tim Merrill and reviewed by David P. Cabitto. The charts were prepared by David P. Cabitto and Greenhorne and O'Mara. Wayne Horne deserves special thanks for designing the illustration for the book's cover. Deborah A.V. Clement designed the illustrations for the chapter title pages.

Finally, the authors acknowledge the generosity of the individuals and public and private agencies who allowed their photographs to be used in this study. They are indebted especially to those who contributed work not previously published.

Contents

List of Figures

Preface

This study replaces *Ethiopia: A Country Study,* which was completed in 1980—six years after a group of military officers overthrew Emperor Haile Selassie I and eventually established a Marxist-Leninist dictatorship. In May 1991, this regime, led by Mengistu Haile Mariam, collapsed, largely because of its inability to defeat two insurgencies in the northern part of the country.

This edition of *Ethiopia: A Country Study* examines the revolutionary government's record from 1974 through the fall of the regime in mid-1991. Subsequent events are discussed in the Introduction. Like its predecessor, this study investigates the historical, social, economic, political, and national security forces that helped determine the nature of Ethiopian society. Sources of information used in the study's preparation included scholarly books, journals, and monographs; official reports of governments and international organizations; numerous periodicals; the authors' previous research and observations; and interviews with individuals who have special competence in Ethiopian and African affairs. Chapter bibliographies appear at the end of the book; brief comments on sources recommended for further reading appear at the end of each chapter.

The available materials on Ethiopia frequently presented problems because of the different transliterations of place-names and personal names used by scholars and other writers. No standardized and universally accepted system has been developed for the transliteration of Amharic (the most widely used language in the country), and even the Ethiopian government's official publications vary in their English renderings of proper names. Insofar as possible, the authors have attempted to reduce the confusion with regard to place-names by adhering to the system adopted by the United States Board on Geographic Names (BGN), except that diacritical markings are eliminated in this study. With regard to personal names, the authors have attempted to use the most common English spellings. The authors also have followed the Amharic tradition of referring only to the first element of a name when using it in a second reference. Thus, Mengistu Haile Mariam becomes Mengistu after the first use.

The reader should exercise caution with regard to dates cited in relation to Ethiopia. Dates used in this book generally are according to the standard, Gregorian (Western) calendar. But life in Ethiopia is actually governed by the Ethiopian calendar, which consists of twelve months of thirty days each and one month of five days (six in leap years) running from September 11 to September 10 according to the Gregorian calendar. The sequence of years in the Ethiopian calendar also differs from the Gregorian calendar, running seven years behind the Gregorian calendar at the beginning of an Ethiopian year and seven years behind at its end.

The reader will note the frequent use in this book of double years, such as 1989/90 or 1990/91, especially in Chapters 2 and 3. These dates do not mean that a two-year period is covered. Rather, they reflect the conversion of Ethiopian calendar years to the Gregorian system. When 1990/91 is used, for example, the date refers to September 11, 1990, to September 10, 1991, or the equivalent of the Ethiopian calendar year of 1983. Some economic data are based on the Ethiopian fiscal year, which runs from July 8 to the following July 7 in the Gregorian calendar, but seven years behind the Gregorian year (eight years behind after December 31). Hence, Ethiopian fiscal year 1990/91 (also seen as EFY 1990/91) corresponds to July 11, 1990, to July 10, 1991, or the equivalent of Ethiopian fiscal year 1983. Concerning economic data in general, it must be noted that there has been a dearth of reliable statistics since 1988, reflecting the state of affairs within the Ethiopian government since that date.

All measurements in this study are presented in the metric system. A conversion table is provided to assist those readers who may not be familiar with metric equivalents (see table 1, Appendix). The book also includes a Glossary to explain terms with which the reader may not be familiar.

Finally, readers will note that the body of the text reflects information available as of July 1991. Certain other portions of the text, however, have been updated: the Introduction discusses significant events that have occurred since the information cutoff date; the Country Profile includes updated information as available; and the Bibliography lists recently published sources thought to be particularly helpful to the reader.

Country Profile

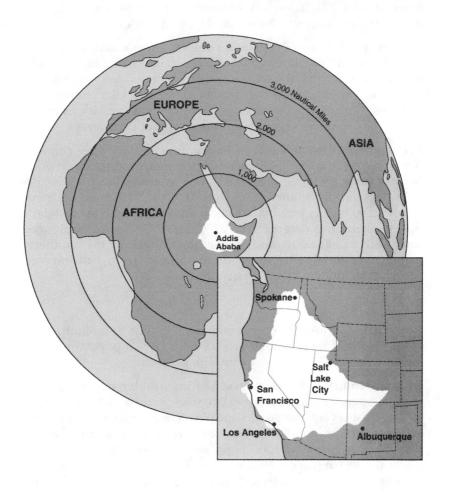

Country

Formal Name: Ethiopia.

Short Form: Ethiopia.

Term for Citizens: Ethiopian(s).

Capital: Addis Ababa.

NOTE—The Country Profile contains updated information as available.

Geography

Size: About 1,221,900 square kilometers; major portion of eastern-most African landmass known as Horn of Africa.

Topography: Massive highland complex of mountains and dissected plateaus divided by Great Rift Valley running generally southwest to northeast and surrounded by lowlands, steppes, or semidesert; northeastern coastline of about 960 kilometers along Red Sea. Great terrain diversity determines wide variations in climate, soils, natural vegetation, and settlement patterns.

Climate: Elevation and geographic location produce three climatic zones: cool zone above 2,400 meters where temperatures range from near freezing to 16°C; temperate zone at elevations of 1,500 to 2,400 meters with temperatures from 16°C to 30°C; and hot zone below 1,500 meters with both tropical and arid conditions and daytime temperatures ranging from 27°C to 50°C. Normal rainy season from mid-June to mid-September (longer in the southern highlands) preceded by intermittent showers from February or March; remainder of year generally dry.

Society

Population: Mid-1992 population estimated at 54 million, with a 3 percent or higher annual growth rate. Urban population estimated at about 11 percent of total population.

Ethnic Groups and Languages: Distinguishable ethnolinguistic entities, some speaking the same language, estimated at more than 100; at least seventy languages spoken as mother tongues. Largest group is the Oromo, with about 40 percent of total population. Roughly 30 percent of total population consists of the Amhara, whose native language—Amharic—is also spoken by additional 20 percent of population as second tongue. Amharic is Ethiopia's official language. The Tigray, speaking Tigrinya, constitute 12 to 15 percent of total population. Large number of smaller groups include Somali, Gurage, Awi, Afar, Welamo, Sidama, and Beja.

Religion: About 50 percent of population Ethiopian Orthodox; Orthodoxy identified mainly with Amhara and Tigray peoples but accepted by other groups as well. About 2 percent Protestant and Roman Catholic combined. Approximately 40 percent adherents of Islam. Remainder of population practiced various indigenous religions.

Education: In 1985/86 (Ethiopian calendar year—see Glossary), 3.1 million children were enrolled in grades one through twelve.

Nearly 2.5 million, or 42 percent of primary school-age children, enrolled in 7,900 primary schools (grades one through six); 363,000 students enrolled in 964 junior secondary schools (grades seven and eight); more than 292,000, or 5.3 percent of secondary school-age children, enrolled in 245 secondary schools (grades nine through twelve). Vocational schools emphasized technical education; in 1985/86 more than 4,200 attended nine technical schools. Intense competition for admission to approximately twelve colleges and universities; more than 18,400 students in various institutions of higher education.

Literacy: Less than 10 percent during imperial regime; had increased to 63 percent by 1984, according to Ethiopian government. Revolutionary government undertook major national literacy campaign, which made significant gains, especially among women.

Health: Malaria and tuberculosis major endemic diseases; also health problems from parasitic and gastroenteritis infections, leprosy, venereal diseases, typhus, typhoid, trachoma, conjunctivitis, and childhood diseases. All complicated by insufficient health facilities, shortage of medical personnel, unsanitary practices, and nutritional deficiencies. Acquired immune deficiency syndrome (AIDS) becoming a greater problem.

Life Expectancy: Fifty years for males and fifty-three for females in 1992.

Economy

Salient Features: Socialist oriented after 1974 revolution, with strong state controls. Thereafter, large part of economy transferred to public sector, including most modern industry and large-scale commercial agriculture, all agricultural land and urban rental property, and all financial institutions; some private enterprise and capital participation permitted in certain sectors. Since mid-1991, a decentralized, market-oriented economy emphasizing individual initiative, designed to reverse a decade of economic decline. In 1993 gradual privatization of business, industry, banking, agriculture, trade, and commerce under way.

Gross Domestic Product (GDP): US$6 billion in 1990; per capita GDP about US$120. Economy grew during late 1970s but declined in early 1980s and stagnated thereafter. GDP in Ethiopian fiscal year (EFY—see Glossary) 1990/91 fell by 5 to 6 percent in real terms, after a 1 percent decline in EFY 1989/90. Agriculture registered modest gains after 1989.

Agriculture and Livestock: Accounted for approximately 40 percent of gross domestic product (GDP), 80 percent of exports, and 80 percent of labor force in 1991; other activities dependent on marketing, processing, and exporting of agricultural products. Production overwhelmingly of subsistence nature with large portion of commodity exports provided by small agricultural monetized sector. Principal crops coffee, pulses, oilseeds, cereals, potatoes, sugarcane, and vegetables. Livestock population believed largest in Africa. Livestock alone accounted for about 15 percent of GDP in 1987.

Industry: Manufacturing severely affected by economic dislocation following revolution. Growth of sector low after 1975. Primary subsectors cement, textiles, food processing, and oil refining. In 1993 smaller enterprises being privatized; larger ones still under state control. Most industry functioning well below capacity.

Energy Sources: Hydroelectric power most important developed and potential source of energy. Domestic mineral fuel resources in 1993 included low-grade lignite and traces of petroleum and natural gas. Potentially important geothermal power exists in Great Rift Valley.

Foreign Trade: Little foreign trade by international standards. Exports almost entirely agricultural commodities; coffee largest foreign exchange earner. Value of imports regularly greater than export receipts. Wide range of trading partners, but most important in 1992 included United States, Germany, Britain, and Japan.

Currency: Birr (pl., birr; no symbol). Prior to October 1, 1992, US$1 equaled 2.07 birr. After devaluation on that date, US$1 equaled 4.94 birr. Significant parallel currency market existed before devaluation.

Transportation and Telecommunications

Roads: Construction of adequate road system greatly hampered by rugged terrain of highlands and normally heavy seasonal rainfall. Approximately 18,000 kilometers of roads in 1991, of which 13,000 kilometers were all-weather roads. Road density lowest in Africa; perhaps three-fourths of farms more than one-half day's walk from an all-weather road.

Railroads: One line operating in 1993 from Addis Ababa to city of Djibouti. Second line from Akordat to Mitsiwa discontinued operation in 1976 because of unprofitability and partly destroyed in later fighting.

xviii

Ports: Two major ports—Aseb and Mitsiwa—both in Eritrea; further access to ocean transport through port of Djibouti; all usable by deep-sea vessels.

Civil Aviation: Important in domestic communications because of underdeveloped state of other means of transportation. International airports at Addis Ababa, Asmera, and Dire Dawa; major airports at a few other towns; remaining airfields little more than landing strips. In 1993 Ethiopian Airlines provided domestic service to some forty-five destinations and international service to Africa, western Europe, India, and China.

Telecommunications: Minimal system. Radio-relay links connected Addis Ababa with Nairobi and Djibouti; other international service via Atlantic Ocean satellite of International Telecommunications Satellite Organization (Intelsat). Limited local telephone service and equipment; four AM radio stations, one shortwave transmitter; television service in ten cities.

Government and Politics

Party and Government: Until 1974 revolution, ruled by an imperial regime whose last emperor was Haile Selassie I. Following revolution, a socialist state based on principles of Marxism-Leninism, led by Workers' Party of Ethiopia. Constitution promulgated in 1987 created People's Democratic Republic of Ethiopia. In theory, National Shengo (National Assembly) highest organ of political power, but real power centered in hands of Mengistu Haile Mariam, president and commander in chief of armed forces.

In May 1991, Mengistu regime overthrown by coalition of forces led by Ethiopian People's Revolutionary Democratic Front (EPRDF). A National Conference in July 1991 created Transitional Government of Ethiopia, consisting of a president and a prime minister, a seventeen-member Council of Ministers, and an eighty-seven-member Council of Representatives. Transitional government to last not longer than two-and-one-half years. Meles Zenawi, former head of EPRDF, elected president by Council of Representatives. In mid-1993 new constitution being drafted to come into force not later than early 1994.

After May 1991, Eritrea controlled by Eritrean People's Liberation Front (EPLF). EPLF set up Provisional Government of Eritrea under its leader, Issaias Afwerki. In a referendum held April 23–25, 1993, more than 98 percent of registered voters favored independence from Ethiopia. In May 1993, Government of Eritrea was formed, consisting of a National Assembly with supreme authority, a State Council with executive powers, and a president. Issaias Afwerki elected president by National Assembly. New government to last not longer than four years, during which a democratic constitution is to be written.

Judicial System: As of mid-1993, new judicial system being established in Ethiopia; judicial system functioning in Eritrea.

Administrative Divisions: In mid-1991 Transitional Government of Ethiopia created twelve autonomous regions on basis of ethnic identity, plus two multiethnic chartered cities (Addis Ababa and Harer). Each region broken into districts (*weredas*), the basic unit of administration. On June 21, 1992, elections were held to fill seats on *wereda* and regional councils.

Foreign Relations: In late 1980s, Ethiopia relied on Soviet Union, Democratic People's Republic of Korea (North Korea), Israel, and various East European countries for military assistance and on Western nations for humanitarian aid and small amounts of economic assistance. After mid-1991, transitional government reoriented Ethiopia's foreign relations from East to West, establishing warm relations with United States and Western Europe and seeking substantial economic aid from Western countries and World Bank. Ethiopia also active in attempts to mediate the civil war in Somalia.

International Agreements and Memberships: Numerous, including Organization of African Unity and United Nations and a number of its specialized agencies, such as World Bank and International Monetary Fund.

National Security

Armed Forces: In mid-1991, combined strength of Ethiopian armed forces about 438,000. Ground forces estimated at 430,000 (including about 200,000 members of People's Militia). Air force estimated at 4,500. Navy estimated at 3,500. After downfall of Mengistu regime, armed forces collapsed and were dismantled by EPRDF. In mid-1993, EPRDF had 100,000 to 120,000 guerrillas under arms; EPLF had between 85,000 and 100,000. Both planned to transform their forces into conventional armies and also to organize air forces and navies.

Combat Units and Major Equipment: Before mid-1991, ground forces organized into five revolutionary armies comprising thirty-one infantry divisions supported by thirty-two tank battalions, forty artillery battalions, twelve air defense battalions, and eight commando brigades. Major weapons systems included T–54/55 and T–62 tanks, various caliber howitzers and guns, antiaircraft guns, and surface-to-air missiles. Air force organized into seven fighter-ground attack squadrons, one transport squadron, and one training squadron. Equipment included 150 combat aircraft. Navy equipment included two frigates and twenty-four patrol and coastal craft.

After downfall of Mengistu government, several insurgent groups, including EPRDF, EPLF, and Oromo Liberation Front, captured a considerable amount of ground equipment; former soldiers sold an unknown quantity of small arms and light equipment throughout Horn of Africa. Naval crews with their vessels and an unknown number of pilots with their aircraft scattered to neighboring countries. Information on military organization, personnel strength, and equipment types and numbers in both Ethiopia and Eritrea unavailable as of mid-1993.

Defense Budget: Estimated at US$472 million in United States fiscal year 1987–88. No figures available for defense expenditures for Ethiopia or Eritrea as of mid-1993.

Police Agencies and Paramilitary Forces: National police included paramilitary Mobile Emergency Police Force, estimated at 9,000. Paramilitary frontier guards. Local law enforcement delegated to civilian paramilitary People's Protection Brigades. As of mid-1993, a national police force functioned throughout Ethiopia. EPLF personnel performed police duties throughout Eritrea.

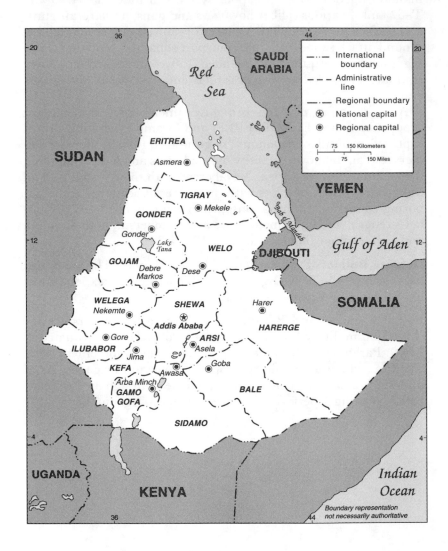

Figure 1. Administrative Divisions of Ethiopia, 1974

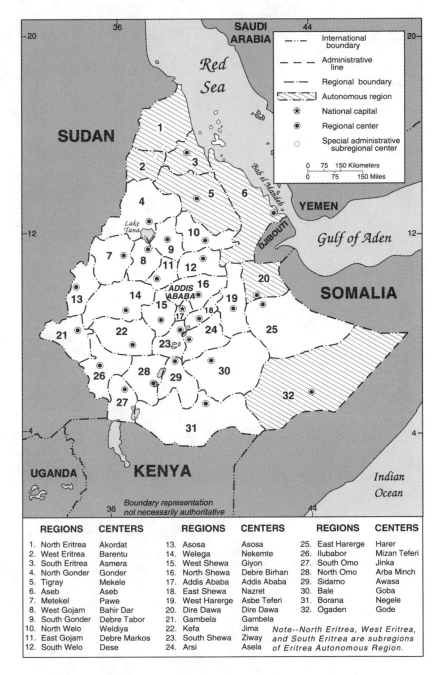

REGIONS	CENTERS	REGIONS	CENTERS	REGIONS	CENTERS
1. North Eritrea	Akordat	13. Asosa	Asosa	25. East Harerge	Harer
2. West Eritrea	Barentu	14. Welega	Nekemte	26. Ilubabor	Mizan Teferi
3. South Eritrea	Asmera	15. West Shewa	Giyon	27. South Omo	Jinka
4. North Gonder	Gonder	16. North Shewa	Debre Birhan	28. North Omo	Arba Minch
5. Tigray	Mekele	17. Addis Ababa	Addis Ababa	29. Sidamo	Awasa
6. Aseb	Aseb	18. East Shewa	Nazret	30. Bale	Goba
7. Metekel	Pawe	19. West Harerge	Asbe Teferi	31. Borana	Negele
8. West Gojam	Bahir Dar	20. Dire Dawa	Dire Dawa	32. Ogaden	Gode
9. South Gonder	Debre Tabor	21. Gambela	Gambela		
10. North Welo	Weldiya	22. Kefa	Jima	Note--North Eritrea, West Eritrea,
11. East Gojam	Debre Markos	23. South Shewa	Ziway	and South Eritrea are subregions
12. South Welo	Dese	24. Arsi	Asela	of Eritrea Autonomous Region.

Source: Based on information from Paul B. Henze, *Ethiopia in 1990: The Revolution Unraveling,*
Santa Monica, California, 1991, 7.

Figure 2. Administrative Divisions of Ethiopia, 1987–91

xxiii

Introduction

FEW AFRICAN COUNTRIES have had such a long, varied, and troubled history as Ethiopia. The Ethiopian state originated in the Aksumite kingdom, a trading state that emerged about the first century A.D. The Askumites perfected a written language; maintained relations with the Byzantine Empire, Egypt, and the Arabs; and, in the mid-fourth century, embraced Christianity. After the rise of Islam in the seventh century, the Aksumite kingdom became internationally isolated as Arabs gradually gained control of maritime trade in the Red Sea. By the early twelfth century, the successors of the Aksumites had expanded southward and had established a new capital and a line of kings called the Zagwe. A new dynasty, the so-called "Solomonic" line, which came to power about 1270, continued this territorial expansion and pursued a more aggressive foreign policy. In addition, this Christian state, with the help of Portuguese soldiers, repelled a near-overpowering Islamic invasion.

Starting about the mid-sixteenth century, the Oromo people, migrating from the southwest, gradually forced their way into the kingdom, most often by warfare. The Oromo, who eventually constituted about 40 percent of Ethiopia's population, possessed their own culture, religion, and political institutions. As the largest national group in Ethiopia, the Oromo significantly influenced the course of the country's history by becoming part of the royal family and the nobility and by joining the army or the imperial government. During the seventeenth and eighteenth centuries, religious and regional rivalries gradually weakened the imperial state until it was little more than a collection of independent and competing fiefdoms.

Ethiopia's modern period (1855 to the present)—represented by the reigns of Tewodros II, Yohannis IV, Menelik II, Zawditu, and Haile Selassie I; by the Marxist regime of Mengistu Haile Mariam; and, since mid-1991, by the Transitional Government of Ethiopia under Meles Zenawi—has been characterized by nation-building as well as by warfare. Tewodros II started the process of recreating a cohesive Ethiopian state by incorporating Shewa into his empire and by suppressing revolts in the country's other provinces. Yohannis IV battled to keep Ethiopia free from foreign domination and to retard the growing power of the Shewan king, Menelik. Eventually, Menelik became emperor and used military force to more than double Ethiopia's size. He also defeated an Italian invasion force that sought to colonize the country.

Struggles over succession to the throne characterized the reign of Zawditu—struggles won by Haile Selassie, the next ruler. After becoming emperor in 1930, Haile Selassie embarked on a nation-wide modernization program. However, the 1935–36 Italo-Ethiopian war halted his efforts and forced him into exile. After returning to Addis Ababa in 1941, Haile Selassie undertook further military and political changes and sought to encourage social and economic development. Although he did initiate a number of fundamental reforms, the emperor was essentially an autocrat, who to a great extent relied on political manipulation and military force to remain in power and to preserve the Ethiopian state. Even after an unsuccessful 1960 coup attempt led by the Imperial Bodyguard, Haile Selassie failed to pursue the political and economic policies necessary to improve the lives of most Ethiopians.

In 1974 a group of disgruntled military personnel overthrew the Ethiopian monarchy. Eventually, Mengistu Haile Mariam, who participated in the coup against Haile Selassie, emerged at the head of a Marxist military dictatorship. Almost immediately, the Mengistu regime unleashed a military and political reign of terror against its real and imagined opponents. It also pursued socialist economic policies that reduced agricultural productivity and helped bring on famine, resulting in the deaths of untold tens of thousands of people. Thousands more fled or perished as a result of government schemes to villagize the peasantry and to relocate peasants from drought-prone areas of the north to better-watered lands in the south and southwest.

Aside from internal dissent, which was harshly suppressed, the regime faced armed insurgencies in the northern part of the country. The longest-running of these was in Eritrea, where the Eritrean People's Liberation Front (EPLF) and its predecessors had been fighting control by the central government since 1961. In the mid-1970s, a second major insurgency arose in Tigray, where the Tigray People's Liberation Front (TPLF), a Marxist-Leninist organization under the leadership of Meles Zenawi, opposed not only the policies of the military government but also the very existence of the government itself.

In foreign affairs, the regime aligned itself with the Soviet Union. As long as the Soviet Union and its allies provided support to Ethiopia's armed forces, the Mengistu government remained secure. In the late 1980s, however, Soviet support waned, a major factor in undermining the ability of government forces to prosecute the wars against the Eritreans and the Tigray. Gradually, the insurgent movements gained the upper hand. By May 1991, the EPLF controlled almost all of Eritrea, and the TPLF, operating as the chief member of a coalition called the Ethiopian People's Revolutionary Democratic Front (EPRDF), had overrun much of the center of the country. Faced with impending defeat, on May 21 Mengistu fled into exile in Zimbabwe; the caretaker government he left behind collapsed a week later. The EPLF completed its sweep of Eritrea on May 24 and 25, and a few days later EPLF chairman Issaias Afwerki announced the formation of the Provisional Government of Eritrea (PGE). Meanwhile, on May 27–28, EPRDF forces marched into Addis Ababa and assumed control of the national government.

After seizing power, Tigrayan and Eritrean leaders confronted an array of political, economic, and security problems that threatened to overwhelm both new governments. Meles Zenawi and Issaias Afwerki committed themselves to resolving these problems and to remaking their respective societies. To achieve these goals, both governments adopted similar strategies, which concentrated on national reconciliation, eventual democratization, good relations with the West, and social and economic development. Each leader, however, pursued different tactics to implement his respective strategy.

The first task facing the new rulers in Addis Ababa was the creation of an interim government. To this end, a so-called National Conference was convened in Addis Ababa from July 1 to July 5. Many political groups from across a broad spectrum were invited to attend, but the EPRDF barred those identified with the former military regime, such as the Workers' Party of Ethiopia and the All-Ethiopia Socialist Movement, as well as those that were opposed to the EPRDF, such as the Ethiopian People's Revolutionary Party and the Coalition of Ethiopian Democratic Forces. A number of international observers also attended, including delegations from the United States, the Soviet Union, and the United Nations (UN).

Although it received accolades for running an open conference, the EPRDF tightly controlled the proceedings. The conference adopted a National Charter, which was signed by representatives of some thirty-one political groups; it established the Transitional Government of Ethiopia (TGE), consisting of executive and legislative branches; and it sanctioned an EPLF–EPRDF agreement that converted Aseb into a free port in exchange for a referendum on Eritrean self-determination to be held within two years. The transitional government was to consist of the offices of president and prime minister and a seventeen-member multiethnic Council of Ministers. To ensure broad political representation, an eighty-seven member Council of Representatives was created, which was to select the new president, draft a new constitution, and oversee a transition to a new national government. The EPRDF occupied thirty-two of the eighty-seven council seats. The Oromo Liberation Front (OLF) received twelve seats, and the TPLF, the Oromo People's Democratic Organization, and the Ethiopian People's Democratic Movement each occupied ten seats. Twenty-seven other groups shared the remaining seats.

The National Charter enshrined the guiding principles for what was expected to be a two-and-one-half-year transitional period. The charter called for creation of a commission to draft a new constitution to come into effect by early 1994. It also committed the transitional government to conduct itself in accordance with the UN Universal Declaration of Human Rights and to pursue a foreign policy based on noninterference in the internal affairs of neighboring states. Perhaps its most significant provisions concerned a new system of internal administration in which the principle of ethnicity was to constitute the basis of local and regional government. The charter recognized the right of all of Ethiopia's nationalities to self-determination, a right that was to be exercised within the context of a federated Ethiopia, and called for creation of district and regional councils on the basis of nationality.

Essentially, the National Conference was a first, basic step in the reconstruction of a viable, legitimate central government. With the end of civil wars all over the country, the aim was to create a balance of competing ethnic and political groups at the center of the state that would allow the wounds of war to heal and economic recovery to begin. Additionally, there was the task of reconciling some segments of the population to the impending loss of Eritrea and of Ethiopia's Red Sea ports.

As the new order got under way, the Council of Representatives elected Meles Zenawi president of the TGE. Then, in order to implement the administrative provisions of the National Charter, the TGE drew up twelve autonomous regions based on ethnic identification and recognized two multiethnic chartered cities—Addis Ababa and Harer. The largest nationalities—the Amhara, Oromo, Somali, and Tigray—were grouped into their own regions, while an attempt was made to put culturally related smaller groups together. Each region was composed of a number of districts (*weredas*), intended to be the basic administrative unit. The largest region—that of the Oromo—contained some 220 *weredas;* the next largest region—that of the Amhara—contained 126, out of a total of 600 *weredas* in all of Ethiopia. Under this system, each *wereda*

*An election official in Dembi Dolo, in Welega, explains procedures
as voters register for district and regional elections, June 1992.*
Courtesy LaVerle Berry

exercised executive, legislative, and judicial authority over local
communities, while the central government remained supreme in
matters of defense, foreign affairs, economic policy, citizenship requirements, and currency.

In order to staff these new administrative units, the TGE scheduled national elections. Originally foreseen for later 1991, these
elections were postponed for administrative and political reasons
into 1992. By then, the authorities had registered almost 200 political parties; few of them, however, had a significant membership or any real influence in shaping government policies. The TGE
held preliminary elections for local governing committees beginning in April and for *wereda* and regional councils on June 21, 1992.

Security problems prevented elections from being held in some
areas, notably among the Afar and the Somali and in Harer. More
important, a corps of some 250 UN observers concluded that the
June elections suffered from a number of serious shortcomings,
including an absence of genuine competition, intimidation of nongovernment parties and candidates, closure of political party offices,
and jailing and even shooting of candidates. Numerous observers
also claimed that various administrative and logistical problems
impaired the electoral process and that many Ethiopians failed to

understand the nature of multiparty politics. As a result, several political parties, including the OLF, the All-Amhara People's Organization, and the Gideo People's Democratic Organization, withdrew a few days before the elections. On June 22, the OLF withdrew from the government and prepared to take up arms once again. Nonetheless, the TGE accepted the results of the elections, although it appointed a commission to investigate irregularities and to take corrective steps.

In the economic arena, the TGE inherited a shattered country. In his first public speech after the EPRDF had captured Addis Ababa, Meles Zenawi indicated that Ethiopia's coffers were empty; moreover, some 7 million people were threatened with starvation because of drought and civil war. Economic performance statistics reflected this gloomy assessment. In Ethiopian fiscal year (EFY—see Glossary) 1990/91, for example, the gross domestic product (GDP—see Glossary) declined by 5.6 percent, the greatest fall since the 1984–85 drought. Preliminary figures indicated a further decline in GDP in EFY 1991/92, although some gains were registered for agriculture.

To resolve these problems, the TGE abandoned the failed policies of the Mengistu regime. It began dismantling the country's command economic system and shifted toward a market-oriented economy with emphasis on private initiative. In December 1992, it adopted a new economic policy whereby the government would maintain control over essential economic sectors such as banking, insurance, petroleum, mining, and chemical industries. However, retail trade, road transport, and a portion of foreign trade were placed in private hands; and farmers could sell their produce at free-market prices, although land remained under government control. While smaller businesses were to be privatized, agriculture was to receive the most attention and investment. By 1993 the state farms of the Mengistu era were being dismantled and turned over to private farmers; similarly, the agricultural cooperatives of prior years had almost all disappeared. A major effort was also being made to steer large numbers of ex-soldiers into farming as a way of increasing production and of providing much-needed employment.

Meanwhile, on October 1, 1992, the TGE devalued Ethiopia's currency to encourage exports and to aid in correcting a chronic balance of payments deficit. The country had in addition begun to receive economic aid from several sources, including the European Community, the World Bank (see Glossary), Japan, Canada, and the United States. Developments such as these provided a solid foundation for future economic improvement—gains that in mid-1993 were still very much in the realm of anticipation. It seemed clear that Ethiopia would remain one of the world's poorest nations for the foreseeable future.

Since the downfall of the Mengistu regime, Ethiopia's human rights record has improved. At the same time, the TGE has failed to end human rights abuses. In the absence of a police force, the TGE delegated policing functions to the EPRDF and to so-called Peace and Stability Committees. On occasion, personnel belonging to these organizations were alleged to have killed, wounded, or tortured criminal suspects. There were also allegations of extrajudicial killings in many areas of the country.

Several incidents in early 1993 raised further questions about human rights in Ethiopia. On January 4, security forces opened fire on university students protesting UN and EPRDF policies toward Eritrea and the upcoming independence referendum. At least one person, and possibly several others, died during the fracas. In early April, the Council of Representatives suspended five southern political parties from council membership for having attended a conference in Paris at which the parties criticized the security situation in the country and the entire transitional process. A few days later, on April 9, more than forty instructors at Addis Ababa University were summarily dismissed. The TGE alleged lack of attention to teaching duties as the reason for its action, but the instructors asserted that they were being punished for having spoken out against TGE policies. These developments came on top of United States Department of State allegations that more than 2,000 officials of the Mengistu regime remained in detention without having been charged after almost twenty months.

One of the most serious dilemmas confronting the TGE concerned its inability to restore security throughout Ethiopia. After the EPRDF assumed power, it dismantled the 440,000-member Ethiopian armed forces. As a result, several hundred thousand ex-military personnel had to fend for themselves. The government's inability to find jobs for these soldiers forced many of them to resort to crime as a way of life. Many of these ex-soldiers contributed to the instability in Addis Ababa and parts of southern, eastern, and western Ethiopia.

To help resolve these problems, the TGE created the Commission for the Rehabilitation of Ex-Soldiers and War Veterans. By mid-1993 this organization claimed that it had assisted in the rehabilitation of more than 159,000 ex-soldiers in various rural areas. Additionally, commission officials maintained that they were continuing to provide aid to 157,000 ex-soldiers who lived in various urban centers.

Apart from the difficulties caused by former soldiers and criminal elements, several insurgent groups hampered the TGE's ability to maintain stability in eastern and western Ethiopia. The situation was particularly troublesome with the OLF. For example, in mid-1991 government forces clashed with OLF units southwest of Dire Dawa over the rights to collect qat revenues. (Qat is a plant that produces a mild narcotic intoxication when chewed and that is consumed throughout the eastern Horn of Africa and in Yemen.) Although the two groups signed a peace agreement in August, tensions still existed, and fighting continued around Dire Dawa and Harer at year's end. In early 1992, EPRDF–OLF relations continued to deteriorate, with armed clashes occurring at several locations throughout eastern and western Ethiopia. After the OLF withdrew from the elections and the government in late June, full-scale fighting broke out in the south and southwest, but OLF forces were too weak to sustain the effort for more than a few weeks. Even so, in April 1993 the OLF announced that it was once again expanding its operations, but many observers doubted this claim and the OLF's ability to launch effective military campaigns against government forces.

The TGE also experienced problems with the Afar pastoralists who inhabit the lowlands along Ethiopia's Red Sea coast, particularly during its first year in power. In early September 1991, some Afar attacked a food relief truck column near the town of Mile on the Addis Ababa-Aseb road and killed at least seven drivers. The EPRDF restored security in this region by shooting armed Afar on sight. Since then, EPRDF-Afar relations have remained tense. Some Afar have associated themselves with the OLF, but many others joined the Afar Liberation Front, which by early 1993 claimed to have 2,500 members under arms.

Elsewhere in eastern Ethiopia, the TGE experienced problems with the Isa and Gurgura Liberation Front (IGLF). On October 4, 1991, clashes between government forces and IGLF rebels resulted in the temporary closure of the Addis Ababa-Djibouti railroad near Dire Dawa and the disruption of trade between the two countries. The fighting also disrupted famine relief distribution to nearly 1 million refugees in eastern Ethiopia. By early 1992, the IGLF still had refused to recognize the EPRDF's right to maintain security in the Isa-populated area around Dire Dawa. By 1993, nonetheless, improved conditions allowed the Addis Ababa-Djibouti railroad to operate on a fairly regular basis.

In western Ethiopia, during the July–September 1991 period, the EPRDF engaged in several battles in Gojam and Gonder with the Ethiopian People's Revolutionary Party, the only major political group excluded from power. Additionally, in Gambela, the EPRDF battled the Gambela People's Liberation Front, which claimed the right to administer Gambela without EPRDF interference. The downfall of the Mengistu regime also created a crisis for approximately 500,000 southern Sudanese who lived in refugee camps in and around Gambela. Although the new government claimed they could remain in Ethiopia, nearly all of the refugees, fearing reprisals for belonging to or supporting southern Sudanese insurgents that the EPRDF opposed, fled toward southern Sudan. As a result, by early 1992 fewer than 15,000 Sudanese refugees remained in western Ethiopia.

In southern Ethiopia, crime was the main security problem. In late March 1992, EPRDF troops reportedly arrested 1,705 armed bandits and captured thousands of weapons, including machine guns and rocket-propelled grenades. Despite this and similar sweeps, many Western observers believed that security problems would continue to plague the EPRDF regime for the foreseeable future because of the large number of available arms and unemployed ex-fighters in the south.

In contrast with the political divisiveness in Ethiopia, nearly all Eritreans appeared to support the EPLF and its goals. As a result, in the first two years after military victory, the PGE was able to move swiftly on a number of fronts. As one of its first acts, the new government expelled thousands of soldiers and personnel of the former Ethiopian army and government in Eritrea, together with their dependents, forcing them across the border into Tigray. The PGE maintained that the expulsions were necessary to free up living quarters and jobs for returning Eritreans and to help reduce budgetary outlays. In October 1992, the government opened schools across Eritrea. A few weeks later, the PGE announced new criminal and civil codes and appointed dozens of judges to run the court system. A National Service Decree made it mandatory for all Eritreans between the ages of eighteen and forty to perform twelve to eighteen months of unpaid service in the armed forces, police, government, or in fields such as education or health.

Perhaps most important, the PGE honored the agreement it had reached with the EPRDF and the OLF in 1991 to postpone a referendum on the question of Eritrean independence for two years. By early 1993, given the general popularity of the PGE and the desire among Eritreans to be free of control from Addis Ababa, the outcome of the referendum was a foregone conclusion. On April 23–25, 1993, the PGE carried out the poll. In a turnout of 98.5 percent of the approximately 1.1 million registered voters, 99.8 percent voted for independence. A 121-member UN observer mission certified that the referendum was free and fair. Within hours, the

United States, Egypt, Italy, and Sudan extended diplomatic recognition to the new country. Thereafter, Eritrea joined the UN, the Organization of Africa Unity, and the Lomé Convention (see Glossary).

A month after the referendum, the EPLF transformed the PGE into the Government of Eritrea, composed of executive, legislative, and judicial branches. Supreme power resided with a new National Assembly, composed of the EPLF's former central committee augmented by sixty additional representatives from the ten provinces into which Eritrea was divided. Aside from formulating internal and external policies and budgetary matters, the assembly was charged with electing a president, who would be head of state and commander in chief of the armed forces. The executive branch consisted of a twenty-four-member State Council, chaired by the president. The judiciary, already in place, continued as before. At its initial meeting on May 21, the assembly elected Issaias Afwerki president. This new political configuration was to last not longer than four years, during which time a democratic constitution was to be drafted and all members of the EPLF would continue to work for the state without salary.

In the months following independence, the Eritrean government enjoyed almost universal popular support. Even such former adversaries as the Eritrean Liberation Front (ELF), the Eritrean Liberation Front-United Organization, and the Eritrean Liberation Front-Revolutionary Council issued statements of support for the referendum and for the new regime. During his first press conference after the referendum, President Issaias stressed that his government would pursue pragmatic and flexible policies. He also discussed prospects for close economic cooperation with Ethiopia and raised the prospect of a future confederation between the two countries. Meanwhile, the president pledged that Aseb would remain a free port for goods in transit to Ethiopia. Additionally, he reaffirmed the EPLF's commitment to the eventual establishment of a multiparty political system, but there would be no political parties based on ethnicity or religion.

Its popularity notwithstanding, the Eritrean government faced many problems and an uncertain future. Economically, the country suffered from the devastation of thirty years of war. Eritrea's forty publicly owned factories operated at no more than one-third capacity, and many of its more than 600 private companies had ceased operations. War damage and drought had caused agricultural production to decline by as much as 40 percent in some areas; as a result, about 80 percent of the population required food aid in 1992. The fighting also had wrecked schools, hospitals, government offices, roads, and bridges throughout the country, while

*A jubilant crowd in Asmera celebrates results of the
independence referendum, April 1993.
Courtesy Paul B. Henze*

bombing had destroyed economically important towns like Mitsiwa
and Nakfa.

To resolve these problems, Eritrea implemented a multifaceted
strategy that concentrated on restarting basic economic activities
and rehabilitating essential infrastructure; encouraging the return
and reintegration of nearly 500,000 Eritrean refugees from neighboring Sudan; and establishing the Recovery and Rehabilitation
Project for Eritrea. Additionally, the Eritrean government reaffirmed its commitment to a liberal investment code, the response
to which by mid-1993 was encouraging. Even so, the Eritrean
government estimated that it needed at least US$2 billion to re-
habilitate the economy and to finance development programs—
aid that it sought largely from Western countries and financial institutions.

Another serious issue confronting the new government concerned
the status of the country's armed forces. Since the country's liberation in 1991, the government had lacked the funds to pay salaries.
Nevertheless, officials adopted a compulsory national service act that
required all former fighters to labor without pay for two years on
various public works projects. When the new Government of Eritrea
extended unpaid compulsory national service for an additional four

years on May 20, 1993, thousands of frustrated former fighters who wanted to be paid and to return at last to their families demonstrated in Asmera. The government responded by promising to begin paying the fighters and by instituting a military demobilization program that would allow volunteers who could fend for themselves to return to their homes.

Eritrea's long-term well-being also depended on President Issaias's ability to preserve the country's unity. Achieving this goal will be difficult. Eritrea's 3.5 million population is split equally between Christians and Muslims; it also is divided into nine ethnic groups, each of which speaks a different language. A reemergence of the historical divisions between the Muslim-dominated ELF and the largely Christian EPLF is possible and could prove to be the young country's undoing. Also, at least some Eritreans doubted President Issaias's pledge to establish a multiparty democracy and viewed with skepticism his determination to prevent the establishment of political parties based on ethnic group or religion. However, as of late 1993, Eritrea remained at peace, and the government enjoyed considerable support. As a result, most Western observers maintained that the country had a good chance of avoiding the turbulence that has plagued much of the rest of the Horn of Africa.

The ultimate fates of Ethiopia and Eritrea are inevitably intertwined. For economic reasons, Ethiopia needs to preserve its access to Eritrean ports, and Eritrea needs food from Ethiopia as well as the revenue and jobs that will be generated by acting as a transshipment point for Ethiopian goods. Also, political and military cooperation will be necessary to prevent conflict between the two nations.

Despite this obvious interdependence, Ethiopia and Eritrea face a difficult future. Many Ethiopians, primarily those who are Amhara, and some Eritreans, largely from the Muslim community, remain opposed to Eritrean independence and the EPLF-dominated government. These malcontents could become a catalyst for antigovernment activities in both countries. Within Ethiopia, the TGE's concept of ethnicity as the basis for organizing political life has aroused controversy and has stymied many of the TGE's policies and programs, thereby reducing chances for the emergence of a democratic government. Additionally, if the EPRDF does not broaden its ethnic base of support and bring such groups as the Amhara and the Oromo into the political process, the likelihood of violence will increase. As of late 1993, it was unclear whether the TGE's plans for a new constitution and national government would resolve these problems or would founder on the shoals of ethnic politics and economic despair.

September 10, 1993   Thomas P. Ofcansky

Chapter 1. Historical Setting

Ethiopian Orthodox cathedral at Aksum, built in the seventeenth century

MODERN ETHIOPIA IS THE PRODUCT of many millennia of interaction among peoples in and around the Ethiopian highlands region. From the earliest times, these groups combined to produce a culture that at any given time differed markedly from that of surrounding peoples. The evolution of this early "Ethiopian" culture was driven by a variety of ethnic, linguistic, and religious groups.

One of the most significant influences on the formation and evolution of culture in northern Ethiopia consisted of migrants from Southwest Arabia. They arrived during the first millennium B.C. and brought Semitic speech, writing, and a distinctive stone-building tradition to northern Ethiopia. They seem to have contributed directly to the rise of the Aksumite kingdom, a trading state that prospered in the first centuries of the Christian era and that united the shores of the southern Red Sea commercially and at times politically. It was an Aksumite king who accepted Christianity in the mid-fourth century, a religion that the Aksumites bequeathed to their successors along with their concept of an empire-state under centralized rulership.

The establishment of what became the Ethiopian Orthodox Church was critical in molding Ethiopian culture and identity. The spread of Islam to the coastal areas of the Horn of Africa in the eighth century, however, led to the isolation of the highlands from European and Middle Eastern centers of Christendom. The appearance of Islam was partly responsible for what became a long-term rivalry between Christians and Muslims—a rivalry that exacerbated older tensions between highlanders and lowlanders and agriculturalists and pastoralists that have persisted to the present day.

Kingship and Orthodoxy, both with their roots in Aksum, became the dominant institutions among the northern Ethiopians in the post-Aksumite period. In the twelfth and thirteenth centuries, a dynasty known as the Zagwe ruled from their capital in the northern highlands. The Zagwe era is one of the most artistically creative periods in Ethiopian history, involving among other things the carving of a large number of rock-hewn churches.

The Zagwe heartland was well south of the old Aksumite domain, and the Zagwe interlude was but one phase in the long-term southward shift of the locus of political power. The successors of the Zagwe after the mid-thirteenth century—the members of the so-called "Solomonic" dynasty—located themselves in the central

3

highlands and involved themselves directly in the affairs of neighboring peoples still farther south and east.

In these regions, the two dominant peoples of what may be termed the "Christian kingdom of Ethiopia," the Amhara of the central highlands and the Tigray of the northern highlands, confronted the growing power and confidence of Muslim peoples who lived between the eastern edge of the highlands and the Red Sea and Gulf of Aden. In religious and ethnic conflicts that reached their climax in the mid-sixteenth century, the Amhara and Tigray turned back a determined Muslim advance with Portuguese assistance, but only after the northern highlands had been overrun and devastated. The advent of the Portuguese in the area marked the end of the long period of isolation from the rest of Christendom that had been near total, except for contact with the Coptic Church of Egypt. The Portuguese, however, represented a mixed blessing, for with them they brought their religion—Roman Catholicism. During the early seventeenth century, Jesuit and kindred orders sought to impose Catholicism on Ethiopia, an effort that led to civil war and the expulsion of the Catholics from the kingdom.

By the mid-sixteenth century, the Oromo people of southwestern Ethiopia had begun a prolonged series of migrations during which they overwhelmed the Muslim states to the east and began settling in the central highlands. A profound consequence of the far-flung settlement of the Oromo was the fusion of their culture in some areas with that of the heretofore dominant Amhara and Tigray.

The period of trials that resulted from the Muslim invasions, the Oromo migrations, and the challenge of Roman Catholicism had drawn to a close by the middle of the seventeenth century. During the next two-and-one-half centuries, a reinvigorated Ethiopian state slowly reconsolidated its control over the northern highlands and eventually resumed expansion to the south, this time into lands occupied by the Oromo.

By the mid-nineteenth century, the Ethiopian state under Emperor Tewodros II (reigned 1855–68) found itself beset by a number of problems, many of them stemming from the expansion of European influence in northeastern Africa. Tewodros's successors, Yohannis IV (reigned 1872–89) and Menelik II (reigned 1889–1913), further expanded and consolidated the state, fended off local enemies, and dealt with the encroachments of European powers, in particular Italy, France, and Britain. Italy posed the greatest threat, having begun to colonize part of what would become its future colony of Eritrea in the mid-1880s.

To one of Menelik's successors, Haile Selassie I (reigned 1930–74), was left the task of dealing with resurgent Italian expansionism.

The disinclination of the world powers, especially those in the League of Nations, to counter Italy's attack on Ethiopia in 1935 was in many ways a harbinger of the indecisiveness that would lead to World War II. In the early years of the war, Ethiopia was retaken from the Italians by the British, who continued to dominate the country's external affairs after the war ended in 1945. A restored Haile Selassie attempted to implement reforms and modernize the state and certain sectors of the economy. For the most part, however, mid-twentieth century Ethiopia resembled what could loosely be termed a "feudal" society.

The later years of Haile Selassie's rule saw a growing insurgency in Eritrea, which had been federated with and eventually annexed by the Ethiopian government following World War II. This insurgency, along with other internal pressures, including severe famine, placed strains on Ethiopian society that contributed in large part to the 1974 military rebellion that ended the Haile Selassie regime and, along with it, more than 2,000 years of imperial rule. The most salient results of the coup d'état were the eventual emergence of Lieutenant Colonel Mengistu Haile Mariam as head of state and the reorientation of the government and national economy from capitalism to Marxism.

A series of crises immediately consumed the revolutionary regime. First, domestic political violence erupted as groups maneuvered to take control of the revolution. Then, the Eritrean insurgency flared at the same time that an uprising in the neighboring region of Tigray began. In mid-1977 Somalia, intent upon wresting control of the Ogaden region from Ethiopia and sensing Addis Ababa's distractions, initiated a war on Ethiopia's eastern frontier. Mengistu, in need of military assistance, turned to the Soviet Union and its allies, who supplied vast amounts of equipment and thousands of Cuban combat troops, which enabled Ethiopia to repulse the Somali invasion.

Misery mounted throughout Ethiopia in the 1980s. Recurrent drought and famine, made worse in the north by virtual civil war, took an enormous human toll, necessitating the infusion of massive amounts of international humanitarian aid. The insurgencies in Eritrea, Tigray, and other regions intensified until by the late 1980s they threatened the stability of the regime. Drought, economic mismanagement, and the financial burdens of war ravaged the economy. At the same time, democratic reform in Eastern Europe and the Soviet Union threatened to isolate the revolutionary government politically, militarily, and economically from its allies.

5

Origins and the Early Periods
Early Populations and Neighboring States

Details on the origins of all the peoples that make up the population of highland Ethiopia were still matters for research and debate in the early 1990s. Anthropologists believe that East Africa's Great Rift Valley is the site of humankind's origins. (The valley traverses Ethiopia from southwest to northeast.) In 1974 archaeologists excavating sites in the Awash River valley discovered 3.5-million-year-old fossil skeletons, which they named *Australopithecus afarensis*. These earliest known hominids stood upright, lived in groups, and had adapted to living in open areas rather than in forests.

Coming forward to the late Stone Age, recent research in historical linguistics—and increasingly in archaeology as well—has begun to clarify the broad outlines of the prehistoric populations of present-day Ethiopia. These populations spoke languages that belong to the Afro-Asiatic super-language family, a group of related languages that includes Omotic, Cushitic, and Semitic, all of which are found in Ethiopia today. Linguists postulate that the original home of the Afro-Asiatic cluster of languages was somewhere in northeastern Africa, possibly in the area between the Nile River and the Red Sea in modern Sudan. From here the major languages of the family gradually dispersed at different times and in different directions—these languages being ancestral to those spoken today in northern and northeastern Africa and far southwestern Asia.

The first language to separate seems to have been Omotic, at a date sometime after 13,000 B.C. Omotic speakers moved southward into the central and southwestern highlands of Ethiopia, followed at some subsequent time by Cushitic speakers, who settled in territories in the northern Horn of Africa, including the northern highlands of Ethiopia. The last language to separate was Semitic, which split from Berber and ancient Egyptian, two other Afro-Asiatic languages, and migrated eastward into far southwestern Asia.

By about 7000 B.C. at the latest, linguistic evidence indicates that both Cushitic speakers and Omotic speakers were present in Ethiopia. Linguistic diversification within each group thereafter gave rise to a large number of new languages. In the case of Cushitic, these include Agew in the central and northern highlands and, in regions to the east and southeast, Saho, Afar, Somali, Sidamo, and Oromo, all spoken by peoples who would play major roles in the subsequent history of the region. Omotic also spawned a large number of languages, Welamo (often called Wolayta) and

Gemu-Gofa being among the most widely spoken of them, but Omotic speakers would remain outside the main zone of ethnic interaction in Ethiopia until the late nineteenth century.

Both Cushitic- and Omotic-speaking peoples collected wild grasses and other plants for thousands of years before they eventually domesticated those they most preferred. According to linguistic and limited archaeological analyses, plough agriculture based on grain cultivation was established in the drier, grassier parts of the northern highlands by at least several millennia before the Christian era. Indigenous grasses such as teff (see Glossary) and eleusine were the initial domesticates; considerably later, barley and wheat were introduced from Southwest Asia. The corresponding domesticate in the better watered and heavily forested southern highlands was ensete, a root crop known locally as false banana. All of these early peoples also kept domesticated animals, including cattle, sheep, goats, and donkeys. Thus, from the late prehistoric period, agricultural patterns of livelihood were established that were to be characteristic of the region through modern times. It was the descendants of these peoples and cultures of the Ethiopian region who at various times and places interacted with successive waves of migrants from across the Red Sea. This interaction began well before the modern era and has continued through contemporary times.

During the first millennium B.C. and possibly even earlier, various Semitic-speaking groups from Southwest Arabia began to cross the Red Sea and settle along the coast and in the nearby highlands. These migrants brought with them their Semitic speech (Sabaean and perhaps others) and script (Old Epigraphic South Arabic) and monumental stone architecture. A fusion of the newcomers with the indigenous inhabitants produced a culture known as pre-Aksumite. The factors that motivated this settlement in the area are not known, but to judge from subsequent history, commercial activity must have figured strongly. The port city of Adulis, near modern-day Mitsiwa, was a major regional entrepôt and probably the main gateway to the interior for new arrivals from Southwest Arabia. Archaeological evidence indicates that by the beginning of the Christian era this pre-Aksumite culture had developed western and eastern regional variants. The former, which included the region of Aksum, was probably the polity or series of polities that became the Aksumite state.

The Aksumite State

The Aksumite state emerged at about the beginning of the Christian era, flourished during the succeeding six or seven centuries,

7

and underwent prolonged decline from the eighth to the twelfth century A.D. Aksum's period of greatest power lasted from the fourth through the sixth century. Its core area lay in the highlands of what is today southern Eritrea, Tigray, Lasta (in present-day Welo), and Angot (also in Welo); its major centers were at Aksum and Adulis. Earlier centers, such as Yeha, also continued to flourish. At the kingdom's height, its rulers held sway over the Red Sea coast from Sawakin in present-day Sudan in the north to Berbera in present-day Somalia in the south, and inland as far as the Nile Valley in modern Sudan. On the Arabian side of the Red Sea, the Aksumite rulers at times controlled the coast and much of the interior of modern Yemen. During the sixth and seventh centuries, the Aksumite state lost its possessions in Southwest Arabia and much of its Red Sea coastline and gradually shrank to its core area, with the political center of the state shifting farther and farther southward.

Inscriptions from Aksum and elsewhere date from as early as the end of the second century A.D. and reveal an Aksumite state that already had expanded at the expense of neighboring peoples. The Greek inscriptions of King Zoskales (who ruled at the end of the second century A.D.) claim that he conquered the lands to the south and southwest of what is now Tigray and controlled the Red Sea coast from Sawakin south to the present-day Djibouti and Berbera areas. The Aksumite state controlled parts of Southwest Arabia as well during this time, and subsequent Aksumite rulers continually involved themselves in the political and military affairs of Southwest Arabia, especially in what is now Yemen. Much of the impetus for foreign conquest lay in the desire to control the maritime trade between the Roman Empire and India and adjoining lands. Indeed, King Zoskales is mentioned by name in the *Periplus of the Erythrean Sea* (the Latin term for the Red Sea is Mare Erythreum), a Greek shipping guide of the first to third centuries A.D., as promoting commerce with Rome, Arabia, and India. Among the African commodities that the Aksumites exported were gold, rhinoceros horn, ivory, incense, and obsidian; in return, they imported cloth, glass, iron, olive oil, and wine.

During the third and fourth centuries, the traditions related to Aksumite rule became fixed. Gedara, who lived in the late second and early third centuries, is referred to as the king of Aksum in inscriptions written in Gi'iz (also seen as Ge'ez), the Semitic language of the Aksumite kingdom. The growth of imperial traditions was concurrent with the expansion of foreign holdings, especially in Southwest Arabia in the late second century A.D. and later in areas west of the Ethiopian highlands, including the kingdom of Meroë.

Meroë was centered on the Nile north of the confluence of the White Nile and Blue Nile. Established by the sixth century B.C. or earlier, the kingdom's inhabitants were black Africans who were heavily influenced by Egyptian culture. It was probably the people of Meroë who were the first to be called *Aithiopiai* ("burnt faces") by the ancient Greeks, thus giving rise to the term *Ethiopia* that considerably later was used to designate the northern highlands of the Horn of Africa and its inhabitants. No evidence suggests that Meroë had any political influence over the areas included in modern Ethiopia; economic influence is harder to gauge because ancient commercial networks in the area were probably extensive and involved much long-distance trade.

Sometime around A.D. 300, Aksumite armies conquered Meroë or forced its abandonment. By the early fourth century A.D., King Ezana (reigned 325–60) controlled a domain extending from Southwest Arabia across the Red Sea west to Meroë and south from Sawakin to the southern coast of the Gulf of Aden. As an indication of the type of political control he exercised, Ezana, like other Aksumite rulers, carried the title *negusa nagast* (king of kings), symbolic of his rule over numerous tribute-paying principalities and a title used by successive Ethiopian rulers into the mid-twentieth century.

The Aksumites created a civilization of considerable distinction. They devised an original architectural style and employed it in stone palaces and other public buildings. They also erected a series of carved stone stelae at Aksum as monuments to their deceased rulers. Some of these stelae are among the largest known from the ancient world. The Aksumites left behind a body of written records, that, although not voluminous, are nonetheless a legacy otherwise bequeathed only by Egypt and Meroë among ancient African kingdoms. These records were written in two languages—Gi'iz and Greek. Gi'iz is assumed to be ancestral to modern Amharic and Tigrinya, although possibly only indirectly. Greek was also widely used, especially for commercial transactions with the Hellenized world of the eastern Mediterranean. Even more remarkable and wholly unique for ancient Africa was the minting of coins over an approximately 300-year period. These coins, many with inlay of gold on bronze or silver, provide a chronology of the rulers of Aksum.

One of the most important contributions the Aksumite state made to Ethiopian tradition was the establishment of the Christian Church. The Aksumite state and its forebears had certainly been in contact with Judaism since the first millennium B.C. and with Christianity beginning in the first century A.D. These interactions probably were rather limited. However, during the second and third centuries, Christianity spread throughout the region. Around A.D. 330–40, Ezana was converted to Christianity and made it the official state religion. The variant of Christianity adopted by the Aksumite state, however, eventually followed the Monophysite belief, which embraced the notion of one rather than two separate natures in the person of Christ as defined by the Council of Chalcedon in 451 (see Ethiopian Orthodox Christianity, ch. 2).

Little is known about fifth-century Aksum, but early in the next century Aksumite rulers reasserted their control over Southwest Arabia, although only for a short time. Later in the sixth century, however, Sassanian Persians established themselves in Yemen, effectively ending any pretense of Aksumite control. Thereafter, the Sassanians attacked Byzantine Egypt, further disrupting Aksumite trade networks in the Red Sea area. Over the next century and a half, Aksum was increasingly cut off from its overseas entrepôts and as a result entered a period of prolonged decline, gradually relinquishing its maritime trading network and withdrawing into the interior of northern Ethiopia.

Ethiopia and the Early Islamic Period

The rise of Islam in the Arabian Peninsula had a significant impact on Aksum during the seventh and eighth centuries. By the time of the Prophet Muhammad's death (A.D. 632), the Arabian Peninsula, and thus the entire opposite shore of the Red Sea, had come under the influence of the new religion. The steady advance of the faith of Muhammad through the next century resulted in Islamic conquest of all of the former Sassanian Empire and most of the former Byzantine dominions.

Despite the spread of Islam by conquest elsewhere, the Islamic state's relations with Aksum were not hostile at first. According to Islamic tradition, some members of Muhammad's family and some of his early converts had taken refuge with the Aksumites during the troubled years preceding the Prophet's rise to power, and Aksum was exempted from the jihad, or holy war, as a result. The Arabs also considered the Aksumite state to be on a par with the Islamic state, the Byzantine Empire, and China as one of the world's greatest kingdoms. Commerce between Aksum and at least some ports on the Red Sea continued, albeit on an increasingly reduced scale.

Problems between Aksum and the new Arab power, however, soon developed. The establishment of Islam in Egypt and the Levant greatly reduced Aksum's relations with the major Christian power, the Byzantine Empire. Although contact with individual Christian churches in Egypt and other lands continued, the Muslim conquests hastened the isolation of the church in Aksum. Limited communication continued, the most significant being with the Coptic Church in Egypt, which supplied a patriarch to the Aksumites. Such contacts, however, were insufficient to counter an ever-growing ecclesiastical isolation. Perhaps more important, Islamic expansion threatened Aksum's maritime contacts, already under siege by Sassanian Persians. Red Sea and Indian Ocean trade, formerly dominated by the Byzantine Empire, Aksum, and Persia, gradually came under the control of Muslim Arabs, who also propagated their faith through commercial activities and other contacts.

Aksum lost its maritime trade routes during and after the mid-seventh century, by which time relations with the Arabs had deteriorated to the point that Aksumite and Muslim fleets raided and skirmished in the Red Sea. This situation led eventually to the Arab occupation of the Dahlak Islands, probably in the early eighth century and, it appears, to an attack on Adulis and the Aksumite fleet. Later, Muslims occupied Sawakin and converted the Beja people of that region to Islam.

By the middle of the ninth century, Islam had spread to the southern coast of the Gulf of Aden and the coast of East Africa, and the foundations were laid for the later extensive conversions of the local populace to Islam in these and adjacent regions. East of the central highlands, a Muslim sultanate, Ifat, was established by the beginning of the twelfth century, and some of the surrounding Cushitic peoples were gradually converted. These conversions of peoples to the south and southeast of the highlands who had previously practiced local religions were generally brought about by the proselytizing efforts of Arab merchants. This population, permanently Islamicized, thereafter contended with the Amhara-Tigray peoples for control of the Horn of Africa.

The Zagwe Dynasty

In response to Islamic expansion in the Red Sea area and the loss of their seaborne commercial network, the Aksumites turned their attention to the colonizing of the northern Ethiopian highlands. The Agew peoples, divided into a number of groups, inhabited the central and northern highlands, and it was these peoples who came increasingly under Aksumite influence. In all probability, this process of acculturation had been going on since the first migrants from Southwest Arabia settled in the highlands, but it seems to have received new impetus with the decline of Aksum's overseas trade and consequent dependence upon solely African resources. As early as the mid-seventh century, the old capital at Aksum had been abandoned; thereafter, it served only as a religious center and as a place of coronation for a succession of kings who traced their lineage to Aksum. By then, Aksumite cultural, political, and religious influence had been established south of Tigray in such Agew districts as Lasta, Wag, Angot, and, eventually, Amhara.

This southward expansion continued over the next several centuries. The favored technique involved the establishment of military colonies, which served as core populations from which Aksumite culture, Semitic language, and Christianity spread to the surrounding Agew population. By the tenth century, a post-Aksumite Christian kingdom had emerged that controlled the central northern highlands from modern Eritrea to Shewa and the coast from old Adulis to Zeila in present-day Somalia, territory considerably larger than the Aksumites had governed. Military colonies were also established farther afield among the Sidama people of the central highlands. These settlers may have been the forerunners of such Semitic-speaking groups as the Argobba, Gafat (extinct), Gurage, and Hareri, although independent settlement of Semitic speakers from Southwest Arabia is also possible. During the eleventh and twelfth centuries, the Shewan region was the scene of renewed Christian expansion, carried out, it appears, by one of the more recently Semiticized peoples—the Amhara.

About 1137 a new dynasty came to power in the Christian highlands. Known as the Zagwe and based in the Agew district of Lasta, it developed naturally out of the long cultural and political contact between Cushitic- and Semitic-speaking peoples in the northern highlands. Staunch Christians, the Zagwe devoted themselves to the construction of new churches and monasteries. These were often modeled after Christian religious edifices in the Holy Land, a locale the Zagwe and their subjects held in special esteem. Patrons of literature and the arts in the service of Christianity, the Zagwe kings were responsible, among other things, for the great churches carved into the rock in and around their capital at Adefa. In time, Adefa became known as Lalibela, the name of the Zagwe king to whose reign the Adefa churches' construction has been attributed.

By the time of the Zagwe, the Ethiopian church was showing the effects of long centuries of isolation from the larger Christian and Orthodox worlds. After the seventh century, when Egypt succumbed to the Arab conquest, the highlanders' sole contact with outside Christianity was with the Coptic Church of Egypt, which

*Medhani Alem Church, one of twelve rock-hewn churches in Lalibela
Courtesy United Nations Educational, Scientific, and Cultural
Organization (G.S. Wade)*

periodically supplied a patriarch, or *abun,* upon royal request. During the long period from the seventh to the twelfth century, the Ethiopian Orthodox Church came to place strong emphasis upon the Old Testament and on the Judaic roots of the church. Christianity in Ethiopia became imbued with Old Testament belief and practice in many ways, which differentiated it not only from European Christianity but also from the faith of other Monophysites, such as the Copts. Under the Zagwe, the highlanders maintained regular contact with the Egyptians. Also, by then the Ethiopian church had demonstrated that it was not a proselytizing religion but rather one that by and large restricted its attention to already converted areas of the highlands. Not until the fourteenth and fifteenth centuries did the church demonstrate real interest in proselytizing among nonbelievers, and then it did so via a reinvigorated monastic movement.

The "Restoration" of the "Solomonic" Line

The Zagwe's championing of Christianity and their artistic achievements notwithstanding, there was much discontent with Lastan rule among the populace in what is now Eritrea and Tigray and among the Amhara, an increasingly powerful people who

13

inhabited a region called Amhara to the south of the Zagwe center at Adefa. About 1270, an Amhara noble, Yekuno Amlak, drove out the last Zagwe ruler and proclaimed himself king. His assumption of power marked yet another stage in the southward march of what may henceforth be termed the "Christian kingdom of Ethiopia" and ushered in an era of increased contact with the Levant, the Middle East, and Europe.

The new dynasty that Yekuno Amlak founded came to be known as the "Solomonic" dynasty because its scions claimed descent not only from Aksum but also from King Solomon of ancient Israel. According to traditions that were eventually molded into a national epic, the lineage of Aksumite kings originated with the offspring of an alleged union between Solomon and the Queen of Sheba, whose domains Ethiopians have variously identified with parts of Southwest Arabia and/or Aksum. Consequently, the notion arose that royal legitimacy derived from descent in a line of Solomonic kings. The Tigray and Amhara, who saw themselves as heirs to Aksum, denied the Zagwe any share in that heritage and viewed the Zagwe as usurpers. Yekuno Amlak's accession thus came to be seen as the legitimate "restoration" of the Solomonic line, even though the Amhara king's northern ancestry was at best uncertain. Nonetheless, his assumption of the throne brought the Solomonic dynasty to power, and all subsequent Ethiopian kings traced their legitimacy to him and, thereby, to Solomon and Sheba.

Under Yekuno Amlak, Amhara became the geographical and political center of the Christian kingdom. The new king concerned himself with the consolidation of his control over the northern highlands and with the weakening and, where possible, destruction of encircling pagan and Muslim states. He enjoyed some of his greatest success against Ifat, an Islamic sultanate to the southeast of Amhara that posed a threat to trade routes between Zeila and the central highlands (see fig. 3).

Upon his death in 1285, Yekuno Amlak was succeeded by his son, Yagba Siyon (reigned 1285–94). His reign and the period immediately following were marked by constant struggles among the sons and grandsons of Yekuno Amlak. This internecine conflict was resolved sometime around 1300, when it became the rule for all males tracing descent from Yekuno Amlak (except the reigning emperor and his sons) to be held in a mountaintop prison that was approachable only on one side and that was guarded by soldiers under a commandant loyal to the reigning monarch. When that monarch died, all his sons except his heir were also permanently imprisoned. This practice was followed with some exceptions until the royal prison was destroyed in the early sixteenth century.

The royal prison was one solution to a problem that would plague the Solomonic line throughout its history: the conflict over succession among those who had any claim to royal lineage.

Amhara Ascendancy

Yekuno Amlak's grandson, Amda Siyon (reigned 1313–44), distinguished himself by at last establishing firm control over all of the Christian districts of the kingdom and by expanding into the neighboring regions of Shewa, Gojam, and Damot and into Agew districts in the Lake Tana area. He also devoted much attention to campaigns against Muslim states to the east and southeast of Amhara, such as Ifat, which still posed a powerful threat to the kingdom, and against Hadya, a Sidama state southwest of Shewa. These victories gave him control of the central highlands and enhanced his influence over trade routes to the Red Sea. His conquests also helped facilitate the spread of Christianity in the southern highlands.

Zara Yakob (reigned 1434–68) was without a doubt one of the greatest Ethiopian rulers. His substantial military accomplishments included a decisive victory in 1445 over the sultanate of Adal and its Muslim pastoral allies, who for two centuries had been a source of determined opposition to the Christian highlanders. Zara Yakob also sought to strengthen royal control over what was a highly decentralized administrative system. Some of his most notable achievements were in ecclesiastical matters, where he sponsored a reorganization of the Orthodox Church, attempted to unify its religious practices, and fostered proselytization among nonbelievers. Perhaps most remarkable was a flowering of Gi'iz literature, in which the king himself composed a number of important religious tracts.

Beginning in the fourteenth century, the power of the *negusa nagast* (king of kings), as the emperor was called, was in theory unlimited, but in reality it was often considerably less than that. The unity of the state depended on an emperor's ability to control the local governors of the various regions that composed the kingdom, these rulers being self-made men with their own local bases of support. In general, the court did not interfere with these rulers so long as the latter demonstrated loyalty through the collection and submission of royal tribute and through the contribution of armed men as needed for the king's campaigns. When the military had to be used, it was under central control but was composed of provincial levies or troops who lived off the land, or who were supported by the provincial governments that supplied them (see Military Tradition in National Life, ch. 5). The result was that the expenses

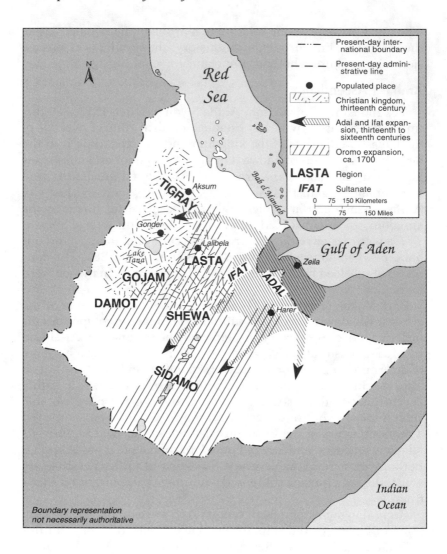

Figure 3. The Early Period, Thirteenth to Seventeenth Centuries

borne by the imperial administration were small, whereas the contributions and tribute provided by the provinces were substantial.

In theory, the emperor had unrestrained control of political and military affairs. In actuality, however, local and even hereditary interests were recognized and respected so long as local rulers paid tribute, supplied levies of warriors, and, in general, complied with royal dictates. Failure to honor obligations to the throne could and often did bring retribution in the form of battle and, if the emperor's forces won, plunder of the district and removal of the local governor. Ethiopian rulers continually moved around the kingdom, an important technique for assertion of royal authority and for collection—and consumption—of taxes levied in kind. The emperor was surrounded by ceremony and protocol intended to enhance his status as a descendant of King Solomon and the Queen of Sheba. He lived in seclusion and was shielded, except on rare occasions, from the gaze of all but his servants and high court officials. Most other subjects were denied access to his person.

The emperor's judicial function was of primary importance. The administration of justice was centralized at court and was conditioned by a body of Egyptian Coptic law known as the *Fetha Nagast* (Law of Kings), introduced into Ethiopia in the mid-fifteenth century (see The Legal System, ch. 5). Judges appointed by the emperor were attached to the administration of every provincial governor. They not only heard cases but also determined when cases could be referred to the governor or sent on appeal to the central government.

The Trials of the Christian Kingdom and the Decline of Imperial Power

From the mid-fifteenth through the mid-seventeenth century, Christian Ethiopians were confronted by the aggressiveness of the Muslim states, the far-reaching migrations of the Oromo, and the efforts of the Portuguese—who had been summoned to aid in the fight against the forces of Islam—to convert them from Monophysite Christianity to Roman Catholicism. The effects of the Muslim and Oromo activities and of the civil strife engendered by the Portuguese left the empire much weakened by the mid-seventeenth century. One result was the emergence of regional lords essentially independent of the throne, although in principle subject to it.

Growth of Regional Muslim States

Beginning in the thirteenth century, one of the chief problems confronting the Christian kingdom, then ruled by the Amhara, was the threat of Muslim encirclement. By that time, a variety of peoples east and south of the highlands had embraced Islam, and some had established powerful sultanates (or shaykhdoms). One of these was the sultanate of Ifat in the northeastern Shewan foothills, and another was centered in the Islamic city of Harer farther east. In the lowlands along the Red Sea were two other important Muslim peoples—the Afar and the Somali. As mentioned previ sly, Ifat posed a major threat to the Christian kingdom, but it was finally defeated by Amda Siyon in the mid-fourteenth century after a protracted struggle. During this conflict, Ifat was supported by other sultanates and by Muslim pastoralists, but for the most part, the Islamicized peoples inhabited small, independent states and were divided by differences in language and culture. Many of them spoke Cushitic languages, unlike the Semitic speakers of Harer. Some were sedentary cultivators and traders, while others were pastoralists. Consequently, unity beyond a single campaign or even the coordination of military activities was difficult to sustain.

Their tendency toward disunity notwithstanding, the Muslim forces continued to pose intermittent threats to the Christian kingdom. By the late fourteenth century, descendants of the ruling family of Ifat had moved east to the area around Harer and had reinvigorated the old Muslim sultanate of Adal, which became the most powerful Muslim entity in the Horn of Africa. Adal came to control the important trading routes from the highlands to the port of Zeila, thus posing a threat to Ethiopia's commerce and, at times, to Christian control of the highlands.

Although the Christian state was unable to impose its rule over the Muslim states to the east, it was strong enough to resist Muslim incursions through the fourteenth century and most of the fifteenth. As the long reign of Zara Yakob came to an end, however, the kingdom again experienced succession problems. It was the monarchs' practice to marry several wives, and each sought to forward the cause of her sons in the struggle for the throne. In those cases where the sons of the deceased king were too young to take office, there could also be conflict within the council of advisers at court. In a polity that had been held together primarily by a strong warrior king, one or more generations of dynastic conflict could lead to serious internal and external problems. Only the persistence of internal conflicts among Muslims generally and within the sultanate of Adal in particular prevented a Muslim onslaught. Through the first quarter of the sixteenth century, relations between Christian and Muslim powers took the form of raids and counterraids. Each side sought to claim as many slaves and as much booty as possible, but neither side attempted to bring the other firmly under its rule.

By the second decade of the sixteenth century, however, a young soldier in the Adali army, Ahmad ibn Ibrahim al Ghazi, had begun to acquire a strong following by virtue of his military successes and in time became the de facto leader of Adal. Concurrently, he acquired the status of a religious leader. Ahmad, who came to be called Grañ (the "Lefthanded") by his Christian enemies, rallied the ethnically diverse Muslims, including many Afar and Somali, in a jihad intended to break Christian power. In 1525 Grañ led

Seventeenth-century Portuguese church beside Lake Tana
Courtesy United Nations Educational, Scientific, and Cultural
Organization (Roger Ferra)

his first expedition against a Christian army and over the next two or three years continued to attack Ethiopian territory, burning churches, taking prisoners, and collecting booty. At the Battle of Shimbra Kure in 1529, according to historian Taddesse Tamrat, "Imam Ahmad broke the backbone of Christian resistance against his offensives." The emperor, Lebna Dengel (reigned 1508–40), was unable to organize an effective defense, and in the early 1530s Grañ's armies penetrated the heartland of the Ethiopian state—northern Shewa, Amhara, and Tigray, devastating the countryside and thereafter putting much of what had been the Christian kingdom under the rule of Muslim governors.

It was not until 1543 that the emperor Galawdewos (reigned 1540–59), joining with a small number of Portuguese soldiers requested earlier by Lebna Dengel, defeated the Muslim forces and killed Grañ. The death of the charismatic Grañ destroyed the unity of the Muslim forces that had been created by their leader's successes, skill, and reputation as a warrior and religious figure. Christian armies slowly pushed the Muslims back and regained control of the highlands. Ethiopians had suffered extraordinary material and moral losses during the struggle against Grañ, and it would be decades or even centuries before they would recover fully. The memory of the bitter war against Grañ remains vivid even today.

Oromo Migrations and Their Impact

In the mid-sixteenth century, its political and military organization already weakened by the Muslim assault, the Christian kingdom began to be pressured on the south and southeast by movements of the Oromo (called Galla by the Amhara). These migrations also affected the Sidama, Muslim pastoralists in the lowlands, and Adal. At this time, the Oromo, settled in far southern Ethiopia, were an egalitarian pastoral people divided into a number of competing segments or groups. They shared, however, a type of age-set system (see Glossary) of social organization called the *gada* system (see Glossary), which was ideally suited for warfare. Their predilection toward warfare, apparently combined with an expanding population of both people and cattle, led to a long-term predatory expansion at the expense of their neighbors after about 1550. Unlike the highland Christians or on occasion the lowland Muslims, the Oromo were not concerned with establishing an empire or imposing a religious system. In a series of massive but uncoordinated movements during the second half of the sixteenth century, they penetrated much of the southern and northern highlands as well as the lowlands to the east, affecting Christians and Muslims equally.

These migrations also profoundly affected the Oromo. Disunited in the extreme, they attacked and raided each other as readily as neighboring peoples in their quest for new land and pastures. As they moved farther from their homeland and encountered new physical and human environments, entire segments of the Oromo population adapted by changing their mode of economic life, their political and social organization, and their religious adherence. Many mixed with the Amhara (particularly in Shewa), became Christians, and eventually obtained a share in governing the kingdom. In some cases, royal family members came from the union of Amhara and Oromo elements. In other cases, Oromo, without losing their identity, became part of the nobility. But no matter how much they changed, Oromo groups generally retained their language and sense of local identity. So differentiated and dispersed had they become, however, that few foreign observers recognized the Oromo as a distinct people until the twentieth century.

In a more immediate sense, the Oromo migration resulted in a weakening of both Christian and Muslim power and drove a wedge between the two faiths along the eastern edge of the highlands. In the Christian kingdom, Oromo groups infiltrated large areas in the east and south, with large numbers settling in Shewa and adjacent parts of the central highlands. Others penetrated as far north as eastern Tigray. The effect of the Oromo migrations was to leave the Ethiopian state fragmented and much reduced in size, with an alien population in its midst. Thereafter, the Oromo played a major role in the internal dynamics of Ethiopia, both assimilating and being assimilated as they were slowly incorporated into the Christian kingdom. In the south, the Sidama fiercely resisted the Oromo, but, as in the central and northern highlands, they were compelled to yield at least some territory. In the east, the Oromo swept up to and even beyond Harer, dealing a devastating blow to what remained of Adal and contributing in a major way to its decline.

Contact with European Christendom

Egyptian Muslims had destroyed the neighboring Nile River valley's Christian states in the fourteenth and fifteenth centuries. Tenuous relations with Christians in western Europe and the Byzantine Empire continued via the Coptic Church in Egypt. The Coptic patriarchs in Alexandria were responsible for the assignment of Ethiopian patriarchs—a church policy that Egypt's Muslim rulers occasionally tried to use to their advantage. For centuries after the Muslim conquests of the early medieval period, this link with the Eastern churches constituted practically all of Ethiopia's administrative connection with the larger Christian world.

A more direct if less formal contact with the outside Christian world was maintained through the Ethiopian Monophysite community in Jerusalem and the visits of Ethiopian pilgrims to the Holy Land. Ethiopian monks from the Jerusalem community attended the Council of Florence in 1441 at the invitation of the pope, who was seeking to reunite the Eastern and Western churches. Westerners learned about Ethiopia through the monks and pilgrims and became attracted to it for two main reasons. First, many believed Ethiopia was the long-sought land of the legendary Christian priest-king of the East, Prester John. Second, the West viewed Ethiopia as a potentially valuable ally in its struggle against Islamic forces that continued to threaten southern Europe until the Turkish defeat at the Battle of Lepanto in 1571.

Portugal, the first European power to circumnavigate Africa and enter the Indian Ocean, displayed initial interest in this potential ally by sending a representative to Ethiopia in 1493. The Ethiopians, in turn, sent an envoy to Portugal in 1509 to request a coordinated attack on the Muslims. Europe received its first written accounts of the country from Father Francisco Alvarez, a Franciscan who accompanied a Portuguese diplomatic expedition to Ethiopia in the 1520s. His book, *The Prester John of the Indies,* stirred further European interest and proved a valuable source for future historians. The first Portuguese forces responded to a request for aid in 1541, although by that time the Portuguese were concerned primarily with strengthening their hegemony over the Indian Ocean trade routes and with converting the Ethiopians to Roman Catholicism. Nevertheless, joining the forces of the Christian kingdom, the Portuguese succeeded eventually in helping to defeat and kill Grañ.

Portuguese Roman Catholic missionaries arrived in 1554. Efforts to induce the Ethiopians to reject their Monophysite beliefs and accept Rome's supremacy continued for nearly a century and engendered bitterness as pro- and anti-Catholic parties maneuvered for control of the state. At least two emperors in this period allegedly converted to Roman Catholicism. The second of these, Susenyos (reigned 1607–32), after a particularly fierce battle between adherents of the two faiths, abdicated in 1632 in favor of his son, Fasiladas (reigned 1632–67), to spare the country further bloodshed. The expulsion of the Jesuits and all Roman Catholic missionaries followed. This religious controversy left a legacy of deep hostility toward foreign Christians and Europeans that continued into the twentieth century. It also contributed to the isolation that followed for the next 200 years.

The Gonder State and the Ascendancy of the Nobility

Emperor Fasiladas kept out the disruptive influences of the foreign Christians, dealt with sporadic Muslim incursions, and in general sought to reassert central authority and to reinvigorate the Solomonic monarchy and the Orthodox Church. He revived the practice of confining royal family members on a remote mountaintop to lessen challenges to his rule and distinguished himself by reconstructing the cathedral at Aksum (destroyed by Grañ) and by establishing his camp at Gonder—a locale that gradually developed into a permanent capital and became the cultural and political center of Ethiopia during the Gonder period.

Although the Gonder period produced a flowering of architecture and art that lasted more than a century, Gonder monarchs never regained full control over the wealth and manpower that the nobility had usurped during the long wars against Grañ and then the Oromo. Many nobles, commanding the loyalty of their home districts, had become virtually independent, especially those on the periphery of the kingdom. Moreover, during Fasiladas's reign and that of his son Yohannis I (reigned 1667–82), there were substantial

The castle of Emperor Yohannis I (1667–82) in Gonder Courtesy United Nations Educational, Scientific, and Cultural Organization (G.S. Wade)

differences between the two monastic orders of the Orthodox Church concerning the proper response to the Jesuit challenge to Monophysite doctrine on the nature of Christ. The positions of the two orders were often linked to regional opposition to the emperor, and neither Fasiladas nor Yohannis was able to settle the issue without alienating important components of the church.

Iyasu I (reigned 1682–1706) was a celebrated military leader who excelled at the most basic requirement of the warrior-king. He campaigned constantly in districts on the south and southeast of the kingdom and personally led expeditions to Shewa and beyond, areas from which royal armies had long been absent. Iyasu also attempted to mediate the doctrinal quarrel in the church, but a solution eluded him. He sponsored the construction of several churches, among them Debre Birhan Selassie, one of the most beautiful and famous of the churches in Gonder.

Iyasu's reign also saw the Oromo begin to play a role in the affairs of the kingdom, especially in the military sense. Iyasu co-opted some of the Oromo groups by enlisting them into his army and by converting them to Christianity. He came gradually to rely almost entirely upon Oromo units and led them in repeated campaigns against their countrymen who had not yet been incorporated into the Amhara-Tigray state. Successive Gonder kings, particularly Iyasu II (reigned 1730–55), likewise relied upon Oromo military units to help counter challenges to their authority from

23

the traditional nobility and for purposes of campaigning in far-flung Oromo territory. By the late eighteenth century, the Oromo were playing an important role in political affairs as well. At times during the first half of the nineteenth century, Oromo was the primary language at court, and Oromo leaders came to number among the highest nobility of the kingdom.

During the reign of Iyoas (reigned 1755–69), son of Iyasu II, the most important political figure was Ras Mikael Sehul, a good example of a great noble who made himself the power behind the throne. Mikael's base was the province of Tigray, which by now enjoyed a large measure of autonomy and from which Mikael raised up large armies with which he dominated the Gonder scene. In 1769 he demonstrated his power by ordering the murder of two kings (Iyoas and Yohannis II) and by placing on the throne Tekla Haimanot II (son of Yohannis II), a weak ruler who did Mikael's bidding. Mikael continued in command until the early 1770s, when a coalition of his opponents compelled him to retire to Tigray, where he eventually died of old age.

Mikael's brazen murder of two kings and his undisguised role as kingmaker in Gonder signaled the beginning of what Ethiopians have long termed the Zemene Mesafint (Era of the Princes), a time when Gonder kings were reduced to ceremonial figureheads while their military functions and real power lay with powerful nobles. During this time, traditionally dating from 1769 to 1855, the kingdom no longer existed as a united entity capable of concerted political and military activity. Various principalities were ruled by autonomous nobles, and warfare was constant.

The five-volume work *Travels to Discover the Source of the Nile* by James Bruce, the Scottish traveler who lived in Ethiopia from 1769 to 1772, describes some of the bloody conflicts and personal rivalries that consumed the kingdom. During the most confused period, around 1800, there were as many as six rival emperors. Provincial warlords were masters of the territories they controlled but were subject to raids from other provinces. Peasants often left the land to become soldiers or brigands. In this period, too, Oromo nobles, often nominally Christian and in a few cases Muslim, were among those who struggled for hegemony over the highlands. The church, still riven by theological controversy, contributed to the disunity that was the hallmark of the Zemene Mesafint.

The Making of Modern Ethiopia

After the mid-nineteenth century, the different regions of the Gonder state were gradually reintegrated to form the nucleus of a modern state by strong monarchs such as Tewodros II, Yohannis

*Seventeenth-century painting depicting St. George and the dragon,
in the church of Debre Birhan Selassie in Gonder
Courtesy United Nations Educational, Scientific, and Cultural
Organization (R. Garraud)*

IV, and Menelik II, who resisted the gradual expansion of European control in the Red Sea area and at the same time staved off a number of other challenges to the integrity of the reunited kingdom.

The Reestablishment of the Ethiopian Monarchy

At the beginning of the nineteenth century, the Gonder state consisted of the northern and central highlands and the lower elevations immediately adjacent to them. This area was only nominally a monarchy, as rival nobles fought for the military title of *ras* (roughly, marshal; literally, head in Amharic) or the highest of all nonroyal titles, *ras-bitwoded*, that combined supreme military command with the duties of first minister at court. These nobles often were able to enthrone and depose princes who carried the empty title of *negusa nagast*.

The major peoples who made up the Ethiopian state were the Amhara and the Tigray, both Semitic speakers, and Cushitic-speaking peoples such as the Oromo and the Agew, many of whom were Christian by the early 1800s. In some cases, their conversion had been accompanied by their assimilation into Amhara culture

25

or, less often, Tigray culture; in other cases, they had become Christian but had retained their languages. The state's largest ethnic group was the Oromo, but the Oromo were neither politically nor culturally unified. Some were Christian, spoke Amharic, and had intermarried with the Amhara. Other Christian Oromo retained their language, although their modes of life and social structure had changed extensively from those of their pastoral kin. At the eastern edge of the highlands, many had converted to Islam, especially in the area of the former sultanates of Ifat and Adal. The Oromo people, whether or not Christian and Amhara in culture, played important political roles in the Zemene Mesafint—often as allies of Amhara aspirants to power but sometimes as *rases* and kingmakers in their own right.

Meanwhile, to the south of the kingdom, segments of the Oromo population—cultivators and suppliers of goods exportable to the Red Sea coast and beyond—had developed kingdoms of their own, no doubt stimulated in part by the examples of the Amhara to the north and the Sidama kingdoms to the south. The seventeenth through nineteenth century was a period not only of migration but also of integration, as groups borrowed usable techniques and institutions from each other. In the south, too, Islam had made substantial inroads. Many Oromo chieftains found Islam a useful tool in the process of centralization as well as in the building of trade networks.

By the second quarter of the nineteenth century, external factors once more affected the highlands and adjacent areas, at least in part because trade among the Red Sea states was being revived. Egypt made incursions along the coast and sought at various times to control the Red Sea ports. Europeans, chiefly British and French, showed interest in the Horn of Africa. The competition for trade, differences over how to respond to Egypt's activities, and the readier availability of modern arms were important factors in the conflicts of the period.

In the mid-nineteenth century, a major figure in Gonder was Kasa Haylu, son of a lesser noble from Qwara, a district on the border with Sudan. Beginning about 1840, Kasa alternated between life as a brigand and life as a soldier of fortune for various nobles, including Ras Ali, a Christian of Oromo origin who dominated the court in Gonder. Kasa became sufficiently effective as an army commander to be offered the governorship of a minor province. He also married Ali's daughter, Tawabech. Nonetheless, Kasa eventually rebelled against Ali, occupied Gonder in 1847, and compelled Ali to recognize him as chief of the western frontier area. In 1848 he attacked the Egyptians in Sudan; however, he suffered a crushing defeat, which taught him to respect modern firepower. Kasa then agreed to a reconciliation with Ali, whom he served until 1852, when he again revolted. The following year, he defeated Ali's army and burned his capital, Debre Tabor. In 1854 he assumed the title *negus* (king), and in February 1855 the head of the church crowned him Tewodros II.

From Tewodros II to Menelik II, 1855-89

Tewodros II's origins were in the Era of the Princes, but his ambitions were not those of the regional nobility. He sought to reestablish a cohesive Ethiopian state and to reform its administration and church. He did not initially claim Solomonic lineage but did seek to restore Solomonic hegemony, and he considered himself the "Elect of God." Later in his reign, suspecting that foreigners considered him an upstart and seeking to legitimize his reign, he added "son of David and Solomon" to his title.

Tewodros's first task was to bring Shewa under his control. During the Era of the Princes, Shewa was, even more than most provinces, an independent entity, its ruler even styling himself *negus*. In the course of subduing the Shewans, Tewodros imprisoned a Shewan prince, Menelik, who would later become emperor himself. Despite his success against Shewa, Tewodros faced constant rebellions in other provinces. In the first six years of his reign, the new ruler managed to put down these rebellions, and the empire was relatively peaceful from about 1861 to 1863. The energy, wealth, and manpower necessary to deal with regional opposition, however, limited the scope of Tewodros's other activities. By 1865 other rebels had emerged, including Menelik, who had escaped from prison and returned to Shewa, where he declared himself *negus*.

In addition to his conflicts with rebels and rivals, Tewodros encountered difficulties with the European powers. Seeking aid from the British government (he proposed a joint expedition to conquer Jerusalem), he became unhappy with the behavior of those Britons whom he had counted on to advance his request, and he took them hostage. In 1868, as a British expeditionary force sent from India to secure release of the hostages stormed his stronghold, Tewodros committed suicide.

Tewodros never realized his dream of restoring a strong monarchy, although he took some important initial steps. He sought to establish the principle that governors and judges must be salaried appointees. He also established a professional standing army, rather than depending on local lords to provide soldiers for his expeditions. He also intended to reform the church, believing the clergy to be ignorant and immoral, but he was confronted by strong opposition when he tried to impose a tax on church lands to help finance government activities. His confiscation of these lands gained him enemies in the church and little support elsewhere. Essentially, Tewodros was a talented military campaigner but a poor politician.

The kingdom at Tewodros's death was disorganized, but those contending to succeed him were not prepared to return to the Zemene Mesafint system. One of them, crowned Tekla Giorgis, took over the central part of the highlands. Another, Kasa Mercha, governor of Tigray, declined when offered the title of *ras* in exchange for recognizing Tekla Giorgis. The third, Menelik of Shewa, came to terms with Tekla Giorgis in return for a promise to respect Shewa's independence. Tekla Giorgis, however, sought to bring Kasa Mercha under his rule but was defeated by a small Tigrayan army equipped with more modern weapons than those possessed by his Gonder forces. In 1872 Kasa Mercha was crowned *negusa nagast* in a ceremony at the ancient capital of Aksum, taking the throne name of Yohannis IV.

Yohannis was unable to exercise control over the nearly independent Shewans until six years later. From the beginning of his reign, he was confronted with the growing power of Menelik, who had proclaimed himself king of Shewa and traced his Solomonic lineage to Lebna Dengel. While Yohannis was struggling against opposing factions in the north, Menelik consolidated his power in Shewa and extended his rule over the Oromo to the south and west. He garrisoned Shewan forces among the Oromo and received military and financial support from them. Despite the acquisition of European firearms, in 1878 Menelik was compelled to submit to Yohannis and to pay tribute; in return, Yohannis recognized Menelik as *negus* and gave him a free hand in territories to the south of Shewa. This agreement, although only a truce in the long-standing rivalry between Tigray and Shewa, was important to Yohannis, who was preoccupied with foreign enemies and pressures. In many of Yohannis's external struggles, Menelik maintained separate relations with the emperor's enemies and continued to consolidate Shewan authority in order to strengthen his own position. In a subsequent agreement designed to ensure the succession in the line of Yohannis, one of Yohannis's younger sons was married to Zawditu, Menelik's daughter.

In 1875 Yohannis had to meet attacks from Egyptian forces on three fronts. The khedive in Egypt envisioned a "Greater Egypt" that would encompass Ethiopia. In pursuit of this goal, an Egyptian force moved inland from present-day Djibouti but was annihilated by Afar tribesmen. Other Egyptian forces occupied Harer, where they remained for nearly ten years, long after the Egyptian cause had been lost. Tigrayan warriors defeated a more ambitious attack launched from the coastal city of Mitsiwa in which the Egyptian forces were almost completely destroyed. A fourth Egyptian army was decisively defeated in 1876 southwest of Mitsiwa.

Italy was the next source of danger. The Italian government took over the port of Aseb in 1882 from the Rubattino Shipping Company, which had purchased it from a local ruler some years before. Italy's main interest was not the port but the eventual colonization of Ethiopia. In the process, the Italians entered into a long-term relationship with Menelik. The main Italian drive was begun in 1885 from Mitsiwa, which Italy had occupied. From this port, the Italians began to penetrate the hinterland, with British encouragement. In 1887, after the Italians were soundly defeated at Dogali by Ras Alula, the governor of northeastern Tigray, they sent a stronger force into the area.

Yohannis was unable to attend to the Italian threat because of difficulties to the west in Gonder and Gojam. In 1887 Sudanese Muslims, known as Mahdists, made incursions into Gojam and Begemdir and laid waste parts of those provinces. In 1889 the emperor met these forces in the Battle of Metema on the Sudanese border. Although the invaders were defeated, Yohannis himself was fatally wounded, and the Ethiopian forces disintegrated. Just before his death, Yohannis designated one of his sons, Ras Mengesha Yohannis of Tigray, as his successor, but this gesture proved futile, as Menelik successfully claimed the throne in 1889.

The Shewan ruler became the dominant personality in Ethiopia and was recognized as Emperor Menelik II by all but Yohannis's son and Ras Alula. During the temporary period of confusion following Yohannis's death, the Italians were able to advance farther into the hinterland from Mitsiwa and establish a foothold in the highlands, from which Menelik was unable to dislodge them. From 1889 until after World War II, Ethiopia was deprived of its maritime frontier and was forced to accept the presence of an ambitious European power on its borders.

The Reign of Menelik II, 1889–1913

By 1900 Menelik had succeeded in establishing control over much of present-day Ethiopia and had, in part at least, gained recognition from the European colonial powers of the boundaries of his empire. Although in many respects a traditionalist, he introduced several significant changes. His decision in the late 1880s to locate the royal encampment at Addis Ababa ("New Flower") in southern Shewa led to the gradual rise of a genuine urban center and a permanent capital in the 1890s, a development that facilitated the introduction of new ideas and technology. The capital's location

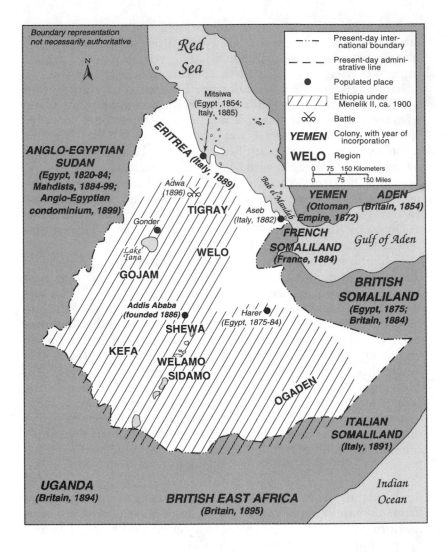

Figure 4. Colonization of the Horn of Africa and Southwest Arabia, 1820– ca. 1900

symbolized the empire's southern reorientation, a move that further irritated Menelik's Tigrayan opponents and some Amhara of the more northerly provinces who resented Shewan hegemony. Menelik also authorized a French company to build a railroad, not completed until 1917, that eventually would link Addis Ababa and Djibouti.

Menelik embarked on a program of military conquest that more than doubled the size of his domain (see fig. 4). Enjoying superior fire power, his forces overran the Kembata and Welamo regions in the southern highlands. Also subdued were the Kefa and other Oromo- and Omotic-speaking peoples.

Expanding south, Menelik introduced a system of land rights considerably modified from that prevailing in the Amhara-Tigray highlands. These changes had significant implications for the ordinary cultivator in the south and ultimately were to generate quite different responses there to the land reform programs that would follow the revolution of 1974 (see The Struggle for Power, 1974–77, this ch.). In the central and northern highlands, despite regional variations, most peasants had substantial inheritable (broadly, *rist*—see Glossary) rights in land. In addition to holding rights of this kind, the nobility held or were assigned certain economic rights in the land, called *gult* (see Glossary) rights, which entitled them to a portion of the produce of the land in which others held *rist* rights and to certain services from the *rist* holders. The Ethiopian Orthodox Church also held land of its own and *gult* rights in land to which peasants held *rist* rights. In the south, all land theoretically belonged to the emperor. He in turn allocated land rights to those he appointed to office and to his soldiers. The rights allocated by the king were more extensive than the *gult* rights prevailing in the north and left most of the indigenous peoples as tenants, with far fewer rights than Amhara and Tigray peasants. Thus, the new landowners in the south were aliens and remained largely so.

At the same time that Menelik was extending his empire, European colonial powers were showing an interest in the territories surrounding Ethiopia. Menelik considered the Italians a formidable challenge and negotiated the Treaty of Wuchale with them in 1889 (see Diplomacy and State Building in Imperial Ethiopia, ch. 4). Among its terms were those permitting the Italians to establish their first toehold on the edge of the northern highlands and from which they subsequently sought to expand into Tigray. Disagreements over the contents of the treaty eventually induced Menelik to renounce it and repay in full a loan Italy had granted as a condition. Thereafter, relations with Italy were further strained as a result of the establishment of Eritrea as a colony and Italy's penetration of the Somali territories.

Italian ambitions were encouraged by British actions in 1891, when, hoping to stabilize the region in the face of the Mahdist threat in Sudan, Britain agreed with the Italian government that Ethiopia should fall within the Italian sphere of influence. France, however, encouraged Menelik to oppose the Italian threat by delineating the projected boundaries of his empire. Anxious to advance French economic interests through the construction of a railroad from Addis Ababa to the city of Djibouti in French Somaliland, France accordingly reduced the size of its territorial claims there and recognized Ethiopian sovereignty in the area.

Italian-Ethiopian relations reached a low point in 1895, when Ras Mengesha of Tigray, hitherto reluctant to recognize the Shewan emperor's claims, was threatened by the Italians and asked for the support of Menelik. In late 1895, Italian forces invaded Tigray. However, Menelik completely routed them in early 1896 as they approached the Tigrayan capital, Adwa. This victory brought Ethiopia new prestige as well as general recognition of its sovereign status by the European powers. Besides confirming the annulment of the Treaty of Wuchale, the peace agreement ending the conflict also entailed Italian recognition of Ethiopian independence; in return, Menelik permitted the Italians to retain their colony of Eritrea.

In addition to attempts on the part of Britain, France, and Italy to gain influence within the empire, Menelik was troubled by intrigues originating in Russia, Germany, and the Ottoman Empire. But, showing a great capacity to play one power off against another, the emperor was able to avoid making any substantial concessions. Moreover, while pursuing his own territorial designs, Menelik joined with France in 1898 to penetrate Sudan at Fashoda and then cooperated with British forces in British Somaliland between 1900 and 1904 to put down a rebellion in the Ogaden by Somali leader Muhammad Abdullah Hassan. By 1908 the colonial powers had recognized Ethiopia's borders except for those with Italian Somaliland.

After Menelik suffered a disabling stroke in May 1906, his personal control over the empire weakened. Apparently responding to that weakness and seeking to avoid an outbreak of conflict in the area, Britain, France, and Italy signed the Tripartite Treaty, which declared that the common purpose of the three powers was to maintain the political status quo and to respect each other's interests. Britain's interest, it was recognized, lay around Lake Tana and the headwaters of the Abay (Blue Nile). Italy's chief interest was in linking Eritrea with Italian Somaliland. France's interest was the territory to be traversed by the railroad from Addis Ababa to Djibouti in French Somaliland.

Apparently recognizing that his political strength was ebbing, Menelik established a Council of Ministers in late 1907 to assist in the management of state affairs. The foremost aspirants to the throne, Ras Mekonnen and Ras Mengesha, had died in 1906. In June 1908, the emperor designated his thirteen-year-old nephew,

Lij Iyasu, son of Ras Mikael of Welo, as his successor. After suffering another stroke in late 1908, the emperor appointed Ras Tessema as regent. These developments ushered in a decade of political uncertainty. The great nobles, some with foreign financial support, engaged in intrigues anticipating a time of troubles as well as of opportunity upon Menelik's death.

Empress Taytu, who had borne no children, was heavily involved in court politics on behalf of her kin and friends, most of whom lived in the northern provinces and included persons who either had claims of their own to the throne or were resentful of Shewan hegemony. However, by 1910 her efforts had been thwarted by the Shewan nobles; thereafter, the empress withdrew from political activity.

The Interregnum

The two years of Menelik's reign that followed the death of Ras Tessema in 1911 found real power in the hands of Ras (later Negus) Mikael of Welo, an Oromo and former Muslim, who had converted to Christianity under duress. Mikael could muster an army of 80,000 in his predominantly Muslim province and commanded the allegiance of Oromo outside it. In December 1913, Menelik died, but fear of civil war induced the court to keep his death secret for some time. Although recognized as emperor, Menelik's nephew, Lij Iyasu, was not formally crowned. The old nobility quickly attempted to reassert its power, which Menelik had undercut, and united against Lij Iyasu. At the outbreak of World War I, encouraged by his father and by German and Turkish diplomats, Lij Iyasu adopted the Islamic faith. Seeking to revive Muslim-Oromo predominance, Lij Iyasu placed the eastern half of Ethiopia under Ras Mikael's control, officially placed his country in religious dependence on the Ottoman sultan-caliph, and established cordial relations with Somali leader Muhammad Abdullah Hassan.

The Shewan nobility immediately secured a proclamation from the head of the Ethiopian Orthodox Church excommunicating Lij Iyasu and deposing him as emperor. Menelik's daughter, Zawditu, was declared empress. Tafari Mekonnen, the son of Ras Mekonnen of Harer (who was a descendant of a Shewan *negus* and a supporter of the nobles), was declared regent and heir to the throne and given the title of *ras*. By virtue of the power and prestige he derived from his achievements as one of Menelik's generals, Habte Giorgis, the minister of war and a traditionalist, continued to play a major role in government affairs until his death in 1926. Although Lij Iyasu was captured in a brief military campaign in 1921 and imprisoned until his death in 1936, his father, Negus Mikael, continued for some time to pose a serious challenge to the government in Addis Ababa. The death of Habte Giorgis in 1926 left Tafari in effective control of the government. In 1928 he was crowned *negus*. When the empress died in 1930, Tafari succeeded to the throne without contest. Seventeen years after the death of Menelik, the succession struggle thus ended in favor of Tafari.

Well before his crowning as *negus*, Tafari began to introduce a degree of modernization into Ethiopia. As early as 1920, he ordered administrative regulations and legal code books from various European countries to provide models for his newly created bureaucracy. Ministers were also appointed to advise the regent and were given official accommodations in the capital. To ensure the growth of a class of educated young men who might be useful in introducing reforms in the years ahead, Tafari promoted government schooling. He enlarged the school Menelik had established for the sons of nobles and founded Tafari Mekonnen Elementary School in 1925. In addition, he took steps to improve health and social services.

Tafari also acted to extend his power base and to secure allies abroad. In 1919, after efforts to gain membership in the League of Nations were blocked because of the existence of slavery in Ethiopia, he (and Empress Zawditu) complied with the norms of the international community by banning the slave trade in 1923. That same year, Ethiopia was unanimously voted membership in the League of Nations. Continuing to seek international approval of the country's internal conditions, the government enacted laws in 1924 that provided for the gradual emancipation of slaves and their offspring and created a government bureau to oversee the process. The exact degree of servitude was difficult to determine, however, as the majority of slaves worked in households and were considered, at least among Amhara and Tigray, to be second-class family members.

Ethiopia signed a twenty-year treaty of friendship with Italy in 1928, providing for an Ethiopian free-trade zone at Aseb in Eritrea and the construction of a road from the port to Dese in Welo. A joint company controlled road traffic. Contact with the outside world expanded further when the emperor engaged a Belgian military mission in 1929 to train the royal bodyguards (see Training, ch. 5). In 1930 negotiations started between Ethiopia and various international banking institutions for the establishment of the Bank of Ethiopia. In the same year, Tafari signed the Arms Traffic Act with Britain, France, and Italy, by which unauthorized persons were denied the right to import arms. The act also recognized the government's right to procure arms against external aggression and to maintain internal order.

Haile Selassie: The Prewar Period, 1930–36

Although Empress Zawditu died in April 1930, it was not until November that Negus Tafari was crowned Haile Selassie I, "Conquering Lion of the Tribe of Judah, Elect of God, and King of Kings of Ethiopia." As emperor, Haile Selassie continued to push reforms aimed at modernizing the country and breaking the nobility's authority. Henceforth, the great *rases* were forced either to obey the emperor or to engage in treasonable opposition to him.

In July 1931, the emperor granted a constitution that asserted his own status, reserved imperial succession to the line of Haile Selassie, and declared that "the person of the Emperor is sacred, his dignity inviolable, and his power indisputable." All power over central and local government, the legislature, the judiciary, and the military remained with the emperor. The constitution was essentially an effort to provide a legal basis for replacing the traditional provincial rulers with appointees loyal to the emperor.

The new strength of the imperial government was demonstrated in 1932 when a revolt led by Ras Hailu Balaw of Gojam in support of Lij Iyasu was quickly suppressed and a new nontraditional governor put in Hailu's place. By 1934 reliable provincial rulers had been established throughout the traditional Amhara territories of Shewa, Gojam, and Begemdir, as well as in Kefa and Sidamo—well outside the core Amhara area. The only traditional leader capable of overtly challenging central rule at this point was the *ras* of Tigray. Other peoples, although in no position to confront the emperor, remained almost entirely outside the control of the imperial government.

Although Haile Selassie placed administrators of his own choosing wherever he could and thus sought to limit the power of the *rases* and other nobles with regional power bases, he did not directly attack the systems of land tenure that were linked to the traditional political order. Abolition of the pattern of *gult* rights in the Amhara-Tigray highlands and the system of land allocation in the south would have amounted to a social and economic revolution that Haile Selassie was not prepared to undertake.

The emperor took nonmilitary measures to promote loyalty to the throne and to the state. He established new elementary and secondary schools in Addis Ababa, and some 150 university-age students studied abroad. The government enacted a penal code in 1930, imported printing presses to provide nationally oriented newspapers, increased the availability of electricity and telephone services, and promoted public health. The Bank of Ethiopia, founded in 1931, commenced issuing Ethiopian currency.

Italian Rule and World War II

Italian Administration in Eritrea

A latecomer to the scramble for colonies in Africa, Italy established itself first in Eritrea (its name was derived from the Latin term for the Red Sea, Mare Erythreum) in the 1880s and secured Ethiopian recognition of its claim in 1889. Despite its failure to penetrate Tigray in 1896, Italy retained control over Eritrea. A succession of Italian chief administrators, or governors, maintained a degree of unity and public order in a region marked by cultural, linguistic, and religious diversity. Eritrea also experienced material progress in many areas before Ethiopia proper did so.

One of the most important developments during the post-1889 period was the growth of an Eritrean public administration. The Italians employed many Eritreans to work in public service—particularly the police and public works—and fostered loyalty by granting Eritreans emoluments and status symbols. The local population shared in the benefits conferred under Italian colonial administration, especially through newly created medical services, agricultural improvements, and the provision of urban amenities in Asmera and Mitsiwa.

After Benito Mussolini assumed power in Italy in 1922, the colonial government in Eritrea changed. The new administration stressed the racial and political superiority of Italians, authorized segregation, and relegated the local people to the lowest level of public employment. At the same time, Rome implemented agricultural improvements and established a basis for commercial agriculture on farms run by Italian colonists.

State control of the economic sphere was matched by tighter political control. Attempts at improving the management of the colony, however, did not transform it into a self-sufficient entity. The colony's most important function was to serve as a strategic base for future aggrandizement.

Mussolini's Invasion and the Italian Occupation

As late as September 29, 1934, Rome affirmed its 1928 treaty of friendship with Ethiopia. Nonetheless, it became clear that Italy wished to expand and link its holdings in the Horn of Africa (see fig. 5). Moreover, the international climate of the mid-1930s provided Italy with the expectation that aggression could be undertaken with impunity. Determined to provoke a casus belli, the Mussolini regime began deliberately exploiting the minor provocations that arose in its relations with Ethiopia.

In December 1934, an incident took place at Welwel in the Ogaden, a site of wells used by Somali nomads regularly traversing the borders between Ethiopia and British Somaliland and Italian Somaliland. The Italians had built fortified positions in Welwel in 1930 and, because there had been no protests, assumed that the international community had recognized their rights over this area. However, an Anglo-Ethiopian boundary commission challenged the Italian position when it visited Welwel in late November 1934 on its way to set territorial boundary markers. On encountering Italian belligerence, the commission's members withdrew but left behind their Ethiopian military escort, which eventually fought a battle with Italian units.

In September 1935, the League of Nations exonerated both parties in the Welwel incident. The long delay and the intricate British and French maneuverings persuaded Mussolini that no obstacle would be placed in his path. An Anglo-French proposal in August 1935—just before the League of Nations ruling—that the signatories to the 1906 Tripartite Treaty collaborate for the purpose of assisting in the modernization and reorganization of Ethiopian internal affairs, subject to the consent of Ethiopia, was flatly rejected by the Italians. On October 3, 1935, Italy attacked Ethiopia from Eritrea and Italian Somaliland without a declaration of war. On October 7, the League of Nations unanimously declared Italy an aggressor but took no effective action.

In a war that lasted seven months, Ethiopia was outmatched by Italy in armaments—a situation exacerbated by the fact that a League of Nations arms embargo was not enforced against Italy. Despite a valiant defense, the next six months saw the Ethiopians pushed back on the northern front and in Harerge. Acting on long-standing grievances, a segment of the Tigray forces defected, as did Oromo forces in some areas. Moreover, the Italians made widespread use of chemical weapons and air power. On March 31, 1936, the Ethiopians counterattacked the main Italian force at Maychew but were defeated. By early April 1936, Italian forces had reached Dese in the north and Harer in the east. On May 2, Haile Selassie left for French Somaliland and exile—a move resented by some Ethiopians who were accustomed to a warrior emperor. The Italian forces entered Addis Ababa on May 5. Four days later, Italy announced the annexation of Ethiopia.

On June 30, Haile Selassie made a powerful speech before the League of Nations in Geneva in which he set forth two choices— support for collective security or international lawlessness. The

Figure 5. The Horn of Africa and Southwest Arabia, Mid-1930s

emperor stirred the conscience of many and was thereafter regarded as a major international figure. Britain and France, however, soon recognized Italy's control of Ethiopia. Among the major powers, the United States and the Soviet Union refused to do so.

In early June 1936, Rome promulgated a constitution bringing Ethiopia, Eritrea, and Italian Somaliland together into a single administrative unit divided into six provinces. On June 11, 1936, Marshal Rodolfo Graziani replaced Marshal Pietro Badoglio, who had commanded the Italian forces in the war. In December the Italians declared the whole country to be pacified and under their effective control. Ethiopian resistance nevertheless continued.

After a failed assassination attempt against Graziani on February 19, 1937, the colonial authorities executed 30,000 persons, including about half of the younger, educated Ethiopian population. This harsh policy, however, did not pacify the country. In November 1937, Rome therefore appointed a new governor and instructed him to adopt a more flexible line. Accordingly, large-scale public works projects were undertaken. One result was the construction of the country's first system of improved roads. In the meantime, however, the Italians had decreed miscegenation to be illegal. Racial separation, including residential segregation, was enforced as thoroughly as possible. The Italians showed favoritism to non-Christian Oromo (some of whom had supported the invasion), Somali, and other Muslims in an attempt to isolate the Amhara, who supported Haile Selassie.

Ethiopian resistance continued, nonetheless. Early in 1938, a revolt broke out in Gojam led by the Committee of Unity and Collaboration, which was made up of some of the young, educated elite who had escaped the reprisal after the attempt on Graziani's life. In exile in Britain, the emperor sought to gain the support of the Western democracies for his cause but had little success until Italy entered World War II on the side of Germany in June 1940. Thereafter, Britain and the emperor sought to cooperate with Ethiopian and other indigenous forces in a campaign to dislodge the Italians from Ethiopia and from British Somaliland, which the Italians seized in August 1940, and to resist the Italian invasion of Sudan. Haile Selassie proceeded immediately to Khartoum, where he established closer liaison with both the British headquarters and the resistance forces within Ethiopia.

Ethiopia in World War II

The wresting of Ethiopia from the occupying Italian forces involved British personnel, composed largely of South African and African colonial troops penetrating from the south, west, and north, supported by Ethiopian guerrillas. It was the task of an Anglo-Ethiopian mission, eventually commanded by Colonel Orde Wingate, to coordinate the activities of the Ethiopian forces in support of the campaign. The emperor arrived in Gojam on January 20, 1941, and immediately undertook the task of bringing the various local resistance groups under his control.

The campaigns of 1940 and 1941 were based on a British strategy of preventing Italian forces from attacking or occupying neighboring British possessions, while at the same time pressing northward from East Africa through Italian Somaliland and eastern Ethiopia to isolate Italian troops in the highlands. This thrust was directed at the Harer and Dire Dawa area, with the objective of cutting the rail link between Addis Ababa and Djibouti. At the same time, British troops from Sudan penetrated Eritrea to cut off Italian forces from the Red Sea. The campaign in the north ended in February and March of 1941 with the Battle of Keren and the defeat of Italian troops in Eritrea. By March 3, Italian Somaliland had fallen to British forces, and soon after the Italian governor initiated negotiations for the surrender of the remaining Italian forces. On May 5, 1941, Haile Selassie reentered Addis Ababa, but it was not until January 1942 that the last of the Italians, cut off near Gonder, surrendered to British and Ethiopian forces.

During the war years, British military officials left responsibility for internal affairs in the emperor's hands. However, it was agreed that all acts relating to the war effort—domestic or international—required British approval. Without defining the limits of authority, both sides also agreed that the emperor would issue "proclamations" and the British military administration would issue "public notices." Without consulting the British, Haile Selassie appointed a seven-member cabinet and a governor of Addis Ababa, but for tactical reasons he announced that they would serve as advisers to the British military administration.

This interim Anglo-Ethiopian arrangement was replaced in January 1942 by a new agreement that contained a military convention. The convention provided for British assistance in the organization of a new Ethiopian army that was to be trained by a British military mission (see Military Tradition in National Life, ch. 5). In addition to attaching officers to Ethiopian army battalions, the British assigned advisers to most ministries and to some provincial governors. British assistance strengthened the emperor's efforts to substitute, as his representatives in the provinces, experienced administrators for the traditional nobility. But such help was rejected whenever proposed reforms threatened to weaken the emperor's personal control.

The terms of the agreement confirmed Ethiopia's status as a sovereign state. However, the Ogaden and certain strategic areas, such as the French Somaliland border, the Addis Ababa-Djibouti railroad, and the Haud (collectively termed the "Reserved Areas"), remained temporarily under British administration. Other provisions set forth recruitment procedures for additional British advisers should they be requested. About the same time, a United States economic mission arrived, thereby laying the groundwork for an alliance that in time would significantly affect the country's direction.

A British-trained national police administration and police force gradually took the place of the police who had served earlier in the retinues of the provincial governors. Opposition to these changes

Italian troops march past billboard of Mussolini during 1936 invasion.
Courtesy Prints and Photographs Division, Library of Congress

was generally minor except for a revolt in 1943 in Tigray—long a stronghold of resistance to the Shewans— and another in the Ogaden, inhabited chiefly by the Somali. British aircraft brought from Aden helped quell the Tigray rebellion, and two battalions of Ethiopian troops suppressed the Ogaden uprising. The 1942 Anglo-Ethiopian agreement enabled the British military to disarm the Somali rebels and to patrol the region.

After Haile Selassie returned to the throne in 1941, the British assumed control over currency and foreign exchange as well as imports and exports. Additionally, the British helped Ethiopia to rehabilitate its national bureaucracy. These changes, as well as innovations made by the Italians during the occupation, brought home to many Ethiopians the need to modernize—at least in some sectors of public life—if the country were to survive as an independent entity.

In addition, the emperor made territorial demands, but these met with little sympathy from the British. Requests for the annexation of Eritrea, which the Ethiopians claimed to be racially, culturally, and economically inseparable from Ethiopia, were received with an awareness on the part of the British of a growing Eritrean sense of separate political identity. Similarly, Italian Somaliland was intended by the British to be part of "Greater Somalia"; thus, the emperor's claims to that territory were also rejected.

The Postwar Period, 1945–60: Reform and Opposition

Despite criticism of the emperor's 1936 decision to go into exile, the concept of the monarchy remained widely accepted after World War II. The country's leaders and the church assumed that victory over the Italians essentially meant the restoration of their traditional privileges. Before long, however, new social classes stirred into life by Haile Selassie's centralizing policies, as well as a younger generation full of frustrated expectations, clashed with forces bent on maintaining the traditional system.

Change and Resistance

The expansion of central authority by appointed officials required a dependable tax base, and that in turn encroached on the established prerogatives of those who had been granted large holdings in the south and of *gult*-holders of the Amhara-Tigray highlands. Consequently, in March 1942, without reference to the restored parliament, the emperor decreed a taxation system that divided all land into one of three categories: fertile, semifertile, and poor. A fixed levy, depending on category, was imposed for each *gasha* (forty hectares) of land.

The nobles of Gojam, Tigray, and Begemdir refused to accept any limitation upon the prevailing land tenure system and successfully battled the government over the issue. The emperor acknowledged defeat by excluding those provinces from the tax. When landlords elsewhere also protested the tax, the emperor exempted them as well, contenting himself with a flat 10 percent tithe on all but church land. But this tax, traditionally collected by landlords, was simply passed on to the tenants. In short, the emperor pursued policies that did not infringe on the rights of the nobility and other large landholders. In 1951, in response to additional pressure from the landlords, Haile Selassie further reduced the land tax payable by landlords and not covered by previous exemptions; the peasant cultivator, as in centuries past, continued to carry the entire taxation burden.

Some reform was also effected within the Ethiopian Orthodox Church. In July 1948, Haile Selassie initiated steps, completed in 1956, by which he, rather than the patriarch of Alexandria, would appoint the *abun,* or patriarch, of the Ethiopian Orthodox Church. Thus, for the first time in sixteen centuries of Ethiopian Christianity, an Ethiopian rather than an Egyptian served as head of the national church. The Ethiopian church, however, continued to recognize the primacy of the Alexandrian see. This appointment was followed by the creation of enough new bishoprics to allow the

Ethiopians to elect their own patriarch. Abuna Basilios, the first Ethiopian archbishop, was elevated to the status of patriarch in 1959. The postwar years also saw a change in the church-state relationship; the vast church landholdings became subject to tax legislation, and the clergy lost the right to try fellow church officials for civil offenses in their own court.

Acutely aware of his international image, Haile Selassie also was active on the diplomatic front (see Foreign Policy, ch. 4). Ethiopia was a founding member of the United Nations (UN) and the Organization of African Unity (OAU). After the postwar relationship with Britain wound down, the emperor in 1953 asked the United States for military assistance and economic support. Although his dependence on Washington grew, Haile Selassie diversified the sources of his international assistance, which included such disparate nations as Italy, China, the Federal Republic of Germany (West Germany), Taiwan, Yugoslavia, Sweden, and the Soviet Union.

Administrative Change and the 1955 Constitution

In pursuit of reform, Haile Selassie faced the recalcitrance of the provincial nobility, other great landholders, and church officials—all of whom intended to maintain their power and privileges. Moreover, some provincial nobility opposed the emperor because of their own long-held claims to the throne. Whatever his intentions as a reformer, Haile Selassie was a political realist and recognized that, lacking a strong military, he had to compromise with the Amhara and Tigray nobility and with the church. And, where required, he made his peace with other ethnic groups in the empire. For example, he eventually granted autonomy over Afar areas that Addis Ababa could not dominate by armed force to the sultan of Aussa. In general, political changes were few and were compromised at the first sign of substantial opposition. In the 1950s, despite his many years as emperor and his international stature, there was almost no significant section of the Ethiopian population on which Haile Selassie could rely to support him in such efforts.

The emperor sought to gain some control over local government by placing it in the hands of the central administration in Addis Ababa. He revised the administrative divisions and established political and administrative offices corresponding to them. The largest of these administrative units were the provinces (*teklay ghizats*), of which there were fourteen in the mid-1960s, each under a governor general appointed directly by Haile Selassie. Each province was subdivided into subprovinces (*awrajas*), districts (*weredas*), and subdistricts (*mikitil weredas*). Although the structure outwardly resembled a modern state apparatus, its impact was largely dissipated by the fact that higher-ranking landed nobles held all the important offices. Younger and better educated officials were little more than aides to the governors general, and their advice more often than not was contemptuously set aside by their superiors.

The emperor also attempted to strengthen the national government. A new generation of educated Ethiopians was introduced to new enlarged ministries, the powers of which were made more specific. The emperor established a national judiciary and appointed its judges. Finally, in 1955 he proclaimed a revised constitution. Apparently, he sought to provide a formal basis for his efforts at centralization and to attract the loyalty of those who gained their livelihood from relatively modern economic activities or who were better educated than most Ethiopians.

The younger leaders were mostly the sons of the traditional elite. Having been educated abroad, they were favorably disposed toward reform and were frequently frustrated and in some cases alienated by their inability to initiate and implement it. The remnants of the small number of educated Ethiopians of an earlier generation had been appointed to high government positions. But whatever their previous concern with reform, they had little impact on traditional methods, and by the mid-1950s even this earlier reformist elite was considered conservative by the succeeding generation.

The new elite was drawn largely from the postwar generation and was generally the product of a half-dozen secondary schools operated by foreign staffs. A majority of the students continued to come from families of the landed nobility, but they were profoundly affected by the presence of students from less affluent backgrounds and by their more democratically oriented Western teachers.

The 1955 constitution was prompted, like its 1931 predecessor, by a concern with international opinion. Such opinion was particularly important at a time when some neighboring African states were rapidly advancing under European colonial tutelage and Ethiopia was pressing its claims internationally for the incorporation of Eritrea, where an elected parliament and more modern administration had existed since 1952.

The bicameral Ethiopian parliament played no part in drawing up the 1955 constitution, which, far from limiting the emperor's control, emphasized the religious origins of imperial power and extended the centralization process. The Senate remained appointive, but the Chamber of Deputies was, at least nominally, elected. However, the absence of a census, the near total illiteracy of the population, and the domination of the countryside by the nobility meant that the majority of candidates who sought election in 1957 were in effect chosen by the elite. The Chamber of Deputies was not altogether a rubber stamp, at times discussing bills and questioning state ministers. However, provisions in the constitution that guaranteed personal freedoms and liberties, including freedom of assembly, movement, and speech, and the due process of law, were so far removed from the realities of Ethiopian life that no group or individual sought to act upon them publicly.

The Attempted Coup of 1960 and Its Aftermath

Haile Selassie's efforts to achieve a measure of change without jeopardizing his own power stimulated rising expectations, some of which he was unwilling or unable to satisfy. Impatient with the rate or form of social and political change, several groups conspired to launch a coup d'état on December 13, 1960, while the emperor was abroad on one of his frequent trips. The leadership of the 1960 revolt came from three groups: the commander of the Imperial Bodyguard, Mengistu Neway, and his followers; a few security officials, including the police chief; and a handful of radical intellectuals related to the officials, including Girmame Neway, Mengistu's brother.

The coup was initially successful in the capital, as the rebels seized the crown prince and more than twenty cabinet ministers and other government leaders. The support of the Imperial Bodyguard, the backbone of the revolt, was obtained without informing the enlisted men—or even a majority of the officers—of the purpose of the rebels' actions. The proclaimed intent of the coup leaders was the establishment of a government that would improve the economic, social, and political position of the general population, but they also appealed to traditional authority in the person of the crown prince. No mention was made of the emperor.

The coup's leaders failed to achieve popular support for their actions. Although university students demonstrated in favor of the coup, army and air force units remained loyal to the emperor, who returned to the capital on December 17. The patriarch of the church, who condemned the rebels as antireligious traitors and called for fealty to the emperor, supported the loyalists. Despite the coup's failure, it succeeded in stripping the monarchy of its claim to universal acceptance and led to a polarization of traditional and modern forces.

Growth of Secessionist Threats

Outside the Amhara-Tigray heartland, the two areas posing the most consistent problems for Ethiopia's rulers were Eritrea and the largely Somali-occupied Ogaden and adjacent regions.

The Liberation Struggle in Eritrea

Eritrea had been placed under British military administration in 1941 after the Italian surrender. In keeping with a 1950 decision of the UN General Assembly, British military administration ended in September 1952 and was replaced by a new autonomous Eritrean government in federal union with Ethiopia. Federation with the former Italian colony restored an unhindered maritime frontier to the country. The new arrangement also enabled the country to gain limited control of a territory that, at least in its inland areas, was more advanced politically and economically.

The Four Power Inquiry Commission established by the World War II Allies (Britain, France, the Soviet Union, and the United States) had failed to agree in its September 1948 report on a future course for Eritrea. Several countries had displayed an active interest in the area. In the immediate postwar years, Italy had requested that Eritrea be returned as a colony or as a trusteeship. This bid was supported initially by the Soviet Union, which anticipated a communist victory at the Italian polls. The Arab states, seeing Eritrea and its large Muslim population as an extension of the Arab world, sought the establishment of an independent state. Some Britons favored a division of the territory, with the Christian areas and the coast from Mitsiwa southward going to Ethiopia and the northwest area going to Sudan.

A UN commission, which arrived in Eritrea in February 1950, eventually approved a plan involving some form of association with Ethiopia. In December the UN General Assembly adopted a resolution affirming the commission's plan, with the provision that Britain, the administering power, should facilitate the UN efforts and depart from the colony no later than September 15, 1952. Faced with this constraint, the British administration held elections on March 16, 1952, for a representative assembly of sixty-eight members. This body, made up equally of Christians and Muslims, accepted the draft constitution advanced by the UN commissioner on July 10. The constitution was ratified by the emperor on September 11, and the assembly, by prearrangement, was transformed into the Eritrean Assembly three days before the federation was proclaimed.

The UN General Assembly resolution of September 15, 1952, adopted by a vote of forty-seven to ten, provided that Eritrea should be linked to Ethiopia through a loose federal structure under the emperor's sovereignty but with a form and organization of internal self-government. The federal government, which for all intents and purposes was the existing imperial government, was to control foreign affairs, defense, foreign and interstate commerce, transportation, and finance. Control over domestic affairs (including police, local administration, and taxation to meet its own budget) was to be exercised by an elected Eritrean assembly on the parliamentary model. The state was to have its own administrative and judicial structure and its own flag.

Almost from the start of federation, the emperor's representative undercut the territory's separate status under the federal system. In August 1955, Tedla Bairu, an Eritrean who was the chief executive elected by the assembly, resigned under pressure from the emperor, who replaced Tedla with his own nominee. He made Amharic the official language in place of Arabic and Tigrinya, terminated the use of the Eritrean flag, and moved many businesses out of Eritrea. In addition, the central government proscribed all political parties, imposed censorship, gave the top administrative positions to Amhara, and abandoned the principle of parity between Christian and Muslim officials. In November 1962, the Eritrean Assembly, many of whose members had been accused of accepting bribes, voted unanimously to change Eritrea's status to that of a province of Ethiopia. Following his appointment of the arch-conservative Ras Asrate Kasa as governor general, the emperor was accused of "refeudalizing" the territory.

The extinction of the federation consolidated internal and external opposition to union (see The Eritrean Movement, ch. 4; The Eritreans, ch. 5). Four years earlier, in 1958, a number of Eritrean exiles had founded the Eritrean Liberation Movement (ELM) in Cairo, under Hamid Idris Awate's leadership. This organization, however, soon was neutralized. A new faction, the Eritrean Liberation Front (ELF), emerged in 1960. Initially a Muslim movement, the ELF was nationalist rather than Marxist and received Iraqi and Syrian support. As urban Christians joined, the ELF became more radical and anticapitalist. Beginning in 1961, the ELF turned to armed struggle and by 1966 challenged imperial forces throughout Eritrea.

The rapid growth of the ELF also created internal divisions between urban and rural elements, socialists and nationalists, and Christians and Muslims. Although these divisions did not take any clear form, they were magnified as the ELF extended its operations and won international publicity. In June 1970, Osman Salah Sabbe, former head of the Muslim League, broke away from the ELF and formed the Popular Liberation Forces (PLF), which led directly to the founding of the Eritrean People's Liberation Front (EPLF) in early 1972. Both organizations initially attracted a large number of urban, intellectual, and leftist Christian youths and projected a strong socialist and nationalist image. By 1975 the EPLF had more than 10,000 members in the field. However, the growth of the EPLF was also accompanied by an intensification of internecine Eritrean conflict, particularly between 1972 and 1974, when casualties were well over 1,200. In 1976 Osman broke with the EPLF and formed the Eritrean Liberation Front-Popular Liberation Front (ELF–PLF). The division reflected differences between combatants in Eritrea and representatives abroad as well as personal rivalries and basic ideological differences, factors important in earlier splits within the Eritrean separatist movement.

Encouraged by the imperial regime's collapse and attendant confusion, the guerrillas extended their control over the whole region by 1977. Ethiopian forces were largely confined to urban centers and controlled the major roads only by day.

Discontent in Tigray

Overt dissidence in Tigray during Haile Selassie's reign centered on the 1943 resistance to imperial rule known as the Weyane. The movement took advantage of popular discontent against Amhara rule but was primarily a localized resistance to imperial rule that depended on three main sources of support. These were the semi-pastoralists of eastern Tigray, including the Azebo and Raya, who believed their traditional Oromo social structure to be threatened; the local Tigray nobility, who perceived their position to be endangered by the central government's growth; and the peasantry, who felt victimized by government officials and their militias.

The course of the Weyane was relatively brief, lasting from May 22 to October 14, 1943. Although the rebels made some initial gains, the imperial forces, supported by British aircraft, soon took the offensive. Poor military leadership, combined with disagreements among the rebel leaders, detracted from the effectiveness of their efforts. After the fall of Mekele, capital of Tigray, on October 14, 1943, practically all organized resistance collapsed. The government exiled or imprisoned the leaders of the revolt. The emperor took reprisals against peasants suspected of supporting the Weyane.

Although a military resolution of the Weyane restored imperial authority to Tigray, the harsh measures used by the Ethiopian military to do so created resentment of imperial rule in many quarters. This resentment, coupled with a long-standing feeling that Shewan Amhara rule was of an upstart nature, lasted through the end of Haile Selassie's reign. After Haile Selassie's demise in 1974, separatist feelings again emerged throughout Tigray.

The Ogaden and the Haud

Ethiopia's entry into the Somali region in modern times dated from the conquest of Harer in the late 1890s by Menelik, who based his actions on old claims of Ethiopian sovereignty. In 1945 Haile Selassie, fearing the possibility of British support for a separate Somali state that would include the Ogaden, claimed Italian Somaliland as a "lost province." In Italian Somaliland, the Somali Youth League (SYL) resisted this claim and in its turn demanded unification of all Somali areas, including those in Ethiopia.

After the British evacuated the Ogaden in 1948, Ethiopian officers took over administration in the city of Jijiga, at one point suppressing a demonstration led by the SYL, which the government subsequently outlawed. At the same time, Ethiopia renounced its claim to Italian Somaliland in deference to UN calls for self-determination. The Ethiopians, however, maintained that self-determination was not incompatible with eventual union.

Immediately upon the birth of the Republic of Somalia in 1960, which followed the merger of British Somaliland and Italian Somaliland, the new country proclaimed an irredentist policy. Somalia laid claim to Somali-populated regions of French Somaliland (later called the French Territory of the Afars and Issas, and Djibouti after independence in 1977), the northeastern corner of Kenya, and the Ogaden, a vast, ill-defined region occupied by Somali nomads extending southeast from Ethiopia's southern highlands that includes a separate region east of Harer known as the Haud. The uncertainty over the precise location of the frontier between Ethiopia and the former Italian possessions in Somalia further complicated these claims. Despite UN efforts to promote an agreement, none was made in the colonial or the Italian trusteeship period.

In the northeast, an Anglo-Ethiopian treaty determined the frontier's official location. However, Somalia contended that it was unfairly placed so as to exclude the herders resident in Somalia from vital seasonal grazing lands in the Haud. The British had administered the Haud as an integral part of British Somaliland, although Ethiopian sovereignty had been recognized there. After it was disbanded in the rest of Ethiopia, the British military administration continued to supervise the area from Harer eastward and did not withdraw from the Haud until 1955. Even then, the British stressed the region's importance to Somalia by requiring the Ethiopians to guarantee the Somali free access to grazing lands.

Somalia refused to recognize any pre-1960 treaties defining the Somali-Ethiopian borders because colonial governments had concluded the agreements. Despite the need for access to pasturage for local herds, the Somali government even refused to acknowledge the British treaty guaranteeing Somali grazing rights in the Haud because it would have indirectly recognized Ethiopian sovereignty over the area.

Within six months after Somali independence, military incidents occurred between Ethiopian and Somali forces along their mutual border. Confrontations escalated again in 1964, when the Ethiopian air force raided Somali villages and encampments inside the Somali border. Hostilities were ended through mediation by the OAU and Sudan. However, Somalia continued to promote irredentism by supporting the Western Somali Liberation Front (WSLF), which was active in the Ogaden. Claims of oil discoveries prompted the resurgence of fighting in 1973.

Revolution and Military Government

In early 1974, Ethiopia entered a period of profound political, economic, and social change, frequently accompanied by violence. Confrontation between traditional and modern forces erupted and changed the political, economic, and social nature of the Ethiopian state.

Background to Revolution, 1960–74

The last fourteen years of Haile Selassie's reign witnessed growing opposition to his regime. After the suppression of the 1960 coup attempt, the emperor sought to reclaim the loyalty of coup sympathizers by stepping up reform. Much of this effort took the form of land grants to military and police officers, however, and no coherent pattern of economic and social development appeared.

In 1966 a plan emerged to confront the traditional forces through the implementation of a modern tax system. Implicit in the proposal, which required registration of all land, was the aim of destroying the power of the landed nobility. But when progressive tax proposals were submitted to parliament in the late 1960s, they were vigorously opposed by the members, all of whom were property owners. Parliament passed a tax on agricultural produce in November 1967, but in a form vastly altered from the government proposal. Even this, however, was fiercely resisted by the landed class in Gojam, and the entire province revolted. In 1969, after two years of military action, the central government withdrew its troops, discontinued enforcement of the tax, and canceled all arrears of taxation going back to 1940.

The emperor's defeat in Gojam encouraged defiance by other provincial landowners, although not on the same scale. But legislation calling for property registration and for modification of landlord-tenant relationships was more boldly resisted in the Chamber of Deputies and the Senate. Debate on these proposals continued until the mid-1970s.

At the same time the emperor was facing opposition to change, other forces were exerting direct or indirect pressure in favor of reform. Beginning in 1965, student demonstrations focused on the need to implement land reform and to address corruption and rising prices. Peasant disturbances, although on a small scale, were especially numerous in the southern provinces, where the imperial government had traditionally rewarded its supporters with land grants. Although it allowed labor unions to organize in 1962, the government restricted union activities. Soon, even the Confederation of Ethiopian Labor Unions (CELU) was criticized as being too subservient to the government. Faced with such a multiplicity of problems, the aging emperor increasingly left domestic issues in the care of his prime minister, Aklilu Habte Wold (appointed in 1961), and turned his attention to foreign affairs.

The Establishment of the Derg

The government's failure to effect significant economic and political reforms over the previous fourteen years—combined with rising inflation, corruption, a famine that affected several provinces (but especially Welo and Tigray) and that was concealed from the outside world, and the growing discontent of urban interest groups—provided the backdrop against which the Ethiopian revolution began to unfold in early 1974. Whereas elements of the urban-based, modernizing elite previously had sought to establish a parliamentary democracy, the initiation of the 1974 revolution was the work of the military, acting essentially in its own immediate interests. The unrest that began in January of that year then spread to the civilian population in an outburst of general discontent.

The Ethiopian military on the eve of the revolution was riven by factionalism; the emperor promoted such division to prevent any person or group from becoming too powerful. Factions included the Imperial Bodyguard, which had been rebuilt since the 1960 coup attempt; the Territorial Army (Ethiopia's national ground force), which was broken into many factions but which was dominated by a group of senior officers called "The Exiles" because they had fled with Haile Selassie in 1936 after the Italian invasion; and the air force. The officer graduates of the Harer Military Academy also formed a distinct group in opposition to the Holeta Military Training Center graduates (see Training, ch. 5).

Conditions throughout the army were frequently substandard, with enlisted personnel often receiving low pay and insufficient food and supplies. Enlisted personnel as well as some of the Holeta graduates came from the peasantry, which at the time was suffering from a prolonged drought and resulting famine. The general perception was that the central government was deliberately refusing to take special measures for famine relief. Much popular discontent over this issue, plus the generally perceived lack of civil freedoms, had created widespread discontent among the middle class, which had been built up and supported by the emperor since World War II.

The revolution began with a mutiny of the Territorial Army's Fourth Brigade at Negele in the southern province of Sidamo on January 12, 1974. Soldiers protested poor food and water conditions; led by their noncommissioned officers, they rebelled and took their commanding officer hostage, requesting redress from the emperor. Attempts at reconciliation and a subsequent impasse promoted the spread of the discontent to other units throughout the military, including those stationed in Eritrea. There, the Second Division at Asmera mutinied, imprisoned its commanders, and announced its support for the Negele mutineers. The Signal Corps, in sympathy with the uprising, broadcast information about events to the rest of the military. Moreover, by that time, general discontent had resulted in the rise of resistance throughout Ethiopia. Opposition to increased fuel prices and curriculum changes in the schools, as well as low teachers' salaries and many other grievances, crystalized by the end of February. Teachers, workers, and eventually students—all demanding higher pay and better conditions of work and education—also promoted other causes, such as land reform and famine relief. Finally, the discontented groups demanded a new political system. Riots in the capital and the continued military mutiny eventually led to the resignation of Prime Minister Aklilu. He was replaced on February 28, 1974, by another Shewan aristocrat, Endalkatchew Mekonnen, whose government would last only until July 22.

On March 5, the government announced a revision of the 1955 constitution—the prime minister henceforth would be responsible to parliament. The new government probably reflected Haile Selassie's decision to minimize change; the new cabinet, for instance, represented virtually all of Ethiopia's aristocratic families. The conservative constitutional committee appointed on March 21 included no representatives of the groups pressing for change. The new government introduced no substantial reforms (although it granted the military several salary increases). It also postponed unpopular changes in the education system and instituted price roll-backs and controls to check inflation. As a result, the general discontent subsided somewhat by late March.

By this time, there were several factions within the military that claimed to speak for all or part of the armed forces. These included the Imperial Bodyguard under the old high command, a group of "radical" junior officers, and a larger number of moderate and radical army and police officers grouped around Colonel Alem Zewd Tessema, commander of an airborne brigade based in Addis Ababa. In late March, Alem Zewd became head of an informal, inter-unit coordinating committee that came to be called the Armed Forces Coordinating Committee (AFCC). Acting with the approval of the new prime minister, Alem Zewd arrested a large number of disgruntled air force officers and in general appeared to support the Endalkatchew government.

Such steps, however, did not please many of the junior officers, who wished to pressure the regime into making major political reforms. In early June, a dozen or more of them broke away from the AFCC and requested that every military and police unit send three representatives to Addis Ababa to organize for further action. In late June, a body of men that eventually totaled about 120, none above the rank of major and almost all of whom remained anonymous, organized themselves into a new body called the Coordinating Committee of the Armed Forces, Police, and Territorial Army. This body soon came to be called the Derg (Amharic for "committee" or "council"—see Glossary). They elected Major Mengistu Haile Mariam chairman and Major Atnafu Abate vice chairman, both outspoken proponents of far-reaching change.

This group of men would remain at the forefront of political and military affairs in Ethiopia for the next thirteen years. The identity of the Derg never changed after these initial meetings in 1974. Although its membership declined drastically during the next few years as individual officers were eliminated, no new members were admitted into its ranks, and its deliberations and membership remained almost entirely unknown. At first, the Derg's officers exercised their influence behind the scenes; only later, during the era of the Provisional Military Administrative Council, did its leaders emerge from anonymity and become both the official as well as the de facto governing personnel.

Because its members in effect represented the entire military establishment, the Derg could henceforth claim to exercise real power and could mobilize troops on its own, thereby depriving the emperor's government of the ultimate means to govern. Although the Derg professed loyalty to the emperor, it immediately began to arrest members of the aristocracy, military, and government who were closely associated with the emperor and the old order. Colonel Alem Zewd, by now discredited in the eyes of the young radicals, fled.

In July the Derg wrung five concessions from the emperor: the release of all political prisoners, a guarantee of the safe return of exiles, the promulgation and speedy implementation of the new constitution, assurance that parliament would be kept in session to complete the aforementioned task, and assurance that the Derg would be allowed to coordinate closely with the government at all levels of operation. Hereafter, political power and initiative lay with the Derg, which was increasingly influenced by a wide-ranging public debate over the future of the country. The demands made of the emperor were but the first of a series of directives or actions that constituted the "creeping coup" by which the imperial system of government was slowly dismantled. Promoting an agenda for lasting changes going far beyond those proposed since the revolution began in January, the Derg proclaimed Ethiopia Tikdem (Ethiopia First) as its guiding philosophy. It forced out Prime Minister Endalkatchew and replaced him with Mikael Imru, a Shewan aristocrat with a reputation as a liberal.

The Derg's agenda rapidly diverged from that of the reformers of the late imperial period. In early August, the revised constitution, which called for a constitutional monarchy, was rejected when it was forwarded for approval. Thereafter, the Derg worked to undermine the authority and legitimacy of the emperor, a policy that enjoyed much public support. The Derg arrested the commander of the Imperial Bodyguard, disbanded the emperor's governing councils, closed the private imperial exchequer, and nationalized the imperial residence and the emperor's other landed and business holdings. By late August, the emperor had been directly accused of covering up the Welo and Tigray famine of the early 1970s that allegedly had killed 100,000 to 200,000 people. After street demonstrations took place urging the emperor's arrest, the Derg formally deposed Haile Selassie on September 12 and imprisoned him. The emperor was too old to resist, and it is doubtful whether he really understood what was happening around him. Three days later, the Armed Forces Coordinating Committee (i.e., the Derg) transformed itself into the Provisional Military Administrative Council (PMAC) under the chairmanship of Lieutenant General Aman Mikael Andom and proclaimed itself the nation's ruling body.

The Struggle for Power, 1974–77

Although not a member of the Derg per se, General Aman had been associated with the Derg since July and had lent his good name

Revolutionary monument extols the virtues of communism.
Courtesy Paul Henze

to its efforts to reform the imperial regime. He was a well-known, popular commander and hero of a war against Somalia in the 1960s. In accordance with the Derg's wishes, he now became head of state, chairman of the Council of Ministers, and minister of defense, in addition to being chairman of the PMAC. Despite his standing, however, General Aman was almost immediately at odds with a majority of the Derg's members on three major issues: the size of the Derg and his role within it, the Eritrean insurgency, and the fate of political prisoners. Aman claimed that the 120-member Derg was too large and too unwieldy to function efficiently as a governing body; as an Eritrean, he urged reconciliation with the insurgents there; and he opposed the death penalty for former government and military officials who had been arrested since the revolution began.

The Derg immediately found itself under attack from civilian groups, especially student and labor groups who demanded the formation of a "people's government" in which various national organizations would be represented. These demands found support in the Derg among a faction composed mostly of army engineers and air force officers. On October 7, the Derg arrested dissidents supporting the civilian demands. By mid-November, Aman, opposed by the majority of the Derg, was attempting unsuccessfully

55

to appeal directly to the army for support as charges, many apparently fabricated, mounted against him within the Derg. He retired to his home and on November 23 was killed resisting arrest. The same evening of what became known as "Bloody Saturday," fifty-nine political prisoners were executed. Among them were prominent civilians such as Aklilu and Endalkatchew, military officers such as Colonel Alem Zewd and General Abiye Abebe (the emperor's son-in-law and defense minister under Endalkatchew), and two Derg members who had supported Aman.

Following the events of Bloody Saturday, Brigadier General Tafari Banti, a Shewan, became chairman of the PMAC and head of state on November 28, but power was retained by Major Mengistu, who kept his post as first vice chairman of the PMAC, with Major Atnafu as second vice chairman. Mengistu hereafter emerged as the leading force in the Derg and took steps to protect and enlarge his power base. Preparations were made for a new offensive in Eritrea, and social and economic reform was addressed; the result was the promulgation on December 20 of the first socialist proclamation for Ethiopia.

In keeping with its declared socialist path, the Derg announced in March 1975 that all royal titles were revoked and that the proposed constitutional monarchy was to be abandoned. In August Haile Selassie died under questionable circumstances and was secretly buried. One of the last major links with the past was broken in February 1976, when the patriarch of the Ethiopian Orthodox Church, Abuna Tewoflos, an imperial appointee, was deposed.

In April 1976, the Derg at last set forth its goals in greater detail in the Program for the National Democratic Revolution (PNDR). As announced by Mengistu, these objectives included progress toward socialism under the leadership of workers, peasants, the petite bourgeoisie, and all antifeudal and anti-imperialist forces. The Derg's ultimate aim was the creation of a one-party system. To accomplish its goals, the Derg established an intermediary organ called the Provisional Office for Mass Organization Affairs (POMOA). Designed to act as a civilian political bureau, POMOA was at first in the hands of the All-Ethiopia Socialist Movement (whose Amharic acronym was MEISON), headed by Haile Fida, the Derg's chief political adviser. Haile Fida, as opposed to other leftists who had formed the Ethiopian People's Revolutionary Party (EPRP), had resourcefully adopted the tactic of working with the military in the expectation of directing the revolution from within (see Political Participation and Repression, ch. 4).

By late 1976, the Derg had undergone an internal reconfiguration as Mengistu's power came under growing opposition and as

Mengistu, Tafari, and Atnafu struggled for supremacy. The instability of this arrangement was resolved in January and February of 1977, when a major shootout at the Grand (Menelik's) Palace in Addis Ababa took place between supporters of Tafari and those of Mengistu, in which the latter emerged victorious. With the death of Tafari and his supporters in the fighting, most internal opposition within the Derg had been eliminated, and Mengistu proceeded with a reorganization of the Derg. This action left Mengistu as the sole vice chairman, responsible for the People's Militia, the urban defense squads, and the modernization of the armed forces—in other words, in effective control of Ethiopia's government and military. In November 1977, Atnafu, Mengistu's last rival in the Derg, was eliminated, leaving Mengistu in undisputed command.

Ethiopia's Road to Socialism

Soon after taking power, the Derg promoted Ye-Itiopia Hibretesebawinet (Ethiopian Socialism). The concept was embodied in slogans such as "self-reliance," "the dignity of labor," and "the supremacy of the common good." These slogans were devised to combat the widespread disdain of manual labor and a deeply rooted concern with status. A central aspect of socialism was land reform. Although there was common agreement on the need for land reform, the Derg found little agreement on its application. Most proposals—even those proffered by socialist countries—counseled moderation in order to maintain production. The Derg, however, adopted a radical approach, with the Land Reform Proclamation of March 1975, which nationalized all rural land, abolished tenancy, and put peasants in charge of enforcement. No family was to have a plot larger than ten hectares, and no one could employ farm workers. Farmers were expected to organize peasant associations, one for every 800 hectares, which would be headed by executive committees responsible for enforcement of the new order. Implementation of these measures caused considerable disruption of local administration in rural areas. In July 1975, all urban land, rentable houses, and apartments were also nationalized, with the 3 million urban residents organized into urban dwellers' associations, or *kebeles* (see Glossary), analogous in function to the rural peasant associations (see Peasant Associations; *Kebeles,* ch. 4).

Although the government took a radical approach to land reform, it exercised some caution with respect to the industrial and commercial sectors. In January and February 1975, the Derg nationalized all banks and insurance firms and seized control of practically every important company in the country. However, retail

57

trade and the wholesale and export-import sectors remained in private hands.

Although the Derg ordered national collective ownership of land, the move was taken with little preparation and met with opposition in some areas, especially Gojam, Welo, and Tigray. The Derg also lost much support from the country's left wing, which had been excluded from power and the decision-making process. Students and teachers were alienated by the government's closure of the university in Addis Ababa and all secondary schools in September 1975 in the face of threatened strikes, as well as the forced mobilization of students in the Development Through Cooperation Campaign (commonly referred to as *zemecha*—see Glossary) under conditions of military discipline. The elimination of the Confederation of Ethiopian Labor Unions (CELU) in favor of the government-controlled All-Ethiopia Trade Union (AETU) in December 1975 further disillusioned the revolution's early supporters. Numerous officials originally associated with the revolution fled the country.

The Mengistu Regime and Its Impact

The transition from imperial to military rule was turbulent. In addition to increasing political discontent, which was particularly intense in the late 1970s, the Derg faced powerful insurgencies and natural calamities throughout the 1980s.

Political Struggles Within the Government

Following the establishment of his supremacy through the elimination of Tafari Banti, Mengistu declared himself Derg chairman in February 1977 and set about consolidating his power. However, several internal and external threats prevented Mengistu from doing this. Various insurgent groups posed the most serious threat to the Derg. The EPRP challenged the Derg's control of the revolution itself by agitating for a broad-based democratic government run by civilians, not by the military. In February 1977, the EPRP initiated terrorist attacks—known as the White Terror—against Derg members and their supporters. This violence immediately claimed at least eight Derg members, plus numerous Derg supporters, and soon provoked a government counteraction—the Red Terror (see Glossary). During the Red Terror, which lasted until late 1978, government security forces systematically hunted down and killed suspected EPRP members and their supporters, especially students. Mengistu and the Derg eventually won this latest struggle for control of the Ethiopian revolution, at a cost to the

EPRP of thousands of its members and supporters imprisoned, dead, or missing.

Also slated for destruction was MEISON, proscribed in mid-1978. In coordination with the government, MEISON had organized the *kebeles* and the peasant associations but had begun to act independently, thus threatening Derg dominance of local governments throughout the country. In response to the political vacuum that would be left as a result of the purging of MEISON, the Derg in 1978 promoted the union of several existing Marxist-Leninist organizations into a single umbrella group, the Union of Ethiopian Marxist-Leninist Organizations (whose Amharic acronym was EMALEDEH). The new organization's duty was similar to that of MEISON—promoting control of Ethiopian socialism and obtaining support for government policies through various political activities. The creation of EMALEDEH symbolized the victory of the Derg in finally consolidating power after having overcome these challenges to its control of the Ethiopian revolution.

War in the Ogaden and the Turn to the Soviet Union

The year 1977 saw the emergence of the most serious external challenge to the revolutionary regime that had yet materialized. The roots of the conflict lay with Somali irredentism and the desire of the Somali government of Mahammad Siad Barre to annex the Ogaden area of Ethiopia. Somalia's instrument in this process was the Western Somali Liberation Front (WSLF), a Somali guerrilla organization, which by February 1977 had begun to take advantage of the Derg's political problems as well as its troubles in Eritrea to attack government positions throughout the Ogaden (see The Somali, ch. 5). The Somali government provided supplies and logistics support to the WSLF. Through the first half of the year, the WSLF made steady gains, penetrating and capturing large parts of the Ogaden from the Dire Dawa area southward to the Kenya border.

The increasingly intense fighting culminated in a series of actions around Jijiga in September, at which time Ethiopia claimed that Somalia's regular troops, the Somali National Army (SNA), were supporting the WSLF. In response, the Somali government admitted giving "moral, material, and other support" to the WSLF. Following a mutiny of the Ethiopian garrison at Jijiga, the town fell to the WSLF. The Mengistu regime, desperate for help, turned to the Soviet Union, its ties to its former military supplier, the United States, having foundered in the spring over the Derg's poor human rights record. The Soviet Union had been supplying equipment and some advisers for months. When the Soviet Union continued to aid Ethiopia as a way of gaining influence in the country, Somalia, which until then had been a Soviet client, responded by abrogating its Treaty of Friendship and Cooperation with Moscow and by expelling all Soviet advisers.

The Soviet turnaround immediately affected the course of the war. Starting in late November, massive Soviet military assistance began to pour into Ethiopia, with Cuban troops deploying from Angola to assist the Ethiopian units. By the end of the year, 17,000 Cubans had arrived and, with Ethiopian army units, halted the WSLF momentum. On February 13, 1978, Mogadishu dispatched the SNA to assist the WSLF, but the Somali forces were driven back toward the border. After the Ethiopian army recapture of Jijiga in early March, the Somali government decided to withdraw its forces from the Ogaden, leaving the Ethiopian army in control of the region. However, in the process of eliminating the WSLF threat, Addis Ababa had become a military client of Moscow and Havana, a situation that had significant international repercussions and that resulted in a major realignment of power in the Horn of Africa.

Eritrean and Tigrayan Insurgencies

After 1974, insurgencies appeared in various parts of the country, the most important of which were centered in Eritrea and Tigray (see Political Dynamics, ch. 4; External and Internal Opponents, ch. 5). The Eritrean problem, inherited from Haile Selassie's regime, was a matter of extensive debate within the Derg. It was a dispute over policy toward Eritrea that resulted in the death of the PMAC's first leader, General Aman, an Eritrean, on November 23, 1974, so-called "Bloody Saturday." Hereafter, the Derg decided to impose a military settlement on the Eritean Liberation Front (ELF) and the Eritrean People's Liberation Front (EPLF). Attempts to invade rebel-held Eritrea failed repeatedly, and by mid-1978 the insurgent groups controlled most of the countryside but not major towns such as Keren, Mitsiwa, Aseb, and a few other places. Despite large commitments of arms and training from communist countries, the Derg failed to suppress the Eritrean rebellion.

By the end of 1976, insurgencies existed in all of the country's fourteen administrative regions (the provinces were officially changed to regions in 1974 after the revolution). In addition to the Eritrean secessionists, rebels were highly active in Tigray, where the Tigray People's Liberation Front (TPLF), formed in 1975, was demanding social justice and self-determination for all Ethiopians. In the southern regions of Bale, Sidamo, and Arsi, the Oromo Liberation Front (OLF) and the Somali Abo Liberation Front (SALF), active since 1975, had gained control of parts of the

Famine scene at Korem, in Welo
Courtesy United Nations Children's Fund (Bert Demmers)

countryside, and the WSLF was active in the Ogaden. Under Ali Mirah's leadership, the Afar Liberation Front (ALF) began armed operations in March 1975, and in 1976 it coordinated some actions with the EPLF and the TPLF.

Despite an influx of military aid from the Soviet Union and its allies after 1977, the government's counterinsurgency effort in Eritrea progressed haltingly. After initial government successes in retaking territory around the major towns and cities and along some of the principal roads in 1978 and 1979, the conflict ebbed and flowed on an almost yearly basis. Annual campaigns by the Ethiopian armed forces to dislodge the EPLF from positions around the northern town of Nakfa failed repeatedly and proved costly to the government. Eritrean and Tigrayan insurgents began to cooperate, the EPLF providing training and equipment that helped build the TPLF into a full-fledged fighting force. Between 1982 and 1985, the EPLF and the Derg held a series of talks to resolve the Eritrean conflict, but to no avail. By the end of 1987, dissident organizations in Eritrea and Tigray controlled at least 90 percent of both regions.

Social and Political Changes

Although Addis Ababa quickly developed a close relationship with the communist world, the Soviet Union and its allies had consistent difficulties working with Mengistu and the Derg. These difficulties were largely the result of the Derg's preoccupation with internal matters and the promotion of Ethiopian variations on what Marxist-Leninist theoreticians regarded as preordained steps on the road to a socialist state. The Derg's status as a military government was another source of concern. Ethiopia's communist allies made an issue of the need to create a civilian "vanguard party" that would rule a people's republic. In a move geared to ensure continued communist support, the Derg formed the Commission to Organize the Party of the Workers of Ethiopia (COPWE) in December 1979, with Mengistu as its chairman. At COPWE's second congress, in January 1983, it was announced that COPWE would be replaced by a genuine communist party. Accordingly, the Workers' Party of Ethiopia (WPE) was proclaimed on September 12, 1984 (see The Workers' Party of Ethiopia, ch. 4).

About the same time, work continued on a new constitution for the planned people's republic. On February 1, 1987, the proposed constitution, which had been submitted to the public for popular debate and changes the prior year, was finally put to a vote. Although the central government claimed an 81 percent approval of the new constitution (with modifications proposed by the public), the circumstances of its review and approval by the general population were called into question. The task of publicizing the document had been entrusted to the *kebeles* and the peasant associations—organizations that had a state security mission as well as local administrative duties. Observers noted that little commentary or dissent was possible under such circumstances. Additional criticism included the charge that the proposed constitution was not designed to address or even understand Ethiopian needs; in fact, many noted that the constitution was "almost an abridged translation of the Soviet Constitution of 1977" (see The 1987 Constitution, ch. 4).

Ethiopia in Crisis: Famine and Its Aftermath, 1984–88

Toward the end of the 1980s, several crises, including famine, economic collapse, and military setbacks in Eritrea and Tigray, confronted the Derg. In addition, as democratic reform swept through the communist world, it became evident that Addis Ababa no longer could rely on its allies for support.

Famine and Economic Collapse

Ethiopia had never recovered from the previous great famine of the early 1970s, which was the result of a drought that affected most of the countries of the African Sahel. The late 1970s again brought signs of intensifying drought. By the early 1980s, large numbers of people in central Eritrea, Tigray, Welo, and parts of Gonder and Shewa were beginning to feel the effects of renewed famine.

By mid-1984 it was evident that another drought and resulting famine of major proportions had begun to affect large parts of northern Ethiopia. Just as evident was the government's inability to provide relief. The almost total failure of crops in the north was compounded by fighting in and around Eritrea, which hindered the passage of relief supplies. Although international relief organizations made a major effort to provide food to the affected areas, the persistence of drought and poor security conditions in the north resulted in continuing need of as well as hazards for famine relief workers. In late 1985, another year of drought was forecast, and by early 1986 the famine had spread to parts of the southern highlands, with an estimated 5.8 million people dependent on relief food. Exacerbating the problem in 1986 were locust and grasshopper plagues.

The government's inability or unwillingness to deal with the 1984–85 famine provoked universal condemnation by the international community. Even many supporters of the Ethiopian regime opposed its policy of withholding food shipments to rebel areas. The combined effects of famine and internal war had by then put the nation's economy into a state of collapse.

The primary government response to the drought and famine was the decision to uproot large numbers of peasants who lived in the affected areas in the north and to resettle them in the southern part of the country. In 1985 and 1986, about 600,000 people were moved, many forcibly, from their home villages and farms by the military and transported to various regions in the south. Many peasants fled rather than allow themselves to be resettled; many of those who were resettled sought later to return to their native regions. Several human rights organizations claimed that tens of thousands of peasants died as a result of forced resettlement (see The Politics of Resettlement, ch. 4).

Another government plan involved villagization, which was a response not only to the famine but also to the poor security situation. Beginning in 1985, peasants were forced to move their homesteads into planned villages, which were clustered around water, schools, medical services, and utility supply points to facilitate distribution of those services. Many peasants fled rather than submit to relocation, which in general proved highly unpopular. Additionally, the government in most cases failed to provide the promised services. Far from benefiting agricultural productivity, the program caused a decline in food production. Although temporarily suspended in 1986, villagization was subsequently resumed.

Government Defeats in Eritrea and Tigray

In March 1988, the EPLF initiated one of its most successful military campaigns by striking at Ethiopian army positions on the Nakfa front north of the town of Afabet, where the Derg had established a base for a new attack against the insurgents. In two days of fighting, the Eritrean rebels annihilated three Ethiopian army divisions, killing or capturing at least 18,000 government troops and seizing large amounts of equipment, including armor and artillery. Subsequently, the town of Afabet, with its military stores, fell to the EPLF, which then threatened all remaining Ethiopian military concentrations in northern Eritrea.

The Ethiopian army's defeat in Eritrea came after setbacks during the preceding week in Tigray. Using the same tactics employed by the EPLF, the TPLF preempted a pending Ethiopian offensive in Tigray with a series of attacks on government positions there in early March. A government attack against central Tigray failed disastrously, with four Ethiopian army divisions reportedly destroyed and most of their equipment captured. In early April, the

TPLF took the town of Adigrat in northern Tigray, cutting the main road link between Addis Ababa and Eritrea.

The March 1988 defeats of the Ethiopian army were catastrophic in terms of their magnitude and crippling in their effect on government strategy in Eritrea and Tigray. The capability of government forces in both regions collapsed as a result. Subsequently, Ethiopian government control of Eritrea was limited to the Keren-Asmera-Mitsiwa triangle and the port of Aseb to the southeast. The TPLF's victories in Tigray ultimately led to its total conquest by the rebels and the expansion of the insurgency into Gonder, Welo, and even parts of Shewa the following year.

The People's Democratic Republic of Ethiopia

On September 10, 1987, after thirteen years of military rule, the nation officially became the People's Democratic Republic of Ethiopia (PDRE) under a new constitution providing for a civilian government. The PMAC was abolished, and in June of that year Ethiopians had elected the National Shengo (National Assembly), a parliament. Despite these changes, members of the now-defunct Derg still ran the government but with different titles. For example, the National Shengo elected Mengistu to be the country's first civilian president; he remained, however, the WPE's general secretary. Other high-ranking Derg and WPE members received similar posts in the new government, including the Derg deputy chairman, Fikre-Selassie Wogderes, who became Ethiopia's prime minister, and Fisseha Desta, WPE deputy general secretary, who became the country's vice president.

Despite outward appearances, little changed in the way the country was actually run. Old Derg members still were in control, and the stated mission of the WPE allowed continued close supervision by the government over much of the urban population. Despite the granting of "autonomy" to Eritrea, Aseb, Tigray, Dire Dawa, and the Ogaden, the 1987 constitution was ambiguous on the question of self-determination for national groups such as the Eritreans, except within the framework of the national government. And although the constitution contained provisions to protect the rights of citizens, the power of peasant associations and *kebeles* was left intact.

Changes in Soviet Policy and New International Horizons

The Soviet Union changed policies toward its allies among the developing countries in the late 1980s; these changes appeared likely to result in significant reductions in its hitherto extensive support of Ethiopia. By then it was evident that the Soviet-Ethiopian relationship had undergone a fundamental reorientation. The change was partly the result of the new directions in Soviet foreign policy undertaken by Mikhail Gorbachev. But other contributing factors were the strong undercurrents of Soviet disapproval of Ethiopia's conduct of its internal affairs and of Addis Ababa's inability to make effective use of the aid that Moscow sent. The implications of this changed policy for Ethiopia were likely to be profound, inasmuch as continued high levels of military assistance were vital to the pursuit of Mengistu's military solution in Eritrea as well as to the fight against other internal insurgencies.

* * *

The literature on Ethiopia is relatively rich and deep, the consequence of Ethiopia's indigenous written tradition, mostly in Gi'iz, and of the extraordinary interest in the country shown by Europeans over the last five centuries. For the early historical period, two works are fundamental: *Aksum: An African Civilisation of Late Antiquity* by Stuart Munro-Hay, and *Church and State in Ethiopia, 1270–1527* by Taddesse Tamrat. Each is the best work on its respective subject and period and likely to remain so for the foreseeable future. In nearly the same league is John Spencer Trimingham's *Islam in Ethiopia,* a standard work and a starting point for the history, culture, and religion of Ethiopia's Muslim peoples, despite its 1952 publishing date.

A comprehensive, up-to-date survey of the country remains to be written, but an older work by Edward Ullendorff, *The Ethiopians: An Introduction to Country and People* (1973), is still quite useful, despite its emphasis on the northern, Semitic-speaking population. As a supplement, the reader might consult the relevant chapters in the eight volumes of *The Cambridge History of Africa,* edited by J.D. Fage and Roland Oliver. Two books by Mordechai Abir, *Ethiopia and the Red Sea* and *Ethiopia: The Era of the Princes,* cover subjects or periods otherwise almost totally neglected, including trade, commerce, and the contributions of the Oromo. Richard K. Pankhurst's *Economic History of Ethiopia, 1800–1935* contains a wealth of information on a wide variety of topics, as do other works by this scholar. Two books by Donald N. Levine, *Wax and Gold* and *Greater Ethiopia: The Evolution of a Multi-Ethnic Society,* provide stimulating and at times provocative analyses of Amhara, Tigray, and (in the latter volume) Oromo cultures but should be consulted only after basics in the field have been mastered. A highly useful reference is the *Historical Dictionary of Ethiopia* by Chris Prouty and Eugene

Rosenfeld, which provides a lexicon of Ethiopian topics as well as an extensive bibliography.

Bahru Zewde's *A History of Modern Ethiopia, 1855–1974* surveys the last century of imperial rule, with an emphasis on the twentieth century. Two biographical histories on nineteenth-century emperors are recommended: *Yohannes IV of Ethiopia* by Zewde Gabre-Sellassie, and *The Life and Times of Menelik II* by Harold G. Marcus. The following are among outstanding works on the reign of Haile Selassie: George W. Baer's *The Coming of the Italian-Ethiopian War;* Christopher S. Clapham's *Haile Selassie's Government;* John Markakis's *Ethiopia: Anatomy of a Traditional Polity;* and Harold G. Marcus's *Haile Selassie I: The Formative Years, 1892–1936.* A new work by Gebru Tareke, *Ethiopia: Power and Protest,* analyzes three major peasant revolts and the response of the imperial government.

An excellent discussion of contemporary Ethiopia that treats both the Haile Selassie era and the revolutionary years is *Ethiopia: Transition and Development in the Horn of Africa* by Mulatu Wubneh and Yohannis Abate. Among the best sources on the military government and its policies are Marina and David Ottaway's *Ethiopia: Empire in Revolution,* still the basic source on the early years of the Derg, and Christopher S. Clapham's *Transformation and Continuity in Revolutionary Ethiopia.* Among periodicals, the *Journal of African History* and *Northeast African Studies* are particularly valuable for scholarly coverage of Ethiopia and the Horn. (For further information and complete citations, see Bibliography.)

Chapter 2. The Society and Its Environment

Traditional council of elders

THE ETHIOPIAN PEOPLE ARE ETHNICALLY heterogeneous, comprising more than 100 groups, each speaking a dialect of one of more than seventy languages. The Amhara, Oromo, and Tigray are the largest groups. With the accession of Menelik II to the throne in 1889, the ruling class consisted primarily of the Amhara, a predominantly Christian group that constitutes about 30 percent of the population and occupies the central highlands. The Oromo, who constitute about 40 percent of the population, are half Orthodox Christians and half Muslims whose traditional alliance with the Amhara in Shewa included participation in public administration and the military. Predominantly Christian, the Tigray occupy the far northern highlands and make up 12 to 15 percent of the population. They or their Eritrean neighbors had been battling the government for nearly three decades and by 1991 had scored many battlefield successes.

According to estimates based on the first census (1984), Ethiopia's population was 51.7 million in 1990 and was projected to reach more than 67 million by the year 2000. About 89 percent of the people live in rural areas, large sectors of which have been ravaged by drought, famine, and war. The regime of Mengistu Haile Mariam embarked on controversial villagization and resettlement programs to combat these problems. Villagization involved the relocation of rural people into villages, while resettlement moved people from drought-prone areas in the north to sparsely populated and resource-rich areas in the south and southwest. The international community criticized both programs for poor implementation and the consequent toll in human lives.

The traditional social system in the northern highlands was, in general, based on landownership and tenancy. After conquest, Menelik II (reigned 1889–1913) imposed the north's imperial system on the conquered south. The government appointed many Amhara administrators, who distributed land among themselves and relegated the indigenous peasants to tenancy. The 1974 revolution swept away this structure of ethnic and class dominance. The Provisional Military Administrative Council (PMAC; also known as the Derg—see Glossary) appointed representatives of the Workers' Party of Ethiopia and the national system of peasant associations to implement land reform. Additionally, the government organized urban centers into a hierarchy of urban dwellers' associations (*kebeles*—see Glossary). Despite these reforms, however, dissatisfaction and covert opposition to the regime continued in the civilian and military sectors.

Prior to the 1974 revolution, the state religion of Ethiopia had been Ethiopian Orthodox Christianity, whose adherents comprised perhaps 40 to 50 percent of the population, including a majority of the Amhara and Tigray. Islam was the faith of about 40 percent of the population, including large segments (perhaps half) of the Oromo and the people inhabiting the contiguous area of the northern and eastern lowlands, such as the Beja, Saho, Afar, and Somali. Adherents of indigenous belief systems were scattered among followers of the two major religions and could be found in more concentrated numbers on the western peripheries of the highlands. In line with its policy that all religions were equally legitimate, the regime in 1975 declared several Muslim holy days national holidays, in addition to the Ethiopian Orthodox holidays that were already observed.

Declaring education one of its priorities, the PMAC expanded the education system at the primary level, especially in small towns and rural areas, which had never had modern schools during the imperial era. The new policy relocated control and operation of primary and secondary schools to the subregion (*awraja*) level, where officials reoriented curricula to emphasize agriculture, handicrafts, commercial training, and other practical subjects. The regime also embarked on a national literacy campaign.

The regime's health policy included expansion of rural health services, promotion of community involvement, self-reliance in health activities, and emphasis on the prevention and control of disease. As with education, the PMAC decentralized health care administration to the local level as part of its effort to encourage community involvement. Despite an emphasis on rural health services, less than a third of the total population had effective health coverage in mid-1991.

Physical Setting

Ethiopia occupies most of the Horn of Africa. The country covers approximately 1,221,900 square kilometers and shares frontiers with Sudan, Kenya, Somalia, and Djibouti. Its Red Sea coastline is about 960 kilometers long. The major physiographic features are a massive highland complex of mountains and plateaus divided by the Great Rift Valley and surrounded by lowlands along the periphery. The diversity of the terrain is fundamental to regional variations in climate, natural vegetation, soil composition, and settlement patterns.

Boundaries: International and Administrative

Except for the Red Sea coastline, only limited stretches of the country's borders are defined by natural features. Most of Ethiopia's borders have been delimited by treaty. The Ethiopia-Somalia boundary has long been an exception, however. One of its sectors has never been definitively demarcated, thanks to disputed interpretations of 1897 and 1908 treaties signed by Britain, Italy, and Ethiopia. This sector was delimited by a provisional "Administrative Line" that was defined by a 1950 Anglo-Ethiopian agreement, when the United Nations (UN) established Somalia as a trust territory. After it became independent in 1960, Somalia refused to recognize any of the border treaties signed between Ethiopia and the former colonial powers. The Somali government also demanded a revision of the boundary that would ensure self-determination for Somali living in the Ogaden. Consequently, the frontier became the scene of recurrent violence and open warfare between Ethiopia and Somalia.

Topography and Drainage

Much of the Ethiopian landmass is part of the East African Rift Plateau. Ethiopia has a general elevation ranging from 1,500 to 3,000 meters above sea level. Interspersed on the landscape are higher mountain ranges and cratered cones, the highest of which, at 4,620 meters, is Ras Dashen Terara northeast of Gonder. The northernmost part of the plateau is Ethiopia's historical core and is the location of the ancient kingdom of Aksum. The national capital of Addis Ababa ("New Flower") is located in the center of the country on the edge of the central plateau (see fig. 6).

Millennia of erosion have produced steep valleys, in places 1,600 meters deep and several kilometers wide. In these valleys flow rapid streams unsuitable for navigation but possessing potential as sources of hydroelectric power and water for irrigation.

The highlands that comprise much of the country are often referred to as the Ethiopian Plateau and are usually thought of as divided into northern and southern parts. In a strict geographical sense, however, they are bisected by the Great Rift Valley into the northwestern highlands and the southeastern highlands, each with associated lowlands. The northwestern highlands are considerably more extensive and rugged and are divided into northern and southern sections by the valley of the Abay (Blue Nile).

North of Addis Ababa, the surface of the plateau is interspersed with towering mountains and deep chasms that create a variety of physiography, climate, and indigenous vegetation. The plateau

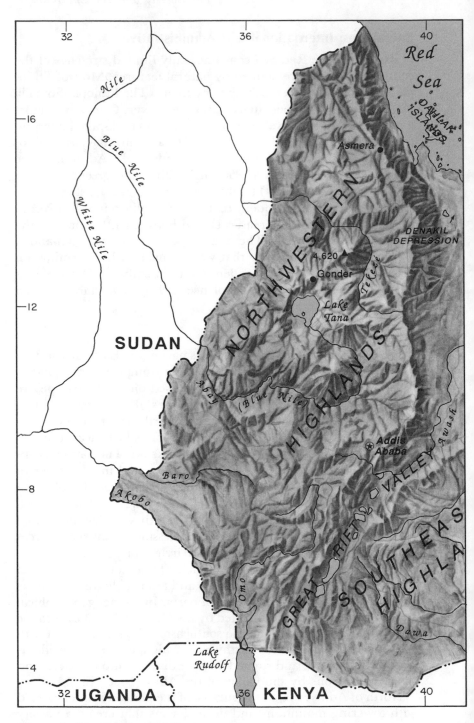

Figure 6. Topography and Drainage

74

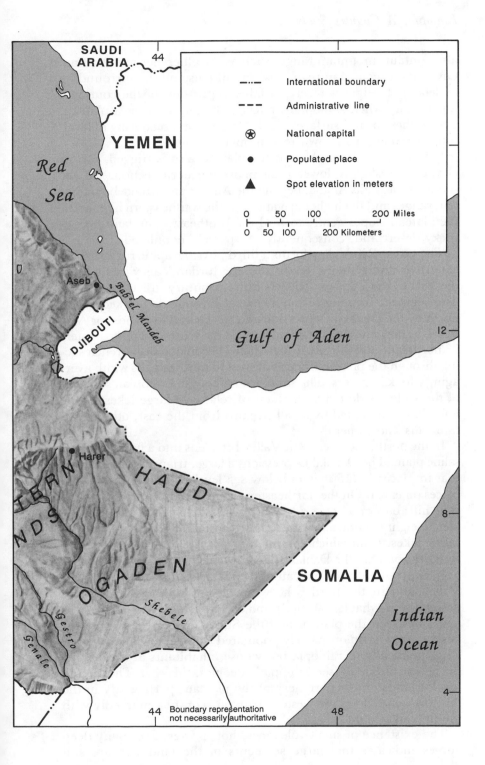

also contains mountain ranges such as the Chercher and Aranna. Given the rugged nature of these mountains and the surrounding tableland, foreigners receive a false impression of the country's topography when Ethiopians refer to the landform as a plateau. Few of these peaks' surfaces are flat except for a scattering of level-topped mountains known to Ethiopians as *ambas*.

Southwest of Addis Ababa, the plateau also is rugged, but its elevation is slightly lower than in its northern section. To the southeast of Addis Ababa, beyond the Ahmar and Mendebo mountain ranges and the higher elevations of the southeastern highlands, the plateau slopes gently toward the southeast. The land here is rocky desert and, consequently, is sparsely populated.

The Great Rift Valley forms a third physiographic region. This extensive fault system extends from the Jordan Valley in the Middle East to the Zambezi River's Shire tributary in Mozambique. The segment running through central Ethiopia is marked in the north by the Denakil Depression and the coastal lowlands, or Afar Plain, as they are sometimes known. To the south, at approximately 9° north latitude, the Great Rift Valley becomes a deep trench slicing through the plateau from southwest to northeast, its width averaging fifty kilometers. The southern half of the Ethiopian segment of the valley is dotted by a chain of relatively large lakes. Some hold fresh water, fed by small streams from the east; others contain salts and minerals.

In the north, the Great Rift Valley broadens into a funnel-shaped saline plain. The Denakil Depression, a large, triangle-shaped basin that in places is 115 meters below sea level, is one of the hottest places on earth. On the northeastern edge of the depression, maritime hills border a hot, arid, and treeless strip of coastal land sixteen to eighty kilometers wide. These coastal hills drain inland into saline lakes, from which commercial salt is extracted. Along the Red Sea coast are the Dahlak Islands, which are sparsely inhabited.

In contrast with the plateau's steep scarps along the Great Rift Valley and in the north, the western and southwestern slopes descend somewhat less abruptly and are broken more often by river exits. Between the plateau and the Sudanese border in the west lies a narrow strip of sparsely populated tropical lowland that belongs politically to Ethiopia but whose inhabitants are related to the people of Sudan (see Ethiopia's Peoples, this ch.). These tropical lowlands on the periphery of the plateau, particularly in the far north and along the western frontier, contrast markedly with the upland terrain.

The existence of small volcanoes, hot springs, and many deep gorges indicates that large segments of the landmass are still geologically unstable. Numerous volcanoes occur in the Denakil area, and hot springs and steaming fissures are found in other northern areas of the Great Rift Valley. A line of seismic faults extends along the length of Eritrea and the Denakil Depression, and small earthquakes have been recorded in the area in recent times.

All of Ethiopia's rivers originate in the highlands and flow outward in many directions through deep gorges. Most notable of these is the Blue Nile, the country's largest river. It and its tributaries account for two-thirds of the Nile River flow below Khartoum in Sudan. Because of the general westward slope of the highlands, many large rivers are tributaries of the Nile system, which drains an extensive area of the central portion of the plateau. The Blue Nile, the Tekezé, and the Baro are among them and account for about half of the country's water outflow. In the northern half of the Great Rift Valley flows the Awash River, on which the government has built several dams to generate power and irrigate major commercial plantations. The Awash flows east and disappears in the saline lakes near the boundary with Djibouti. The southeast is drained by the Genale and Shebele rivers and their tributaries, and the southwest is drained by the Omo.

Climate

Diverse rainfall and temperature patterns are largely the result of Ethiopia's location in Africa's tropical zone and the country's varied topography. Altitude-induced climatic conditions form the basis for three environmental zones—cool, temperate, and hot—which have been known to Ethiopians since antiquity as the *dega,* the *weina dega,* and the *kolla,* respectively.

The cool zone consists of the central parts of the western and eastern sections of the northwestern plateau and a small area around Harer. The terrain in these areas is generally above 2,400 meters in elevation; average daily highs range from near freezing to 16°C, with March, April, and May the warmest months. Throughout the year, the midday warmth diminishes quickly by afternoon, and nights are usually cold. During most months, light frost often forms at night and snow occurs at the highest elevations.

Lower areas of the plateau, between 1,500 and 2,400 meters in elevation, constitute the temperate zone. Daily highs there range from 16°C to 30°C.

The hot zone consists of areas where the elevation is lower than 1,500 meters. This area encompasses the Denakil Depression, the Eritrean lowlands, the eastern Ogaden, the deep tropical valleys of the Blue Nile and Tekezé rivers, and the peripheral areas along the Sudanese and Kenyan borders. Daytime conditions are torrid, and daily temperatures vary more widely here than in the other two regions. Although the hot zone's average annual daytime temperature is about 27°C, midyear readings in the arid and semiarid areas along the Red Sea coast often soar to 50°C and to more than 40°C in the arid Ogaden. Humidity is usually high in the tropical valleys and along the seacoast.

Variations in precipitation throughout the country are the result of differences in elevation and seasonal changes in the atmospheric pressure systems that control the prevailing winds. Because of these factors, several regions receive rainfall throughout most of the year, but in other areas precipitation is seasonal. In the more arid lowlands, rainfall is always meager.

In January the high pressure system that produces monsoons in Asia crosses the Red Sea. Although these northeast trade winds bring rain to the coastal plains and the eastern escarpment in Eritrea, they are essentially cool and dry and provide little moisture to the country's interior. Their effect on the coastal region, however, is to create a Mediterranean-like climate. Winds that originate over the Atlantic Ocean and blow across Equatorial Africa have a marked seasonal effect on much of Ethiopia. The resulting weather pattern provides the highlands with most of its rainfall during a period that generally lasts from mid-June to mid-September.

The main rainy season is usually preceded in April and May by converging northeast and southeast winds that produce a brief period of light rains, known as *balg*. These rains are followed by a short period of hot dry weather, and toward the middle of June violent thunderstorms occur almost daily. In the southwest, precipitation is more evenly distributed and also more abundant. The relative humidity and rainfall decrease generally from south to north and also in the eastern lowlands. Annual precipitation is heaviest in the southwest, scant in the Great Rift Valley and the Ogaden, and negligible in the Denakil Depression.

Population

Size, Distribution, and Growth

Ethiopia's population was estimated at 51.7 million in 1990. According to the nation's only census, conducted in 1984, Ethiopia's population was about 42 million. But the census was far from comprehensive. The rural areas of Eritrea and Tigray were excluded because of hostilities. In addition, the population in the southern parts of Bale and Harerge could only be estimated because of the prevalence of pastoral nomadism.

The 1984 census revealed that Ethiopia's population was about 89 percent rural, and this percentage did not appear to have changed by the late 1980s (see table 2, Appendix). This segment included many nomadic and seminomadic peoples. The Ethiopian population always has been predominantly rural, engaging in sedentary agricultural activities such as the cultivation of crops and livestock-raising in the highlands. In the lowlands, the main activities traditionally have been subsistence farming by seminomadic groups and seasonal grazing of livestock by nomadic people.

The distribution of Ethiopia's population generally is related to altitude, climate, and soil. These physical factors explain the concentration of population in the highlands, which are endowed with moderate temperatures, rich soil, and adequate rainfall. About 14 percent of the population lives in areas above 2,400 meters (cool climatic zone), about 75 percent between 1,500 and 2,400 meters (temperate zone), and only 11 percent below 1,500 meters (hot climatic zone), although the hot zone encompasses more than half of Ethiopia's territory. Localities with elevations above 3,000 meters and below 1,500 meters are sparsely populated, the first because of cold temperatures and rugged terrain, which limit agricultural activity, and the second because of high temperatures and low rainfall, except in the west and southwest.

Although census data indicated that overall density was about thirty-seven people per square kilometer, density varied from over 100 per square kilometer for Shewa and seventy-five for Arsi to fewer than ten in the Ogaden, Bale, the Great Rift Valley, and the western lowlands adjoining Sudan. There was also great variation among the populations of the various administrative regions (see table 3, Appendix).

In 1990 officials estimated the birth rate at forty-five births per 1,000 population and the total fertility rate (the average number of children that would be born to a woman during her lifetime) at about seven per 1,000 population. Census findings indicated that the birth rate was higher in rural areas than in urban areas. Ethiopia's birth rate, high even among developing countries, is explained by early and universal marriage, kinship and religious beliefs that generally encourage large families, a resistance to contraceptive practices, and the absence of family planning services for most of the population. Many Ethiopians believe that families with many children have greater financial security and are better situated to provide for their elderly members.

In the absence of a national population policy or the provision of more than basic health services, analysts consider the high birth rate likely to continue. A significant consequence of the high birth rate is that the population is young; children under fifteen years of age made up nearly 50 percent of the population in 1989 (see

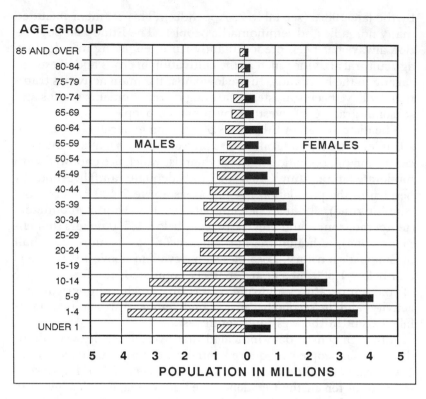

Source: Based on information from United Nations, *Demographic Yearbook, 1989,* New York, 1991, 166–67.

Figure 7. Population by Age and Sex, 1989

fig. 7). Thus, a large segment of the population was dependent and likely to require heavy expenditures on education, health, and social services.

In 1990 the death rate was estimated at fifteen per 1,000 population (down from 18.1 per 1,000 in 1984). This also was a very high rate but typical of poor developing countries. The high death rate was a reflection of the low standard of living, poor health conditions, inadequate health facilities, and high rates of infant mortality (116 per 1,000 live births in 1990; 139 per 1,000 in 1984) and child mortality. Additional factors contributing to the high death rate include infectious diseases, poor sanitation, malnutrition, and food shortages. Children are even more vulnerable to such deprivations. In Ethiopia half of the total deaths involve children under five years of age. In addition, drought and famine in the 1980s, during which more than 7 million people needed food aid, interrupted the normal evolution of mortality and fertility and un-doubtedly left many infants and children with stunted physical and mental capabilities. Life expectancy in 1990 was estimated at forty-nine years for males and fifty-two years for females.

Generally, birth rates, infant mortality rates, and overall mortality rates were lower in urban areas than in rural areas. As of 1990, urban residents had a life expectancy of just under fifty-three years, while rural residents had a life expectancy of forty-eight years. The more favorable statistics for urban areas can be explained by the wider availability of health facilities, greater knowledge of sanitation, easier access to clean water and food, and a slightly higher standard of living.

There has been a steady increase in the population growth rate since 1960. Based on 1984 census data, population growth was estimated at about 2.3 percent for the 1960–70 period, 2.5 percent for the 1970–80 period, and 2.8 percent for the 1980–85 period. Population projections compiled in 1988 by the Central Statistical Authority (CSA) projected a 2.83 percent growth rate for 1985–90 and a 2.96 percent growth rate for 1990–95. This would result in a population of 57.9 million by 1995. Estimated annual growth for 1995–2000 varied from 3.03 percent to 3.16 percent. Population estimates ranged from 67.4 million to 67.8 million by the year 2000. The CSA projected that Ethiopia's population could range from 104 million to 115 million by the year 2015. The International Development Association (IDA) provided a more optimistic estimate. Based on the assumption of a gradual fertility decline, such as might be caused by steady economic development without high priority given to population and family planning programs, the population growth rate might fall to about 2.8 percent per annum in 1995–2000 and to 2.1 percent in 2010–15, resulting in a population of 93 million in 2015.

Analysts believed that reducing the population growth rate was a pressing need, but one that could only be addressed through a persistent and comprehensive nationwide effort over the long term. As of mid-1991, the Ethiopian regime had shown no commitment to such a program.

Variations in population growth existed among administrative regions. Kefa, Sidamo, and Shewa had the highest average growth rates for the 1967–84 period, ranging from 4.2 percent for Kefa to 3.5 percent for Sidamo and Shewa. Whereas Shewa's population growth was the result of Addis Ababa's status as the administrative, commercial, and industrial center of Ethiopia, Kefa and Sidamo grew primarily because of agricultural and urban development. The population in administrative regions such as Harerge,

Welo, and Tigray, which had been hard hit by famine and insurrection, grew at slow rates: 1.3 percent, 1 percent, and 0.2 percent, respectively. Generally, the population of most central and western administrative regions grew more rapidly than did the population of the eastern and northern administrative regions.

Urbanization

Ethiopia was under-urbanized, even by African standards. In the late 1980s, only about 11 percent of the population lived in urban areas of at least 2,000 residents. There were hundreds of communities with 2,000 to 5,000 people, but these were primarily extensions of rural villages without urban or administrative functions. Thus, the level of urbanization would be even lower if one used strict urban structural criteria. Ethiopia's relative lack of urbanization is the result of the country's history of agricultural self-sufficiency, which has reinforced rural peasant life. The slow pace of urban development continued until the 1935 Italian invasion. Urban growth was fairly rapid during and after the Italian occupation of 1936–41. Urbanization accelerated during the 1960s, when the average annual growth rate was about 6.3 percent. Urban growth was especially evident in the northern half of Ethiopia, where most of the major towns are located.

Addis Ababa was home to about 35 percent of the country's urban population in 1987. Another 7 percent resided in Asmera, the second largest city. Major industrial, commercial, governmental, educational, health, and cultural institutions were located in these two cities, which together were home to about 2 million people, or one out of twenty-five Ethiopians. Nevertheless, many small towns had emerged as well. In 1970 there were 171 towns with populations of 2,000 to 20,000; this total had grown to 229 by 1980.

The period 1967–75 saw rapid growth of relatively new urban centers (see table 4, Appendix). The population of six towns—Akaki, Arba Minch, Awasa, Bahir Dar, Jijiga, and Shashemene—more than tripled, and that of eight others more than doubled. Awasa, Arba Minch, Metu, and Goba were newly designated capitals of administrative regions and important agricultural centers. Awasa, capital of Sidamo, had a lakeshore site and convenient location on the Addis Ababa-Nairobi highway. Bahir Dar was a newly planned city on Lake Tana and the site of several industries and a polytechnic institute. Akaki and Aseb were growing into important industrial towns, while Jijiga and Shashemene had become communications and service centers.

Urban centers that experienced moderate growth tended to be more established towns, such as Addis Ababa, Dire Dawa, and

Debre Zeyit. A few old provincial capitals, such as Gonder, also experienced moderate growth, but others, such as Harer, Dese, Debre Markos, and Jima, had slow growth rates because of competition from larger cities. By the 1990s, Harer was being overshadowed by Dire Dawa, Dese by Kembolcha, and Debre Markos by Bahir Dar.

Overall, the rate of urban growth declined from 1975 to 1987. With the exception of Aseb, Arba Minch, and Awasa, urban centers grew an average of about 40 percent over that twelve-year period. This slow growth is explained by several factors. Rural-to-urban migration had been largely responsible for the rapid expansion during the 1967–75 period, whereas natural population growth may have been mostly responsible for urban expansion during the 1975–84 period. The 1975 land reform program provided incentives and opportunities for peasants and other potential migrants to stay in rural areas. Restrictions on travel, lack of employment, housing shortages, and social unrest in some towns during the 1975–80 period also contributed to a decline in rural-to-urban migration.

Although the male and female populations were about equal, men outnumbered women in rural areas. More women migrated to the urban centers for a variety of reasons, including increased job opportunities.

As a result of intensified warfare in the period 1988–91, all urban centers received a large influx of population, resulting in severe overcrowding, shortages of housing and water, overtaxed social services, and unemployment. In addition to beggars and maimed persons, the new arrivals comprised large numbers of young people. These included not only primary and secondary school students but also an alarming number of orphans and street children, estimated at well over 100,000. Although all large towns shared in this influx, Addis Ababa, as the national capital, was most affected. This situation underscored the huge social problems that the Mengistu regime had neglected for far too long.

Resettlement and Villagization

Drought and famine have been frequent occurrences in Ethiopia. In fact, it was the imperial government's attempt to hide the effects of the 1973–74 famine that aroused world indignation and eventually contributed to Haile Selassie I's demise (see The Establishment of the Derg, ch. 1). Between 1984 and 1986, drought and famine again hit Ethiopia and may have claimed as many as 1 million lives and threatened nearly 8 million more (see The Politics of Drought and Famine, ch. 4). Even worse disaster was averted when the international community mounted a massive effort to airlift food and medical supplies to famine victims.

The government embarked on forced resettlement and villagi-zation in the mid-1980s as part of a national program to combat drought, avert famine, and increase agricultural productivity. Resettlement, the regime's long-term solution to the drought problem, involved the permanent relocation of about 1.5 million people from the drought-prone areas of the north to the south and southwest, where population was relatively sparse and so-called virgin, arable land was plentiful (see Government Rural Programs, ch. 3; The Politics of Resettlement, ch. 4).

Development specialists agreed on the need for resettlement of famine victims in Ethiopia, but once the process had begun, there was widespread criticism that resettlement was poorly planned and haphazardly executed and thus increased the number of famine deaths. Moreover, critics charged that the government forcibly relo-cated peasants, in the process breaking up thousands of families. Thousands also died of malaria and sleeping sickness because of poor sanitation and inadequate health care in newly settled areas. A Paris-based international doctors' organization, Doctors Without Borders (Médecins sans Frontières), estimated that the forced reset-tlement and mass deportation of peasants for purposes of resettle-ment endangered the lives of 300,000 because of shortages of food, water, and medicine. Other international organizations accused the Ethiopian government of moving peasants to resettlement areas without adequate preparation of such basic items as housing, water, seeds, and tools. Because of widespread criticism, the Mengistu regime temporarily halted the resettlement program in mid-1986 after 600,000 people had been relocated, but the program resumed in November 1987.

Some sources voiced suspicion that the regime's primary mo-tive in resettlement was to depopulate the northern areas where it faced insurgencies. Resettlement, the argument went, would reduce the guerrillas' base of support. But this argument did not take into account the strength of the Tigray People's Liberation Front (TPLF) (see The Tigrayan Movement, ch. 4; The Tigray, ch. 5). Another Western objection to the resettlement program re-lated to the long-term government policy concerning peasant farms. Western countries, on whose support the resettlement program de-pended, did not want to sponsor a plan in which recruits labored for communist-style collectives and state farms.

The villagization program, the regime's plan to transform rural society, started in earnest in January 1985 (see The Politics of Vil-lagization, ch. 4). If completed, the program might have uprooted

Cornfields surround a village in Ansokia Valley, 350 kilometers north of Addis Ababa.
Courtesy World Vision (Bruce Brander)

and relocated more than 30 million peasants over a nine-year period. The regime's rationale for the program was that the existing arrangement of dispersed settlements made it difficult to provide social services and to use resources, especially land and water, efficiently. The relocation of the peasants into larger villages (with forty to 300 families, or 200 to 2,500 people) would give rural people better access to amenities such as agricultural extension services, schools, clinics, water, and electricity cooperative services and would strengthen local security and the capacity for self-defense. Improved economic and social services would promote more efficient use of land and other natural resources and would lead to increased agricultural production and a higher standard of living.

More specifically, the Ethiopian government perceived villagization as a way to hasten agricultural collectivization. Most peasant farming in Ethiopia was still based on a traditional smallholding system, which produced 90 percent of farm output, employed about 80 percent of the labor force, and accounted for 94 percent of cultivable land in 1985. State farms and cooperative farms were responsible for only 4 percent and 2 percent, respectively, of cultivated land.

By the end of 1988, more than 12 million people had been relocated in villages in twelve of the fourteen administrative regions.

The exceptions were Eritrea and Tigray, where insurgents were waging war against the regime. In 1989 the total reached about 13 million people. Some regions implemented villagization more rapidly than others. In Harerge, where the program began in 1985, more than 90 percent of the population had been relocated to villages by early 1987, whereas in Gonder and Welo the program was just beginning. In Ilubabor more than 1 million peasants had been relocated to 2,106 villages between December 1985 and March 1989. Nomadic peoples and shifting cultivators were not affected by villagization.

The verdict on villagization was not favorable. Thousands of people fled to avoid villagization; others died or lived in deplorable conditions after being forcibly resettled. Moreover, the program's impact on rural peasants and their social and economic well-being remained to be assessed. There were indications that in the short term, villagization may have further impoverished an already poor peasantry. The services that were supposed to be delivered in new villages, such as water, electricity, health care clinics, schools, transportation, and agricultural extension services, were not being provided because the government lacked the necessary resources. Villagers therefore resorted to improvised facilities or reverted to old ways of doing things. Villagization also reduced the productive capacity of the peasants by depriving them of the opportunity for independent organization and action. By increasing the distance peasants had to travel to work on their land and graze their cattle, villagization wasted time and effort. Denied immediate access to their fields, the peasants were also prevented from guarding their crops from birds and other wild animals.

In the long run, analysts believed that villagization would be counterproductive to a rational land use system and would be damaging ecologically. Concentrating people in a central area would, in time, intensify pressure on available water and grazing and lead to a decline in soil fertility and to a poorer peasantry. The ecological damage could be averted by the application of capital investment in infrastructure, such as irrigation and land-intensive agricultural technology and strict application of land rotation to avert overgrazing. But resources were unavailable for such agricultural investment.

The most bitter critics of villagization, such as Survival International, a London-based human rights organization, argued that the Mengistu regime's noneconomic objective in villagization was control of the population. Larger villages would facilitate the regime's control over the population, cut rebels off from peasant support, and discourage dissident movements. Indeed, some observers believed that the reason for starting villagization in Harerge and Bale was nothing less than to suppress support of the Oromo Liberation Front (OLF).

After the government's announcement of the new economic policy in March 1990, peasants were given the freedom to join or abandon cooperatives and to bring their produce to market. Hence, the Mengistu regime abandoned one of the strong rationales for villagization and, in effect, the whole program as well.

Refugees, Drought, and Famine

In Ethiopia, a predominantly rural society, the life of peasants is rooted in the land, from which they eke out a meager existence. Through the ages, they have faced frequent natural disasters, armed conflict, and political repression, and in the process they have suffered hunger, societal disruption, and death.

Periodic crop failures and losses of livestock often occur when seasonal rains fail or when unusually heavy storms cause widespread flooding. Pastoral nomads, who move seasonally in search of water and grazing, often are trapped when drought inhibits rejuvenation of the denuded grasslands, which their overgrazing produces. During such times, a family's emergency food supplies diminish rapidly, and hunger and starvation become commonplace until weather conditions improve and livestock herds are subsequently rejuvenated. For centuries, this has been the general pattern of life for most Ethiopian peasants; the insurgent movements in Eritrea, Tigray, and the Ogaden have only served to exacerbate the effects of these natural calamities (see The Eritreans; The Tigray; The Somali, ch. 5).

A drought that began in 1969 continued as dry weather brought disaster to the Sahel and swept eastward through the Horn of Africa. By 1973 the attendant famine had threatened the lives of hundreds of thousands of Ethiopian nomads, who had to leave their home grounds and struggle into Somalia, Djibouti, Kenya, and Sudan, seeking relief from starvation. By the end of 1973, famine had claimed the lives of about 300,000 peasants of Tigray and Welo, and thousands more had sought relief in Ethiopian towns and villages.

After assuming power in 1974, the military regime embarked on a program to improve the condition of peasants, but famine and hunger continued despite this effort, which was supplemented by substantial foreign assistance. Moreover, the escalation of the military campaign against the insurgent movements in Eritrea, Tigray, and the Ogaden forced thousands of Ethiopians to flee into neighboring countries.

The 1977–78 Ogaden War and the 1978 drought in eastern Ethiopia forced large numbers of people across the southeastern frontier into Somalia. After the defeat of Somali forces in the Ogaden, the government launched a counteroffensive against Eritrean guerrillas, and several hundred thousand Ethiopians sought refuge in Sudan. Meanwhile, in the Ogaden, international relief agencies estimated the number of refugees entering Somali refugee camps at more than 1,000 a day. Most were women and children, and many suffered from dehydration, malnutrition, and diseases such as dysentery, malaria, and tuberculosis. There were more than 700,000 reported refugees scattered in twenty-six makeshift camps, where the absence of sanitation and inadequate medical assistance were compounding the misery created by the food shortages.

By mid-1980 most observers considered the refugee crisis in the Horn of Africa to be the world's worst. During the 1980s, the crisis intensified, as 2.5 million people in the region abandoned their homes and sought asylum in neighboring countries. Although drought, famine, government repression, and conflict with insurgents were the principal causes of large-scale refugee migrations, other factors such as resettlement and villagization in Ethiopia and conflicts in southern Sudan and northern Somalia also generated refugees. Sudan's war against the Sudanese People's Liberation Army (SPLA) forced many Sudanese into Ethiopia. In northern Somalia, the Somali National Movement (SNM) had been fighting Somali government forces, and in the process hundreds of thousands of Somali fled into Ethiopia.

Several factors were responsible for the refugee crisis in Ethiopia. The repressive Mengistu regime was ruthless in its treatment of both real and imagined opponents (see Human Rights, ch. 5). During the so-called Red Terror (see Glossary) of 1977–78, government security forces killed thousands of students and urban professionals. Because human rights violations characterized the government's policy toward dissidents, there was a constant exodus of young and educated people. The regime also found itself engaged in continuous civil war with one or more of the insurgent groups, which had a devastating impact on the people, the land, and the economy. The fighting not only generated hundreds of thousands of refugees but also displaced thousands of other people from their farms and villages. Forcible villagization and resettlement also generated refugees. In Harerge alone, the forced imposition of villagization prompted 33,000 people to flee to Somalia.

Famine also contributed to Ethiopia's refugee crises. The 1984–85 famine resulted in the death or displacement of hundreds of thousands of people within Ethiopia and forced about 100,000 into Somalia, 10,000 into Djibouti, and more than 300,000 into Sudan.

In 1987 another drought threatened 5 million people in Eritrea and Tigray. This time, however, the international community was better prepared to get food to the affected areas in time to prevent starvation and massive population movements. However, insurgents belonging to the TPLF and the Eritrean People's Liberation Front (EPLF) attacked convoys carrying food supplies or denied them access to rebel-held areas because they believed the government would use relief convoys to cover the movement of military supplies. The consequence was more deaths and more refugees.

International relief agencies considered the 1990 famine more critical because of the scarcity of rain after 1987. Mitsiwa was one of the Eritrean ports where ships unloaded food and medical supplies for distribution to famine victims in Eritrea. Following the EPLF's capture of Mitsiwa in February 1990 and the government's bombing of the city in an effort to dislodge the insurgents, the port was out of action. A few months later, however, the EPLF and the Ethiopian government reached an agreement that allowed the port to reopen. In addition, the government lost control of Tigray in early 1989 and was reluctant to allow food shipments to go through rebel-held territory until May 1990, when the rebels, the government, the UN, and donor officials agreed to move grain supplies from Dese to Tigray. Food could not be airlifted into Tigray because fighting had destroyed the airport in Mekele, capital of Tigray. Sudan was the only nation through which food shipments could come to Tigray and Eritrea. Both the Relief Society of Tigray and the Eritrean Relief Association—arms of the TPLF and EPLF, respectively—operated overland food convoys from Sudan to Tigray and Eritrea. But poor road conditions and the fact that convoys had to operate at night to avoid Ethiopian air force attacks prevented adequate supplies from reaching affected regions. Consequently, about 3 million people were threatened with death and starvation in Eritrea and Tigray.

Disagreements persist concerning the number of Ethiopian refugees in Somalia in the late 1980s. A UN survey estimated the number of Ethiopian refugees in Somalia at 450,000 to 620,000. The United States Catholic Relief Services, however, estimated that about 410,000 refugees had returned to Ethiopia, leaving about 430,000 in Somali refugee camps. At the same time, more than 350,000 Somali of the Isaaq clan-family (see Glossary) fled northern Somalia for Ethiopia after mid-1988. Most of these people remained in camps run by the Office of the United Nations High Commissioner for Refugees (UNHCR).

Djibouti was home to about 45,000 Ethiopian refugees from the Ogaden by late 1978. These people had fled after Somalia's defeat in the Ogaden War. In 1983 the UNHCR began a repatriation program, which resulted in the departure of 15,000 former refugees by mid-1984. But the 1984 drought in Ethiopia brought an additional influx of 10,000 refugees into Djibouti. Slow, steady repatriation continued through 1989, by which time there were only 1,500 Ethiopian refugees in Djibouti.

A large influx of Ethiopian refugees into Sudan occurred in 1978, during the escalation of the conflict between Eritrean insurgents and the Mengistu regime. The influx continued into 1983, when the refugees numbered about 132,500. The 1984 drought and famine forced 160,000 refugees into Sudan in 1984 and more than 300,000 by April 1985. By June 1985, in anticipation of summer rains in Tigray, 55,000 Tigrayans left Sudan, followed by another 65,000 in 1986, but only a small percentage of refugee Eritreans returned to Ethiopia.

Ethiopia also had been host to refugees from southern Sudan since 1983. As the conflict in southern Sudan between the SPLA and the Sudanese regime intensified, more refugees fled into western Ethiopia, where the Sudanese refugees numbered about 250,000 in early 1988 and perhaps 400,000 by early 1991.

Ethiopia's Peoples

A simple ethnic classification of Ethiopia's population is not feasible. People categorized on the basis of one criterion, such as language, may be divided on the basis of another. Moreover, ethnicity—a people's insistence that it is distinctive and its behavior on the basis of that insistence—is a subjective response to both historical experience and current situations. A group thus distinguished may not be the same as that established on the basis of objective criteria.

Historically, entities defining themselves in ethnic terms reacted or adapted to Amhara domination in various ways. Affecting their adaptation was the degree of Amhara domination—in some areas Amhara were present in force, while in others they established a minimal administrative presence—and the extent of ethnic mixing. In some areas, historical differences and external conditions led to disaffection and attempts at secession, as in multiethnic Eritrea and in the Ogaden. In others, individuals adapted to the Amhara. Often they understood the change not so much as a process of becoming Amhara as one of taking on an Ethiopian (and urban) identity.

Ethnic Groups, Ethnicity, and Language

One way of segmenting Ethiopia's population is on the basis of language. However, the numbers in each category are uncertain, and estimates are often in conflict. At present, at least seventy languages are spoken as mother tongues, a few by many millions, others by only a few hundred persons. The number of distinct social units exceeds the number of languages because separate communities sometimes speak the same language. More than fifty of these languages—and certainly those spoken by the vast majority of Ethiopia's people—are grouped within three families of the Afro-Asiatic super-language family: Semitic (represented by the branch called Ethio-Semitic and by Arabic), Cushitic, and Omotic. In addition, about 2 percent of the population speak the languages of four families—East Sudanic, Koman, Berta, and Kunema—of the Nilo-Saharan super-language family.

Most speakers of Ethio-Semitic languages live in the highlands of the center and north. Speakers of East Cushitic languages are found in the highlands and lowlands of the center and south, and other Cushitic speakers live in the center and north; Omotic speakers live in the south; and Nilo-Saharan speakers live in the southwest and west along the border with Sudan. Of the four main ethno-linguistic groups of Ethiopia, three—the Amhara, Tigray, and Oromo—generally live in the highlands; the fourth—the Somali—live in the lowlands to the southeast (see fig. 8).

Ethio-Semitic Language Groups

The most important Ethio-Semitic language is Amharic. It was the empire's official language and is still widely used in government and in the capital despite the Mengistu regime's changes in language policy. Those speaking Amharic as a mother tongue numbered about 8 million in 1970, a little more than 30 percent of the population. A more accurate count might show them to constitute a lesser proportion. The total number of Amharic speakers, including those using Amharic as a second language, may constitute as much as 50 percent of the population.

The Amhara are not a cohesive group, politically or otherwise. From the perspective of many Amhara in the core area of Gonder, Gojam, and western Welo, the Amhara of Shewa (who constituted the basic ruling group under Menelik II and Haile Selassie) are not true descendants of the northern Amhara and the Tigray and heirs to the ancient kingdom of Aksum. Regional variations notwithstanding, the Amhara do not exhibit the differences of religion and mode of livelihood characteristic of the Oromo, for example,

91

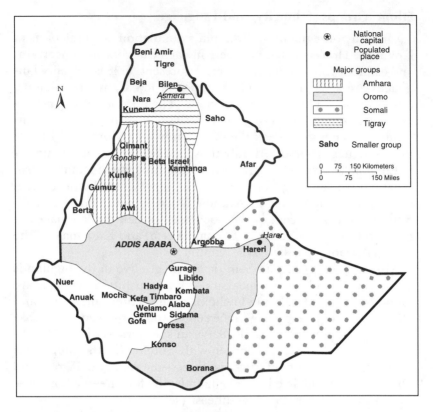

Source: Based on information from Mulatu Wubneh and Yohannis Abate, *Ethiopia,* Boulder, Colorado, 1988, 129; and M. Lionel Bender (ed.), *The Non-Semitic Languages of Ethiopia,* East Lansing, 1976.

Figure 8. Principal Ethnolinguistic Groups, 1991

who constitute Ethiopia's largest linguistic category. With a few exceptions, the Amhara are Ethiopian Orthodox Christians and are highland plow agriculturists.

The Tigray (whose language is Tigrinya) constitute the second largest category of Ethio-Semitic speakers. They made up about 14 percent of the population in 1970. Like the Amhara, the Tigray are chiefly Ethiopian Orthodox Christians, and most are plow agriculturists. Despite some differences in dialect, Tigray believe, as anthropologist Dan Franz Bauer has noted, ''that they have a common tenuous kinship with other Tigray regardless of their place of residence.''

The number of persons speaking other Ethio-Semitic languages is significantly smaller than the number who speak Amharic and

Tigrinya. Moreover, unlike the Amhara and Tigray, members of other Ethio-Semitic groups do not share the Aksumite heritage and Orthodox Christianity, and their traditional economic base is different.

Of the seven Ethio-Semitic languages found among the Gurage of southern Shewa, four are single tongues and three are dialect clusters, each encompassing four or five dialects. All correspond to what anthropologist William A. Shack calls tribes, which, in turn, consist of independent clan (see Glossary) chiefdoms. Although most people accept the name Gurage, they are likely to specify a tribal name in addition.

The traditional social organization and religion of the Gurage resemble those of the neighboring East Cushitic-speaking Sidama and related peoples. In some cases, Orthodox Christianity or Islam has displaced the traditional religious system, in whole or in part. The Gurage traditionally depended on the ensete plant (known locally as false banana) rather than grain for their staple food and used the hoe rather than the plow.

In 1970 there were more than 500,000 speakers of Gurage tongues, but no single group numbered more than 100,000. Substantial numbers, perhaps 15 to 20 percent of all Gurage, live in urban centers, particularly Addis Ababa, where they work at a range of manual tasks typically avoided by the Amhara and the Tigray.

In 1970 a total of 117,000 persons were estimated to speak Tigre, which is related to Tigrinya; but that figure was likely an underestimate. The ten or so Eritrean groups or clusters of groups speaking the language do not constitute an ethnic entity, although they share an adherence to Islam. Locally, people traditionally used the term *Tigre* to refer to what has been called the serf class, as opposed to the noble class, in most Tigre-speaking groups.

Perhaps the most numerous of the Tigre-speaking peoples are the Beni Amir, a largely pastoral people living in the semiarid region of the north and west along the Sudanese border. A large number of the Beni Amir also speak Beja, a North Cushitic language. Other groups are, in part at least, cultivators, and some, who live along the Red Sea coast and on nearby islands, gain some of their livelihood from fishing.

Except for the fact that the distinction between nobles and serfs seems at one time to have been pervasive, little is known of early social and political organization among these groups except for the Beni Amir, who were organized in a tribal federation with a paramount chief. The other groups seem to have been autonomous units.

The Hareri are of major historical importance, and their home was in that part of Ethiopia once claimed by Somali irredentists. The Hareri (''people of the city'') established the walled city of Harer as early as the thirteenth century A.D. Harer was a major point from which Islam spread to Somalia and then to Ethiopia.

The Argobba consist of two groups. Living on the hilly slopes of the Great Rift Valley escarpment are small groups of Northern Argobba. The Southern Argobba live southwest of Harer. Northern Argobba villages, interspersed among Amharic- or Oromo-speaking communities, stretch from an area at roughly the latitude of Addis Ababa to southeasternmost Welo. Most Argobba speak either Amharic or Oromo in addition to their native tongue.

Cushitic Language Groups

The Oromo, called Galla by the Amhara, constitute the largest and most ubiquitous of the East Cushitic-speaking peoples. Oromo live in many regions as a result of expansion from their homeland in the central southern highlands beginning in the sixteenth century. Although they share a common origin and a dialectically varied language, Oromo groups changed in a variety of ways with respect to economic base, social and political organization, and religion as they adapted to different physical and sociopolitical environments and economic opportunities.

Even more uncertain than estimates of the Amhara population are estimates for the Oromo. The problem stems largely from the imperial government's attempts to downplay the country's ethnic diversity. Government estimates put the number of Oromo speakers at about 7 million in 1970—about 28 percent of the total population of Ethiopia. By contrast, the OLF claimed there were 18 million Oromo in 1978, well over half of a total population roughly estimated that year at 31 million. Anthropologist P.T.W. Baxter, taking into account the lack of a census (until 1984) and the political biases affecting estimates, asserted that the Oromo were almost certainly the largest ethnic group in Ethiopia, making up somewhere between a third and just over half its population. A widely accepted estimate in the late 1980s was 40 percent.

The Oromo provide an example of the difficulties of specifying the boundaries and nature of an ethnic group. Some Oromo groups, such as the Borana, remain pastoralists. But others, the great majority of the people, have become plow cultivators or are engaged in mixed farming. A few groups, particularly the pastoralists, retain significant features of the traditional mode of social and political organization marked by generation and age-set systems (see

Glossary) and the absence of a centralized political structure; others, such as those who established kingdoms along the Gibe River, developed hierarchial systems. Cutting across the range of economic and political patterns are variations in religious belief and practice. Again, the pastoralists usually adhere to the indigenous system. Other groups, particularly those in Shewa and Welega, have been influenced by Orthodox Christianity, and still others have been converted to Islam. Here and there, missionary Protestantism has had minor successes. Moreover, the Oromo sections and subsections have a long history of conflict. Sometimes this conflict has been the outcome of competition for land; sometimes it has resulted from strife between those allied with the Amhara and those resisting the expansion of the empire. Some Oromo adapted to Amhara dominance, the growth of towns, and other changes by learning Amharic and achieving a place in the empire's political and economic order. But they had not thereby become Amhara or lost their sense of being Oromo.

In the far south live several groups speaking languages of the Oromic branch of Lowland East Cushitic and in many cases sharing features of Oromo culture. Most have been cultivators or mixed farmers, and some have developed distinctive features, such as the highlands-dwelling Konso, who live in walled communities of roughly 1,500 persons. All these groups are small and are often subdivided. With an estimated population of 60,000 in 1970, the Konso are the largest of these groups.

Three other Lowland East Cushitic groups—the Somali, Afar, and Saho—share a pastoral tradition (although some sections of each group have been cultivators for some time), commitments of varying intensity to Islam, and social structures composed of autonomous units defined as descent groups (see Glossary). In addition, all have a history of adverse relations with the empire's dominant Orthodox Christian groups and with Ethiopian governments in general.

The largest of the three groups are the Somali, estimated to number nearly 900,000 in 1970. Many Somali clans and lineages living predominantly in Ethiopia have close links with or are members of such groups in Somalia. The number of Somali in Ethiopia in the late 1980s—given the Ogaden War and the movement of refugees—was uncertain.

Somali society is divided into groups of varying genealogical depth based on putative or traceable common patrilineal descent. The largest of these groups is the clan-family (see Glossary), which is in turn divided into clans, which are further divided into lineages (see Glossary) and sublineages (see Glossary). The clan-family has no concrete political, economic, or social functions. The other groups do, however, and these functions often entail political and economic competition and sometimes conflict between parallel social units.

The government estimated that the Afar (called Denakil or Adal by their neighbors) numbered no more than 363,000 in 1970. Despite their relatively small numbers, they were of some importance because of their location between the highlands and the Red Sea, their antipathy to Ethiopian rule, and the quasi-autonomy of a part of the Afar under the sultan of Aussa before the 1974 revolution.

Except for several petty centralized states under sultans or shaykhs, the Afar are fragmented among tribes, subtribes, and still smaller divisions and are characterized by a distinction between noble and commoner groups, about which little is known. Most Afar are pastoralists but are restricted in their nomadism by the need to stay close to permanent wells in extremely arid country. A number of them in the former sultan of Aussa's territory have long been settled cultivators in the lower Awash River valley, although the imperial government initiated a program to settle others along the middle Awash.

Saho is a linguistic rather than an ethnic category. The groups speaking the language include elements from the Afar, the Tigray, Tigre speakers, and others, including some Arabs. Almost all are pastoralists. Most are Muslims, but several groups—those heavily influenced by the Tigray—are Ethiopian Orthodox Christians.

Little is known about the political and social systems of the ten or so groups making up the total estimated Saho-speaking population of 120,000, but each group seems to be divided into segments. None was ever marked by the noble-serf distinction characteristic of Tigre speakers to their north, and all were said to elect their chiefs.

The speakers of the Highland East Cushitic languages (sometimes called the Sidamo languages after a version of the name of their largest component) numbered more than 2 million in 1970. The two largest groups were the Sidama (857,000) and the Hadya-Libido speakers (700,000). Kembata-Timbaro-Alaba speakers and the Deresa made up the rest. Each of these two groups numbered about 250,000 in 1970. As the hyphenated names suggest, two or more autonomous groups speaking dialects of the same language have been grouped together. In fact, most Sidama, although calling themselves by a single name in some contexts, traditionally are divided into a number of localized and formerly politically autonomous patrilineal clans, each under a chief.

The Sidama and other Highland East Cushitic speakers are cultivators of ensete and of coffee as a cash crop. In areas below 1,500 meters in elevation, however, the Sidama keep cattle.

The Sidama and other groups have retained their traditional religious systems, although some have been responsive to Protestant missionaries. Others, such as the Alaba, the Hadya, and the Timbaro, have accepted Islam. Only the Kembata are converts to Orthodox Christianity.

There are six groups of Central Cushitic (Agew) speakers, five of which live in the central highlands surrounded by Amhara. The Bilen in the extreme northern highlands form an enclave between the Tigray and the Tigre speakers. Agew-speaking groups total between 100,000 and 125,000 persons. They are the remnants of a population thought to have been the inhabitants of much of the central and northern highlands when Semitic-speaking migrants arrived millennia ago to begin the process that led to the formation of such groups as the Tigray and the Amhara. It is likely that Agew speakers provided much of the basic stock from which the Amhara and Tigray were drawn.

The largest of the Agew-speaking groups are the Awi (whose language is Awngi), estimated to number 50,000 in 1970. The linguistically related but geographically separate Kunfel numbered no more than 2,000. The Awi and the Qimant, numbering about 17,000, retain their traditional religious system; but the Kunfel and the Xamtanga, totaling about 5,000, are apparently Orthodox Christians. The Bilen have been much influenced by Islam, and many have begun to speak the Tigre of their Islamic neighbors as a second tongue.

A special case is the Beta Israel (their own name; others call them Falasha or Kayla), who numbered about 20,000 in 1989, most of whom emigrated to Israel in late 1984 and in May 1991. Perhaps preceding the arrival of Christianity in the fourth century A.D., a group of Agew speakers adopted a form of Judaism, although their organization and many of their religious practices resemble those of their Orthodox Christian neighbors. The precise origins and nature of the Judaic influence are matters of dispute. Most Beta Israel speak Amharic as a first language. Agew occurs in their liturgy, but the words are not understood.

Except for the Beta Israel, all Agew-speaking groups are plow agriculturists (the Kunfel augment their livelihood by hunting). The Beta Israel had been cultivators until deprived of their right to hold land after a major conflict with the Amhara and their refusal to convert to Christianity in the fifteenth century. They then became craftsmen, although many later returned to the land as tenants.

The sole group speaking a Northern Cushitic tongue is the Beja, a Muslim pastoral group that numbered about 20,000 in 1970. (Many more live in neighboring Sudan.) Their language is influenced by Arabic, and the Beja have come to claim Arab descent since their conversion to Islam. Like many of the other nomadic pastoralists in the area, they traditionally were segmented into tribes and smaller units, based on actual or putative descent from a common male ancestor and characterized by considerable autonomy, although federated under a paramount chief.

Omotic Language Groups

Between the lakes of southern Ethiopia's Great Rift Valley and the Omo River (in a few cases west of the Omo) live many groups that speak languages of the Omotic family. As many as eighty groups have been distinguished, but various sets of them speak dialects of the same language. Together they were estimated to number 1.3 million in 1970. Of these, the Welamo (often called Wolayta) are the most numerous, estimated to number more than 500,000 in 1970. Gemu-Gofa is a language spoken by perhaps forty autonomous groups, estimated at 295,000 in 1970 in the Gemu highlands. Kefa-Mocha, spoken by an estimated 170,000, is the language of two separate groups (one, commonly called Mocha, calls itself Shekatcho). Of the two, Kefa is the larger.

The relatively limited area in which they live, the diversity of their languages, and other linguistic considerations suggest that the ancestors of the speakers of Omotic languages have been in place for many millennia. Omotic speakers have been influenced linguistically and otherwise by Nilo-Saharan groups to the west and by East Cushitic groups surrounding them. As a result of the early formation of ancestral Omotic-speaking groups, external influences, and the demands of varied physical and social environments, the Omotic speakers have developed not only linguistic diversity but also substantial differences in other respects. Most Omotic-speaking peoples, for example, are hoe cultivators, relying on the cultivation of ensete at higher altitudes and of grains below approximately 1,500 meters. They also practice animal husbandry. Many in the Gemu highlands are artisans, principally weavers. Their craftwork has become attractive as the demand for their work in Addis Ababa and other urban centers has increased. In the capital these people are commonly called Dorze, although that is the name of just one of their groups.

Except for the Kefa—long influenced by Orthodox Christianity—and a small number of Muslims, Omotic speakers have retained their indigenous religious systems, although a few have been

Tall cacti in southern Ethiopia
Courtesy United Nations (O. Monsen)

influenced by European missionaries. Most of these groups originally had chiefs or kings. Among the exceptions are larger entities
such as the Welamo and the Kefa, both characterized by centralized political systems that exacted tribute from neighboring peoples.

Nilo-Saharan Language Groups

In the far southwest and along the country's western border live
several peoples speaking Nilo-Saharan languages. The most numerous of these are the Nuer and Anuak, both members of the East
Sudanic family. Most Nuer are found in Sudan, whereas the Anuak
live almost entirely in Ethiopia. Most of these people are hoe cultivators of grains, but many have cattle. A few, such as the Nuer,
are seminomadic.

The Kunema are found in western Tigray. Perhaps because of
the long Italian influence in Eritrea, they have been most affected
by foreign religious influences. Although Orthodox Christianity
had little or no impact on them, the Kunema often accepted the
teachings of Protestant and Roman Catholic missionaries. Two
other groups, the Berta and the Nara, have been influenced by
Islam. Otherwise, these peoples have retained their traditional religious systems. Koman speakers consist of several groups who live
along the Ethio-Sudan border in western Welega. Among these
little-known peoples are the Gumuz, who, along with the Berta,

are also called Bani Shangul. In the past, these peoples were often the object of slave raids by their neighbors in Ethiopia and Sudan.

Occupational Castes

Sixty to seventy groups scattered throughout Ethiopia traditionally were on the periphery of local social systems. Many authorities refer to them as occupational castes. Characterized by endogamy and also by specialization in one or more occupations considered unclean or degrading, they have been excluded from ordinary interaction with members of the host community, although one group acted as ritual functionaries for its host. The members of a caste group typically speak the local language, but some also have a language of their own or speak a variation on the local one. They also tend to be physically distinguishable from members of the host group. Their most common occupational specialties are woodworking, beekeeping, and ritual functions. Another group, consisting primarily of hunters, at one time provided royal guards for the traditional ruler of one host society.

Ethnic and Social Relations

Interethnic Relations

Ethnicity in Ethiopia is an enormously complex concept. No ethnic entity has been untouched by others. Groups in existence in the twentieth century are biological and social amalgams of several preexisting entities. The ingredients are often discernible only by inference, particularly if the mixing took place long ago. Nonetheless, such mixing led to the formation of groups that think of themselves and are considered by others as different. For instance, in the prerevolutionary period there were thousands of non-Amhara who had acquired the wherewithal to approximate the life-style of wealthy Amhara and had in fact gained recognition as Amhara. Such mixing has continued, and the boundaries of ethnic groups also continue to change.

Interethnic relations in prerevolutionary Ethiopia did not conform to a single model and were complex because of the nature of Amhara contact with other groups and the internal social and economic dynamics of the groups. Each group reacted differently to Amhara dominance. What makes this analysis even more complex is that the Amhara themselves do not constitute a cohesive group. Indeed, the tendency to see Ethiopia before (and, by some accounts, after) the revolution as dominated by Amhara has obscured the complexity of interethnic relations.

The Amhara are found predominantly in Gojam, Gonder, in parts of Welo such as Lasta and Wag, and in parts of Shewa such as Menz. Amhara from one area view those from other areas as different, and there is a long history of conflicts among Amhara nobles aspiring to be kings or kingmakers.

Intraprovincial and interprovincial conflict between Amhara nobles and their followers was quite common. Some aspects of intra-Amhara friction may be seen in the relations of Shewan Amhara to other Amhara and to other Ethiopians. Shewan Amharic speakers are on the southern periphery of the territory occupied by the Amhara. They made their presence felt in much of the Shewa region relatively late, except in areas such as Menz, which had always been Amhara. Thus, the Shewans over the centuries developed a culture and a society that emerged from Oromo, Amhara, and perhaps other groups. Whereas the southern people considered Shewan Orthodox Christians as Amhara, people from older Amhara areas such as Gojam and Gonder thought of such persons as Shewans or sometimes even as Oromo.

During the imperial regime, Amhara dominance led to the adoption of Amharic as the language of government, commerce, and education. Other forms of Amhara dominance occurred in local government, where Amhara served as representatives of the central government or became landholders.

Reaction to the Amhara varied even within individual ethnic groups. Some resisted the Amhara bitterly, while others aided them. In its most extreme form, resistance to Amhara dominance resulted in enduring separatist movements, particularly in Eritrea, Tigray, and the Ogaden. The separatist movement in Eritrea reflects a somewhat different historical experience from that of other areas of Ethiopia. Despite Eritrea's seeming unity, ethnic and religious differences among Eritreans abounded. For example, the Kunema, a Nilo-Saharan-speaking people who formed an enclave among Eritrea's Muslims and Christians and who have long been treated as inferior by some groups that make up the Eritrean independence movement, historically have provided an island of support for the central government.

Perhaps the only region to which the Amhara did not bring their sense of superiority was Tigray, home of the people who lay claim to the Aksumite heritage. The Amhara did not come to Tigray as receivers of land grants, and government administrators were often Tigrayan themselves. Tigray perspectives on the Amhara were, however, influenced negatively by a number of historical factors. For example, the son of the only emperor of Tigray origin to have ruled Ethiopia, Yohannis IV (reigned 1872–89), was deprived of the throne by Menelik II, an Amhara. In 1943 the imperial regime brutally repressed a Tigray rebellion called the Weyane.

Ethiopia's Ogaden region, inhabited primarily by ethnic Somali, was the scene of a series of Ethiopian-Somali struggles in 1964, 1977–78, and intermittently after that until 1987. Somalia supported self-determination for Ogaden Somali. Although Somalia and Ethiopia signed a joint communiqué in 1988 to end hostilities, Mogadishu refused to abandon its claim to the Ogaden. Moreover, in 1989 and 1990, the Ogaden region was home to about 350,000 Isaaq Somali from northern Somalia who had escaped persecution by the regime of Mahammad Siad Barre.

In April 1976, the PMAC promulgated its Program for the National Democratic Revolution (PNDR), which accepted the notions of self-determination for nationalities and regional autonomy. In compliance with the program, the PMAC created the Institute for the Study of Ethiopian Nationalities in 1983 to develop administrative and political proposals to accommodate all the country's major nationalities. As a result of the institute's findings, the government expressed a desire to abolish Ethiopia's fourteen administrative regions and to create thirty regions, of which five—Eritrea, Tigray, Aseb, Dire Dawa, and the Ogaden—were to be autonomous. Eritrean and Tigrayan leaders denounced the plan as nothing more than an attempt to perpetuate government control of Eritrea and Tigray. Their military campaigns to wrest control of the two regions from the Mengistu regime eventually succeeded.

The PMAC undermined the patterns of ethnic relations prevailing in imperial Ethiopia and eliminated the basis for Amhara dominance. However, postrevolutionary Ethiopia continued to exhibit ethnic tension. Traits based on ethnicity and religion are deeply ingrained and are not susceptible to elimination by ideology.

Social Relations

Ethiopia's ethnic and cultural diversity has affected social relations. Most lowland people are geographically and socially isolated from the highland population. Moreover, rural inhabitants, who constitute about 89 percent of the total population, generally live their lives without coming into contact with outsiders. Exposure to other ethnic groups usually occurs by means of relatively limited contact with administrators, tax collectors, and retail merchants. By contrast, the towns are a mosaic of social and ethnic diversity. Since the early 1940s, towns fulfilling administrative and economic functions have proliferated. In Addis Ababa, it is common for families and groups from disparate social and economic classes to live side by side. Only in recent years, with unprecedented urbanization, have upper-income residential zones emerged. Smaller urban centers have tended to be fairly homogeneous in ethnic and religious makeup. But with increasing urbanization, towns are expected to be the scene of increased interaction among different ethnic groups and social classes.

Traditionally, among the most important factors in social relations in Ethiopia has been religion (see Religious Life, this ch.). Ethiopian emperors nurtured the country's identity with Christianity, although there were at least as many Muslims as Christians in the country. Although the imperial regime did not impose Orthodox Christianity on Muslims and pagans, very few non-Christians held high positions in government and the military. In many cases, Muslims gravitated to commerce and trade, occupations relatively untainted by religious discrimination.

The Mengistu regime downplayed the role of religion in the state's life and disestablished the Ethiopian Orthodox Church. Moreover, the 1987 constitution guaranteed freedom of religion. In principle, all religions had equal status in relation to the state.

Muslims live throughout Ethiopia, but large concentrations can be found in Bale, Eritrea, Harerge, and Welo. Muslims also belong to many ethnic groups, a factor that may prevent them from exerting political influence commensurate with their numbers. Centuries of conflict between the Christian kingdom and its Muslim antagonists, recent apprehensions about Arab nationalism, and Arab support for Eritrean separatism and Somali irredentism all continue to perpetuate Ethiopian historical fears of "Islamic encirclement." Such historically rooted religious antagonism has persisted in creating a social barrier between Christians and Muslims.

Those who profess traditional religious beliefs are interspersed among Christians and Muslims. Such groups include the Sidama, the Gurage, the Oromo of Arsi and Borana, and the Nilotic groups along the Ethiopia-Sudan border. They have no political influence and are scorned socially by Muslims and Christians.

The existence of more than seventy languages has been another barrier to social communication and national integration. The imperial government, recognizing the importance of a national language, adopted Amharic as the official tongue. The use of Amharic became mandatory in government, education, radiobroadcasts, and newspapers. But the government's promotion of Amharic entailed the suppression of other major languages, which aroused opposition and accusations of cultural imperialism. Language policy changed under the Mengistu regime, which attempted to reverse the trend by dropping Amharic as a requirement in schools for non-Amharic speakers. The new policy recognized several languages widely spoken in specific areas—such as Oromo, Tigrinya, Welamo, and Somali—for use in schools at the lower levels (see Primary and

Secondary Education since 1975, this ch.). Addis Ababa also authorized the use of the five languages mentioned above, as well as Afar, in radiobroadcasts and literacy campaigns. Nevertheless, Amharic remained the language of government, and anyone who aspired to a national role had to learn to speak and write Amharic.

The most preferred occupations traditionally have been in government, the military, the clergy, and farming, with commerce and trade considered less important and consequently usually left to Muslims and foreigners. All major Ethiopian ethnic units include hereditary groups of artisans and craftsmen. Their occupations historically have been held in low esteem by the dominant groups. Prior to 1974, artisans and craftsmen could not own land or hold political office and could not participate in local meetings or assemblies. Dominant groups in their respective areas generally treated them as subjects.

Social status in Ethiopia during the centuries of imperial rule depended on one's landholdings, which provided the basis for class formation and social stratification. The emperor, the nobility, and landlords occupied the social hierarchy's highest positions. Under them were smallholding farmers, followed by millions of landless peasants who cultivated rented land. In the twentieth century, most of the southern landlord class consisted of Christian settlers from the north, whereas the tenants were mostly non-Christians and natives of the area. Thus, ethnic and cultural differences exacerbated class distinctions, which, in turn, adversely affected social relations (see Rural Society, this ch.).

With the dissolution of the imperial system and the nationalization of urban and rural land, social stratification and community relations based on landholding largely disappeared. The military regime wanted to create a classless society, but the social hierarchy based on landholdings simply was replaced by one based on political power and influence. National and regional party members, government ministers, military officers, and senior civil servants had enormous political sway and enjoyed the economic perquisites that the nobility and landlords once possessed.

After Ethiopia's liberation from Italian occupation in 1941, education played an important role in social relations by creating a "new nobility" and a middle class whose position and status were largely independent of landownership. This new group consisted of educated children of the nobility, commoners who had achieved distinction for their loyalty to the emperor, and others with advanced education whose skills were needed to modernize the bureaucracy and military. The postwar education system, the new government bureaucracy, and the modern sector of the economy also encouraged the growth of a middle class employed in the public and private sectors. Members of the small educated class that filled the bureaucracy and the professions during the postwar imperial period by and large retained their positions under Mengistu, although many left the country because of disenchantment with his regime.

The educated group was generally less attached to religion and tradition than was the rest of Ethiopian society. Members' education, income, occupation, and urban life-style likewise set them apart. They had more in common with educated people from other ethnic groups and frequently married across ethnic lines, although rarely across religious lines. Nevertheless, in the last decade or so before the 1974 revolution, some younger and better-educated non-Amhara expressed continued, even heightened, ethnic awareness through membership in urban-based self-help associations, which the Mengistu regime later banned. Although this educated group played a vital role in the emperor's downfall, it had little influence on the military government.

Many of the PMAC's policies were perceived as inimical to the interests of major ethnic and class groups. Despite the regime's tentative efforts—such as land reform—to defuse some longstanding grievances, opposition based on ethnic, religious, and class interests continued.

Social System

Rural areas, which contain an estimated 89 percent of the population, make up most of the country; it is the urban centers, however, that generate most of the country's political, administrative, cultural, and commercial activities. The towns and cities are also home to a variety of people forced to live on the margins of society by the Mengistu regime—absentee landlords whose rural lands and urban property had been confiscated by the state, as well as erstwhile activists who had aspired to genuine democratic reforms and had seen their hopes dashed.

Prior to the 1974 revolution, most Ethiopians conducted their daily lives in accordance with norms peculiar to each community or region. Ethnic groups characterized by common features of social organization and values were, on closer examination, actually quite diverse. As important as local structures were, the societies they characterized were not autonomous. Those that came closest to self-sufficiency were the eastern nomads. In the inaccessible and inhospitable areas inhabited by these groups, representatives of the central government were scarce. Elsewhere, each community was bound to a region and through it to the imperial center by layers

105

of social and political strata. Binding these strata together even tighter was a complex system of land rights.

Modifications introduced after World War II, particularly with respect to land rights, had little effect on the essential characteristics of the social order. The regime that took power in 1974 attempted to replace the old rural order with a new one based on the principle that land should be distributed equitably. Even though most rural areas supported the government's efforts to bring about such a change, the ultimate shape of the social and economic order remained uncertain as the 1990s began.

Rural Society

Political scientist John Markakis has observed, "The social structure of traditional Amhara-Tigray society [represented] the classic trinity of noble, priest, and peasant. These groups [were] distinguished not only through the division of labor, distinct social status, and a clear awareness of such distinctions expressed and justified in ideological terms, but also through differences in their relationships to the only means of production: land." In the northern highlands, land was usually held by the kin group, the state, and the church and, through each of these, by individuals. Private ownership in the Western sense came later and was abolished in 1975.

Anthropologist Allan Hoben is considered to have made the most thorough analysis of Amhara land tenure and its relation to social structure. According to his findings, the cognatic descent group (see Glossary), comprising men and women believed to be descended from a common ancestor through both males and females, ultimately held a block of land. As in cognatic descent systems elsewhere, men and women could belong to several such landholding groups. The descent group and each of its segments had a representative who looked after its collective interests. This agent, the respected elders, and politically influential members of the group or its segments acted in disputes over rights to land. The land was called *rist* (see Glossary) land, and the rights held or claimed in it were *rist* rights. An Amhara had claims not to a specific piece of land but to a portion of it administered by the descent group or a segment of this group. The person holding such rights was called *ristegna*. In principle, *rist* rights guaranteed security of tenure. Litigation over such rights was common, however. Most northern highland peasants held at least some *rist* land, but some members of pariah groups and others were tenants.

Peasants were subject to claims for taxes and labor from those above them, including the church. The common term for peasant, derived from the word for tribute, was *gebbar*. Taxes and fees were comprehensive, multiple, and burdensome. In addition, the peasant had to provide labor to a hierarchy of officials for a variety of tasks. It was only after World War II that administrative and fiscal reforms ended many of these exactions.

The state exercised another set of rights over land, including land held in *rist*. The emperor was the ultimate and often immediate arbiter of such rights, called *gult* (see Glossary) rights, and the recipient was called *gultegna*. There was considerable variation in the content and duration of the *gult* rights bestowed on any person.

Gult rights were the typical form of compensation for an official until the government instituted salaries in the period after World War II. Many *gult* grants were for life, or were hereditary, and did not depend on the performance of official duties. The grants served to bind members of noble families and the local gentry to the emperor.

The emperor also granted hereditary possession (*rist gult*) of state land to members of the higher nobility or the royal family. Peasants on such land became tenants of the grantee and paid rent in addition to the usual taxes and fees. Lieutenants who shared in the tribute represented the absentee landlords.

Those who benefited from the allocation of *gult* rights included members of the royal family (*masafint,* or princes), the nobility (*makuannent*), the local gentry, low-level administrators, and persons with local influence. Until the twentieth century, the chief duties of the *makuannent* were administrative and military. Membership in the *makuannent* was not fixed, and local gentry who proved able and loyal often assumed higher office and were elevated to the nobility. It was possible for a commoner to become a noble and for the son of a noble—even one with a hereditary title—to lose status and wealth unless he demonstrated military or other capabilities. Although there was a gap in living standards between peasant and noble, cultural differences were not profound. Consequently, the Amhara and Tigray lacked the notion of a hereditary class of nobles. Although it is possible to divide the Amhara and Tigray populations of the late nineteenth and much of the twentieth centuries in terms of rank, social status, power, and wealth, those who fell into various categories did not necessarily constitute distinct strata.

The pattern of land allocation in the southern territories incorporated into the empire by Menelik II differed in important ways from the pattern in the north. Moreover, the consequences of allocation and the administrative regime imposed by Menelik II and Haile Selassie varied, depending on the way in which particular ethnic groups or regions became subject to Ethiopian rule, on the nature of the preexisting sociopolitical structure, and on the territory's economic appeal.

Supposedly, the government divided conquered land in the south on the one-third (*siso*) principle, by which two-thirds went to the state and the remainder to the indigenous population. In fact, the proportion of the land taken by the state ranged from virtually none to more than two-thirds. In areas such as Jima, which had capitulated to Menelik II without resistance, the state took no occupied land, although it later took over unoccupied land and granted much of it to leading imperial officials. Other northerners, attracted by the coffee-growing potential of the Jima area, bought land in that region. In areas inhabited by nomads, all the land was state land, little was granted, and the pastoralists used it as before.

The government allocated state-held land to a variety of claimants. The emperor retained a substantial portion of the most fertile land. Churches also received large amounts of land in the south as northern governors implemented the imperial policy of establishing Orthodox Christian churches in conquered territory and as northern clergy came in numbers to serve them. Each church received *samon* grants, according to which the church held the rights to tribute in perpetuity, and the tribute from those working the land went solely to the support of the church (or local monastery). No part of it went through the secular hierarchy to the emperor. The nobility, including the leaders of Menelik's conquering armies (many of whom became governors in the south), received *rist gult* rights over large areas occupied by peasants. *Rist gult* holders, secure in their rights, allocated land rights of various kinds to kinsmen and retainers. The government granted *rist gult* rights over smaller parcels of land to officials at any level for loyal service. Remaining land was divided between the indigenous population and traditional leaders (*balabats*—see Glossary), who acquired some of the best land. People who had been on the land thus became tenants (*gebbars*).

Peasants from the north went south as soldiers and settlers. If the soldiers and their heirs continued to perform military or other service, they received land that remained in the family. If they arrived as settlers, the government gave them small parcels of land or allowed them to buy land from the state at low cost. Such land, unencumbered by the residual rights of a kin group but requiring the payment of state taxes, was thus held in an arrangement much like that applied to freehold land. Generally, settlers were armed and were expected to support local officials with force.

Most of the southern population consisted of indigenous peoples, largely deprived of the rights they had held under local systems.

Peasant from Bale
Courtesy United Nations
(John Isaac)

Grandmother carrying
child in Borana
Courtesy United Nations
(Ray Witlin)

They, like Amhara and Tigray peasants, were called *gebbars,* but they held no *rist* land and therefore had little security of tenure. The situation of the southern *gebbars* depended on the rights granted by the state over the land on which they lived. Those working land granted to a minor official paid tribute through him. If the land reverted to state control, the *gebbar* became a tributary of the state. As salaries for officials became the rule after World War II, the land that formerly served as compensation in lieu of salary was granted in permanent possession (in effect, became freehold land) to those holding contingent rights or to others. In these circumstances, the *gebbars* became tenants.

The basis of southern social stratification was, as in the north, the allocation of political office and rights in land by the emperor. The method of allocating rights in land and of appointing government officials in the south gave rise to a structure of status, power, and wealth that differed from the arrangement in the north and from the earlier forms of sociopolitical organization in the area. Those appointed as government officials in the south were northerners—mainly Amhara, Tigray, and educated Oromo—virtually all of whom were Orthodox Christians who spoke Amharic. This meant that social stratification coincided with ethnicity. However, the path to social mobility and higher status, as in the north, was education and migration to urban areas.

In 1966, under growing domestic pressure for land reform, the imperial government abolished *rist gult* in the north and south and *siso gult* in the south. Under the new system, the *gultegna* and the *gebbar* paid taxes to the state. In effect, this established rights of private ownership. The abolition of *rist gult* left the northern Amhara and Tigray peasant a *rist* holder, still dependent on the cognatic descent group to verify his rights to *rist* land. But at least he was formally freed of obligations to the *gult* holder.

Typically, the landholders and many northern provincial officials came from families with at least several generations of status, wealth, and power in the province—situations they owed not to Menelik II or to Haile Selassie but to earlier emperors or to great provincial lords. These nobles had some claim to the peasants' loyalty, inasmuch as all belonged to the same ethnic group and shared the same values. Peasants often saw attacks on the northern nobility as challenges to the entire system of which they were a part, including their right to *rist* land.

By contrast, whether or not they were descended from the older nobility, southern landholders were more dependent on the central government for their status and power. They were confronted with an ethnically different peasantry and lacked a base in the culture and society of the locality in which they held land.

In 1975 the revolution succeeded in eliminating the nobility and landlord classes. Those individual group members who avoided being killed, exiled, or politically isolated were able to do so because they had in some way already modified or surrendered their rights and privileges.

Land reform affected huge numbers of people throughout Ethiopia. However, there were regional differences in its execution. Peasant associations carried out land redistribution in the south, motivated not only by economic need but also by their antipathy toward the landlords. In the north, the government preserved *rist* tenure, and the peasant associations concerned themselves mainly with litigation over *rist* rights. Moreover, northern peasants were not driven by the ethnic and class hatred characteristic of southern peasants.

The 1975 Peasant Associations Organization and Consolidation Proclamation granted local self-government to peasant associations. Subsequently, peasant associations established judicial tribunals to deal with certain criminal and civil cases, including those involving violations of association regulations. Armed units, known as peasant defense squads, enforced decisions. Additionally, peasant associations had economic powers, including the right to establish service cooperatives as a prelude to collective ownership (although there was little peasant enthusiasm for the latter). The revolutionary government also established a hierarchy of administrative and development committees in districts, subregions, and regions to coordinate the work of the bodies at each administrative level. The Workers' Party of Ethiopia (WPE) later supplemented the work of these committees. Only a few officials spoke for peasants at the district and subregional levels, and rarely, if at all, were peasants represented in regional organizations, where civilians and military members of the central government were in control (see Peasant Associations, ch. 4).

Urban Society

After World War II, towns, commerce, and bureaucracy gradually became more significant in Ethiopia. Except for Addis Ababa and some Red Sea ports, towns were small, and urbanization had proceeded more slowly than in many other African countries. City and town life had not been a feature of Ethiopian society, and trade was not a full-time occupation for Ethiopians except for itinerant Muslims and Arabized peoples on the Red Sea coast. Manufacturing had arrived only recently, and the role of Ethiopians, except

111

as unskilled laborers, was minimal. Ownership and management, with relatively few exceptions, were in the hands of foreigners.

Most Ethiopians who entered into occupations not associated with the land or with traditional methods of administration worked for the central government, which had expanded to bring Ethiopia under the emperor's control, to provide essential services, and to generate economic development. During the 1940s, Ethiopia's few educated persons, who usually came from families of the nobility and gentry, joined the government.

Beginning in the 1950s, relatively younger Ethiopians with higher education developed hopes and expectations for democratic institutions. Still small in number, perhaps 7,000 to 8,000 by 1970, they were more ethnically varied in origin than the older educated group, although Amhara and Tigray were still represented disproportionately (as they were even among secondary school graduates). These would-be reformers were frequently frustrated by the older ways of the senior officials, who were dependent on Haile Selassie and beholden to him. Nevertheless, sustained opposition to the regime did not occur, largely because even middle- and lower-level government employees were better off than the peasants, small traders, and some of the gentry.

Small traders and craftsmen, below educated government workers in income and status, had little influence on the government, which tended to encourage larger-scale capital-intensive ventures typically requiring foreign investment and management. Although an increasing number of Christians were involved in commercial activities, small traders remained largely a Muslim group. Skilled craftsmen who were not of the traditional pariah groups often belonged to small ethnic groups, such as the weavers (often called Dorze) of Gamo Gofa.

At the bottom of the urban social scale were workers of varied ethnic origins, generally unskilled in a labor market crowded with unskilled workers ready to replace them. Neither government policy, the weak labor unions, nor the condition of the labor market gave them social or political leverage. By the late 1960s, inflation and a lack of jobs for university and secondary school graduates intensified disgruntlement. Urban-based agitation by students, labor, and the military eventually toppled the imperial regime.

Those who had served in senior positions in the imperial government and the military establishment were dismissed, imprisoned, executed, or they fled the country. The survivors of the old social structure were younger persons in government service: bureaucrats, teachers, and technicians. Some benefited from the nationalization of private enterprises and expansion of the government apparatus, filling posts held by senior officials or foreign specialists before the revolution. But this group was excluded from power, and some became militant opponents of the new regime's radical policies.

The position of the middle class—traders and artisans—varied. Generally, the status of Muslim traders rose after the new regime disestablished the Ethiopian Orthodox Church. As economic conditions worsened and consumer goods became scarce, however, traders became scapegoats and subject to violent attacks.

Notwithstanding allusions to the proletariat's revolutionary role, the urban working class—mainly in Addis Ababa and its environs—gained neither status nor power. The military government replaced the Confederation of Ethiopian Labor Unions (CELU) with the All-Ethiopia Trade Union (AETU) when the CELU leadership started opposing the direction of the revolution. The AETU focused its activities on supporting the government policy of emphasizing production rather than on advancing worker rights. The AETU—unlike the CELU—was a hierarchy rather than a confederation; unions at the base accepted policy decisions made at higher levels. In the next few years, the government had difficulty enforcing this policy. Deteriorating economic conditions caused strikes and demonstrations. In addition, violence often broke out between workers and government officials (see Labor Unions, ch. 3).

The urban equivalents of the peasant associations were the *kebeles* (see *Kebeles*, ch. 4). Initially, mid- and lower-level bureaucrats were elected to posts in these associations, but the military government soon purged them for opposing the revolutionary regime. New laws excluded from elective office for one year those who had owned rental property and members of their households. Thus, not only were the wealthy excluded from participation, but also many middle-class investors who had built and rented low-cost housing and who were far from rich were excluded as well. This exclusion also deprived many students and other young people of a role in the *kebeles*. Those who worked full time away from the neighborhood tended to be unwilling to take on *kebele* positions. Partly by default and partly with the PMAC's encouragement, elections in 1976 filled *kebele* posts with (in the words of John Markakis and Nega Ayele) "persons of dubious character, indeterminate occupation, busybodies and opportunists of all sorts . . . . Militia units [attached to the urban associations] charged with local security mustered the perennially unemployed, the shiftless and hangers-on, young toughs and delinquents, who were instantly transformed into revolutionary proletarian fighters." These individuals perpetrated crimes against people they disliked or dis-agreed with.

The *kebeles* engaged in some of the revolution's most brutal blood-letting. Increasing criticism eventually forced the regime to restrain them. After the populace recognized the PMAC's permanence, more people participated in *kebele* administration. By 1990 the *kebeles* were part of the grass-roots WPE organization.

The Role of Women

There have been few studies concerning women in Ethiopia, but many observers have commented on the physical hardship that Ethiopian women experience throughout their lives. Such hard-ship involves carrying loads over long distances, grinding corn manually, working in the homestead, raising children, and cook-ing. Ethiopian women traditionally have suffered sociocultural and economic discrimination and have had fewer opportunities than men for personal growth, education, and employment. Even the civil code affirmed the woman's inferior position, and such rights as ownership of property and inheritance varied from one ethnic group to another.

As in other traditional societies, a woman's worth is measured in terms of her role as a mother and wife. Over 85 percent of Ethio-pian women reside in rural areas, where peasant families are en-gaged primarily in subsistence agriculture. Rural women are integrated into the rural economy, which is basically labor inten-sive and which exacts a heavy physical toll on all, including chil-dren. The revolution had little impact on the lives of rural women. Land reform did not change their subordinate status, which was based on deep-rooted traditional values and beliefs. An improve-ment in economic conditions would improve the standard of liv-ing of women, but real change would require a transformation of the attitudes of governments and men regarding women.

There have been some changes for women in urban areas, where education, health care, and employment outside the home have become more available. Although a few women with higher edu-cation have found professional employment, most hold low-paying jobs. About 40 percent of employed women in urban areas worked in the service sector, mainly in hotels, restaurants, and bars, ac-cording to a 1976 government survey. Employment in production and related areas (such as textiles and food processing) accounted for 25 percent of the female work force, followed by sales, which accounted for about 11 percent. The survey also showed that women factory workers in Addis Ababa earned about a quarter of the wages men earned for the same type of work. These differences existed despite a 1975 proclamation stipulating equal pay for equal work for men and women.

Following the revolution, women made some gains in economic and political areas. The Revolutionary Ethiopia Women's Association (REWA), which claimed a membership of over 5 million, took an active part in educating women. It encouraged the creation of women's organizations in factories, local associations, and in the civil service. Some women participated in local organizations and in peasant associations and *kebeles*. However, the role of women was limited at the national level. In 1984, for example, the government selected only one woman as a full member of the Central Committee of the WPE. Of the 2,000 delegates who attended the WPE's inaugural congress in 1984, only 6 percent were women.

On a more positive note, the Mengistu regime could claim success in increasing literacy among women (see Literacy, this ch.). The enrollment of women in primary and secondary schools increased from about 32 percent in 1974/75 (Ethiopian calendar year—see Glossary) to 39 percent in 1985/86, although the rate of enrollment of urban women far exceeded the rate for rural women.

Religious Life

The 1955 constitution stated, "The Ethiopian Orthodox Church, founded in the fourth century on the doctrines of Saint Mark, is the established church of the Empire and is, as such, supported by the state." The church was the bulwark of the state and the monarchy and became an element in the ethnic identity of the dominant Amhara and Tigray. By contrast, Islam spread among ethnically diverse and geographically dispersed groups at different times and therefore failed to provide the same degree of political unity to its adherents. Traditional belief systems were strongest in the lowland regions, but elements of such systems characterized much of the popular religion of Christians and Muslims as well. Beliefs and rituals varied widely, but fear of the evil eye, for example, was widespread among followers of all religions.

Officially, the imperial regime tolerated Muslims. For example, the government retained Muslim courts, which dealt with family and personal law according to Islamic law. However, the imperial authorities gradually took over Muslim schools and discouraged the teaching of Arabic. Additionally, the behavior of Amhara administrators in local communities and the general pattern of Christian dominance tended to alienate Muslims.

The revolution brought a major change in the official status of the Ethiopian Orthodox Church and other religions. In 1975 the Mengistu regime disestablished the church, which was a substantial landholder during the imperial era, and early the next year removed its patriarch. The PMAC declared that all religions were equal, and a number of Muslim holy days became official holidays in addition to the Christian holidays already honored. Despite these changes, divisions between Muslims and Christians persisted.

Demography and Geography of Religious Affiliation

Statistical data on religious affiliation, like those on ethnic groups, are unreliable. Most Orthodox Christians are Amhara and Tigray, two groups that together constitute more than 40 percent of the population. When members of these two groups are combined with others who have accepted Orthodoxy, the total Christian population might come to roughly 50 percent of all Ethiopians.

Muslims have been estimated to constitute 40 percent of the population. The largest ethnic group associated with Islam is the Somali. Several other much smaller Islamic groups include the Afar, Argobba, Hareri, Saho, and most Tigre-speaking groups in northern Eritrea (see Ethiopia's Peoples, this ch.). Oromo also constitute a large proportion of the total Muslim population. There are also Muslims in other important ethnic categories, e.g., the Sidamo speakers and the Gurage. In the far north and the east, and to some extent in the south, Islamic peoples surround Orthodox Christians.

The only people (variously estimated at 5 to 15 percent of the population) who have had little if any contact with Orthodox Christianity or Islam live in the far south and the west. Included among adherents of indigenous religions are most of those speaking Nilo-Saharan languages and many of those speaking Omotic and Cushitic, including sections of the Oromo, such as the pastoral Borana. It is among these peoples that the few converts to missionary Christianity—Protestant and Roman Catholic—are to be found.

Ethiopian Orthodox Christianity

John Markakis has remarked of Ethiopia that "the dominant element in this culture and its major distinguishing feature is the Christian religion." Yet almost all of the analysis of Orthodox Christianity as practiced by Ethiopians has focused on the Amhara and Tigray. The meaning of that religion for the Oromo and others is not clear. For some Oromo who achieved significant political power in Amhara kingdoms in the eighteenth century and after, adherence to Christianity seemed to be motivated by nothing more than expediency.

By the mid-twentieth century, some educated Amhara and Tigray had developed skepticism, not so much of doctrine—although that also occurred—as of the church's political and economic role. They had developed similar feelings toward the

Worshipers dressed in white shammas *attend a service at Holy Trinity Cathedral in Addis Ababa.*
Courtesy World Vision (Bruce Brander)

clergy, most of whom were poorly educated. Nevertheless, the effects of the church's disestablishment and of the continuing social upheaval and political repression impelled many Ethiopians to turn to religion for solace.

Organization of the Church and the Clergy

The Ethiopian Orthodox Church's headquarters was in Addis Ababa. The boundaries of the dioceses, each under a bishop, followed provincial boundaries; a patriarch (*abun*) headed the church. The ultimate authority in matters of faith was the Episcopal Synod. In addition, the Church Council, a consultative body that included clergy and laity, reviewed and drafted administrative policy.

Beginning in 1950, the choice of the *abun* passed from the Coptic Church of Egypt in Alexandria to the Episcopal Synod in Addis Ababa. When Abuna Tewoflos was ousted by the government in 1976, the church announced that nominees for patriarch would be chosen from a pool of bishops and monks—archbishops were disqualified—and that the successful candidate would be chosen on the basis of a vote by clergy and laity. The new *abun* was a fifty-eight-year-old monk who took the name of Tekla Haimanot, after a fourteenth-century Ethiopian saint.

117

From the Christian peasant's point of view, the important church figures are the local clergy. The priest has the most significant role. An estimated 10 to 20 percent of adult male Amhara and Tigray were priests in the 1960s—a not extraordinary figure, considering that there were 17,000 to 18,000 churches and that the celebration of the Eucharist required the participation of at least two priests and three deacons, and frequently included more. Large churches had as many as 100 priests; one was said to have 500.

There are several categories of clergy, collectively referred to as the *kahinat* (priests, deacons, and some monks) and the *debteras* (priests who have lost their ordination because they are no longer ritually pure, or individuals who have chosen not to enter the priesthood). A boy between the ages of seven and ten who wishes to become a deacon joins a church school and lives with his teacher—a priest or *debtera* who has achieved a specified level of learning—and fellow students near a church. After about four years of study, the diocesan bishop ordains him a deacon.

After three or four years of service and additional study, a deacon can apply to be ordained a priest. Before doing so, he has to commit himself to celibacy or else get married. Divorce and remarriage or adultery result in a loss of ritual purity and loss of one's ordination.

A priest's chief duty is to celebrate the Eucharist, a task to which he is assigned for a fixed period of weeks or months each year. He also officiates at baptisms and funeral services and attends the feasts (provided by laymen) associated with these and other events. His second important task is to act as confessor, usually by arrangement with specific families.

Most priests come from the peasantry, and their education is limited to what they acquire during their training for the diaconate and in the relatively short period thereafter. They are, however, ranked according to their learning, and some acquire far more religious knowledge than others.

Debteras often have a wider range of learning and skills than what is required for a priest. *Debteras* act as choristers, poets, herbalists, astrologers, fortune-tellers, and scribes (for those who cannot read).

Some monks are laymen, usually widowers, who have devoted themselves to a pious life. Other monks undertake a celibate life while young and commit themselves to advanced religious education. Both kinds of monks might lead a hermit's life, but many educated monks are associated with the great monastic centers, which traditionally were the sources of doctrinal innovation or dispute that had sometimes riven the Ethiopian Orthodox Church.

Nuns are relatively few, usually older women who perform largely domestic tasks in the churches.

Faith and Practice

The faith and practice of most Orthodox Christians combine elements from Monophysite Christianity as it has developed in Ethiopia over the centuries and from a non-Christian heritage rejected by more educated church members but usually shared by the ordinary priest. According to Monophysite doctrine, Christ is a divine aspect of the trinitarian God. Broadly, the Christian elements are God (in Amharic, Egziabher), the angels, and the saints. A hierarchy of angelic messengers and saints conveys the prayers of the faithful to God and carries out the divine will. When an Ethiopian Christian is in difficulty, he or she appeals to these angels and saints as well as to God. In more formal and regular rituals, priests communicate on behalf of the community, and only priests may enter the inner sanctum of the usually circular or octagonal church where the ark (*tabot*) dedicated to the church's patron saint is housed. On important religious holidays, the ark is carried on the head of a priest and escorted in procession outside the church. The ark, not the church, is consecrated. Only those who feel pure, have fasted regularly, and have generally conducted themselves properly may enter the middle ring to take communion. At many services, most parish members remain in the outer ring, where *debteras* sing hymns and dance.

Weekly services constitute only a small part of an Ethiopian Orthodox Christian's religious observance. Several holy days require prolonged services, singing and dancing, and feasting. An important religious requirement, however, is the keeping of fast days. Only the clergy and the very devout maintain the full schedule of fasts, comprising 250 days, but the laity is expected to fast 165 days per year, including every Wednesday and Friday and the two months that include Lent and the Easter season.

In addition to standard holy days, most Christians observe many saint's days. A man might give a small feast on his personal saint's day. The local voluntary association (called the *maheber*) connected with each church honors its patron saint with a special service and a feast two or three times a year.

Belief in the existence of active spirits—many malevolent, some benevolent—is widespread among Ethiopians, whether Christian, Muslim, or pagan. The spirits called *zar* can be male or female and have a variety of personality traits. Many peasants believe they can prevent misfortune by propitiating the *zar*.

The protective *adbar* spirits belong to the community rather than to the individual or family. The female *adbar* is thought to protect the community from disease, misfortune, and poverty, while the male *adbar* is said to prevent fighting, feuds, and war and to bring good harvests. People normally pay tribute to the *adbars* in the form of honey, grains, and butter.

Myths connected with the evil eye (*buda*) vary, but most people believe that the power rests with members of lowly occupational groups who interact with Amhara communities but are not part of them. To prevent the effects of the evil eye, people wear amulets or invoke God's name. Because one can never be sure of the source of illness or misfortune, the peasant has recourse to wizards who can make diagnoses and specify cures. *Debteras* also make amulets and charms designed to ward off satanic creatures.

The belief system, Christian and other, of peasant and priest was consonant with the prerevolutionary social order in its stress on hierarchy and order. The long-range effects on this belief system of a Marxist-Leninist regime that ostensibly intended to destroy the old social order were difficult to evaluate in mid-1991. Even though the regime introduced some change in the organization of the church and clergy, it was not likely that the regime had succeeded in significantly modifying the beliefs of ordinary Christians.

Islam

Basic Teachings of Islam

Islam is a system of religious beliefs and an all-encompassing way of life. Muslims believe that God (Allah) revealed to the Prophet Muhammad the rules governing society and the proper conduct of society's members. Therefore, it is incumbent on the individual to live in a manner prescribed by the revealed law and incumbent on the community to build the perfect human society on earth according to holy injunctions. Islam recognizes no distinctions between church and state. The distinction between religious and secular law is a recent development that reflects the more pronounced role of the state in society and of Western economic and cultural penetration. Religion has a greater impact on daily life in Muslim countries than it has had in the largely Christian West since the Middle Ages.

Islam came to Ethiopia by way of the Arabian Peninsula, where in A.D. 610, Muhammad—a merchant of the Hashimite branch of the ruling Quraysh tribe in the Arabian town of Mecca—began to preach the first of a series of revelations he said had been granted him by God through the angel Gabriel. A fervent monotheist, Muhammad denounced the polytheism of his fellow Meccans. Because the town's economy was based in part on a thriving pilgrimage business to the shrine called the Kaaba and to numerous other pagan religious sites in the area, Muhammad's censure earned him the enmity of the town's leaders. In 622 he and a group of followers accepted an invitation to settle in the town of Yathrib, later known as Medina (the city), because it was the center of Muhammad's activities. The move, or hijra, known in the West as the hegira, marks the beginning of the Islamic era and of Islam as a force in history; indeed, the Muslim calendar begins in 622. In Medina, Muhammad continued to preach, and he eventually defeated his detractors in battle. He consolidated the temporal and the spiritual leadership in his person before his death in 632. After Muhammad's death, his followers compiled those of his words regarded as coming directly from God into the Quran, the holy scriptures of Islam. Others of his sayings and teachings, recalled by those who had known him, became the hadith. The precedent of Muhammad's personal behavior is called the sunna. Together, these works form a comprehensive guide to the spiritual, ethical, and social life of the orthodox Sunni Muslim.

The duties of Muslims form the five pillars of Islam, which set forth the acts necessary to demonstrate and reinforce the faith. These are the recitation of the *shahada* ("There is no god but God [Allah], and Muhammad is his prophet."), *salat* (daily prayer), *zakat* (almsgiving), *sawm* (fasting), and hajj (pilgrimage). The believer is to pray in a prescribed manner after purification through ritual ablutions each day at dawn, midday, midafternoon, sunset, and nightfall. Prescribed genuflections and prostrations accompany the prayers, which the worshiper recites facing toward Mecca. Whenever possible, men pray in congregation at the mosque with an imam, or prayer leader, and on Fridays they make a special effort to do so. The Friday noon prayers provide the occasion for weekly sermons by religious leaders. Women may also attend public worship at the mosque, where they are segregated from the men, although women usually pray at home. A special functionary, the muezzin, intones a call to prayer to the entire community at the appropriate hour. Those out of earshot determine the time by the position of the sun.

The ninth month of the Muslim calendar is Ramadan, a period of obligatory fasting in commemoration of Muhammad's receipt of God's revelation. Throughout the month, all but the sick and weak, pregnant or lactating women, soldiers on duty, travelers on necessary journeys, and young children are enjoined from eating, drinking, smoking, or sexual intercourse during the daylight hours. Those adults who are excused are obliged to endure an equivalent fast at their earliest opportunity. A festive meal breaks the daily fast and inaugurates a night of feasting and celebration. The pious well-to-do usually perform little or no work during this period, and some businesses close for all or part of the day. Because the months of the lunar year revolve through the solar year, Ramadan falls at various seasons in different years. A considerable test of discipline at any time of the year, a fast that falls in summertime imposes severe hardship on those who must do physical work.

All Muslims, at least once in their lifetimes, are strongly encouraged to make the hajj to Mecca to participate in special rites held there during the twelfth month of the lunar calendar. Muhammad instituted this requirement, modifying pre-Islamic custom, to emphasize sites associated with God and Abraham (Ibrahim), considered the founder of monotheism and father of the Arabs through his son Ismail.

Other tenets of the Muslim faith include the jihad (holy war) and the requirement to do good works and to avoid all evil thoughts, words, and deeds. In addition, Muslims agree on certain basic principles of faith based on the teachings of the Prophet Muhammad: there is one God, who is a unitary divine being, in contrast to the trinitarian belief of Christians; Muhammad, the last of a line of prophets beginning with Abraham and including Moses (Musa) and Jesus (Isa), was chosen by God to present His message to humanity; and there is to be a general resurrection on the last, or judgment, day.

During his lifetime, Muhammad was spiritual and temporal leader of the Muslim community. Religious and secular law merged, and all Muslims traditionally have been subject to sharia, or religious law. A comprehensive legal system, sharia developed gradually through the first four centuries of the Islamic era, primarily through the accretion of interpretations and precedents set by various judges and scholars.

After Muhammad's death, Muslim community leaders chose Abu Bakr, the Prophet's father-in-law and one of his earliest followers, to succeed him. At that time, some persons favored Ali ibn Abu Talib, Muhammad's cousin and the husband of his daughter Fatima, but Ali and his supporters (the Shiat Ali, or Party of Ali) eventually recognized the community's choice. The next two caliphs (successors)—Umar, who succeeded in A.D. 634, and Uthman, who took power in 644—enjoyed the recognition of the entire community. When Ali finally succeeded to the caliphate in 656, Muawiyah, governor of Syria, rebelled in the name of his murdered kinsman Uthman. After the ensuing civil war, Ali moved his capital to the area of present-day Iraq, where he was murdered shortly thereafter.

Ali's death ended the last of the so-called four orthodox caliphates and the period in which the entire community of Islam recognized a single caliph. Muawiyah proclaimed himself caliph from Damascus. The Shiat Ali refused to recognize him or his line, the Umayyad caliphs, and withdrew in the great schism to establish the dissident sect, known as the Shia, who supported the claims of Ali's line to the caliphate based on descent from the Prophet. The larger faction, the Sunnis, adhered to the position that the caliph must be elected, and over the centuries they have represented themselves as the orthodox branch.

Early in Islam's history the Sufism movement emerged. It stressed the possibility of emotional closeness to God and mystical knowledge of God in contrast to the intellectual and legalistic emphasis of orthodox Sunni theology. By the twelfth century, this tendency had taken a number of forms. Orders, each emphasizing specific disciplines (ways) of achieving that closeness and knowledge, were organized. Disdained by orthodox Islamic theologians, Sufi orders nevertheless became an integral part of Islam, although their importance varied regionally.

Local Character of Belief and Practice

Ethiopian Muslims are adherents of the dominant Sunni, or orthodox, branch of Islam. Shia are not represented in Ethiopia. The beliefs and practices of Ethiopian Muslims are embodied in a more or less integrated amalgam of three elements: the Islam of the Quran and the sharia, the worship of saints and the rituals and organization of religious orders, and the still-important remnant of pre-Islamic patterns. Islam in the traditional sense is dominant only on the Eritrean coast among Arab and Arab-influenced populations and in Harer and a few other towns.

In general, the most important practices of the Islamic faith, particularly regular prayer and fasting during the month of Ramadan, are observed in urban centers rather than in the smaller towns and villages and more among settled peoples than among nomads. Records of the pilgrimage to Mecca by Ethiopian Muslims are scarce.

Under Haile Selassie, Muslim communities could bring matters of personal and family law and inheritance before Islamic courts; many did so and probably continued to do so under the revolutionary regime. However, many Muslims dealt with such matters in terms of customary law. For example, the Somali and

123

other pastoralists tended not to follow the requirement that daughters inherit half as much property as sons, particularly when livestock was at issue. In parts of Eritrea, the tendency to treat land as the corporate property of a descent group (lineage or clan) precluded following the Islamic principle of division of property among one's heirs.

In Ethiopia's Muslim communities, as in neighboring Sudan and Somalia, the faithful are associated with, but not necessarily members of, specific orders. Nevertheless, although formal and informal attachment to Sufi orders is widespread, the emphasis is less on contemplative and disciplined mysticism than on the powers of the founders and other leaders of local branches of the orders. Most believe that these persons possess extraordinary powers to intercede with God and have the ability to promote the fertility of women and cure illness. In many cases, these individuals are recognized as saints. People visit their tombs to pray for their help or their intercession with God.

Indigenous Religions

Among indigenous religious systems, the names of certain deities and spirits recur frequently, especially among groups speaking related languages. Certain features of these traditional belief systems are broadly similar—for example, the existence of a supreme god identified with the sky and relatively remote from the everyday concerns of the people and addressed through spirits. Surface similarities notwithstanding, the configuration of the accepted roster of spirits, the rituals addressed to them, the social units (some based on the territorial community, others on common descent, generation, or sex) participating in specific rituals, and the nature and functions of religious specialists are peculiar to each ethnic group or subsection. Common to almost all indigenous systems is a range of spirits, some closely resembling in name and function the spirits recognized by neighboring Christians or Muslims.

Among the Oromo, especially those not fully Christianized, there is a belief in a supreme god called Waka, represented by spirits known as *ayanas*. The *ayanas* are mediators between the high god and human beings and are themselves approached through the *kallu,* a ritual specialist capable of being possessed by these spirits. The *kallu* is said to communicate directly with Waka and bless the community in his name. By contrast, some pastoral Oromo, such as the Guji and Borana, are regarded as monotheists.

Foreign Missions

In a 1944 decree, Haile Selassie forbade missionaries from attempting to convert Ethiopian Orthodox Christians, and they had

Priest conducting a
service at a church
in Debre Markos
Courtesy United Nations (Y. Levy)

little success in proselytizing among Muslims. Most missionaries focused their activities on adherents of local religions—but still with only little success. In the 1960s, there were about 900 foreign missionaries in Ethiopia, but many were laypersons. This fact was consistent with the emphasis of many such missions on the education and vocational training of the people they sought to serve. One obstacle to the missions' success in the rural areas may have been the imperial government's insistence that Amharic be used as the medium of religious instruction except in the earliest stages of missionary activity. There was also some evidence that Ethiopian Orthodox priests residing outside the Amhara and Tigray heartland, as well as local administrators, were hostile to the missionaries.

In the late 1960s, there were 350,000 to 400,000 Protestants and Catholics in Ethiopia, roughly 1.5 percent of the population. About 36 percent of these were Catholics, divided among those adhering to the Ethiopian rite (about 60 percent) and those following the Latin rite. The three bishops were Ethiopians. Protestants were divided among a number of denominations. The largest, nearly equaling in number the size of the Catholic congregation, consisted of adherents to the Fellowship of Evangelical Believers, the Ethiopian branch of the Sudan Interior Mission. The next largest group, about half as large, was the Ethiopian Evangelical Church Mekane Yesus, an entity that was fostered jointly by Scandinavian, German, and American Lutheran groups. This group claimed 400,000 members in the late 1970s and had an Ethiopian head. Several other groups, including the Bethel Evangelical Church (sponsored by the American United Presbyterian Church) and the Seventh-Day Adventists, had between 5,000 and 15,000 members each.

Many missionaries and other observers claimed that the revolutionary regime opposed missions and harassed the clergy and communicants. Although the government denied these accusations, its approach to those accused of not accepting its authority suggests that the mission churches and the regime had not reached a modus vivendi.

Education

Education in Ethiopia was oriented toward religious learning until after World War II, when the government began to emphasize secular learning as a means to achieve social mobility and national development. By 1974, despite efforts by the government to improve the situation, less than 10 percent of the total population was literate. There were several reasons for this lack of progress. According to Teshome G. Wagaw, a former educator at Haile Selassie I University, the primary failure of the education system was its inability to "satisfy the aspirations of the majority of the people and to prepare in any adequate way those passing through its ranks." Teshome described the system as elitist, inflexible, and unresponsive to local needs. He was equally critical of the distribution of educational opportunity, which favored a few administrative regions and urban centers at the expense of a predominantly illiterate rural population. The education system also suffered from inadequate financing.

In the early 1990s, the problems Ethiopians faced in making their education system responsive to national needs remained formidable. Social and political change had affected many traditional elements of national life, but it was too soon to predict what effect the changes would have on the progress of education.

Education During Imperial Rule

Until the early 1900s, formal education was confined to a system of religious instruction organized and presented under the aegis of the Ethiopian Orthodox Church. Church schools prepared individuals for the clergy and for other religious duties and positions. In the process, these schools also provided religious education to the children of the nobility and to the sons of limited numbers of tenant farmers and servants associated with elite families. Such schools mainly served Amhara and Tigray inhabitants of the central highlands. Toward the end of the nineteenth century, Menelik

II had also permitted the establishment of European missionary schools. At the same time, Islamic schools provided some education for a small part of the Muslim population.

At the beginning of the twentieth century, the education system's failure to meet the needs of people involved in statecraft, diplomacy, commerce, and industry led to the introduction of government-sponsored secular education. The first public school was established in Addis Ababa in 1907, and a year later a primary school opened in Harer. Foreign languages, elementary mathematics, and rudimentary science were taught in French to a limited number of students, along with Amharic and religious subjects.

In 1925 the government adopted a plan to expand secular education, but ten years later there were only 8,000 students enrolled in twenty public schools. A few students also studied abroad on government scholarships. Schools closed during the Italian occupation of 1936–41. After the restoration of Ethiopian independence, schools reopened, but the system faced shortages of teachers, textbooks, and facilities. The government recruited foreign teachers for primary and secondary schools to offset the teacher shortage. By 1952 a total of 60,000 students were enrolled in 400 primary schools, eleven secondary schools, and three institutions offering college-level courses. In the 1960s, 310 mission and privately operated schools with an enrollment of 52,000 supplemented the country's public school system.

In May 1961, Ethiopia hosted the United Nations-sponsored Conference of African States on the Development of Education. Among other things, the conference highlighted Ethiopia's educational deficiencies. The Ethiopian education system, especially in primary and secondary education, was ranked at the bottom among African nations. There were school and teacher shortages, a high dropout rate, and low overall attendance rates (about 10 percent among all school-age children in the country), especially among females, non-Christians, and rural children. Embarrassed by this record, the Ministry of Education developed a new education policy, which was in effect until 1974. Designed in conjunction with the objectives of the government's second and third five-year development plans, extending from 1962 to 1973, the policy gave precedence to the establishment of technical training schools, although academic education also was expanded. Curriculum revisions introduced a mix of academic and nonacademic subjects. But Amharic became the language of instruction for the entire primary cycle, which handicapped any child who had a different primary language.

Under the revised system, the two-year junior secondary schools offered a general academic program for individuals who wished to continue their education. A number of vocational subjects prepared others to enter technical or vocational schools. Some practical experience in the use of tools was provided, which qualified graduates as semiskilled workers. The curriculum in the four-year senior secondary schools prepared students for higher education in Ethiopia or abroad. Successful completion of the cycle also qualified some for specialized agricultural or industrial institutes. Others were qualified for intermediate positions in the civil service, the armed forces, or private enterprises.

There were two institutions of higher education: Haile Selassie I University in Addis Ababa, formed by imperial charter in 1961, and the private University of Asmera, founded by a Roman Catholic religious order based in Italy.

Between 1961 and 1971, the government expanded the public school system more than fourfold, and it declared universal primary education a long-range objective. In 1971 there were 1,300 primary and secondary schools and 13,000 teachers, and enrollment had reached 600,000. In addition, many families sent their children to schools operated by missionary groups and private agencies. But the system suffered from a shortage of qualified personnel, a lack of funds, and overcrowded facilities. Often financed with foreign aid, school construction usually proceeded faster than the training and certification of teachers. Moreover, many teachers did not stay long in the profession. Sources such as the United States Peace Corps and teachers from the National Service program (university students who taught for one year after completing their junior year) served only as stopgaps. In addition, most schools were in the major towns. Crowded and understaffed, those schools in small towns and rural areas provided a poor education.

The inadequacies of public education before the mid-1970s resulted partly from the school financing system. To finance primary education, the government levied a special tax on agricultural land. Local boards of education supervised the disbursement of tax receipts. (The central government financed secondary and higher education.) The system's inequities fostered the expansion of primary education in wealthier regions rather than in poorer ones. Moreover, urban inhabitants, who did not have to pay the tax but who were predominantly represented in the schools, sent their children at the expense of the taxpaying rural landowners and poor peasants. The government attempted to rectify this imbalance in 1970 by imposing an education tax on urban landowners and a 2 percent tax on the personal income of urban residents. But the Ministry of Finance treated the funds collected as part of the general revenue and never spent the money for its intended purpose.

Despite the fact that money spent on education increased from 10 percent of total government expenditures in 1968 to 20 percent in the early 1970s, funding remained inadequate. Expenditure on education was only 1.4 to 3 percent of the gross national product (GNP—see Glossary) between 1968 and 1974, compared with 2.5 to 6 percent for other African countries during the same period.

Under the pressure of growing public dissatisfaction and mounting student activism in the university and secondary schools, the imperial government initiated a comprehensive study of the education system. Completed in July 1972, the Education Sector Review (ESR) recommended attaining universal primary education as quickly and inexpensively as possible, ruralizing the curricula through the inclusion of informal training, equalizing educational opportunities, and relating the entire system to the national development process.

The ESR criticized the education system's focus on preparing students for the next level of academic study and on the completion of rigid qualifying examinations. Also criticized was the government's lack of concern for the young people who dropped out before learning marketable skills, a situation that contributed to unemployment. The report stated that, by contrast, "The recommended system would provide a self-contained program at each level that would be terminal for most students."

The report was not published until February 1974, which gave time for rumors to generate opposition among students, parents, and the teachers' union to the ESR recommendations. Most resented what they considered the removal of education from its elite position. Many teachers also feared salary reductions. Strikes and widespread disturbances ensued, and the education crisis became a contributing factor in the imperial regime's fall later that year.

Primary and Secondary Education since 1975

After the overthrow of imperial rule, the provisional military government dismantled the feudal socioeconomic structure through a series of reforms that also affected educational development. By early 1975, the government had closed Haile Selassie I University and all senior secondary schools and had deployed some 60,000 students and teachers to rural areas to participate in the government's Development Through Cooperation Campaign (commonly referred to as *zemecha*—see Glossary). The campaign's stated purposes were to promote land reform and improve agricultural production, health, and local administration and to teach peasants about the new political and social order.

In 1975 the new regime nationalized all private schools, except church-affiliated ones, and made them part of the public school system. Additionally, the government reorganized Haile Selassie I University and renamed it Addis Ababa University. It also initiated reforms of the education system based partly on ESR recommendations and partly on the military regime's socialist ideology. However, no meaningful education occurred (except at the primary level) from 1975 to 1978 because of the social turmoil, which pitted the regime against numerous opposition forces, including students.

Beginning in 1975, a new education policy emphasized improving learning opportunities in the rural areas as a means of increasing economic productivity. In the mid-1980s, the education system was still based on a structure of primary, secondary, and higher education levels, much as it was during the imperial regime. However, the government's objective was to establish an eight-year unified education system at the primary level. Preliminary to implementing this program, officials tested a new curriculum in seventy pilot schools. This curriculum emphasized expanded opportunities for nonacademic training. The new approach also decentralized control and operation of primary and secondary schools to the subregional level, where the curriculum addressed local requirements. In each case, committees drawn from the peasant associations and *kebeles* and augmented by at least one teacher and one student over the age of sixteen from each school administered the public schools. Students used free textbooks in local languages. In late 1978, the government expanded the program to include nine languages, and it adopted plans to add five others.

There were also changes in the distribution and number of schools and the size and composition of the student body. The military regime worked toward a more even distribution of schools by concentrating its efforts on small towns and rural areas that had been neglected during the imperial regime. With technical assistance from the Ministry of Education, individual communities performed all primary school construction. In large part because of such community involvement, the number of primary schools grew from 3,196 in 1974/75 to 7,900 in 1985/86 (the latest years for which figures were available in mid-1991), an average increase of 428 schools annually (see table 5, Appendix). The number of primary schools increased significantly in all regions except three, including Eritrea and Tigray, where there was a decline because of continuing insurgencies. In Addis Ababa, the number of primary

Students in a school near Holeta
Courtesy International Development Association (Ray Muldoon)

schools declined because of the closure or absorption of nongovernment schools, especially religious ones, into the government system.

Primary school enrollment increased from about 957,300 in 1974/75 to nearly 2,450,000 in 1985/86. There were still variations among regions in the number of students enrolled and a disparity in the enrollment of boys and girls. Nevertheless, while the enrollment of boys more than doubled, that of girls more than tripled (see table 6, Appendix). Urban areas had a higher ratio of children enrolled in schools, as well as a higher proportion of female students, compared with rural areas.

The number of junior secondary schools almost doubled, with fourfold increases in Gojam, Kefa, and Welega. Most junior secondary schools were attached to primary schools.

The number of senior secondary schools almost doubled as well, with fourfold increases in Arsi, Bale, Gojam, Gonder, and Welo. The prerevolutionary distribution of schools had shown a concentration in the urban areas of a few administrative regions. In 1974/75 about 55 percent of senior secondary schools were in Eritrea and Shewa, including Addis Ababa. In 1985/86 the figure was down to 40 percent. Although there were significantly fewer girls enrolled at the secondary level, the proportion of females in the school system at all levels and in all regions increased from about 32 percent in 1974/75 to 39 percent in 1985/86.

The number of teachers also increased, especially in senior secondary schools (see table 7, Appendix). However, this increase had not kept pace with student enrollment. The student-teacher ratio went from forty-four to one in 1975 to fifty-four to one in 1983 in primary schools and also increased from thirty-five to one in 1975 to forty-four to one in 1983 in secondary schools.

Although the government achieved impressive improvements in primary and secondary education, prospects for universal education in the near future were not bright. In 1985/86, the latest year for which government statistics were available, enrollment in the country's primary, junior secondary, and senior secondary schools totaled 3.1 million students, up from the nearly 785,000 enrolled a decade earlier. Only about 2.5 million (42 percent) of the 6 million primary school-age children were enrolled in school in 1985/86. Junior secondary school enrollments (grades seven and eight) amounted to 363,000, while at the secondary school level (grades nine through twelve), only 292,385 out of 5.5 million, or 5.3 percent, attended school. In addition, prospects for continued study for most primary school graduates were slim. In 1985/86 there was only one junior secondary school for every eight primary schools and only one senior secondary school for every four junior secondary schools. There were many primary school students for whom space would not be available and who therefore would most likely end up on the job market, where work already was scarce for people with limited educations.

School shortages also resulted in crowding, a situation aggravated by the rural-urban influx of the late 1980s. Most schools operated on a morning and afternoon shift system, particularly in urban areas. A teacher shortage exacerbated the problems created by crowded classrooms. In addition to these problems were those of the destruction and looting of educational facilities as a result of fighting in northern regions. By 1990/91 destruction was especially severe in Eritrea, Tigray, and Gonder, but looting of schools was reported in other parts of the country as well.

Higher and Vocational Education since 1975

In 1977 the revolutionary regime issued Proclamation No. 109, which created the Commission for Higher Education. This document also outlined the main objectives of higher education institutions as follows: to train individuals for high-level positions in accordance with the national plan of development and to provide qualified medium-level personnel to meet the immediate needs of the economy; to improve the quality of education, strengthen and expand tertiary-level institutions, and establish new research and training centers; and to contribute to a better standard of living among the masses by developing science, technology, the arts, and literature.

Additionally, Addis Ababa reoriented institutions of higher education to reflect the new regime's objectives and modified admission criteria to benefit students from small towns and rural areas. But the government also assigned many students to specialize in certain fields, which denied them the opportunity to decide on careers of their choosing.

Higher education expanded modestly in the period after 1975. The College of Agriculture at Alemaya, which was part of Addis Ababa University, was granted independent university status in 1985. A postgraduate studies program was established in 1978, which had an enrollment of 246 students in 1982/83, of whom fifteen were women. Graduate programs were offered in several fields, including engineering, natural science, agriculture, the social sciences, and medicine. Several research institutes supported these institutions of higher education. Addis Ababa University also provided an evening extension program offering courses in many fields.

Other diploma-granting independent colleges trained middle-level manpower in several fields. These included the College of Teacher Education, the Junior College of Commerce, and the Municipal Technical College, all in Addis Ababa. There were also junior colleges of agriculture in Ambo and Jima, the Institute of Animal Health Assistants in Debre Zeyit, and the Institute of Health Sciences in Jima. Altogether, there were approximately twelve colleges or universities in the country in the early 1990s, with intense competition among students for admission.

Enrollment in higher education grew from 4,500 in 1970 to more than 18,400 in 1985/86, of whom nearly 11 percent were women. But enrollment was low, considering the size of the population. Space limitations at the colleges and universities caused the government to raise admission standards. To narrow the gap somewhat, the number of students sent abroad on scholarships and fellowships grew from an annual average of 433 during 1969–73 to about 1,200 during 1978–82.

The number of Ethiopians on teaching staffs also grew. The faculty of Addis Ababa University increased from 437 in 1970 to 1,296 in 1983, with a corresponding increase in Ethiopian faculty from 48 percent to 74 percent of this total during the same period.

There was also more emphasis on the creation of technical and vocational schools, most of which were operated by the government.

The Ministry of Education operated or supervised nine such schools scattered around the country. These schools had an enrollment of more than 4,200 in 1985/86, and their graduates were in great demand by industries. With Soviet assistance, Ethiopia established its first polytechnic institute, in Bahir Dar, in the 1960s. It trained personnel in agromechanics, industrial chemistry, electricity, and textile and metal-working technology. In addition, a system of general polytechnic education had been introduced into the senior secondary school curriculum so that those who did not continue their education still could venture into the skilled job market.

The government also introduced vocational training to upgrade peasant skills. The peasant training centers, operated by the Ministry of Agriculture, provided training in vocational trades related to agriculture for periods ranging from three weeks to six months. The country had twelve such centers, which trained more than 200,000 farmers from 1974 to 1988.

Literacy

Among the revolutionary regime's few successes was the national literacy campaign. The literacy rate, under 10 percent during the imperial regime, increased to about 63 percent by 1984, according to government figures. Others sources, however, estimated it at around 37 percent. In 1990/91 an adult literacy rate of just over 60 percent was still being reported in government as well as in some international reports. As with the 1984 data, it several wise to exercise caution with regard to the latest figure. As some observers pointed out, defining just what the term "literacy" means presented a problem; in addition, the military government's desire to report as high a literacy rate as possible had to be taken into account.

The national literacy campaign began in early 1975 when the government mobilized more than 60,000 students and teachers, sending them all over the country for two-year terms of service. This experience was crucial to the creation in 1979 of the National Literacy Campaign Coordinating Committee (NLCCC) and a nationwide effort to raise literacy levels. The government organized the campaign in rounds, which began in urban centers and spread outward to the remote parts of the country up to Round 12. Officials originally conducted the literacy training in five languages: Amharic, Oromo, Tigrinya, Welamo, and Somali. The number of languages was later expanded to fifteen, which represented about 93 percent of the population. By the end of Round 12, in the late 1980s, about 17 million people had been registered, of whom 12 million had passed the literacy test. Women represented about half of those enrolled.

According to government sources, about 1.5 million people eventually worked in the campaign. They included students, civil servants, teachers, military personnel, housewives, and members of religious groups, all of whom, it was claimed, offered their services freely. Adult literacy classes used primary and secondary school facilities in many areas. Officials distributed more than 22 million reading booklets for beginners and more than 9 million texts for postliteracy participants. The Ministry of Education also stocked reading centers with appropriate texts. These books focused on topics such as agriculture, health, and basic technology. To consolidate the gains from the literacy campaign, the government offered follow-up courses for participants up to grade four, after which they could enroll in the regular school system. In addition, national newspapers included regular columns for new readers. The literacy campaign received international acclaim when the United Nations Educational, Scientific, and Cultural Organization (UNESCO) awarded Ethiopia the International Reading Association Literacy Prize in 1980.

Foreign Educational Assistance

The regime's efforts to resolve the country's educational problems received considerable support from abroad. The initial cost of reorienting the education system toward national development goals through improving opportunities in remote rural areas had been estimated at US$34.7 million. Of this amount, US$23 million was received from the International Development Association (IDA). By late 1978, the European Community had contributed US$2.6 million to help with the government's education development plan. The German Democratic Republic (East Germany) sent teachers, training specialists, and curriculum development experts. The Soviet Union provided hundreds of scholarships. In 1978 there were 1,200 Ethiopian children (aged nine to fifteen years) from poor families who attended two special schools in Cuba for an undetermined period. Other students followed this initial group. In 1990 the Swedish International Development Authority granted US$10.5 million for elementary education. This aid helped make possible the construction of about 300 schools. The Swedish agency already had contributed to the construction of 7,000 elementary schools.

Health and Welfare

The main cause of many of Ethiopia's health problems is the relative isolation of large segments of the population from the modern sector. Additionally, widespread illiteracy prevents the

135

dissemination of information on modern health practices. A shortage of trained personnel and insufficient funding also hampers the equitable distribution of health services. Moreover, most health institutions were concentrated in urban centers prior to 1974 and were concerned with curative rather than preventive medicine.

Western medicine came to Ethiopia during the last quarter of the nineteenth century with the arrival of missionary doctors, nurses, and midwives. But there was little progress on measures to cope with the acute and endemic diseases that debilitated large segments of the population until the government established its Ministry of Public Health in 1948. The World Health Organization (WHO), the United Nations Children's Fund (UNICEF), and the United States Agency for International Development (AID) provided technical and financial assistance to eliminate the sources of health problems.

In addition to establishing hospitals, health centers, and outpatient clinics, the government initiated programs to train Ethiopian health care personnel so that they could supplement the private institutions that existed in a few major urban centers. The few government campaigns that exhorted the people to cooperate in the fight against disease and unhealthful living conditions were mainly directed at the urban population.

By the mid-1970s, the number of modern medical facilities had increased relatively slowly—particularly in rural areas, where at least 80 percent of the people still did not have access to techniques or services that would improve health conditions (see table 8; table 9, Appendix). Forty-six percent of the hospital beds were concentrated in Addis Ababa, Asmera, Dire Dawa, and Harer. In the absence of modern medical services, the rural population continued to rely on traditional folk medicine. According to official statistics, in 1983/84 there were 546 physicians in the country to serve a population of 42 million, a ratio of roughly one physician per 77,000 people, one of the worst ratios in the world. Less than 40 percent of the population was within reach of modern health services.

As in most developing countries in the early 1990s, Ethiopia's main health problems were communicable diseases caused by poor sanitation and malnutrition and exacerbated by the shortage of trained manpower and health facilities. Mortality and morbidity data were based primarily on health facility records, which may not reflect the real incidence of disease in the population. According to such records, the leading causes of hospital deaths were dysentery and gastroenteritis (11 percent), tuberculosis (11 percent), pneumonia (11 percent), malnutrition and anemia (7 percent), liver diseases including hepatitis (6 percent), tetanus (3 percent), and malaria (3 percent). The leading causes of outpatient morbidity in children under age five were upper respiratory illnesses, diarrhea, eye infections including trachoma, skin infections, malnutrition, and fevers. Nearly 60 percent of childhood morbidity was preventable. The leading causes of adult morbidity were dysentery and gastrointestinal infections, malaria, parasitic worms, skin and eye diseases, venereal diseases, rheumatism, malnutrition, fevers, upper respiratory tract infections, and tuberculosis. These diseases were endemic and quite widespread, reflecting the fact that Ethiopians had no access to modern health care.

Tuberculosis still affected much of the population despite efforts to immunize as many people as possible. Venereal diseases, particularly syphilis and gonorrhea, were prevalent in towns and cities, where prostitution contributed to the problem. The high prevalence of worms and other intestinal parasites indicated poor sanitary facilities and education and the fact that potable water was available to less than 14 percent of the population. Tapeworm infection was common because of the popular practice of eating raw or partially cooked meat.

Schistosomiasis, leprosy, and yellow fever were serious health hazards in certain regions of the country. Schistosomiasis, a disease caused by a parasite transmitted from snails to humans through the medium of water, occurred mainly in the northern part of the highlands, in the western lowlands, and in Eritrea and Harerge. Leprosy was common in Harerge and Gojam and in areas bordering Sudan and Kenya. The incidence of typhoid, whooping cough, rabies, cholera, and other diseases had diminished in the 1970s because of school immunization programs, but serious outbreaks still plagued many rural areas. Frequent famine made health conditions even worse.

Smallpox has been stamped out in Ethiopia, the last outbreak having occurred among the nomadic population in the late 1970s. Malaria, which is endemic in 70 percent of the country, was once a scourge in areas below 1,500 meters elevation. Its threat had declined considerably as a result of government efforts supported by WHO and AID, but occasional seasonal outbreaks were common. The most recent occurrence was in 1989, and the outbreak was largely the result of heavy rain, unusually high temperatures, and the settling of peasants in new locations. There was also a report of a meningitis epidemic in southern and western Ethiopia in 1989, even though the government had taken preventive measures by vaccinating 1.6 million people. The logistics involved in reaching the 70 percent of Ethiopians who lived more than three days' walk from a health center with refrigerated vaccines and penicillin prevented the medical authorities from arresting the epidemic.

Acquired immune deficiency syndrome (AIDS) was a growing problem in Ethiopia. In 1985 the Ministry of Health reported the country's first AIDS case. In subsequent years, the government sponsored numerous AIDS studies and surveys. For example, in 1988 the country's AIDS Control and Prevention Office conducted a study in twenty-four towns and discovered that an average of 17 percent of the people in each town tested positive for the human immunodeficiency virus (HIV), the precursor of full-blown AIDS. A similar survey in Addis Ababa showed that 24 percent tested positive.

In 1990 Mengistu Mihret, head of the Surveillance and Research Coordination Department of the AIDS Control and Prevention Office, indicated that AIDS was spreading more rapidly in heavily traveled areas. According to the Ministry of Health, there were two AIDS patients in the country in 1986, seventeen in 1987, eighty-five in 1988, 188 in 1989, and 355 as of mid-1990. Despite this dramatic growth rate, the number of reported AIDS cases in Ethiopia was lower than in many other African countries. However, the difference likely reflected the comparatively small amount of resources being devoted to the study of AIDS.

Starting in 1975, the regime embarked on the formulation of a new health policy emphasizing disease prevention and control, rural health services, and promotion of community involvement and self-reliance in health activities. The ground for the new policy was broken during the student *zemecha* of 1975/76, which introduced peasants to the need for improved health standards. In 1983 the government drew up a ten-year health perspective plan that was incorporated into the ten-year economic development plan launched in September 1984. The goal of this plan was the provision of health services to 80 percent of the population by 1993/94. To achieve such a goal would have required an increase of over 10 percent in annual budget allocations, which was unrealistic in view of fiscal constraints.

The regime decentralized health care administration to the local level in keeping with its objective of community involvement in health matters. Regional Ministry of Health offices gave assistance in technical matters, but peasant associations and *kebeles* had considerable autonomy in educating people on health matters and in constructing health facilities in outlying areas. Starting in 1981, a hierarchy of community health services, health stations, health centers, rural hospitals, regional hospitals, and central referral hospitals were supposed to provide health care. By the late 1980s,

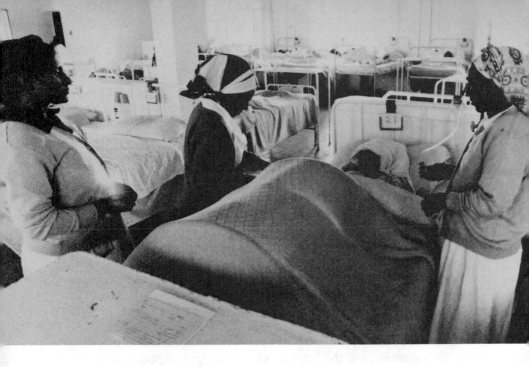

Nurses comfort a patient at a hospital in Addis Ababa.
Courtesy World Vision (Bruce Brander)

however, these facilities were available to only a small fraction of the country's population.

At the bottom of the health-care pyramid was the community health service, designed to give every 1,000 people access to a community health agent, someone with three months of training in environmental sanitation and the treatment of simple diseases. In addition to the community health agent, there was a traditional birth attendant, with one month of training in prenatal and postnatal care and safe delivery practices. As of 1988, only about a quarter of the population was being served by a community health agent or a traditional birth attendant. Both categories were made up of volunteers chosen by the community and were supported by health assistants.

Health assistants were full-time Ministry of Health workers with eighteen months of training, based at health stations ultimately to be provided at the rate of one health station per 10,000 population. Each health station was ultimately to be staffed by three health assistants. Ten health stations were supervised by one health center, which was designed to provide services for a 100,000-person segment of the population. The Regional Health Department supervised health centers. Rural hospitals with an average of seventy-five beds and general regional hospitals with 100 to 250 beds provided referral services for health centers. The six central referral hospitals were organized to provide care in all important specialties, train health professionals, and conduct research. There were a few specialized hospitals for leprosy and tuberculosis, but overall the lack of funds meant emphasis on building health centers and health stations rather than hospitals.

Trained medical personnel were also in short supply. As noted previously, the ratio of citizens to physicians was one of the worst in the world. Of 4,000 positions for nurses, only half were filled, and half of all health stations were staffed by only one health assistant instead of the planned three. There were two medical schools—in Addis Ababa and Gonder—and one school of pharmacy, all managed by Addis Ababa University. The Gonder medical school also trained nurses and sanitation and laboratory technicians. The Ministry of Health ran three nursing schools and eleven schools for health assistants. Missionaries also ran two such schools. The regime increased the number of nurses to 385 and health assistants to 650 annually, but the health budget could not support this many new graduates. The quality of graduates had also not kept pace with the quantity of graduates.

Since 1974 there have been modest improvements in national expenditures on public health. Between 1970 and 1975, the government spent about 5 percent of its total budget on health programs. From 1975 to 1978, annual expenditures varied between 5.5 and 6.6 percent of outlays, and for the 1982–88 period total expenditures on the Ministry of Health were about 4 percent of total government expenditures. This was a low figure but comparable to that for other low-income African countries. Moreover, much of the real increases of 7 to 8 percent in the health budget went to salaries.

A number of countries were generous in helping Ethiopia meet its health care needs. Cuba, the Soviet Union, and a number of East European countries provided medical assistance. In early 1980, nearly 300 Cuban medical technicians, including more than 100 physicians, supported local efforts to resolve public health problems. Western aid for long-term development of Ethiopia's health sector was modest, averaging about US$10 million annually, the lowest per capita assistance in sub-Saharan Africa. The main Western donors included Italy and Sweden. International organizations, namely UNICEF, WHO, and the United Nations Population Fund, also extended assistance.

* * *

Much of the literature on Ethiopian society is based on research concluded before the 1974 revolution. However, an increasing number of post-1974 works contain useful information on both the imperial and the revolutionary periods.

An excellent linguistic study is *Language in Ethiopia,* edited by M. Lionel Bender et al. John Markakis's *Ethiopia: Anatomy of a Traditional Polity* provides a useful assessment of Ethiopia's prerevolutionary social order with particular reference to the political ramifications of social stratification, interethnic relations, and land control. Donald N. Levine's *Greater Ethiopia: The Evolution of a Multi-Ethnic Society* analyzes the main structural features of the traditional Amhara, Tigrayan, and Oromo sociocultural systems. Allan Hoben's *Land Tenure among the Amhara of Ethiopia* and Ambaye Zekarias's *Land Tenure in Eritrea (Ethiopia)* examine the land tenure system in the Amhara highlands and in Eritrea, respectively. Taddesse Tamrat's *Church and State in Ethiopia, 1270–1527* and John Spencer Trimingham's *Islam in Ethiopia* are useful for an understanding of the role of religion in Ethiopia.

Richard K. Pankhurst's *An Introduction to the Medical History of Ethiopia* provides useful insight into the evolution of health practices in Ethiopia. *Implementing Educational Policies in Ethiopia* by Fassil R. Kiros examines the revolutionary government's attempts to reform Ethiopia's education system. Desta Asayehegn's *Socio-Economic and Educational Reforms in Ethiopia, 1942–1974* analyzes the educational changes made during Haile Selassie's last thirty-two years on the throne. (For further information and complete citations, see Bibliography.)

Chapter 3. The Economy

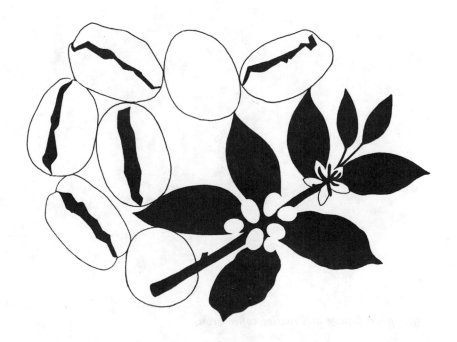

Coffee plant foliage and roasted coffee beans

RESTRUCTURING THE ECONOMY along socialist lines and achieving sustained economic growth were the two major economic objectives of the Provisional Military Administrative Council when it assumed power in 1974. After the 1974 revolution, the pace of economic restructuring was accelerated by a barrage of legislation. A key part of the effort to reshape the economy was the implementation of Africa's most ambitious land reform program, which included nationalization of both rural and urban land. Most of Ethiopia's industries, large-scale agricultural farms, and financial institutions were brought under the control of the government, and both rural and urban communities were organized into a hierarchy of associations. Pursuit of the military regime's second objective—sustained economic growth—was less successful. Drought, regional conflicts, inflexible government policy, and lack of confidence by the private sector seriously affected the economy. Falling productivity, soaring inflation, growing dependence on foreign aid and loans, high unemployment, and a deteriorating balance of payments all combined to create a deepening economic crisis. In 1990 Ethiopia had a gross national product of US$6 billion and a per capita income of about US$120, one of the lowest per capita incomes of any country in the world.

Following the 1974 revolution, the socialist government developed a series of annual plans and a ten-year perspective plan to revitalize the war-ravaged economy. Although the annual plans helped the regime deal with some urgent economic problems, such as shortages of food and consumer goods, decline in productivity, lack of foreign exchange, and rising unemployment, these plans failed to move the country significantly closer to attaining its long-term development objectives. In 1984/85 (Ethiopian calendar year—see Glossary) the military government launched a new ten-year perspective plan, which represented a renewed commitment to economic growth and structural transformation of the economy. However, the economy continued to deteriorate. In response, the regime introduced several additional reforms. For instance, the 1988 Investment Code allowed unlimited participation of the private sector in certain areas of the economy. In January 1988, under pressure from aid donor countries, the government agreed to restructure agricultural and farm price policies. Finally, in March 1990 President Mengistu Haile Mariam announced the end of the country's

Marxist economic system and the beginning of a mixed economy. Despite these reforms, the economy failed to improve.

Growth and Structure of the Economy
Developments up to 1974

By African standards, Ethiopia is a potentially wealthy country, with fertile soil and good rainfall over large regions. Farmers produce a variety of grains, including wheat, corn, and millet. Coffee also grows well on southern slopes. Herders can raise cattle, sheep, and goats in nearly all parts of the country. Additionally, Ethiopia possesses several valuable minerals, including gold and platinum.

Unlike most sub-Saharan African countries, Ethiopia's resources have enabled the country to maintain contacts with the outside world for centuries. Since ancient times, Ethiopian traders exchanged gold, ivory, musk, and wild animal skins for salt and luxury goods, such as silk and velvet. By the late nineteenth century, coffee had become one of Ethiopia's more important cash crops. At that time, most trade flowed along two major trade routes, both of which terminated in the far southwest in the Kefa-Jima region. From there, one route went north to Mitsiwa via Gonder and Adwa, the other along the Awash River valley to Harer and then on to Berbera or Zeila on the Red Sea.

Despite its many riches, Ethiopia never became a great trading nation. Most Ethiopians despised traders, preferring instead to emulate the country's warriors and priests. After establishing a foothold in the country, Greek, Armenian, and Arab traders became the economic intermediaries between Ethiopia and the outside world. Arabs also settled in the interior and eventually dominated all commercial activity except petty trade.

When their occupation of Ethiopia ended in 1941, the Italians left behind them a country whose economic structure was much as it had been for centuries. There had been some improvements in communications, particularly in the area of road building, and attempts had been made to establish a few small industries and to introduce commercial farming, particularly in Eritrea, which Italy had occupied since 1890. But these changes were limited. With only a small proportion of the population participating in the money economy, trade consisted mostly of barter. Wage labor was limited, economic units were largely self-sufficient, foreign trade was negligible, and the market for manufactured goods was extremely small.

During the late 1940s and 1950s, much of the economy remained unchanged. The government focused its development efforts on expansion of the bureaucratic structure and ancillary services. Most farmers cultivated small plots of land or herded cattle. Traditional and primitive farming methods provided the population with a subsistence standard of living. In addition, many nomadic peoples raised livestock and followed a life of seasonal movement in drier areas. The agricultural sector grew slightly, and the industrial sector represented a small part of the total economy.

By the early 1950s, Emperor Haile Selassie I (reigned 1930–74) had renewed calls for a transition from a subsistence economy to an agro-industrial economy. To accomplish this task, Ethiopia needed an infrastructure to exploit resources, a material base to improve living conditions, and better health, education, communications, and other services. A key element of the emperor's new economic policy was the adoption of centrally administered development plans. Between 1945 and 1957, several technical missions, including one each from the United States, the Food and Agriculture Organization of the United Nations (FAO), and Yugoslavia, prepared a series of development plans. However, these plans failed to achieve any meaningful results, largely because basic statistical data were scarce and the government's administrative and technical capabilities were minimal.

In 1954/55 the government created the National Economic Council to coordinate the state's development plans. This agency, which was a policy-making body chaired by the emperor, devoted its attention to improving agricultural and industrial productivity, eradicating illiteracy and diseases, and improving living standards for all Ethiopians. The National Economic Council helped to prepare Ethiopia's first and second five-year plans.

The First Five-Year Plan (1957–61) sought to develop a strong infrastructure, particularly in transportation, construction, and communications, to link isolated regions. Another goal was the establishment of an indigenous cadre of skilled and semiskilled personnel to work in processing industries to help reduce Ethiopia's dependence on imports. Lastly, the plan aimed to accelerate agricultural development by promoting commercial agricultural ventures. The Second Five-Year Plan (1962–67) signaled the start of a twenty-year program to change Ethiopia's predominantly agricultural economy to an agro-industrial one. The plan's objectives included diversification of production, introduction of modern processing methods, and expansion of the economy's productive capacity to increase the country's growth rate. The Third Five-Year Plan (1968–73) also sought to facilitate Ethiopia's economic well-being by raising manufacturing and agro-industrial performance. However, unlike its predecessors, the third plan expressed the government's willingness to expand educational opportunities and to improve peasant agriculture. Total investment for the First Five-Year Plan reached 839.6 million birr (for value of the birr—see Glossary), about 25 percent above the planned 674 million birr figure; total expenditure for the Second Five-Year Plan was 13 percent higher than the planned 1,694 million birr figure. The allocation for the Third Five-Year Plan was 3,115 million birr.

Several factors hindered Ethiopia's development planning. Apart from the fact that the government lacked the administrative and technical capabilities to implement a national development plan, staffing problems plagued the Planning Commission (which prepared the first and second plans) and the Ministry of Planning (which prepared the third). Many project managers failed to achieve plan objectives because they neglected to identify the resources (personnel, equipment, and funds) and to establish the organizational structures necessary to facilitate large-scale economic development.

During the First Five-Year Plan, the gross national product (GNP—see Glossary) increased at a 3.2 percent annual rate as opposed to the projected figure of 3.7 percent, and growth in economic sectors such as agriculture, manufacturing, and mining failed to meet the national plan's targets. Exports increased at a 3.5 percent annual rate during the first plan, whereas imports grew at a rate of 6.4 percent per annum, thus failing to correct the negative balance of trade that had existed since 1951.

The Second Five-Year Plan and Third Five-Year Plan anticipated that the economy would grow at an annual rate of 4.3 percent and 6.0 percent, respectively. Officials also expected agriculture, manufacturing, and transportation and communications to grow at respective rates of 2.5, 27.3, and 6.7 percent annually during the Second Five-Year Plan and at respective rates of 2.9, 14.9, and 10.9 percent during the Third Five-Year Plan. The Planning Commission never assessed the performance of these two plans, largely because of a shortage of qualified personnel.

However, according to data from the Ethiopian government's Central Statistical Authority, during the 1960/61 to 1973/74 period the economy achieved sustained economic growth. Between 1960 and 1970, for example, Ethiopia enjoyed an annual 4.4 percent average growth rate in per capita gross domestic product (GDP—see Glossary). The manufacturing sector's growth rate more than doubled (from 1.9 percent in 1960/61 to 4.4 percent in 1973/74), and the growth rate for the wholesale, retail trade, transportation, and communications sectors increased from 9.3 percent to 15.6 percent.

Relative to its neighbors, Ethiopia's economic performance was mixed. Ethiopia's 4.4 percent average per capita GDP growth rate was higher than Sudan's 1.3 percent rate or Somalia's 1 percent rate. However, Kenya's GDP grew at an estimated 6 percent annual rate, and Uganda achieved a 5.6 percent growth rate during the same 1960/61 to 1972/73 period.

By the early 1970s, Ethiopia's economy not only had started to grow but also had begun to diversify into areas such as manufacturing and services. However, these changes failed to improve the lives of most Ethiopians. About four-fifths of the population were subsistence farmers who lived in poverty because they used most of their meager production to pay taxes, rents, debt payments, and bribes. On a broader level, from 1953 to 1974 the balance of trade registered annual deficits. The only exception was 1973, when a combination of unusually large receipts from the export of oilseeds and pulses and an unusually small rise in import values resulted in a favorable balance of payments of 454 million birr. With the country registering trade deficits, the government attempted to restrict imports and to substitute locally produced industrial goods to improve the trade balance. Despite these efforts, however, the unfavorable trade balance continued. As a result, foreign grants and loans financed much of the balance of payments deficit.

Postrevolution Period

The 1974 revolution resulted in the nationalization and restructuring of the Ethiopian economy. After the revolution, the country's economy can be viewed as having gone through four phases (see table 10, Appendix).

Internal political upheaval, armed conflict, and radical institutional reform marked the 1974–78 period of the revolution. There was little economic growth; instead, the government's nationalization measures and the highly unstable political climate caused economic dislocation in sectors such as agriculture and manufacturing. Additionally, the military budget consumed a substantial portion of the nation's resources. As a result of these problems, GDP increased at an average annual rate of only 0.4 percent. Moreover, the current account deficit and the overall fiscal deficit widened, and the retail price index jumped, experiencing a 16.5 percent average annual increase.

In the second phase (1978–80), the economy began to recover as the government consolidated power and implemented institutional reforms. The government's new Development Through Cooperation Campaign (commonly referred to as *zemecha*—see Glossary) also contributed to the economy's improvement. More

149

important, security conditions improved as internal and external threats subsided. In the aftermath of the 1977-78 Ogaden War and the decline in rebel activity in Eritrea, Addis Ababa set production targets and mobilized the resources needed to improve economic conditions. Consequently, GDP grew at an average annual rate of 5.7 percent. Benefiting from good weather, agricultural production increased at an average annual rate of 3.6 percent, and manufacturing increased at an average annual rate of 18.9 percent, as many closed plants, particularly in Eritrea, reopened. The current account deficit and the overall fiscal deficit remained below 5 percent of GDP during this period.

In the third phase (1980-85), the economy experienced a setback. Except for Ethiopian fiscal year (EFY—see Glossary) 1982/83, the growth of GDP declined. Manufacturing took a downturn as well, and agriculture reached a crisis stage. Four factors accounted for these developments. First, the 1984-85 drought affected almost all regions of the country. As a result, the government committed scarce resources to famine relief efforts while tabling long-term development projects. Consequently, the external accounts (as shown in the current account deficit and the debt service ratio) and the overall fiscal deficit worsened, despite international drought assistance totaling more than US$450 million. Notwithstanding these efforts, close to 8 million people became famine victims during the drought of the mid-1980s, and about 1 million died. Second, the manufacturing sector stagnated as agricultural inputs declined. Also, many industries exhausted their capacity to increase output; as a result, they failed to meet the rising demand for consumer items. Third, the lack of foreign exchange and declining investment reversed the relatively high manufacturing growth rates of 1978-80. Finally, Ethiopia's large military establishment created a major burden on the economy. Defense expenditures during this time were absorbing 40 to 50 percent of the government's current expenditure (see Defense Costs, ch. 5).

In the fourth period (1985-90), the economy continued to stagnate, despite an improvement in the weather in EFY 1985/86 and EFY 1986/87, which helped reverse the agricultural decline. GDP and the manufacturing sector also grew during this period, GDP increasing at an average annual rate of 5 percent. However, the lingering effects of the 1984-85 drought undercut these achievements and contributed to the economy's overall stagnation. During the 1985-90 period, the current account deficit and the overall fiscal deficit worsened to annual rates of 10.6 and 13.5 percent, respectively, and the debt service ratio continued to climb.

Rug-weaving room at a government-run crafts center in Addis Ababa
Courtesy Food and Agriculture Organization of the United
Nations (S. Pierbattistin)

Role of Government

The imperial government presided over what was, even in the mid-twentieth century, essentially a feudal economy, with aristocrats and the church owning most arable land and tenant farmers who paid exorbitant rents making up the majority of the nation's agriculturalists. Acting primarily through the Ministry of Finance, the emperor used fiscal and monetary strategies to direct the local economy. The various ministries, although not always effective, played a key role in developing and implementing programs. The government conducted negotiations with the ministries to allocate resources for plan priorities.

Officials formulated actual operations, however, without adhering to plan priorities. This problem developed partly because the relationship between the Planning Commission, responsible for formulating national objectives and priorities, and the Ministry of Finance, responsible for resource planning and management, was not clearly defined. The Ministry of Finance often played a pivotal role, whereas the Planning Commission was relegated to a minor role. Often the Planning Commission was perceived as merely another bureaucratic layer. The ultimate power to approve

151

budgets and programs rested with the emperor, although the Council of Ministers had the opportunity to review plans.

After the revolution, the government's role in determining economic policies changed dramatically. In January and February 1975, the government nationalized or took partial control of more than 100 companies, banks and other financial institutions, and insurance companies. In March 1975, the regime nationalized rural land and granted peasants "possessing rights" to parcels of land not to exceed ten hectares per grantee. In December 1975, the government issued Proclamation No. 76, which established a 500,000 birr ceiling on private investment and urged Ethiopians to invest in enterprises larger than cottage industries. This policy changed in mid-1989, when the government implemented three special decrees to encourage the development of small-scale industries, the participation of nongovernmental bodies in the hotel industry, and the establishment of joint ventures.

Under the Provisional Military Administrative Council (PMAC; also known as the Derg—see Glossary), Ethiopia's political system and economic structure changed dramatically, and the government embraced a Marxist-Leninist political philosophy. Planning became more ambitious and more pervasive, penetrating all regions and all sectors of the society, in contrast to the imperial period. Article 11 of the 1987 constitution legitimized these changes by declaring that "the State shall guide the economic and social activities of the country through a central plan." The Office of the National Council for Central Planning (ONCCP), which replaced the Planning Commission and which was chaired by Mengistu as head of state, served as the supreme policy-making body and had the power and responsibility to prepare the directives, strategies, and procedures for short- and long-range plans. The ONCCP played a pivotal role in mediating budget requests between other ministries and the Ministry of Finance. The government also sought to improve Ethiopia's economic performance by expanding the number of state-owned enterprises and encouraging barter and countertrade practices (see Industry and Energy; Foreign Trade, this ch.).

On March 5, 1990, President Mengistu delivered a speech to the Workers' Party of Ethiopia (WPE) Central Committee in which he declared the failure of the Marxist economic system imposed by the military regime after the 1974 overthrow of Emperor Haile Selassie. He also announced the adoption of a new strategy for the country's future progress and development. Mengistu's proposals included decentralization in planning and a free-market, mixed economy in which the private and public sectors would play complementary roles. The new strategy would permit Ethiopian and foreign private individuals to invest in foreign and domestic trade, industry, construction, mining, and agriculture and in the country's development in general. Although Mengistu's new economic policy attracted considerable attention, many economists were skeptical about Ethiopia's ability to bring about a quick radical transformation of its economic policies. In any case, the plan proved irrelevant in view of the deteriorating political and military situation that led to the fall of the regime in 1991.

The Budgetary Process

During the imperial period, the government initiated the budget cycle each year on the first day of Tikimt (October 11) by issuing a "call for budget proposals." Supposedly, the various ministries and agencies adhered to deadlines in completing the budgetary process. These organizations submitted current and capital budget proposals to the Ministry of Finance; the Council of Ministers reviewed all requests. The ultimate power for approval rested with the emperor.

After the revolution, the government developed new guidelines on budget preparation and approval. Addis Ababa issued annual budget "calls" in July or August, with preliminary information and guidance. The new guidelines required ministries and agencies to complete their proposals by January, when budget hearings would begin. The hearings included discussions with ministries in which requests would be aligned with allocations, and justifications for requests would be evaluated. After the ministries submitted their current budget proposals to the Ministry of Finance for review, with a copy to the ONCCP, the ONCCP executive committee would approve, disapprove, or change the requests. Conversely, ministries would send capital budget proposals to the ONCCP with a copy to the Ministry of Finance. The ONCCP would conclude a similar process of budget hearings, which would include a review of adherence to guidelines, justifications for requests, and conformity to investment priorities identified in the national plan. Thus, under the new system, the Ministry of Finance developed the current budget, and the ONCCP developed the capital budget. Draft current and capital budgets prepared by the Ministry of Finance and the ONCCP, respectively, would then be reconciled with estimates of revenues, domestic resources, and other sources of funding such as loans and aid. The consolidated current and capital budgets then would go to the Council of Ministers for review and recommendations. The final approval was the head of state's prerogative (see Banking and Monetary Policy, this ch.).

Revenue and Expenditures

Resources were allocated among the various sectors of the economy differently in the imperial and revolutionary periods. Under the emperor, the government dedicated about 36 percent of the annual budget to national defense and maintenance of internal order. Toward the end of the imperial period, the budgets of the various ministries increased steadily while tax yields stagnated. With a majority of the population living at a subsistence level, there was limited opportunity to increase taxes on personal or agricultural income. Consequently, the imperial government relied on indirect taxes (customs, excise, and sales) to generate revenues. For instance, in the early 1970s taxes on foreign trade accounted for close to two-fifths of the tax revenues and about one-third of all government revenues, excluding foreign grants. At the same time, direct taxes accounted for less than one-third of tax revenues.

The revolutionary government changed the tax structure in 1976, replacing taxes on agricultural income and rural land with a rural land-use fee and a new tax on income from agricultural activities. The government partially alleviated the tax collection problem that existed during the imperial period by delegating the responsibility for collecting the fee and tax on agriculture to peasant associations, which received a small percentage of revenues as payment. Whereas total revenue increased significantly, to about 24 percent of GDP in EFY 1988/89, tax revenues remained stagnant at around 15 percent of GDP. In EFY 1974/75, total revenue and tax revenue had been 13 and 11 percent of GDP, respectively. Despite the 1976 changes in the tax structure, the government believed that the agricultural income tax was being underpaid, largely because of underassessments by peasant associations.

The government levied taxes on exports and imports. In 1987 Addis Ababa taxed all exports at 2 percent and levied an additional export duty and a surtax on coffee. Import taxes included customs duties and a 19 percent general import transaction tax. Because of a policy of encouraging new capital investment, the government exempted capital goods from all import taxes. Among imports, intermediate goods were taxed on a scale ranging from 0 to 35 percent, consumer goods on a scale of 0 to 100 percent, and luxuries at a flat rate of 200 percent. High taxes on certain consumer goods and luxury items contributed to a flourishing underground economy in which the smuggling of some imports, particularly liquor and electronic goods, played an important part.

Although tax collection procedures proved somewhat ineffective, the government maintained close control of current and capital expenditures. The Ministry of Finance oversaw procurements and audited ministries to ensure that expenditures conformed to budget authorizations.

Current expenditures as a proportion of GDP grew from 13.2 percent in EFY 1974/75 to 26.1 percent in EFY 1987/88. This growth was largely the result of the increase in expenditures for defense and general services following the 1974 revolution. During the 1977–78 Ogaden War, for example, when the Somali counteroffensive was under way, defense took close to 60 percent of the budget. That percentage declined after 1979, although it remained relatively higher than the figure for the prerevolutionary period. Between 1974 and 1988, about 40 to 50 percent of the budget was dedicated to defense and government services.

Economic and social services received less than 30 percent of government funds until EFY 1972/73, when a rise in educational outlays pushed them to around 40 percent. Under the Mengistu regime, economic and social service expenditures remained at prerevolutionary levels: agriculture's share was 2 percent, while education and health received an average of 14 and 4 percent, respectively.

Banking and Monetary Policy

The 1974 revolution brought major changes to the banking system. Prior to the emergence of the Marxist government, Ethiopia had several state-owned banking institutions and private financial institutions. The National Bank of Ethiopia (the country's central bank and financial adviser), the Commercial Bank of Ethiopia (which handled commercial operations), the Agricultural and Industrial Development Bank (established largely to finance state-owned enterprises), the Savings and Mortgage Corporation of Ethiopia, and the Imperial Savings and Home Ownership Public Association (which provided savings and loan services) were the major state-owned banks. Major private commercial institutions, many of which were foreign owned, included the Addis Ababa Bank, the Banco di Napoli, and the Banco di Roma. In addition, there were several insurance companies.

In January and February 1975, the government nationalized and subsequently reorganized private banks and insurance companies. By the early 1980s, the country's banking system included the National Bank of Ethiopia; the Addis Ababa Bank, which was formed by merging the three commercial banks that existed prior to the revolution; the Ethiopian Insurance Corporation, which incorporated all of the nationalized insurance companies; and the new Housing and Savings Bank, which was responsible for making loans for new housing and home improvement. The government placed all banks and financial institutions under the National Bank of Ethiopia's control and supervision. The National Bank of Ethiopia regulated currency, controlled credit and monetary policy, and administered foreign-currency transactions and the official foreign-exchange reserves. A majority of the banking services were concentrated in major urban areas, although there were efforts to establish more rural bank branches throughout the country. However, the lending strategies of the banks showed that the productive sectors were not given priority. In 1988, for example, about 55 percent of all commercial bank credit financed imports and domestic trade and services. Agriculture and industry received only 6 and 13 percent of the commercial credit, respectively.

To combat inflation and reduce the deficit, the government adopted a conservative fiscal management policy in the 1980s. The government limited the budget deficit to an average of about 14 percent of GDP in the five years ending in EFY 1988/89 by borrowing from local sources. For instance, in EFY 1987/88 domestic borrowing financed about 38 percent of the deficit. Addis Ababa also imposed measures to cut back capital expenditures and to lower inflation. However, price controls, official overvaluing of the birr, and a freeze on the wages of senior government staff have failed to control inflation. By 1988 inflation was averaging 7.1 percent annually, but it turned sharply upward during 1990 as war expenditures increased and was estimated at 45 percent by mid-1991. Moreover, money supply, defined as currency in circulation and demand deposits with banks (except that of the National Bank of Ethiopia), rose with the expansion in government budget deficits, which reached about 1.6 billion birr in EFY 1988/89. To help resolve this deficit problem and numerous other economic difficulties, Addis Ababa relied on foreign aid (see Balance of Payments and Foreign Assistance, this ch.).

Labor Force

Ethiopia's first and only national census, conducted in 1984, put the population at 42 million, which made Ethiopia the third most populous country in Africa, after Egypt and Nigeria. The census also showed that by 1994 Ethiopia's population would reach 56 million. According to World Bank (see Glossary) projections, Ethiopia will have a population of 66 million by the year 2000 (other estimates suggested that the population would be more than 67 million).

156

The 1984 census indicated that 46.6 percent of the population consisted of children under fifteen years of age, which indicated a relatively high rate of dependence on the working population for education, health, and social services. Such a high dependency rate often is characteristic of a country in transition from a subsistence to a monetized economy. Because of limited investment resources in the modern sector, not all the working-age population can be absorbed, with the result that unemployment can become a growing social and economic problem for an economy in transition.

The 1988/89 economically active labor force was estimated to be 21 million, of which 19.3 million were in rural areas and 1.7 million in urban areas. Estimates of the labor force's annual growth ranged from 1.8 to 2.9 percent.

The labor force's occupational distribution showed that in 1990 some 80 percent of the labor force worked in agriculture, 8 percent in industry, and 12 percent in services. These figures had changed slightly from the 1965 figures of 86, 5, and 9 percent, respectively. Thus, while agriculture's proportionate share of the labor force fell, the other two sectors gained. This trend reflects a modernizing society that is diversifying its economy by expanding secondary and tertiary sectors.

Unemployment

Generally, it is difficult to measure unemployment in less developed countries such as Ethiopia because of the lack of reliable records and the existence of various informal types of work. However, based on Ministry of Labor surveys and numerous other analyses, a general assessment of unemployment in Ethiopia can be made. According to the Ministry of Labor, the unemployment rate increased 11.5 percent annually during the 1979–88 period; by 1987/88 there were 715,065 registered unemployed workers in thirty-six major towns. Of those registered, 134,117 ultimately found jobs, leaving the remaining 580,948 unemployed. The urban labor force totaled 1.7 million in 1988/89. The Ministry of Labor indicated that the government employed 523,000 of these workers. The rest relied on private employment or self-employment for their livelihood.

According to the government, rural unemployment was virtually nonexistent. A 1981/82 rural labor survey revealed that 97.5 percent of the rural labor force worked, 2.4 percent did not work because of social reasons, and 0.1 percent had been unemployed during the previous twelve months. However, it is important to note that unemployment, as conventionally defined, records only

*Young women from a producers' cooperative weave baskets
to be sold as souvenirs.
Courtesy Food and Agriculture Organization of the
United Nations (F. Mattiol)*

part of the story; it leaves out disguised unemployment and under-employment, which were prevalent in both urban and rural areas. For instance, the same rural labor force survey found that 50 percent of those working were unpaid family workers. What is important about unemployment in Ethiopia is that with an expansion of the labor force, the public sector—with an already swollen payroll and acute budgetary problems—was unlikely to absorb more than a tiny fraction of those entering the labor market.

Labor Unions

The 1955 constitution guaranteed the right to form workers' associations. However, it was not until 1962 that the Ethiopian government issued the Labor Relations Decree, which authorized trade unions. In April 1963, the imperial authorities recognized the Confederation of Ethiopian Labor Unions (CELU), which represented twenty-two industrial labor groups. By 1973 CELU had 167 affiliates with approximately 80,000 members, which represented only about 30 percent of all eligible workers.

CELU never evolved into a national federation of unions. Instead, it remained an association of labor groups organized at the local level. The absence of a national constituency, coupled with other problems such as corruption, embezzlement, election fraud, ethnic and regional discrimination, and inadequate finances, prevented CELU from challenging the status quo in the industrial sector. Nevertheless, CELU sponsored several labor protests and strikes during the first decade of its existence. After 1972 CELU became more militant as drought and famine caused the death of up to 200,000 people. The government responded by using force to crush labor protests, strikes, and demonstrations.

Although many of its members supported the overthrow of Haile Selassie, CELU was the first labor organization to reject the military junta and to demand the creation of a people's government. On May 19, 1975, the Derg temporarily closed CELU headquarters on the grounds that the union needed to be reorganized. Furthermore, the military authorities asserted that workers should elect their future leaders according to the aims and objectives of Ethiopian socialism. This order did not rescind traditional workers' rights, such as the right to organize freely, to strike, and to bargain collectively over wages and working conditions. Rather, it sought to control the political activities of the CELU leadership. As expected, CELU rejected these actions and continued to demand democratic changes and civilian rights. In January 1977, the Derg replaced CELU (abolished December 1975) with the All-Ethiopia Trade Union (AETU). The AETU had 1,341 local

chapters, known as workers' associations, with a total membership of 287,000. The new union thus was twice as large as CELU
had ever been. The government maintained that the AETU's purpose was to educate workers about the need to contribute their share
to national development by increasing productivity and building
socialism.

In 1978 the government replaced the AETU executive committee after charging it with political sabotage, abuse of authority, and
failure to abide by the rules of democratic centralism. In 1982 a
further restructuring of the AETU occurred when Addis Ababa
issued the Trade Unions' Organization Proclamation. An uncom-
promising Marxist-Leninist document, this proclamation emphasized the need "to enable workers to discharge their historical
responsibility in building the national economy by handling with
care the instruments of production as their produce, and by enhancing the production and proper distribution of goods and services." A series of meetings and elections culminated in a national
congress in June 1982, at which the government replaced the leadership of the AETU. In 1986 the government relabeled the AETU
the Ethiopia Trade Union (ETU).

In 1983/84 the AETU claimed a membership of 313,434. The
organization included nine industrial groups, the largest of which
was manufacturing, which had accounted for 29.2 percent of the
membership in 1982/83, followed by agriculture, forestry, and fishing with 26.6 percent, services with 15.1 percent, transportation
with 8.1 percent, construction with 8.0 percent, trade with 6.2 per-
cent, utilities with 3.7 percent, finance with 2.4 percent, and mining with 0.7 percent. A total of 35.6 percent of the members lived
in Addis Ababa and another 18.0 percent in Shewa. Eritrea and
Tigray accounted for no more than 7.5 percent of the total membership. By the late 1980s, the AETU had failed to regain the ac-
tivist reputation its predecessors had won in the 1970s. According
to one observer, this political quiescence probably indicated that
the government had successfully co-opted the trade unions.

Wages and Prices

Prior to the revolution, the Central Personnel Agency formulated and regulated wage policies. At the time of the military
takeover, there was no minimum wage law; wages and salaries depended much on demand. There was, however, some legislation
that defined pay scales. For instance, Notice 49 of 1972 defined
pay scales and details regarding incremental steps for civil servants.
Similarly, the Ethiopian Workers Commission had developed pay-
scale guidelines based on skill, experience, and employment. In

1974 CELU asked for a 3 birr daily minimum wage, which the imperial government eventually granted.

After the revolution, the government's policy was to control wage growth to reduce pay scales. For parastatal and public enterprise workers earning 650 birr or less per month (real income, i.e., income adjusted for inflation) and civil servants earning 600 birr or less per month, the government allowed incremental pay increases. But for those above these cutoff points, there was a general salary freeze. However, promotions sometimes provided a worker a raise over the cutoff levels.

Given inflation, the salary freeze affected the real income of many workers. For instance, the starting salary of a science graduate in 1975 was 600 birr per month. In 1984 the real monthly income of a science graduate had dropped to 239 birr. Similarly, the highest civil servant's maximum salary in 1975 was 1,440 birr per month; the real monthly income of the same civil servant in 1984 was 573 birr.

Data on real wages of manufacturing workers and the behavior of price indexes provide further evidence of worsening living standards after the revolution. In 1985/86 the average real monthly income of an industrial worker was 65.6 percent of the 1974/75 level (see table 11, Appendix). The general trend shows that real income fell as consumer prices continued to increase. The retail price index for Addis Ababa rose from 375.2 in 1980/81 (1963 = 100) to 480.0 in 1987/88. This rise in the retail price index included increases in the cost of food (27 percent), household items (38 percent), and transportation (17 percent) (see table 12, Appendix).

Price increases mainly affected urban wage earners on fixed incomes, as purchases of necessities used larger portions of their pay. The government's wage freeze and the controls it placed on job transfers and changes made it difficult for most urban wage earners to improve their living standards. The freeze on wages and job changes also reduced productivity.

Agriculture

Accounting for over 40 percent of GDP, 80 percent of exports, and 80 percent of the labor force, agriculture remained in 1991 the economy's most important sector (see fig. 9). Ethiopia has great agricultural potential because of its vast areas of fertile land, diverse climate, generally adequate rainfall, and large labor pool. Despite this potential, however, Ethiopian agriculture has remained underdeveloped. Because of drought, which has persistently affected the country since the early 1970s, a poor economic base (low productivity, weak infrastructure, and low level of technology), and the

Mengistu government's commitment to Marxism-Leninism, the agricultural sector has performed poorly. For instance, according to the World Bank, between 1980 and 1987 agricultural production dropped at an annual rate of 2.1 percent, while the population grew at an annual rate of 2.4 percent. Consequently, the country faced a tragic famine that resulted in the death of nearly 1 million people from 1984 to 1986.

During the imperial period, the development of the agricultural sector was retarded by a number of factors, including tenancy and land reform problems, the government's neglect of the agricultural sector (agriculture received less than 2 percent of budget allocations even though the vast majority of the population depended on agriculture), low productivity, and lack of technological development. Moreover, the emperor's inability to implement meaningful land reform perpetuated a system in which aristocrats and the church owned most of the farmland and in which most farmers were tenants who had to provide as much as 50 percent of their crops as rent. To make matters worse, during the 1972–74 drought and famine the imperial government refused to assist rural Ethiopians and tried to cover up the crisis by refusing international aid. As a result, up to 200,000 Ethiopians perished.

Although the issue of land reform was not addressed until the 1974 revolution, the government had tried to introduce programs to improve the condition of farmers. In 1971 the Ministry of Agriculture introduced the Minimum Package Program (MPP) to bring about economic and social changes. The MPP included credit for the purchase of items such as fertilizers, improved seeds, and pesticides; innovative extension services; the establishment of cooperatives; and the provision of infrastructure, mainly water supply and all-weather roads. The program, designed for rural development, was first introduced in a project called the Chilalo Agricultural Development Unit (CADU). The program later facilitated the establishment of similar internationally supported and financed projects at Ada (just south of Addis Ababa), Welamo, and Humera. By 1974 the Ministry of Agriculture's Extension and Project Implementation Department (EPID) had more than twenty-eight areas with more than 200 extension and marketing centers. Although the MPPs improved the agricultural productivity of farmers, particularly in the project areas, there were many problems associated with discrimination against small farmers (because of a restrictive credit system that favored big landowners) and tenant eviction.

Imperial government policy permitting investors to import fertilizers, pesticides, tractors and combines, and (until 1973) fuel free

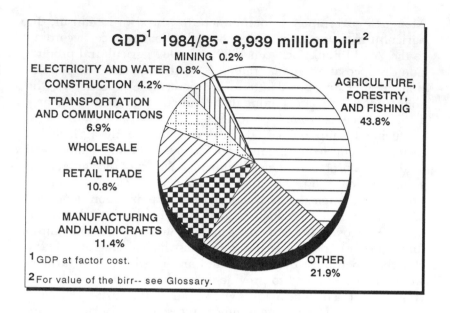

Figure 9. Gross Domestic Product (GDP) by Sector, Ethiopian Fiscal Year 1984/85

of import duties encouraged the rapid expansion of large-scale commercial farming. As a result, agriculture continued to grow, albeit below the population growth rate. According to the World Bank, agricultural production increased at an average annual rate of 2.1 percent between 1965 and 1973, while population increased at an average annual rate of 2.6 percent during the same period.

Agricultural productivity under the Derg continued to decline. According to the World Bank, agricultural production increased at an average annual rate of 0.6 percent between 1973 and 1980 but then decreased at an average annual rate of 2.1 percent between 1980 and 1987. During the same period (1973–87), population increased at an average annual rate of 2.6 percent (2.4 percent for 1980–87). The poor performance of agriculture was related to several factors, including drought; a government policy of controlling prices and the free movement of agricultural products from surplus to deficit areas; the unstable political climate; the dislocation of the rural community caused by resettlement, villagization, and conscription of young farmers to meet military obligations; land tenure difficulties and the problem of land fragmentation; the lack of resources such as farm equipment, better seeds, and fertilizers; and the overall low level of technology.

President Mengistu's 1990 decision to allow free movement of goods, to lift price controls, and to provide farmers with security of tenure was designed to reverse the decline in Ethiopia's agricultural sector. There was much debate as to whether or not these reforms were genuine and how effectively they could be implemented. Nonetheless, agricultural output rose by an estimated 3 percent in 1990–91, almost certainly in response to the relaxation of government regulation. This modest increase, however, was not enough to offset a general decrease in GDP during the same period.

Land Use and Land Reform

Land Use

Of Ethiopia's total land area of 1,221,480 square kilometers, the government estimated in the late 1980s that 15 percent was under cultivation and 51 percent was pastureland. It was also estimated that over 60 percent of the cultivated area was cropland. Forestland, most of it in the southwestern part of the country, accounted for 4 percent of the total land area, according to the government. These figures varied from those provided by the World Bank, which estimated that cropland, pastureland, and forestland accounted for 13, 41, and 25 percent, respectively, of the total land area in 1987.

Inaccessibility, water shortages, and infestations of disease-causing insects, mainly mosquitoes, prevented the use of large parcels of potentially productive land. In Ethiopia's lowlands, for example, the presence of malaria kept farmers from settling in many areas.

Most agricultural producers were subsistence farmers with small holdings, often broken into several plots. Most of these farmers lived on the highlands, mainly at elevations of 1,500 to 3,000 meters. The population in the lowland peripheries (below 1,500 meters) was nomadic, engaged mainly in livestock raising.

There are two predominant soil types in the highlands. The first, found in areas with relatively good drainage, consists of red-to-reddish-brown clayey loams that hold moisture and are well endowed with needed minerals, with the exception of phosphorus. These types of soils are found in much of Ilubabor, Kefa, and Gamo Gofa. The second type consists of brownish-to-gray and black soils with a high clay content. These soils are found in both the northern and the southern highlands in areas with poor drainage. They are sticky when wet, hard when dry, and difficult to work. But with proper drainage and conditioning, these soils have excellent agricultural potential.

Sandy desert soils cover much of the arid lowlands in the northeast and in the Ogaden area of southeastern Ethiopia. Because of

165

low rainfall, these soils have limited agricultural potential, except in some areas where rainfall is sufficient for the growth of natural forage at certain times of the year. These areas are used by pastoralists who move back and forth in the area following the availability of pasture for their animals.

The plains and low foothills west of the highlands have sandy and gray-to-black clay soils. Where the topography permits, they are suitable for farming. The soils of the Great Rift Valley often are conducive to agriculture if water is available for irrigation. The Awash River basin supports many large-scale commercial farms and several irrigated small farms.

Soil erosion has been one of the country's major problems. Over the centuries, deforestation, overgrazing, and practices such as cultivation of slopes not suited to agriculture have eroded the soil, a situation that worsened considerably during the 1970s and 1980s, especially in Eritrea, Tigray, and parts of Gonder and Welo. In addition, the rugged topography of the highlands, the brief but extremely heavy rainfalls that characterize many areas, and centuries-old farming practices that do not include conservation measures have accelerated soil erosion in much of Ethiopia's highland areas. In the dry lowlands, persistent winds also contribute to soil erosion.

During the imperial era, the government failed to implement widespread conservation measures, largely because the country's complex land tenure system stymied attempts to halt soil erosion and improve the land. After 1975 the revolutionary government used peasant associations to accelerate conservation work throughout rural areas. The 1977 famine also provided an impetus to promote conservation. The government mobilized farmers and organized "food for work" projects to build terraces and plant trees. During 1983–84 the Ministry of Agriculture used "food for work" projects to raise 65 million tree seedlings, plant 18,000 hectares of land, and terrace 9,500 hectares of land. Peasant associations used 361 nurseries to plant 11,000 hectares of land in community forest. Between 1976 and 1985, the government constructed 600,000 kilometers of agricultural embankments on cultivated land and 470,000 kilometers of hillside terraces, and it closed 80,000 hectares of steep slopes for regeneration. However, the removal of arable land for conservation projects has threatened the welfare of increasing numbers of rural poor. For this reason, some environmental experts maintain that large-scale conservation work in Ethiopia has been ineffective.

Land Reform

Until the 1974 revolution, Ethiopia had a complex land tenure system. In Welo Province, for example, there were an estimated

111 types of land tenure. The existence of so many land tenure systems, coupled with the lack of reliable data, has made it difficult to give a comprehensive assessment of landownership in Ethiopia. However, the tenure system can be understood in a rudimentary way if one examines it in the context of the basic distinction between landownership patterns in the north and those in the south.

Historically, Ethiopia was divided into the northern highlands, which constituted the core of the old Christian kingdom, and the southern highlands, most of which were brought under imperial rule by conquest. This north-south distinction was reflected in land tenure differences. In the northern provinces—particularly Gojam, Begemdir and Simen (called Gonder after 1974), Tigray, highland Eritrea, parts of Welo, and northern Shewa—the major form of ownership was a type of communal system known as *rist* (see Glossary). According to this system, all descendants (both male and female) of an individual founder were entitled to a share, and individuals had the right to use (a usufruct right) a plot of family land. *Rist* was hereditary, inalienable, and inviolable. No user of any piece of land could sell his or her share outside the family or mortgage or bequeath his or her share as a gift, as the land belonged not to the individual but to the descent group (see Glossary). Most peasants in the northern highlands held at least some *rist* land, but there were some members belonging to minority ethnic groups who were tenant farmers.

The other major form of tenure was *gult* (see Glossary), an ownership right acquired from the monarch or from provincial rulers who were empowered to make land grants. *Gult* owners collected tribute from the peasantry and, until 1966 (when *gult* rights were abolished in principle), exacted labor service as payment in kind from the peasants. Until the government instituted salaries in the twentieth century, *gult* rights were the typical form of compensation for an official.

Other forms of tenure included *samon, mengist,* and *maderia* land. *Samon* was land the government had granted to the Ethiopian Orthodox Church in perpetuity. Traditionally, the church had claimed about one-third of Ethiopia's land; however, actual ownership probably never reached this figure. Estimates of church holdings range from 10 to 20 percent of the country's cultivated land. Peasants who worked on church land paid tribute to the church (or monastery) rather than to the emperor. The church lost all its land after the 1974 revolution. The state owned large tracts of agricultural land known as *mengist* and *maderia. Mengist* was land registered as government property, and *maderia* was land granted mainly to government officials, war veterans, and other patriots in lieu of a pension or salary. Although it granted *maderia* land for life, the state possessed a reversionary right over all land grants. Government land comprised about 12 percent of the country's agricultural land.

In general, absentee landlordism in the north was rare, and landless tenants were few. For instance, tenancy in Begemdir and Simen and in Gojam was estimated at about 2 percent of holdings. In the southern provinces, however, few farmers owned the land on which they worked. Southern landownership patterns developed as a result of land measurement and land grants following the Ethiopian conquest of the region in the late nineteenth and early twentieth centuries. After conquest, officials divided southern land equally among the state, the church, and the indigenous population. Warlords who administered the occupied regions received the state's share. They, in turn, redistributed part of their share to their officers and soldiers. The government distributed the church's share among the church hierarchy in the same manner. Officials divided the rest between the traditional leaders (*balabats*—see Glossary) and the indigenous people. Thus, the loss of two-thirds of the land to the new landlords and the church made many local people tenants (*gebbars*). Tenancy in the southern provinces ranged between 65 and 80 percent of the holdings, and tenant payments to landowners averaged as high as 50 percent of the produce.

In the lowland periphery and the Great Rift Valley, the traditional practice of transhumance and the allocation of pastoral land according to tribal custom remained undisturbed until after World War II. These two areas are inhabited by pastoralists, including the Afar and Isa in eastern Eritrea, Welo, and Harerge; the Somali in the Ogaden; the Borana in Sidamo and Bale; and the Kereyu in the Great Rift Valley area of Shewa. The pastoral social structure is based on a kinship system with strong interclan connections; grazing and water rights are regulated by custom. Until the 1950s, this pastoral life remained largely undisturbed by the highlanders, who intensely disliked the hot and humid lowland climate and feared malaria. Beginning in the 1950s, however, the malaria eradication programs made irrigation agriculture in these areas possible. The government's desire to promote such agriculture, combined with its policy of creating new tax revenues, created pressure on many pastoralists, especially the Afar and the Arsi (a division of the Oromo). Major concessionaires, such as the Tendaho Cotton Plantation (managed until the 1974 revolution by the British firm Mitchell Cotts) and the Wonji Sugar Plantation (managed by HVA, a Dutch company), acquired large tracts of traditional Afar and Arsi grazing land and converted it into large-scale commercial farms. The loss of grazing land to these concessions significantly affected traditional migration patterns for grazing and water.

In the northern and southern parts of Ethiopia, peasant farmers lacked the means to improve production because of the fragmentation of holdings, a lack of credit, and the absence of modern facilities. Particularly in the south, the insecurity of tenure and high rents killed the peasants' incentive to improve production.

By the mid-1960s, many sectors of Ethiopian society favored land reform. University students led the land reform movement and campaigned against the government's reluctance to introduce land reform programs and the lack of commitment to integrated rural development. By 1974 it was clear that the archaic land tenure system was one of the major factors responsible for the backward condition of Ethiopia's agriculture and the onset of the revolution. On March 4, 1975, the Derg announced its land reform program. The government nationalized rural land without compensation, abolished tenancy, forbade the hiring of wage labor on private farms, ordered all commercial farms to remain under state control, and granted each peasant family so-called "possessing rights" to a plot of land not to exceed ten hectares.

Tenant farmers in southern Ethiopia, where the average tenancy was as high as 55 percent and rural elites exploited farmers, welcomed the land reform. But in the northern highlands, where communal ownership (*rist*) dominated and large holdings and tenancy were exceptions, many people resisted land reform. Despite the special provision for communal areas (Article 19 of the proclamation gave peasants in the communal areas "possessing rights" to the land they were tilling at the time of the proclamation) and the PMAC's efforts to reassure farmers that land reform would not affect them negatively, northerners remained suspicious of the new government's intentions. The reform held no promise of gain for most northerners; rather, many northern farmers perceived land reform as an attack on their rights to *rist* land. Resistance intensified when *zemecha* (see Glossary) members campaigned for collectivization of land and oxen.

Land reform had the least impact on the lowland peripheries, where nomads traditionally maintained their claims over grazing lands. The new proclamation gave them rights of possession to land they used for grazing. Therefore, the nomads did not perceive the new program as a threat. However, in the Afar area of the lower Awash Valley, where large-scale commercial estates had thrived, there was opposition to land reform, led mainly by tribal leaders (and large landowners), such as Ali Mirah, the sultan of Aussa.

The land reform destroyed the feudal order; changed landowning patterns, particularly in the south, in favor of peasants and small landowners; and provided the opportunity for peasants to participate in local matters by permitting them to form associations. However, problems associated with declining agricultural productivity and poor farming techniques still were prevalent.

Government attempts to implement land reform also created problems related to land fragmentation, insecurity of tenure, and shortages of farm inputs and tools. Peasant associations often were periodically compelled to redistribute land to accommodate young families or new households moving into their area. The process meant not only smaller farms but also the fragmentation of holdings, which were often scattered into small plots to give families land of comparable quality. Consequently, individual holdings were frequently far smaller than the permitted maximum allotment of ten hectares. A 1979 study showed that around Addis Ababa individual holdings ranged from 1.0 to 1.6 hectares and that about 48 percent of the parcels were less than one-fourth of a hectare in size. Another study, of Dejen *awraja* (subregion) in Gojam, found that land fragmentation had been exacerbated since the revolution. For example, during the pre-reform period, sixty-one out of 200 farmer respondents owned three or four parcels of land; after the reform, the corresponding number was 135 farmers.

The second problem related to security of tenure, which was threatened by increasing pressure to redistribute land and to collectivize farms. Many peasants were reluctant to improve their land because they were afraid that they would not receive adequate compensation for upgrades. The third problem developed as a result of the military government's failure to provide farmers with basic items like seeds, oxen, and fertilizer. For instance, one study of four communities in different parts of Ethiopia found that up to 50 percent of the peasants in some areas lacked oxen and about 40 percent did not have plows.

Government Rural Programs

In 1984 the founding congress of the Workers' Party of Ethiopia (WPE) emphasized the need for a coordinated strategy based on socialist principles to accelerate agricultural development. To implement this strategy, the government relied on peasant associations and rural development, cooperatives and state farms, resettlement and villagization, increased food production, and a new marketing policy.

Peasant Associations and Rural Development

Articles 8 and 10 of the 1975 Land Reform Proclamation required that peasants be organized into a hierarchy of associations

Planting cotton in the Awash Valley
Courtesy United Nations

Food distribution point
at Senafe, 1988
Courtesy International Committee
of the Red Cross (T. Gassman)

that would facilitate the implementation of rural development programs and policies. Accordingly, after the land reform announcement, the government mobilized more than 60,000 students to organize peasants into associations. By the end of 1987, there were 20,367 peasant associations with a membership of 5.7 million farmers. Each association covered an area of 800 hectares, and members included tenants, landless laborers, and landowners holding fewer than ten hectares. Former landowners who had held more than ten hectares of land could join an association only after the completion of land redistribution. An umbrella organization known as the All-Ethiopia Peasants' Association (AEPA) represented local associations. Peasant associations assumed a wide range of responsibilities, including implementation of government land use directives; adjudication of land disputes; encouragement of development programs, such as water and land conservation; construction of schools, clinics, and cooperatives; organization of defense squads; and tax collection. Peasant associations also became involved in organizing forestry programs, local service and production cooperatives, road construction, and data collection projects, such as the 1984 census.

Cooperatives and State Farms

Starting in 1976, the government encouraged farmers to form cooperatives. Between 1978 and 1981, the PMAC issued a series of proclamations and directives outlining procedures for the formation of service cooperatives and producers' cooperatives. Service cooperatives provided basic services, such as the sale of farm inputs and consumer items that were often rationed, the provision of loans, the education of peasant association members in socialist philosophy, and the promotion of cottage industries.

The producers' cooperatives alleviated shortages of inputs (because farmers could pool resources) and problems associated with the fragmentation of landholdings. The government ordered the creation of these cooperatives because of its belief that small farmers were inefficient and were unable to take advantage of economies of scale.

The producers' cooperatives developed in three stages. The first stage was the *melba,* an elementary type of cooperative that required members to pool land (with the exception of plots of up to 2,000 square meters, which could be set aside for private use) and to share oxen and farm implements. The second stage, *welba,* required members to transfer their resources to the cooperative and reduce private plots to 1,000 square meters. The third stage, the *weland,* abolished private land use and established advanced forms of cooperatives, whose goal was to use mechanized farming with members organized into production brigades. Under this system, income would be distributed based on labor contributions.

The government provided a number of inducements to producers' cooperatives, including priority for credits, fertilizers, improved seed, and access to consumer items and building materials. According to the ten-year plan, more than half of the country's cultivated land would be organized into producers' cooperatives by 1994.

Despite the incentives, farmers responded less than enthusiastically. Farmers saw the move to form cooperatives as a prelude to the destruction of their "family farms." By 1985/86 there were only 2,323 producers' cooperatives, of which only 255 were registered. Some critics argued that the resistance of farmers caused the government to formulate its resettlement and villagization programs.

A major component of the government's agricultural policy since the 1974 revolution has been the development of large-scale state farms. After the 1975 land reform, the Derg converted a majority of the estimated 75,000 hectares of large, commercial farms owned by individuals and cooperatives into state farms. Since then, the government has expanded the size of state farms. In 1987/88 there were about 216,000 hectares of state farmland, accounting for 3.3 percent of the total cultivated area. The ten-year plan indicated that state farms would be expanded to 468,000 hectares by 1994, accounting for 6.4 percent of the cultivated land.

The primary motive for the expansion of state farms was the desire to reverse the drop in food production that has continued since the revolution. After the 1975 land reform, peasants began withholding grain from the market to drive up prices because government price-control measures had created shortages of consumer items such as coffee, cooking oil, salt, and sugar. Additionally, increased peasant consumption caused shortages of food items such as teff (see Glossary), wheat, corn, and other grains in urban areas. The problem became so serious that Mengistu lashed out against the individual and petit burgeois tendencies of the peasantry and their capitalist mentality on the occasion of the fourth anniversary of military rule in September 1978. Mengistu and his advisers believed that state farms would produce grain for urban areas and raw materials for domestic industry and would also increase production of cash crops such as coffee to generate badly needed foreign exchange. Accordingly, state farms received a large share of the country's resources for agriculture; from 1982 to 1990, this totaled about 43 percent of the government's agricultural investment. In 1983 state farms received 76 percent of the total allocation of chemical fertilizers, 95 percent of the improved seeds, and 81 percent of agricultural credit. In terms of subsidies, between 1982/83 and 1985/86 the various state farm corporations received more than 90 million birr in direct subsidies. Despite the emphasis on state farms, state farm production accounted for only 6 percent of total agricultural output in 1987 (although meeting 65 percent of urban needs), leaving peasant farmers responsible for over 90 percent of production.

The stress on large-scale state farms was under attack by Western donors, who channeled their agricultural aid to the peasant sector. These donors maintained that experiences elsewhere in Africa and in Eastern Europe and the Soviet Union had shown that state farms were inefficient and a drain on scare resources.

Resettlement and Villagization

The policy of encouraging voluntary resettlement went back to 1958, when the government established the first known planned resettlement in Sidamo. Shortly after the 1974 revolution, it became Derg policy to accelerate resettlement. Article 18 of the 1975 Land Reform Proclamation stated that "the government shall have the responsibility to settle peasants or to establish cottage industries to accommodate those who, as a result of distribution of land . . . remain with little or no land." Accordingly, in 1975/76 there were eighty-eight settlement centers accommodating 38,818 households. The government conducted most of these resettlement programs under the auspices of the Relief and Rehabilitation Commission (RRC) and the Ministry of Agriculture. By 1982 there were 112 planned settlements populated by more than 120,000 people. The settlements were concentrated mainly in the south and southwest. In 1984 Addis Ababa announced its intention to resettle 1.5 million people from the drought-affected northern regions to the south and southwest, where arable land was plentiful. By 1986 the government had resettled more than 600,000 people to three settlement areas. More than 250,000 went to Welega; about 150,000 settled in the Gambela area of Ilubabor; and just over 100,000 went to Pawe, the largest planned resettlement in Gojam and largely sustained by Italian financial support. In addition, another 78,000 went to Kefa, Shewa, and western Gonder.

In mid-1986 the government halted the resettlement program, largely to fend off the negative reaction from the international community. But in November 1987 the program resumed, and in March 1988 Mengistu spoke of the need to move at least 7 million people. He claimed resettlement would resolve the country's recurring drought problem and would ease population pressure from northern areas where the land had been badly overused. Western donors and governments, whom Addis Ababa expected to help with the program, remained apprehensive of the government's intentions, however. Some believed that the plan to resettle 1.5 million people by 1994 was unrealistic, given the country's strained finances. Others argued that resettlement was a ploy to depopulate areas of resistance, weaken the guerrillas' support base, and deny them access to recruits, particularly in Eritrea and Tigray. Additional arguments against resettlement included charges of human rights violations, forced separations of families, and lack of medical attention in resettlement centers, which resulted in thousands of deaths from malaria and sleeping sickness.

Although many of these charges were valid, some criticisms may have been unfounded. For instance, the claim that the resettlement was a ploy to depopulate the rebel areas may not have been valid, given that by 1986 only 15 percent of the 600,000 resettled peasants were from Tigray and none were from Eritrea. More than 80 percent of those resettled were from Welo and Shewa.

In 1985 the government initiated a new relocation program known as villagization. The objectives of the program, which grouped scattered farming communities throughout the country into small village clusters, were to promote rational land use; conserve resources; provide access to clean water and to health and education services; and strengthen security. Government guidelines stipulated that villages were to house 200 to 300 households, with 100-square-meter compounds for each family.

In 1985 Addis Ababa established a national coordinating committee to oversee the villagization plan's implementation. By March 1986, about 4.6 million people in Shewa, Arsi, and Harerge had been relocated into more than 4,500 villages. Although the government had villagized about 13 million people by 1989, international criticism, deteriorating security conditions, and lack of resources doomed the plan to failure. Nevertheless, Mengistu remained committed to the villagization concept.

Opponents of villagization argued that the scheme was disruptive to agricultural production because the government moved many farmers during the planting and harvesting seasons. There also was concern that villagization could have a negative impact on fragile local resources, particularly on water and grazing land; accelerate the spread of communicable diseases; and increase problems with plant pests and diseases. In early 1990, the government essentially abandoned villagization when it announced new economic policies

175

that called for free-market reforms and a relaxation of centralized planning.

Agricultural Production

The effect of the PMAC's land reform program on food production and its marketing and distribution policies were among two of the major controversies surrounding the revolution. Available data on crop production show that land reform and the various government rural programs had a minimal impact on increasing the food supply, as production levels displayed considerable fluctuations and low growth rates at best (see table 13, Appendix).

Major Cash Crops

The most important cash crop in Ethiopia was coffee. During the 1970s, coffee exports accounted for 50 to 60 percent of the total value of all exports, although coffee's share dropped to 25 percent as a result of the economic dislocation following the 1974 revolution. By 1976 coffee exports had recovered, and in the five years ending in 1988/89, coffee accounted for about 63 percent of the value of exports. Domestically, coffee contributed about 20 percent of the government's revenue. Approximately 25 percent of Ethiopia's population depended directly or indirectly on coffee for its livelihood.

Ethiopia's coffee is almost exclusively of the arabica type, which grows best at altitudes between 1,000 and 2,000 meters. Coffee grows wild in many parts of the country, although most Ethiopian coffee is produced in the southern and western regions of Kefa, Sidamo, Ilubabor, Gamo Gofa, Welega, and Harerge.

Reliable estimates of coffee production in Ethiopia were unavailable as of mid-1991. However, some observers indicated that Ethiopia produced between 140,000 and 180,000 tons annually. The Ethiopian government placed coffee production at 187,000 tons in 1979/80, 233,000 tons in 1983/84, and 172,000 tons in 1985/86. Estimates for 1986/87 and 1987/88 were put at 186,000 and 189,000 tons, respectively. Preliminary figures from other sources indicated that coffee production continued to rise in 1988/89 and 1989/90 but registered a sharp decline of perhaps as much as one-third during 1990/91. About 44 percent of the coffee produced was exported. Although the potential for local coffee consumption was high, the government, eager to increase its hard-currency reserves, suppressed domestic consumption by controlling coffee sales. The government also restricted the transfer of coffee from coffee-producing areas to other parts of the country. This practice made the price of local coffee two to three times higher than the price of exported coffee.

About 98 percent of the coffee was produced by peasants on small holdings of less than a hectare, and the remaining 2 percent was produced by state farms. Some estimates indicated that yields on peasant farms were higher than those on state farms. In the 1980s, as part of an effort to increase production and to improve the cultivation and harvesting of coffee, the government created the Ministry of Coffee and Tea Development, which was responsible for production and marketing. The ten-year plan called for an increase in the size of state farms producing coffee from 14,000–15,000 hectares to 50,000 hectares by 1994. However, given the strain on the government's financial resources and the consistently declining coffee price in the world market, this may have been an unrealistic goal.

The decline in world coffee prices, which began in 1987, reduced Ethiopia's foreign-exchange earnings. In early 1989, for example, the price of one kilogram of coffee was US$0.58; by June it had dropped to US$0.32. Mengistu told the 1989 WPE party congress that at US$0.32 per kilogram, foreign-exchange earnings from coffee would drop by 240 million birr, and government revenue would be reduced by 140 million birr by the end of 1989. Such declines not only hampered the government's ability to implement its political, economic, and social programs but also reduced Addis Ababa's capacity to prosecute its war against various rebel groups in northern Ethiopia.

Before the revolution, pulses and oilseeds played an important role, second only to coffee, in Ethiopia's exports. In EFY 1974/75, pulses and oilseeds accounted for 34 percent of export earnings (about 163 million birr), but this share declined to about 3 percent (about 30 million birr) in EFY 1988/89 (see table 14, Appendix). Three factors contributed to the decline in the relative importance of pulses and oilseeds. First, the recurring droughts had devastated the country's main areas where pulses and oilseeds were produced. Second, because peasants faced food shortages, they gave priority to cereal staples to sustain themselves. Finally, although the production cost of pulses and oilseeds continued to rise, the government's price control policy left virtually unchanged the official procurement price of these crops, thus substantially reducing net income from them. The Ethiopian Pulses and Oilseeds Corporation, the agency responsible for exporting two-thirds of these crops, reported losses in EFY 1982/83 and EFY 1983/84. In EFY 1983/84, the corporation received export subsidies of more than 9 million birr. Subsequently, production of both crops failed to improve; by 1988 the output index, whose base year was 1972 (100), was 85.3 for pulses and 15.8 for oilseeds. Given the country's economic and political problems and the ongoing war in the north, there was little prospect of improvement.

Cotton is grown throughout Ethiopia below elevations of about 1,400 meters. Because most of the lowlands lack adequate rainfall, cotton cultivation depends largely on irrigation. Before the revolution, large-scale commercial cotton plantations were developed in the Awash Valley and the Humera areas. The Tendaho Cotton Plantation in the lower Awash Valley was one of Ethiopia's largest cotton plantations. Rain-fed cotton also grew in Humera, Bilate (in Sidamo), and Arba Minch (in Gamo Gofa).

Since the revolution, most commercial cotton has been grown on irrigated state farms, mostly in the Awash Valley area. Production jumped from 43,500 tons in 1974/75 to 74,900 tons in 1984/85. Similarly, the area of cultivation increased from 22,600 hectares in 1974/75 to 33,900 hectares in 1984/85.

Major Staple Crops

Ethiopia's major staple crops include a variety of cereals, pulses, oilseeds, and coffee. Grains are the most important field crops and the chief element in the diet of most Ethiopians. The principal grains are teff, wheat, barley, corn, sorghum, and millet. The first three are primarily cool-weather crops cultivated at altitudes generally above 1,500 meters. Teff, indigenous to Ethiopia, furnishes the flour for *injera,* an unleavened bread that is the principal form in which grain is consumed in the highlands and in urban centers throughout the country. Barley is grown mostly between 2,000 and 3,500 meters. A major subsistence crop, barley is used as food and in the production of *tella,* a locally produced beer.

Sorghum, millet, and corn are cultivated mostly in warmer areas at lower altitudes along the country's western, southwestern, and eastern peripheries. Sorghum and millet, which are drought resistant, grow well at low elevations where rainfall is less reliable. Corn is grown chiefly between elevations of 1,500 and 2,200 meters and requires large amounts of rainfall to ensure good harvests. These three grains constitute the staple foods of a good part of the population and are major items in the diet of the nomads.

Pulses are the second most important element in the national diet and a principal protein source. They are boiled, roasted, or included in a stew-like dish known as *wot,* which is sometimes a main dish and sometimes a supplementary food. Pulses, grown widely at all altitudes from sea level to about 3,000 meters, are

Fruit stall in Addis Ababa
Courtesy Paul Henze

more prevalent in the northern and central highlands. Pulses were a particularly important export item before the revolution.

The Ethiopian Orthodox Church traditionally has forbidden consumption of animal fats on many days of the year. As a result, vegetable oils are widely used, and oilseed cultivation is an important agricultural activity. The most important oilseed is the indigenous niger seed (*neug*), which is grown on 50 percent or more of the area devoted to oilseeds. Niger seed is found mostly in the northern and central highlands at elevations between 1,800 and 2,500 meters. Flaxseed, also indigenous, is cultivated in the same general area as niger seed. The third most important oilseed is sesame, which grows at elevations from sea level to about 1,500 meters. In addition to its domestic use, sesame is also the principal export oilseed. Oilseeds of lesser significance include castor beans, rapeseed, groundnuts (peanuts), and safflower and sunflower seeds. Most oilseeds are raised by small-scale farmers, but sesame was also grown by large-scale commercial farms before the era of land reform and the nationalization of agribusiness.

Ensete, known locally as false banana, is an important food source in Ethiopia's southern and southwestern highlands. It is cultivated principally by the Gurage, Sidama, and several other ethnic groups in the region. Resembling the banana but bearing an inedible fruit, the plant produces large quantities of starch in its underground rhizome and an above-ground stem that can reach a height of several meters. Ensete flour constitutes the staple food of the local people. Taro, yams, and sweet potatoes are commonly grown in the same region as the ensete.

The consumption of vegetables and fruits is relatively limited, largely because of their high cost. Common vegetables include onions, peppers, squash, and a cabbage similar to kale. Demand for vegetables has stimulated truck farming around the main urban areas such as Addis Ababa and Asmera. Prior to the revolution, urbanization increased the demand for fruit, leading to the establishment of citrus orchards in areas with access to irrigation in Shewa, Arsi, Harerge, and Eritrea. The Mengistu regime encouraged fruit and vegetable production. Fresh fruits, including citrus and bananas, as well as fresh and frozen vegetables, became important export items, but their profitability was marginal. The Ethiopian Fruit and Vegetable Marketing Enterprise (EFVME), which handled about 75 percent of Ethiopia's exports of fruits and vegetables in 1984–85, had to receive government subsidies because of losses.

Ethiopia's demand for grain continued to increase because of population pressures, while supply remained short, largely because of drought and government agricultural policies, such as price controls, which adversely affected crop production. Food production had consistently declined throughout the 1980s. Consequently, Ethiopia became a net importer of grain worth about 243 million birr annually from 1983/84 to 1987/88. The food deficit estimate for the 1985/89 period indicated that production averaged about 6 million tons while demand reached about 10 million tons, thus creating an annual deficit of roughly 4 million tons. Much of the food deficit was covered through food aid. Between 1984/85 and 1986/87, at the height of the drought, Ethiopia received more than 1.7 million tons of grain, about 14 percent of the total food aid for Africa. In addition, Ethiopia spent 341 million birr on food purchases during the 1985–87 period.

Livestock

Livestock production plays an important role in Ethiopia's economy. Estimates for 1987 indicated that livestock production contributed one-third of agriculture's share of GDP, or nearly 15 percent of total GDP. Hides and skins constituted the second largest export earner, averaging about 15 percent of the total export value during the period 1984/85 to 1988/89; live animals averaged around 3 percent of the total value of exports during the same period.

Although varying from region to region, the role of livestock in the Ethiopian economy was greater than the figures suggest. Almost the entire rural population was involved in some way with animal husbandry, whose role included the provision of draft power, food, cash, transportation, fuel, and, especially in pastoral areas, social prestige. In the highlands, oxen provided draft power in crop production. In pastoral areas, livestock formed the basis of the economy. Per capita meat consumption was high by developing countries' standards, an estimated thirteen kilograms annually. According to a 1987 estimate, beef accounted for about 51 percent of all meat consumption, followed by mutton and lamb (19 percent), poultry (15 percent), and goat (14 percent).

Ethiopia's estimated livestock population of about 78.4 million in 1988 was believed to be Africa's largest. There were approximately 31 million cattle, 23.4 million sheep, 17.5 million goats, 5.5 million horses and mules, 1 million camels, and 57 million poultry. Livestock was distributed throughout the country, with the greatest concentration in the highlands, where more than 90 percent of these animals were located. The raising of livestock always has been largely a subsistence activity.

Ethiopia has great potential for increased livestock production, both for local use and for export. However, expansion was constrained by inadequate nutrition, disease, a lack of support services such as extension services, insufficient data with which to plan improved services, and inadequate information on how to improve animal breeding, marketing, and processing. The high concentration of animals in the highlands, together with the fact that cattle are often kept for status, reduces the economic potential of Ethiopian livestock.

Both the imperial and the Marxist governments tried to improve livestock production by instituting programs such as free vaccination, well-digging, construction of feeder roads, and improvement of pastureland, largely through international organizations such as the World Bank and the African Development Bank. The Mengistu regime also opened veterinary stations at Bahir Dar, Buno Bedele, and Debre Zeyit to provide treatment and vaccination services.

Cattle in Ethiopia are almost entirely of the zebu type and are poor sources of milk and meat. However, these cattle do relatively well under the traditional production system. About 70 percent of the cattle in 1987 were in the highlands, and the remaining 30 percent were kept by nomadic pastoralists in the lowland areas. Meat and milk yields are low and losses high, especially among calves and young stock. Contagious diseases and parasitic infections are major causes of death, factors that are exacerbated by malnutrition and starvation. Recurring drought takes a heavy toll on the animal population, although it is difficult to determine the extent of losses. Practically all animals are range-fed. During the rainy seasons, water and grass are generally plentiful, but with the onset of the dry season, forage is generally insufficient to keep animals nourished and able to resist disease.

Most of Ethiopia's estimated 41 million sheep and goats are raised by small farmers who used them as a major source of meat and cash income. About three-quarters of the total sheep flock is in the highlands, whereas lowland pastoralists maintain about three-quarters of the goat herd. Both animals have high sales value in urban centers, particularly during holidays such as Easter and New Year's Day.

Most of the estimated 7 million equines (horses, mules, and donkeys) are used to transport produce and other agricultural goods. Camels also play a key role as pack animals in areas below 1,500 meters in elevation. Additionally, camels provide pastoralists in those areas with milk and meat.

Poultry farming is widely practiced in Ethiopia; almost every farmstead keeps some poultry for consumption and for cash sale. The highest concentration of poultry is in Shewa, in central Welo, and in northwestern Tigray. Individual poultry farms supply eggs and meat to urban dwellers. By 1990 the state had begun to develop large poultry farms, mostly around Addis Ababa, to supply hotels and government institutions.

Fishing

Ethiopia's many lakes, rivers, and reservoirs and its approximately 960 kilometers of Red Sea coastline are fertile fishing grounds. However, fishing contributed less than 1 percent of GDP in 1987. The ten-year plan in 1983/84 estimated that the country had the potential to produce more than 92,000 tons of fish—66,000 tons from the Red Sea and the remaining 26,000 tons from lakes and rivers. But actual production in 1983/84 was estimated at 600 to 1,200 tons.

Fresh fish are consumed along the Red Sea coast, in Asmera, and in the vicinity of the Great Rift Valley lakes. Outside these areas, however, the domestic market for fish is small. Two factors account for this low level of local fish consumption. First, fish has not been integrated into the diet of most of the population. Second, because of religious influences on consumption patterns, the demand for fish is only seasonal. During Lent, for example, Christians who abstain from eating meat, milk, and eggs consume fish.

There was considerable commercial fishing activity in the Red Sea prior to 1974, chiefly consisting of private foreign companies that exported most of their catch after processing the fish onshore. For instance, in 1970 private companies exported about 9,140 tons of fish. After the 1974 revolution, most commercial fishing companies left Ethiopia, which reduced fish exports.

The Mengistu regime encouraged the establishment of fishery associations and cooperatives along the Red Sea coast and in the Great Rift Valley lakes area. In 1978 the government established the Fish Production and Marketing Corporation (FPMC) to help improve the Ethiopian fish industry. The following year, the Ministry of Agriculture created the Fisheries Resources Development Department to help improve fish breeding, control, and marketing. The FPMC received loans from the Agricultural and Industrial Development Bank and aid from the European Community (EC) to purchase various types of transportation equipment and to establish modern shops and cold storage.

In late 1990, the Red Sea Fishery Resources Development Project, which is managed by the Food and Agriculture Organization of the United Nations (FAO), received funding from the United Nations Development Programme (UNDP) and the Capital Development Fund to purchase motor boats, fishing nets, and other accessories for five fishermen's cooperatives in Aseb. The government hoped this equipment would help increase production and eventually enable the five cooperatives to extract 450 tons of fish annually. Nevertheless, the 1988/89 fish production of sixty tons fell by more than half in 1989/90 because of security problems in the area.

Forestry

In the late nineteenth century, about 30 percent of the country was covered with forest. The clearing of land for agricultural use and the cutting of trees for fuel gradually changed the scene, and today forest areas have dwindled to less than 4 percent of Ethiopia's total land. The northern parts of the highlands are almost devoid of trees. However, about 4.5 million hectares of dense forest exist in the southern and southwestern sections of the highlands. Some of these include coniferous forests, found at elevations above 1,600 meters, but a majority of the forestland consists primarily of woodlands found in drier areas of the highlands and in the drier areas bordering the highlands.

Lumber from the coniferous forests is important to the construction industry. The broadleaf evergreen forests furnish timber that is used in construction and in the production of plywood. The woodlands are a major source of firewood and charcoal. Certain trees—boswellia and species of commiphora—are of special economic significance. Both grow in the arid lowlands and produce gums that are the bases for frankincense and myrrh. A species of acacia found in several parts of the country is a source of gum arabic used in the manufacture of adhesives, pharmaceutical products, and confectionery. The eucalyptus, an exotic tree introduced in the late nineteenth century and grown mainly near urban areas, is a valuable source of telephone and telegraph poles, tool handles, furniture, and firewood. It is also a major source of the material from which fiberboard and particleboard are made.

Data on forestry's contribution to the economy are not readily available, largely because most GDP tables aggregate data on forestry, fishing, and hunting. In 1980/81 forestry accounted for 2.5 percent of GDP at constant 1960/61 factor cost and 5.4 percent of the share attributable to the agricultural sector.

Before 1974 about half of the forestland was privately owned or claimed, and roughly half was held by the government. There was little government control of forestry operations prior to the revolution. The 1975 land reform nationalized forestland and sawmills, which existed mostly in the south. The government controlled harvesting of forestland, and in some cases individuals had to secure permits from local peasant associations to cut trees. But this measure encouraged illegal logging and accelerated the destruction of Ethiopia's remaining forests. To ensure that conservation activity conformed with government policy and directives on land use, reforestation programs were organized through the Ministry of Agriculture or district offices that planed, coordinated, and monitored all work. The local peasant associations lacked decision-making authority.

Reforestation programs resulted in the planting of millions of seedlings in community forests throughout Ethiopia. A variety of Non-Governmental Organizations (NGOs), which had to organize their activities through the local peasant association, supplemented government efforts to rehabilitate Ethiopia's forests. However, critics maintain that both systems caused communal resources to be developed at the expense of private needs. As a result, reforestation programs did not perform well. Seedling survival rates varied from as low as 5 to 20 percent in some areas to 40 percent in others, largely because of inadequate care and premature cutting by peasants. In late 1990, Addis Ababa was in the process of launching the Ethiopian Forestry Action Plan (EFAP) to improve forestry conservation, increase public participation in reforestation projects, and prevent further depletion of existing forest resources.

It remained to be seen whether this plan would improve the state of Ethiopia's forests.

Government Marketing Operations

Private traders and the Agricultural Marketing Corporation (AMC), established in 1976, marketed Ethiopia's agricultural output. The AMC was a government agency whose objective was to influence the supply and price of crops. It purchased grain from peasant associations at fixed prices. The AMC set quotas of grain purchases to be delivered by peasant associations and cooperatives and also bought from private wholesalers, who were required to sell half of their purchases at predetermined prices. State farms sold their output to the AMC. Although the AMC had agents in all regions, it was particularly active in the major cereal-producing regions, namely, Gojam, Shewa, Arsi, and Gonder. In 1981/82, out of the AMC's purchases of 257,000 tons of grain, Gojam accounted for 32 percent of the purchases, and Arsi, Shewa, and Gonder accounted for 23, 22, and 10 percent, respectively. The government's price controls and the AMC's operations had led to the development of different price systems at various levels. For instance, the 1984/85 official procurement price for 100 kilograms of teff was 42 birr at the farm level and 60 birr when the AMC purchased it from wholesalers. But the same quantity of teff retailed at 81 birr at food stores belonging to the urban dwellers' associations (*kebeles*—see Glossary) in Addis Ababa and sold for as much as 181 birr in the open market. Such wide price variations created food shortages because farmers as well as private merchants withheld crops to sell on the black market at higher prices.

Industry and Energy

Manufacturing

Prior to 1957, when Ethiopia initiated a series of five-year development plans, cottage and handicraft industries met most of the population's needs for manufactured goods such as clothes, ceramics, machine tools, and leather goods. Various factors—including the lack of basic infrastructure, the dearth of private and public investment, and the lack of any consistent public policy aimed at promoting industrial development—contributed to the insignificance of manufacturing. Throughout much of the 1960s and early 1970s, manufacturing activity increased as the government's five-year plans diversified the economy by encouraging agro-industrial activity and by substituting domestically produced goods for imported items. Thus, according to the World Bank, manufacturing production increased at an annual rate of 6.1 percent between 1965 and 1973. During the same period, agriculture grew at an annual 2.1 percent rate, and services grew at an annual 6.7 percent rate. Despite this favorable growth rate, manufacturing in 1975 accounted for less than 5 percent of GDP and employed only about 60,000 people. Handicrafts, such as weaving, pottery, blacksmithing, leather working, and jewelry making, along with other small-scale industries, accounted for another 5 percent of GDP. In 1984/85 manufacturing and handicrafts together accounted for 11.4 percent of GDP.

In 1975 the PMAC nationalized more than 100 industries and took partial control of some of them. The main characteristics of the manufacturing sector inherited by the revolution included a predominance of foreign ownership and foreign managerial, professional, and technical staffing; heavy emphasis on light industries; inward orientation and relatively high tariffs; capital-intensiveness; underutilized capacity; minimal linkage among the different sectors; and excessive geographical concentration of industries in Addis Ababa.

After nationalization, there was an exodus of foreigners who had owned and operated the industrial enterprises. The war in Eritrea and labor strikes and demonstrations also closed the approximately 30 percent of the country's plants that had been located in that region.

The economic dislocation that followed the revolution had a significant impact on the manufacturing sector. Private-sector capital investment ceased, and labor's marginal productivity began to decline. In performance terms, the manufacturing sector's output after 1975 grew haltingly. Manufacturing had grown at an average annual rate of 6.1 percent between 1965 and 1973. A period of decline from 1974/75 to 1977/78 and an average annual growth rate of 18.9 percent for 1978/79 and 1979/80 were followed by a reduction of the growth rate to about 3.1 percent per annum between 1980/81 and 1984/85 and 3.8 percent per annum from 1985/86 to 1988/89.

The manufacturing sector's performance paralleled developments in other parts of the country. In the revolution's early days, the dislocation caused by nationalization, the flight of managers, the wars in Eritrea and the Ogaden, and local strife in many areas disrupted production and hurt productivity. *Zemecha* production campaigns, which focused on increasing capacity utilization, characterized the late 1970s. As a result of these campaigns, Ethiopia achieved growth rates of 27.3 and 10.5 percent, respectively, in 1978/79 and 1979/80. By 1985 capacity utilization estimates of many

Coffee seedlings at Bulbulo Nursery near Agaro, in Kefa
Courtesy Paul Henze

industries ranged between 70 and 100 percent, and many plants operated in three shifts. These figures were high by African standards.

Manufacturing productivity began to decline by 1980 because of a downturn in agricultural production and a shortage of foreign exchange to import raw materials. Analysts expected the manufacturing sector's productivity to decline further in the 1990s as equipment aged and spare-parts shortages grew. In response to the downward trend, in 1987/88 the government planned to invest 342 million birr in industrial enterprises to increase production capacity. In 1989 the government issued Proclamation No. 11, which enunciated policies intended to attract foreign investment. Finally, in March 1990 Mengistu announced the replacement of Ethiopia's socialist economic system with a mixed economy. Among the proposed changes were that private investors would by permitted to participate in all parts of the economy with no limit on the amount of capital invested (see Role of Government, this ch.).

Industrial Development Policy

Between 1950 and 1960, the imperial government enacted legislation and implemented a new policy to encourage foreign investment. This new policy provided investor benefits in the form of tax exemptions, remittances of foreign exchange, import and export duty relief, tax exemptions on dividends, and the provision of financing through the Ethiopian Investment Corporation and the Development Bank of Ethiopia. In addition, the government guaranteed protection to industrial enterprises by instituting high tariffs and by banning the importation of commodities that might adversely affect production of domestic goods. Protected items included sugar, textiles, furniture, and metal. The government also participated through direct investment in enterprises that had high capital costs, such as oil refineries and the paper and pulp, glass and bottle, tire, and cement industries. In 1963, with the Second Five-Year Plan under way, the government enacted Proclamation No. 51. The proclamation's objective was to consolidate other investment policies enacted up to that period, to extend benefits to Ethiopian investors (previous legislation had limited the benefits to foreigners only), and to create an Investment Committee that would oversee investment programs. In 1966 Addis Ababa enacted Proclamation No. 242, which elevated the Investment Committee's status as an advisory council to that of an authorized body empowered to make independent investment decisions. Thus, by the early 1970s, Ethiopia's industrialization policy included a range of fiscal incentives, direct government investment, and equity participation in private enterprises.

The government's policy attracted considerable foreign investment to the industrial sector. For instance, in 1971/72 the share of foreign capital in manufacturing industries amounted to 41 percent of the total paid-up capital. Many foreign enterprises operated as private limited companies, usually as a branch or subsidiary of multinational corporations. The Dutch had a major investment (close to 80 percent) in the sugar industry. Italian and Japanese investors participated in textiles; and Greeks maintained an interest in shoes and beverages. Italian investors also worked in building, construction, and agricultural industries.

In 1975 the PMAC nationalized most industries and subsequently reorganized them into state-owned corporations. On February 7, 1975, the government released a document outlining socialist Ethiopia's economic policy. The policy identified three manufacturing areas slated for state involvement: basic industries that produced goods serving other industries and that had the capacity to create linkages in the economy; industries that produced essential goods for the general population; and industries that made drugs, medicine, tobacco, and beverages. The policy also grouped areas of the public and private sectors into activities reserved for the state, activities where state and private capital could operate jointly, and activities left to the private sector.

The 1975 nationalization of major industries scared off foreign private investment. Private direct investment, according to the National Bank of Ethiopia, declined from 65 million birr in 1974 to 12 million birr in 1977. As compensation negotiations between the Ethiopian government and foreign nationals dragged on, foreign investment virtually ceased. The United States Congress invoked the Hickenlooper Amendment, which had the effect of prohibiting the use of United States funds for development purposes until Ethiopia had settled compensation issues with United States nationals. During 1982 and 1983, the Mengistu regime settled claims made by Italian, Dutch, Japanese, and British nationals. Negotiation to settle compensation claims by United States nationals continued until 1985, when Ethiopia agreed to pay about US$7 million in installments to compensate United States companies.

Issued in 1983, the PMAC's Proclamation No. 235 (the Joint Venture Proclamation) signaled Ethiopia's renewed interest in attracting foreign capital. The proclamation offered incentives such as a five-year period of income tax relief for new projects, import and export duty relief, tariff protection, and repatriation of profits and capital. It limited foreign holdings to a maximum of 49 percent and the duration of any joint venture to twenty-five years. Although the proclamation protected investors' interests from expropriation, the government reserved the right to purchase all shares in a joint venture "for reasons of national interest." The proclamation failed to attract foreign investment, largely because foreign businesses were hesitant to invest in a country whose government recently had nationalized foreign industries without a level of compensation these businesses considered satisfactory.

In 1989 the government issued Special Decree No. 11, a revision of the 1983 proclamation. The decree allowed majority foreign ownership in many sectors, except in those related to public utilities, banking and finance, trade, transportation, and communications, where joint ventures were not allowed. The decree also removed all restrictions on profit repatriation and attempted to provide more extensive legal protection of investors than had the 1983 proclamation.

President Mengistu's March 1990 speech to the Central Committee of the WPE was a turning point in Ethiopia's recent economic history. Acknowledging that socialism had failed, Mengistu proposed implementing a mixed economy. Under the new system, the private sector would be able to participate in all parts of the economy with no limit on capital investment (Ethiopia had a

US$250,000 ceiling on private investment); developers would be allowed to build houses, apartments, and office buildings for rent or sale; and commercial enterprises would be permitted to develop industries, hotels, and a range of other enterprises on government-owned land to be leased on a concessionary basis. Additionally, state-owned industries and businesses would be required to operate on a profit basis, with those continuing to lose money to be sold or closed. Farmers would receive legal ownership of land they tilled and the right to sell their produce in a free market. Whereas there were many areas yet to be addressed, such as privatization of state enterprises and compensation for citizens whose land and property had been confiscated, these proposals generated optimism among some economists about Ethiopia's economic future. However, some observers pointed out that Mengistu's proposals only amounted to recognition of existing practices in the underground economy.

Energy Resources

Ethiopia is one of the few African countries with the potential to produce hydroelectric and geothermal power. As of mid-1991, however, no comprehensive assessment of this potential was available, although some estimates indicated that the total potential could be as much as 143 billion kilowatts. The main sources of this potential were thought to be the Abay (Blue Nile; 79.9 billion kilowatts), the Shebele (21.6 billion kilowatts), and the Omo (16.1 billion kilowatts). The remaining 25.9 billion kilowatts would come from rivers such as the Tekezé, Awash, Baro, Genale, and Mereb.

Ethiopia's first large hydroelectric generating facilities were constructed in the Awash River basin. The three plants—Awash I (Koka) with 54,000 kilowatts capacity, Awash II with 32,000 kilowatts capacity, and Awash III with 32,000 kilowatts capacity—were finished between 1960 and 1972. In 1974 the Fincha River facility in central Welega opened with a generating capacity of 84,000 kilowatts. Other major power-generating facilities included those at Bahir Dar (7,680 kilowatts) and Aba Samuel (6,560 kilowatts). The total installed capacity of thermal generating units amounted to 210,084 kilowatts in 1985/86.

Electric power production in 1985/86 totaled 998.7 million kilowatt-hours, 83 percent of which was produced by hydroelectric power installations. Thermal generating units produced the remaining 17 percent. The thermal generating units in the public utility system, many of which were comparatively small, had a generating capacity of 95,635 kilowatts in 1985. Major units were located close to Asmera (31,900 kilowatts), Dire Dawa (4,500 kilowatts), Addis Ababa (3,100 kilowatts), and Aseb (3,100 kilowatts). In 1985/86 various business enterprises and local communities owned electrical generators of unspecified capacity.

The regional electrical distribution system included an interconnected system and a self-contained system. By 1988 most power generating sources, including all major hydroelectric power plants, were interconnected in a power grid. The interconnected system served more than 100 towns. Power from the Awash, Fincha, and Aba Samuel stations ran the central system, the largest component of the interconnected system. The Bahir Dar interconnected system, which served parts of Gojam and Gonder, and the Eritrean Region Electricity Supply Agency (ERESA) were two of the other major systems. A majority of the self-contained systems got their power from thermal power plants, with the power often being used for domestic purposes and to run small mills.

The Ethiopian Electric Light and Power Authority (ELPA), a government corporation, operated most of the country's power systems. Prior to the revolution, ELPA incorporated more than forty electric power stations and generated about 80 percent of the nation's total electrical output. Two Italian firms, Società Elettrica dell'Africa Orientale and Compagnia Nazionale Impresse Elettriche, chiefly serving Eritrea, produced another 16.5 percent of the country's electrical energy. Independent stations generated the remaining 3 to 4 percent. In 1975 the government nationalized all private utility companies and placed them under ELPA. Since then, utility services have been reserved exclusively to the state. In 1987 ELPA served about 170 towns and produced about 92 percent of the national electrical output. Mass organizations, sugar factories, and the Aseb refinery administered the remaining 8 percent.

In 1985/86, of the total 847.7 million kilowatt-hours of power sold by ELPA, 59 percent was for industrial use, 29 percent for domestic use, 10 percent for commercial use, and the remaining 2 percent for other uses such as street lighting and agriculture. By 1987 about 9 percent of the total population (4.3 million people) were using electricity.

Ethiopia's second commercial energy resource is oil. Despite reports of natural gas reserves and traces of petroleum, Ethiopia still depends on imported crude oil, which accounted for an average of about 12 percent of the value of imports during the period 1982/83 to 1987/88. Exploration for petroleum and natural gas in the Ogaden and the Red Sea basin has been going on for many years. In May 1988, International Petroleum, a subsidiary of Canada's International Petroleum Corporation (IPC), signed a production sharing and exploration license for the Denakil block, which covers 34,000 square kilometers on and off shore along the Red Sea coast. The IPC also has conducted geothermal studies and undertaken mapping projects. In late 1990, the government announced that geologists had discovered oil in western Ilubabor, with an expected deposit ranging from 100 million to 120 million tons.

Since the early 1970s, there has been exploration and development of geothermal resources in the Great Rift Valley. In early 1972, the United Nations Development Programme (UNDP) conducted preliminary explorations in the area and detected what appeared to be one of the world's largest potential sources of geothermal power. In mid-1979 the EEC, assisted by the UNDP, provided a grant to aid exploration in the valley's lake region. In 1984 Ethiopia reported the discovery of a promising geothermal source in the Lake Langano area. However, no indication has been provided as to when production will start. The primary energy sources for most Ethiopians are charcoal, animal manure, and firewood. Some estimates indicate that as much as 96 percent of the country's total energy consumption is based on these traditional sources.

Mining

Ethiopia's minerals industry has been only of minor importance, contributing an average of less than 0.2 percent of GDP at constant factor cost between 1984/85 and 1988/89. Although it had reported the existence of a wide range of minerals throughout the country, the government had authorized little exploration. Thus, there are no reliable estimates of the extent of mineral resources. However, there has been some small-scale mining for minerals such as gold, platinum, salt, limestone, and clay. Gold has been mined at Adola (in Sidamo) for many years. In 1981/82 output at this site in southern Ethiopia averaged around 500 kilograms per annum. However, by 1985/86 production had dropped to 293 kilograms. In 1987 the government reported the discovery of large gold deposits in Lege Dimbi, also in Sidamo. Observers believed that prospectors mined an annual average of 7.5 to 8 kilograms of platinum in the Yubdo area in Welega.

Stretching inland from the Red Sea coast, the Denakil Depression has large salt deposits. Production averaged some 20,000 tons annually. Other major salt sources are found at Aseb and around Mitsiwa, also on the Red Sea. According to some estimates, Ethiopia produces about 300,000 tons of marine and mined salt annually.

However, this supply fails to satisfy domestic needs because the government exports salt to improve its hard-currency reserves.

A large potash deposit, estimated at 140 to 150 million tons, is located in Tigray's Dallol area. Production has averaged less than 1 million tons per year.

Large iron ore deposits are scattered throughout the country. During the Italian colonial period, a few companies started iron-mining operations in Eritrea but abandoned them after the Italian occupation ended in 1941. In the late 1980s, prospectors identified iron ore deposits estimated at 20 million tons in the Agametta region (near Mitsiwa) and another 160,00 tons of iron ore in Welega and Bale.

Copper, lead, and zinc deposits are found near Debarwa, thirty-five kilometers southwest of Asmera. In 1973 the Ethio-Nippon Mining Share Company started mining copper in Debarwa. However, the Eritrean war forced an end to operations two years later.

Limestone is excavated near Mitsiwa, Dire Dawa, and Addis Ababa. The limestone is used chiefly at the cement works operating in those cities.

Transportation and Telecommunications

A lack of resources, coupled with military and political instability, has retarded the growth of a transportation infrastructure in Ethiopia, even though development of such a system traditionally has been a government objective. The Haile Selassie regime allocated an average of 700 million birr of the planned budget for the development of transportation during the three five-year development plans (1957–74). In 1975, when the PMAC articulated its socialist economic policy, the government assumed control of all transportation and communication facilities. The military government continued to expand and improve the transportation infrastructure by using its own funds and by securing loans from international organizations such as the World Bank. In 1991 the transportation system included 13,000 kilometers of all-weather roads, a 781-kilometer railroad connecting Addis Ababa and Djibouti, twenty-five airports, and another twenty airfields (see fig. 10).

Roads

Road transport was the means of movement for about 93 percent of freight and 95 percent of all passengers. In 1991, in addition to the 13,000 kilometers of all-weather roads, of which about 4,000 were asphalted and 8,900 were all-weather gravel roads, there were 4,900 kilometers of rural dirt roads, making a total of nearly 18,000 kilometers of all types of roads. Centered in Addis Ababa, the road system radiated in all directions in a spoke-like pattern. However, substantial parts of the country, notably in the west, southwest, and southeast, still lacked all-weather connections to this network. Only about 12 percent of the population had ready access to roads. Most roads in the national network were concentrated in the central, eastern, and northern highlands.

During the 1936–41 Italian occupation, road building increased. Mobility helped Italy consolidate its rule over Ethiopia, initiate development projects, and pacify unstable areas. By 1941 there were about 7,000 kilometers of roads, of which about half were surfaced with asphalt. After liberation, road construction and maintenance stagnated because of a lack of funds, equipment, and expertise until 1951, when the government established the Imperial Highway Authority. With the help of World Bank funds and with technical assistance from the United States Bureau of Public Roads, the development of Ethiopia's highway system continued.

The Imperial Highway Authority played a major role in the construction of roads until the revolution. The Derg restructured the Imperial Highway Authority as the Ethiopian Road Authority and the Rural Roads Task Force. The government created the latter to develop rural roads outside the main system and to extend feeder roads within the main system. The World Bank, which had financed four previous highway programs, funded this project. In addition, the African Development Bank and the EC provided assistance for road construction and maintenance. Despite these efforts, Ethiopia's road network remained primitive and quite limited, even by African standards. This shortcoming had tragic consequences during the 1984–85 famine, when the lack of good roads contributed to Ethiopia's inability to distribute food to famine victims. As a result, many thousands of Ethiopians perished. In 1991 completion of an adequate nationwide highway system continued to be one of Ethiopia's major development challenges.

Railroads

Ethiopia's two original rail systems were the Franco-Ethiopian Railroad (FER) and the Akordat-Mitsiwa railroad. A French company, the Compagnie Impériale des Chemins de Fers Ethiopiens, built the FER by authority of Emperor Menelik II. Construction began in 1897 at the port city of Djibouti, and the final link reached Addis Ababa in 1917. In 1959 the Ethiopian government acquired a 50 percent holding in the line.

By the early 1960s, however, Ethiopia had taken steps to reduce its dependence on the FER, which could be disrupted by natural disaster or an attack by antigovernment forces. Nevertheless, Ethiopia suffered economically when sabotage associated with the 1977–78 Ogaden War temporarily closed the FER. As an alternate to the FER, the government expanded the port of Aseb and constructed a highway between Addis Ababa and Aseb. The opening of the Addis Ababa-Aseb highway prompted the FER to improve the railroad to remain competitive. In particular, the FER expanded investment in diesel locomotion, new rolling stock, and track. Despite these efforts, competition between the rail and road systems remained intense. For example, in 1986/87 the FER moved 335,400 tons of freight compared with a high of 375,000 tons in the mid-1960s. One of the major reasons for the decline was attacks on the rail line by rebel groups.

An Italian company completed construction of the Akordat-Mitsiwa line in 1922. The Ethiopian government acquired ownership of the line after World War II. In the mid-1960s, the volume of freight and passenger traffic stagnated. By the early 1970s, the railroad's equipment was old, and the line was in need of track improvements. In the mid-1970s, operation ceased to be viable because of the threat posed by Eritrean guerrillas and the realization that existing road facilities could handle the railroad's traffic. For these reasons, the government closed the line in 1976, and it was partially destroyed in later fighting.

Ports

Ethiopia had two major ports, Aseb and Mitsiwa, on the Red Sea coast. These ports accounted for about 93 percent of Ethiopia's export-import trade. The port of Djibouti, which operated as a free port, handled the remaining 7 percent of Ethiopia's seaborne freight. All three ports handled deep-sea vessels, possessed some mechanized cargo-handling equipment, and offered covered and open storage facilities.

The port of Aseb was connected by road with Addis Ababa. Developed by the imperial government in the late 1950s, Aseb, together with Djibouti, principally served Ethiopia's central and southern areas. In 1988 Aseb handled about 71 percent of the export-import trade. In EFY 1986/87, more than 2.8 million tons of cargo transited Aseb, of which about 66 percent consisted of imports, including about 792,000 tons of crude oil for Aseb's refinery. Although the port of Aseb was not threatened, antigovernment forces repeatedly attacked the Addis Ababa-Aseb highway.

Mitsiwa was connected to Asmera by road and by rail. Until the Eritrean People's Liberation Front (EPLF) captured Mitsiwa in early 1990, the port handled traffic bound mainly for the northern part of the country. Also, the Ethiopian navy had stationed most of its ships at Mitsiwa. In EFY 1986/87, Mitsiwa handled about 470,000 tons of cargo, of which imports made up about 14 percent.

Developments during the 1986–87 drought, when food aid donated to Ethiopia rotted in storage facilities and ships waited for weeks to unload their cargo, demonstrated the inadequacy of the port of Aseb. In 1988 the government announced plans to build a new terminal at Aseb with a US$11 million loan from the European Investment Bank. This multipurpose terminal for general cargo, container ships, and roll-on/roll-off vessels was to consist of a 6,400-square-meter transit shed. The government expected the first berth to be completed in 1991 and the rest of the work to be done by 1992.

In addition to the major ports, there is a limited inland water transportation system. The Baro River is navigable and is used to transport goods to Sudan. Traders also transport local goods on Lake Tana in the northwest and Lake Abaya and Lake Chamo in the south. In EFY 1986/87, about 2,000 tons of cargo transited local waterways. A total of 98 percent of this activity was on Lake Tana.

Air Transport

Distance, terrain, and an underdeveloped road system made air transport an important part of Ethiopia's transportation network. Ethiopian Airlines (EAL), a government-owned corporation that began operations in 1946, provided domestic and international air service. The airline served some forty-five cities and towns in Ethiopia and operated international flights that, in early 1991, included service to twenty-one cities in eighteen African countries; to western European destinations such as London, Paris, Frankfurt, Rome, and Athens; and to India and China. Many international and several regional airlines also provided regular service between Ethiopia and other countries.

International airports were located at Addis Ababa, Asmera, and Dire Dawa. Addis Ababa's Bole International Airport served more than 195,000 passengers in EFY 1986/87, while the Asmera and Dire Dawa airports handled 108,000 and 81,000 passengers, respectively, during the same period. Bole International Airport and the airport at Asmera were capable of handling larger aircraft, such as the Boeing 747.

EAL had an excellent reputation because of its safety record. It was also one of the few profitable African airlines. EAL also had provided training and maintenance services to more than a dozen other African and Middle Eastern airlines. In late 1986, EAL assembled the first agro-aircraft to support the nation's agricultural development and the agro-aviational needs of other African countries. New facilities included an expanded catering network, a gas production plant, and base maintenance shops for ground equipment. EAL also had an ongoing program to automate airline activities such as maintenance and engineering, ticket accounting, and crew and corporate data management.

Although it refrained from interfering in EAL operations, the Mengistu government opposed the airline's plans to expand into areas such as hotel construction and management, tourism, and catering, which the government reserved for state corporations, which operated at a loss. In June 1989, EAL announced plans to spend US$1.2 billion on new aircraft; in early 1991, EAL received Western credits to acquire five new Boeing 757s and to refinance two Boeing 767s.

Telecommunications

Ethiopia's telecommunications system was rudimentary. Broadcast facilities were concentrated in a few cities, and telephones were limited primarily to government offices and businesses in Addis Ababa and regional capitals. Long-distance and international communications to two neighboring countries went via two radio-relay links: a modern 960-channel system that went south from Addis Ababa to Nairobi, and an older, twenty-four-channel system that paralleled the railroad line from Addis Ababa to Djibouti. Other parts of the country were linked by old and unreliable open-wire lines. International service, other than to Kenya and Djibouti, passed through the Atlantic Ocean satellite of the International Telecommunications Satellite Organization (Intelsat) via a ground station just north of the capital. This ground station was capable of providing over 100 simultaneous high-quality telephone, data, and television links with the rest of the world.

In 1989 Ethiopia counted only 109,000 telephones, or two sets per 1,000 inhabitants, one of the lowest per capita figures in the world. Only 84 percent of service was automatic; the rest still used outdated manual systems. Over two-thirds of the telephones were in Addis Ababa or Asmera; the remainder were scattered throughout a few of the larger towns or regional capitals. Most users were either government offices or businesses. International direct dial was available to some users in Addis Ababa. Local or long-distance calling was difficult, however, with frequent busy signals for uncompleted calls.

Broadcast service was also limited. In mid-1991 the country counted four medium-wave AM radio stations, two in Addis Ababa and one each in Asmera and Harer. A shortwave transmitter south of the capital broadcast "Voice of Ethiopia" programming in English, French, Amharic, Arabic, and Somali to surrounding countries. Ten cities had low-power television stations. In mid-1991 the nation had an estimated 9 million radio receivers and 100,000 television sets.

Foreign Trade

Both the imperial and the Marxist governments tried to improve Ethiopia's balance of trade, the former by encouraging exports and the latter by curtailing imports. However, Ethiopia's foreign trade balance has basically been in deficit since 1953, with the exception of 1975, when a combination of unusually large receipts from sales of oilseeds and pulses resulted in a surplus. In general, foreign trade has grown faster than the national economy, particularly in the early 1970s, but it has accounted for only a small percentage of the national economy. In EFY 1972/73, exports and imports accounted for 13 and 12 percent of GDP, respectively. By EFY 1988/89, exports had declined to 8 percent of GDP, and imports had jumped to 21 percent. Virtually all machinery and equipment had to be imported, as well as intermediate goods for agriculture and industry, including fertilizer and fuel. Increased cereal shipments accounted for the growth in imports. In the 1980s, Ethiopia faced several famines and droughts. Consequently, the country, which had been virtually self-sufficient in food supplies in the 1970s, became a net importer of food worth as much as 243 million birr annually during the period EFY 1983/84 to EFY 1987/88. The military government failed to correct the country's historical trade deficit, despite efforts to regulate exports and imports. Consequently, during the 1980s the trade picture worsened as imports grew rapidly and foreign aid slowed.

Exports

Ethiopia's exports in EFY 1988/89 were primarily agricultural products (see table 14, Appendix). The only significant nonagricultural exports were petroleum products such as heating oil, which had no use in Ethiopia, from the Aseb refinery.

The value of exports increased during the 1980s, and by EFY 1988/89 exports had almost twice the value they had in 1973. However, the composition of exports had remained essentially the same, although the relative share of the various agricultural exports had changed. Coffee, the major export, still averaged about

63 percent of the value of exports during the five years ending in EFY 1988/89. The relative share of oilseeds and pulses, however, had changed dramatically. Pulses and oilseeds, which accounted for about 15 percent and 19 percent, respectively, of the total value of exports in EFY 1974/75, dropped to 1.9 and 1.4 percent, respectively, of the total value of exports in EFY 1988/89. Droughts, famines, the peasants' preference for cereals and other staples, and the rising cost of producing pulses and oilseeds accounted for the decline in the export of these two products. Exports of livestock and livestock products averaged 18 percent of the value of exports for the five years ending in EFY 1988/89, which was slightly higher than the prerevolution share of 16 percent.

After the 1974 revolution, exports' relative share of GDP declined, largely because domestic production grew more slowly than total demand. This could be attributed to the agricultural crisis associated with the country's recurring droughts and famines and the dislocation of the farm economy resulting from the revolution. Total domestic production, measured by GDP, grew at an average annual rate of 0.9 percent per year during the 1980–87 period while exports declined at an average annual rate of 0.6 percent. During the same period, the population grew at an average 2.4 percent annual rate. Consequently, Ethiopia's export share of 8 percent of GDP in EFY 1988/89 was one of the world's lowest.

The direction of Ethiopia's post-1974 exports remained essentially the same as in the prerevolution period, despite the government's change of policy and realignment with the Soviet Union and Eastern Europe. About 79 percent of Ethiopia's exports went to Western countries, primarily the United States, the Federal Republic of Germany (West Germany), and Japan. Ethiopia's export trade with the Soviet Union, one of its major allies, was less than 4 percent in the five years ending in 1987; prior to 1974, the Soviet Union had accounted for less than 1 percent of Ethiopia's imports. Beginning in 1979, Addis Ababa sought to encourage exports to the Soviet Union and other socialist countries by encouraging barter and countertrade. Ethiopia used this technique to market products such as spices, natural gums, some pulses, frozen meats, and handicraft items, which are not reliable hard-currency earners. In exchange, Ethiopia usually received consumer goods, industrial machinery, or construction machinery. Although reliable figures on the volume of barter and countertrade were unavailable, it appeared unlikely that the figure exceeded US$50 to US$55 million in any year.

Imports

Ethiopia's major category of import items was consumer goods, which accounted for about one-third of the value of imports during the period EFY 1984/85 to EFY 1988/89. Capital goods, primarily machinery and transportation equipment, accounted for another 39 percent, with fuel, semifinished goods, and durable consumer goods accounting for the other third of the value of imports. A major structural change in Ethiopia's imports was the relative increase in the importation of food items. During the three years ending in EFY 1986/87, cereals and other food items accounted for 22 percent of the total value of imports; in 1974 cereal and food items had accounted for only 4.6 percent. As a result, the share of nondurable consumer items jumped from 16.8 percent in 1974 to 34.2 percent in 1985. It dropped to 24.9 percent in EFY 1986/87.

Imports provided the capital and intermediate goods upon which industry depended. Imports also satisfied most of the country's demand for nonfood consumer goods, such as automobiles, radios, televisions, pharmaceuticals, and textiles. In the five years ending in EFY 1986/87, the relative share of the value of transportation and transportation equipment increased, reflecting the country's increasing demand for trucks and other heavy road vehicles needed to transport food to areas affected by drought and famine.

Most of Ethiopia's imports came from Western countries. Italy, the United States, West Germany, and Japan, in order of importance, accounted for 45 percent of total imports in 1987. The Soviet Union accounted for 16 percent of the value of imports in 1987. By contrast, Ethiopia's exports to the Soviet Union amounted to only 5 percent of total exports in 1987. The relatively high proportion of imports from the Soviet Union was largely because of oil; in 1987 Ethiopia received virtually all its crude petroleum from the Soviet Union. In 1987 the United States remained Ethiopia's major trading partner despite cool relationships between the two countries; the United States ranked first in buying Ethiopia's exports and third in satisfying Ethiopia's import needs.

Balance of Payments and Foreign Assistance

Ethiopia has experienced chronic balance of payments difficulties since 1953, with the exception of a few years. The major factor in the deteriorating balance of payments was the worsening situation of merchandise trade. The trade deficit that existed during the imperial years continued to grow after the revolution, despite the introduction of import controls. Since EFY 1981/82, the value of merchandise imports has been roughly double the value of exports (see table 15, Appendix).

Since 1974 there has been low growth in the overall volume and value of exports. Coffee, Ethiopia's principal export, accounted for about 60 percent of total merchandise exports, although this level fluctuated in the 1980s. Coffee exports reached an all-time high of 98,000 tons in EFY 1983/84 but dropped to 73,000 tons in EFY 1987/88. Similarly, coffee receipts declined as the world price of coffee plummeted. The share of noncoffee exports has not shown any significant change. Exports of oilseeds and pulses have declined since imperial times. Industrial exports consistently contributed only about 8 percent of the total value of merchandise exports. In contrast to the slow increase in the volume and value of exports, imports grew by nearly 7 percent during the decade ending in EFY 1988/89. This trend reflected Ethiopia's growing dependence on imports and the decline of foreign-financed investment and domestic savings. A high growth rate in import prices accompanied the high growth rate in imports. The result of these deteriorating terms of trade was a severe trade balance problem.

To finance its trade deficit, the government has depended on foreign aid. These import finance funds were in addition to the large volume of development project aid and commodity assistance the international community has provided to Ethiopia since the end of World War II. The volume of official development assistance jumped from US$134 million in 1975 to US$212 million in 1980 and to US$635 million in 1987. Most external financial assistance came from Western nations. By the late 1980s, Ethiopia was the principal African recipient of concessionary funding and the largest recipient of EC aid. In 1988 Ethiopia received US$141 million from the EC under the provisions of the Lomé Convention (see Glossary). An additional US$230 million was later allocated under the Lomé Convention. Bilateral assistance, mainly from European countries, also increased in the late 1980s. World Bank lending for various projects covering agriculture, education, housing, road construction, and power development reached US$400 to US$500 million by 1988. Despite this aid, however, Ethiopia still received the smallest amount of aid per capita of all developing countries. The 1987 per capita aid level was US$14, compared with a US$23 group average for all developing countries.

Reliance on foreign aid has created economic problems for Addis Ababa. In 1987 Ethiopia's total external debt amounted to US$2.6 billion, of which US$2.4 billion was long-term debt (excluding military debt). Addis Ababa owed more than one-third of the total to multinational agencies and the remainder to bilateral creditors. Economists estimated the EFY 1986/87 cost of servicing this long-term debt to be 28.4 percent of export earnings and projected the figure to rise to 40 percent of export earnings by 1990.

Economic Prospects

Under the imperial regime, economic progress was sluggish. The country's agricultural and industrial performance was poor. Efforts by the emperor to bring Ethiopia into the twentieth century enjoyed some success in limited areas, such as the emergence of Ethiopian Airlines; however, on the whole, imperial Ethiopia's economic policies must be judged a failure. As a result, many Ethiopians supported the 1974 revolution in hopes that it would improve their standard of living.

Between 1974 and 1975, Ethiopia's Marxist government carried out a wide range of political, economic, and social reforms. Unfortunately, these reforms promised more than they delivered. Gradually, the country's economy deteriorated. By 1990–91 Ethiopia's economy was in a steep decline, from which recovery will be difficult. During the last year of the military government, GDP declined by 5 percent in real terms, and inflation soared. Defense expenditures accounted for 40 to 60 percent of the national budget. Merchandise exports fell to their lowest level since 1974, and a collapse in international coffee prices (during the 1979–89 period, coffee accounted for an average of 55 percent of total exports) reduced foreign-exchange reserves to an all-time low. More important, insurgencies had spread to new areas of central and northern Ethiopia; recurring cycles of drought and famine again threatened millions of Ethiopians; and ill-conceived Marxist economic policies further eroded the country's economic performance. As a result of these and numerous other problems, the World Bank classified Ethiopia as the world's poorest country. Mengistu's early 1990 adoption of a new economic policy failed to reinvigorate Ethiopia's ailing economy. Without massive and genuine political, economic, and social reforms, it appeared unlikely that Ethiopia could harness its resources and improve the lives of its citizens anytime soon.

*   *   *

Much of the literature about Ethiopia's economy examines land tenure and land reform. Some of the more useful works about the imperial era include John Markakis's *Ethiopia: Anatomy of a Traditional Polity* and John M. Cohen and Dov Weintraub's *Land and Peasants in Imperial Ethiopia*. A considerable amount of literature deals with land reform in the post-1974 period. Essential studies include Dessalegn Rahmato's *Agrarian Reform in Ethiopia,* Haile Yesus Abegaz's *The Organization of State Farms in Ethiopia after the Land Reform of 1975,* Keith Griffin and Roger Hay's "Problems of Agricultural Development in Socialist Ethiopia," and Ajit Kumar Ghose's "Transforming Feudal Agriculture." Kidane Mengisteab's *Ethiopia: Failure of Land Reform and Agricultural Crisis* analyzes the relationship between inadequate land reform policies and recurring famines during the imperial and revolutionary periods. Marina Ottaway's *The Political Economy of Ethiopia* includes chapters that offer a critical analysis of Ethiopia's economic crisis.

For general statistical materials, the best sources are the annual *Ethiopia: Statistical Abstract* published by the Ethiopian government's Central Statistical Authority and the *Annual Report* of the National Bank of Ethiopia. The most up-to-date data are available in the bank's *Quarterly Bulletin.* The *Country Reports* published quarterly and the *Country Profiles* published annually by the Economist Intelligence Unit also contain a great deal of useful economic information. (For further information and complete citations, see Bibliography.)

Chapter 4. Government and Politics

Main gate of Jubilee Palace, Addis Ababa

THE FINAL CONGRESS of Ethiopia's Provisional Military Administrative Council marked a watershed in modern Ethiopian history. The congress, held in the capital city of Addis Ababa, was the prelude to the inauguration, in 1987, of the People's Democratic Republic of Ethiopia, which would be guided by a vanguard Marxist-Leninist party and regime. At least nominally, thirteen years of rule by the military regime were at an end. When the Provisional Military Administrative Council had assumed power in 1974, there were no clear signs that it was committed to a Marxist-Leninist model of social transformation; neither was there any indication that it was sincere about its pledge to return Ethiopia to civilian rule. In fact, within months of seizing power, the new regime began systematically to buttress the already preeminent role of the military as the vanguard of the revolution.

Until its collapse in 1974, the Ethiopian imperial state had attempted to construct an absolutist but modernizing autocracy, a regime committed to preserving tradition while carefully guiding society into the twentieth century. Emperor Haile Selassie I, who ruled the country from 1930 to 1974, portrayed himself as a strong but compassionate leader, a model for all African statesmen. However, at a very fundamental level, the imperial state constructed by Haile Selassie was tenuously held together by a top-heavy, secularized bureaucracy and an imperial myth. Once the myth that the emperor was unassailable had been broken, the new regime began the process of reconstituting state institutions. This process was slow but methodical, and by 1989 the fruits of this institutional transformation were definitely in evidence.

The tasks of social, political, and economic reconstruction facing the new regime in 1974 were formidable. To meet these challenges, the regime attempted to fashion a new ideological foundation for society. The Provisional Military Administrative Council favored a Marxist-Leninist development model because of the organizational power it promised. The approach taken was statist and based on the principles of scientific socialism as interpreted in the Soviet Union from the time of Joseph Stalin to that of Leonid Brezhnev. At an operational level, this choice required the state's reorganization and reconstitution, the redistribution of wealth and property, the creation of a capacity for central planning, the pursuit of a state socialist development strategy under the guidance of a vanguard party of "revolutionary democrats," and the establishment of a constitutionally based "people's republic."

Ethiopia's turn toward Marxism-Leninism first became evident in early 1976 with the enunciation of the Program for the National Democratic Revolution. This document, which reflected the views of those regime members who espoused Marxism-Leninism long before they seized power, committed the regime to a noncapitalist approach to development based on the principles of scientific socialism. For the next decade, the ruling group used ideology and new socialist institutions to implement and legitimize its policies. Even when particular economic strategies were chosen, the regime seemed to be motivated by political objectives rather than driven by ideological zeal. Chief among the objectives were establishing the regime's political control and securing popular legitimacy.

By 1989 it was evident that the government had failed to consolidate its rule. Natural catastrophes such as drought and famine had taken a heavy toll. Furthermore, the regime not only was unable to control the general population, but also dozens of top-ranking officials had defected to the West, where they bitterly denounced the government. With military morale at its lowest point since 1974, disaffected senior officers attempted a coup d'état in May 1989. In addition, numerous opposition groups waged military campaigns against the government. Most notable among these were the Eritrean People's Liberation Front and the Tigray People's Liberation Front, the latter operating with several other antigovernment groups in an umbrella organization known as the Ethiopian People's Revolutionary Democratic Front. By early 1991, these groups controlled large stretches of territory in north-central Ethiopia and were poised to seize even more.

Moreover, by this time the Soviet Union, in the spirit of Mikhail Gorbachev's *glasnost* (openness), had abandoned its uncritical support of Ethiopia's revolution. The winds of democracy that were sweeping across much of the communist world also meant that Ethiopia could no longer rely on its Soviet and East European allies for military and economic assistance. These developments forced the government to reconsider its efforts to deal with its opponents through military rather than political means. However, by early 1991 the government had failed to reach a negotiated settlement with the Eritrean People's Liberation Front and the Ethiopian People's Revolutionary Democratic Front. Thereafter, both groups launched renewed attacks that by late May brought the insurgents to power. The leaders of both insurgencies disavowed the state socialism of the military government and pledged themselves to democratic principles and free-market economics. Eritrea was also expected to become an independent country.

The Workers' Party of Ethiopia

Toward Party Formation

As early as 1976, the Soviet Union had encouraged Addis Ababa's new leaders to create a civilian-based vanguard party. The Ethiopian head of state and leader of the Provisional Military Administrative Council (PMAC; also known as the Derg—see Glossary), Lieutenant Colonel Mengistu Haile Mariam, initially had resisted, arguing that the revolution had taken place without such a party and that there was no need for haste in creating one. However, in the late 1970s, in the wake of the regime's near collapse under the weight of armed opposition to its rule, Mengistu believed the creation of a vanguard party would accomplish the regime's goals of gaining political control over the general population and of securing popular legitimacy. Therefore, in December 1979 Mengistu announced the creation of the Commission to Organize the Party of the Workers of Ethiopia (COPWE).

The establishment of mass organizations, such as the All-Ethiopia Trade Union, the All-Ethiopia Urban Dwellers' Association, and the All-Ethiopia Peasants' Association, preceded the creation of COPWE. The Revolutionary Ethiopia Youth Association, the Revolutionary Ethiopia Women's Association, the Working People's Control Committees, and various professional associations were instituted after COPWE's establishment. The idea behind the proliferation of mass organizations was to create a party that would neutralize "narrow nationalism," or sectarianism, and that would be based on broad, yet clearly defined, class interests. In response to the fiasco that resulted from efforts to create a union of Marxist-Leninist organizations in the mid-1970s, the Derg determined that the party should be one of individuals, not of political organizations. To the extent that individual interests were represented, this was to be done through mass organizations.

Mass organizations not only represented their membership at party congresses but also guarded their interests on an everyday basis. The mass organizations had educational and developmental roles. The basic units of political consciousness and involvement, then, would be party cells at work sites or in mass organizations. Individuals could belong to more than one mass organization at a time.

In determining COPWE membership, the regime tried to give the impression that a broadly representative organization had been created. Between 1,200 and 1,500 delegates from all regions and all walks of life attended the three congresses. However, the diversity of the delegates was questionable. For example, at COPWE's first congress, in 1980, more than a third of the delegates were members of the armed forces or residents of the Addis Ababa area.

The first congress unveiled the membership of the COPWE Central Committee and the Secretariat. The Secretariat, which was supervised by the top Derg leadership, consisted mainly of civilian ideologues. The Secretariat was responsible for the day-to-day administration of Central Committee business. Regional branches under the direction of military officers in each region complemented COPWE's central leadership. However, the positions of chief regional administrator and COPWE representative were divided in late 1981, with the party posts assuming greater importance. Within a year of the first congress, it was clear that COPWE was being transformed into a party that could be used by the state as an instrument of control.

By mid-1983 the COPWE bureaucracy stretched from the national center to the fourteen regions and thence to the subregional level, to peasant associations and urban dwellers' associations (*kebeles*—see Glossary), and on down to the party cell level. At that time, there were an estimated 6,500 COPWE party cells, with a total membership estimated at 30,000 to 50,000.

Party membership, however, was not open to all. The main criterion for acceptability was loyalty to the regime rather than ideological sophistication. Although Mengistu had stressed the need for ideological purity and for only a few "committed communists," concern over ideological purity appeared to be a facade for the Derg's efforts to neutralize or preempt its opponents and thus establish the party's exclusive role in defining the normative order.

Once COPWE was in place, the Derg projected itself into the most important sectors of the central bureaucracy. Derg members served as the administrators of twelve of the fourteen regions. An additional thirty Derg members took up influential posts in subregional administration and in central ministries. After 1978 the presence of military personnel in the bureaucracy expanded so greatly that not only members of the Derg but also other trusted military men served in such roles.

The organizational model followed by COPWE was Soviet inspired. Even though there was tension between self-styled communists and nationalists in the Derg, there was an understanding that their collective position as a ruling group was unassailable. This could be seen in the distribution of power within COPWE. The most important policy-making bodies in COPWE were the

Executive Committee, whose seven members all came from the Derg, and the Central Committee, which consisted of ninety-three full members and thirty alternates. Of the 123 members of the Central Committee, seventy-nine were military men or police officers. There were at least twenty Derg members in this group, and others held important regional posts in the bureaucracy as well as in COPWE. At the time of COPWE's demise, military personnel represented more than 50 percent of the congress that established the vanguard party.

The Vanguard Party

The government announced the formation of the Workers' Party of Ethiopia (WPE) on September 12, 1984, the tenth anniversary of the revolution. Regional and local COPWE branches were transformed into WPE instruments, and it was announced that party congresses would be held at five-year intervals. These congresses would be responsible for electing the party Central Committee, a body of 183 members as of 1987. The Central Committee normally met twice a year. Among its duties was the election of the WPE's Political Bureau, the general secretary, and members of the WPE Secretariat. However, the Central Committee was too large and diverse to serve as an effective decision-making body. Although in the late 1980s more than half of the Central Committee's full members were former police or former military personnel, the Central Committee also included peasants, workers, trade union members, and representatives of various mass organizations.

The WPE Political Bureau had eleven full members and six alternate members. The Derg's Standing Committee and the COPWE Executive Committee had comprised the Derg's seven most influential members. The additional four members appointed to the WPE were two civilian ideologues and two career technocrats, who in the years leading up to the WPE's inauguration had become responsible for the day-to-day direction of party matters and who evidently had Mengistu's confidence.

The WPE's Political Bureau was the country's most important decision-making body. Although the Political Bureau's decisions were always made in secret, there was evidence that General Secretary Mengistu's wishes generally prevailed, no matter what the opposition. One observer suggested that whatever power or influence other Political Bureau members exerted was owed more to their closeness to Mengistu than to any formal positions they might occupy or to their personal qualities. The Political Bureau, therefore, was little more than a forum for the articulation of policies already determined personally by Mengistu.

The paramount position of the WPE was enshrined in the 1987 constitution, which stated that the party should be ''the formulator of the country's development process and the leading force of the state and in society.'' Indeed, the WPE had become more important than the central government in determining the direction of national and local policies. Local party leaders sometimes possessed a great deal of latitude in determining approaches to policy in their regions as long as their decisions did not conflict with objectives determined in Addis Ababa. At the national level, highly politicized party representatives often exercised greater influence than the Western-trained bureaucrats in government ministries. It appeared that the government bureaucracy had to follow the lead of the party and often found its policies and procedures overridden by political decisions.

At the national level, individuals from the military, the government bureaucracy, and those ethnic groups (especially Amhara and Tigray) that had historically endorsed the notion of a unitary, ''Greater Ethiopia'' dominated the WPE. However, below the level of the regional first secretary of the WPE, the military and ethnic origins of party leadership became less important.

The 1987 Constitution

The primary task facing the WPE following its formation in 1984 was to devise the new national constitution that would inaugurate the People's Democratic Republic of Ethiopia (PDRE). In March 1986, a 343-member Constitutional Commission was formed to draft a new constitution based on the principles of scientific socialism. Eventually, the 122 full and alternate members of the WPE Central Committee who had been appointed to its membership dominated the commission.

The Constitutional Commission had its origins in the Institute for the Study of Ethiopian Nationalities, which the Derg had established in March 1983 to find solutions to problems resulting from Ethiopia's extreme ethnic diversity. The institute was staffed mostly by academics from Addis Ababa University, who continued to serve as advisers to the Constitutional Commission. The commission's diverse membership included religious leaders, artists, writers, doctors, academics, athletes, workers, and former nobility. There was also an attempt by those who chose appointees to the commission to make sure that all major ethnic nationalities had representation in the body.

For about six months, the commission debated the details of the new constitution. In June 1986, it issued a 120-article draft document. The government printed and distributed 1 million copies

City Hall, Addis Ababa
Courtesy Thomas Ofcansky

to *kebeles* and peasant associations throughout the country. During the next two months, the draft was discussed at about 25,000 locations. The regime used this method of discussion to legitimize the constitution-making process and to test the mood of the populace. In some cases, people attended constitutional discussion sessions only after pressure from local WPE cadres, but in other cases attendance was voluntary. Where popular interest was apparent, it centered on issues such as taxes, the role of religion, marriage, the organization of elections, and citizenship rights and obligations. By far the most controversial draft provision was the one that outlawed polygamy, which caused a furor among Muslims. Few questions were raised about the document's failure to address the nationalities problem and the right to self-determination. According to government officials, the citizenry submitted more than 500,000 suggested revisions. In August the commission reconvened to consider proposed amendments. In all, the commission accepted ninety-five amendments to the original draft. Most of the changes, however, were cosmetic.

The referendum on the constitution was held on February 1, 1987, and Mengistu announced the results three weeks later. He reported that 96 percent of the 14 million people eligible to participate (adults eighteen years of age and older) actually voted. Eighty-one percent of the electorate endorsed the constitution, while 18 percent opposed it (1 percent of the ballots were invalid). Although this was the first election in Ethiopia's history based on universal suffrage, the presence of communist cadres throughout the country ensured that the constitution would be adopted. In Tigray and Eritrea, however, the regime held referenda only in urban centers because much of these territories was controlled by the Tigray People's Liberation Front and the Eritrean People's Liberation Front, respectively (see Political Dynamics, this ch.). In other places, such as parts of Welo and Gonder regions, the vote took place amid heightened security measures.

The constitution officially took effect on February 22, 1987, when the People's Democratic Republic of Ethiopia was proclaimed, although it was not until September that the new government was fully in place and the PMAC formally abolished (see The People's Democratic Republic of Ethiopia, ch. 1). The document, which established the normative foundations of the republic, consisted of seventeen chapters and 119 articles. The preamble traced Ethiopia's origins back to antiquity, proclaimed the historical heroism of its people, praised the country's substantial natural and human resources, and pledged to continue the struggle against imperialism, poverty, and hunger. The government's primary concern was proclaimed to be the country's development through the implementation of the Program for the National Democratic Revolution (PNDR). In the process, it was assumed that the material and technical bases necessary for establishing socialism would be created.

The constitution attempted to situate Ethiopia in the context of the worldwide movement of so-called "progressive states" and made no direct reference to Africa. Critics claim that the constitution was no more than an abridged version of the 1977 Soviet constitution, with the exception that strong powers were assigned to the newly created office of the president. A second difference between the Ethiopian and Soviet constitutions is that the former declared the country to be a unitary state rather than a union of republics. It was reported that the problem of nationalities was hotly debated in the Constitutional Commission, as well as in the WPE Central Committee, but the regime would not abandon its desire to create a single multiethnic state rather than a federation.

The Social Order

Chapter 1 of the constitution defined Ethiopia's social order. The People's Democratic Republic of Ethiopia (PDRE) was declared to be "a state of working peasants in which the intelligentsia, the revolutionary army, artisans, and other democratic sections of society participate.'' The commitment to socialist construction was reaffirmed, as was the idea of egalitarianism within the context of a unitary state. The official language remained Amharic. The functioning and organization of the country was proclaimed to be based on the principles of democratic centralism, under which representative party and state organs are elected by lower bodies. The vanguard character of the WPE was asserted, and its roles as well as those of mass organizations were spelled out.

Chapter 2 dealt with the country's economic system. The state was dedicated to the creation of a "highly interdependent and integrated national economy" and to the establishment of conditions favorable to development. In addition, the constitution committed the state to central planning; state ownership of the means of production, distribution, and exchange; and expansion of cooperative ownership among the general population.

Chapter 3 addressed social issues, ranging from education and the family to historical preservation and cultural heritage. The family was described as the basis of society and therefore deserving of special attention by means of the joint efforts of state and society. In addition, the constitution pledged that health insurance and other social services would be expanded through state leadership.

National defense was the subject of Chapter 4. The first article asserted the nation's need to defend its sovereignty and territorial integrity and to safeguard the accomplishments of the revolution. It was declared that the Ethiopian people had a historical responsibility to defend the country. The defense force was to be the army of the country's working people. The army's fundamental role would be to secure peace and socialism.

Foreign policy objectives were spelled out in four brief articles in Chapter 5 and were based on the principles of proletarian internationalism, peaceful coexistence, and nonalignment. In many respects, the language of this section resembled that of a constitution of a Warsaw Pact country in the days before *glasnost*.

Citizenship, Freedoms, Rights, and Duties

Chapters 6 and 7 were concerned with defining citizenship and spelling out the freedoms, rights, and duties of citizens. The language was egalitarian, and Ethiopians were declared to be equal before the law, regardless of nationality, sex, religion, occupation, and social or other status. They had the right to marry, to work, to rest, to receive free education, and to have access to health care and to a fair trial. Ethiopians were guaranteed freedom of conscience and religion. As was not the case in imperial Ethiopia, religion and the state were proclaimed to be separate institutions. Citizens were assured the freedoms of movement, speech, press, assembly, peaceful demonstration, and association. Regarding political participation, citizens had the right to vote and the right to be elected to political office. Their duties included national military service, protection of socialist state property, protection of the environment, and observance of the constitution and laws of the country.

In spite of the attention the constitution paid to basic freedoms, until the last days of the regime international human rights organizations were virtually unanimous in condemning the Mengistu regime. Summary execution, political detention, torture, and forced migration represented only some of the violations cited by these groups (see Human Rights, ch. 5).

National Shengo (National Assembly)

The constitution's most detailed sections related to the central government's organization and activities. In these sections, the document described the various state organs and explained their relationship to one another.

The supreme organ of state power was the National Shengo (National Assembly). Its responsibilities included amending the constitution; determining foreign, defense, and security policy; establishing the boundaries, status, and accountability of administrative regions; and approving economic plans. The National Shengo was also responsible for establishing the Council of State; the Council of Ministers, ministries, state committees, commissions, and state authorities; the Supreme Court; the Office of the Prosecutor General; the National Workers' Control Committee; and the Office of the Auditor General. In addition, the National Shengo elected the president and officials of the Council of State and approved the appointment of other high-ranking authorities.

Candidates to the National Shengo had to be nominated by regional branches of the WPE, mass organizations, military units, and other associations recognized by law. Balloting for seats in the National Shengo was required to be secret, and all individuals eighteen years of age and above were eligible to vote. Elected members served five-year terms, and the body met in regular session once each year. These sessions were usually public but might on occasion be held *in camera*. In 1987 the National Shengo had 835 members.

Council of State

The Council of State, consisting of the president of the republic, several vice presidents, a secretary, and other members, was an organ of the National Shengo. The Council of State served as the most active oversight arm of the government, and it exercised the national legislative role when the National Shengo was not in session. In addition to its normal functions, the Council of State was empowered to establish a defense council and might be assigned special duties by the National Shengo (see Command and Force Structure, ch. 5). The Council of State had the further authority to issue decrees in the pursuit of the duties stipulated by law or assigned by the National Shengo. The power of this organ was evident in the constitutional provision that stated, "When compelling circumstances warrant it, the Council of State may, between sessions of the National Shengo, proclaim a state of emergency, war, martial law, mobilization or peace."

The President

The 1987 constitution established the office of president. Theoretically, the Council of State ruled along with the president and exercised legislative oversight in relation to other branches of government. In reality, however, the office of the president in particular and the executive branch in general were the most powerful branches of government. The president was able to act with considerable independence from the National Shengo.

Although the constitution stipulated that the president was accountable to the National Shengo, Mengistu demonstrated repeatedly that there was no authority higher than his own office. By law he was responsible for presenting members of his executive staff and the Supreme Court to the National Shengo for election. At the same time, the president, "when compelling circumstances warrant it" between sessions of the National Shengo, could appoint or relieve the prime minister, the deputy prime minister, and other members of the Council of Ministers; the president, the vice president, and Supreme Court judges; the prosecutor general; the chairman of the National Workers' Control Committee; and the auditor general. The National Shengo was by law supposed to act on such decrees in its next regular session, but this appeared to be only pro forma.

The president, who could be elected to an indefinite number of successive five-year terms, had to submit nominations for appointment to the Council of Ministers (his cabinet) to the National Shengo for approval. However, by the time nominations reached the National Shengo for consideration, their appointment was a foregone conclusion. In practice, President Mengistu would chose individuals for particular offices without any apparent input from the National Shengo, the WPE, or the Council of State.

The president, who was also commander in chief of the armed forces, was also responsible for implementing foreign and domestic policy, concluding international treaties, and establishing diplomatic missions. If he deemed it necessary, the president could rule by decree.

Council of Ministers

The Council of Ministers, defined in the constitution as "the Government," was the government's highest executive and administrative organ. The body consisted of the prime minister, the deputy prime minister, the ministers, and other members as determined by law. Members were accountable to the National Shengo, but between sessions they were accountable to the president and the Council of State. Members of this council were chosen from regularly elected members of the National Shengo and served five-year terms, unless they resigned or were removed by the president. For example, in early November 1989 Prime Minister Fikre-Selassie Wogderes resigned his office, allegedly for health reasons. However, some reports maintained that he was forced out by Mengistu because of his apparent loss of enthusiasm for the regime's policies. At the same time, Mengistu reshuffled his cabinet. Significantly, these events occurred weeks after the annual session of the National Shengo had concluded.

The Council of Ministers was responsible for the implementation of laws and regulations and for the normal administrative functions of national government. It prepared social and economic development plans, the annual budget, and proposals concerning foreign relations. In their respective areas of responsibility, members of the Council of Ministers were the direct representatives of the president and the government; and because they typically held parallel offices within the WPE, as a group they tended to be the most significant political actors in the government.

In 1991 there were twenty-one ministries. Portfolios consisted of the Ministry in Charge of the General Plan and the ministries of agriculture; coffee and tea development; communications and transport; construction; culture and sports affairs; domestic trade; education and fine arts; finance; foreign affairs; foreign trade; health; industry; information; internal affairs; labor and social affairs; law and justice; mines, energy, and water resources; national defense; state farms; and urban development and housing. In addition to these ministries, there were several other important state authorities, such as the Office of the National Council for Central Planning, the Institute for the Study of Ethiopian Nationalities, the Relief and Rehabilitation Commission, and the National Bank of Ethiopia.

Judicial System

The constitution provided for Ethiopia's first independent judiciary. Traditionally, the Supreme Court and various lower courts were the responsibility of the Ministry of Law and Justice. After Haile Selassie's overthrow, much of the formal structure of the existing judicial structure remained intact. Over the years, regional and district level courts were reformed somewhat. However, the new constitutional provisions had the potential to change Ethiopia's national judicial system significantly.

The constitution stipulated that judicial authority was vested in "one Supreme Court, courts of administrative and autonomous regions, and other courts established by law." Supreme Court judges were elected by the National Shengo; those who served at the regional level were elected by regional *shengos* (assemblies). In each case, the judges served terms concurrent with that of the *shengo* that elected them. The Supreme Court and higher courts at the regional level were independent of the Ministry of Law and Justice, but judges could be recalled by the relevant *shengo*.

The Supreme Court was responsible for administering the national judicial system. The court's powers were expanded to oversee all judicial aspects of lesser courts, not just cases appealed to it. At the request of the prosecutor general or the president of the Supreme Court, the Supreme Court could review any case from another court. Noteworthy is the fact that, in addition to separate civil and criminal sections, the court had a military section. In the late 1980s, it was thought that this development might bring the military justice system, which had been independent, into the normal judicial system. However, it became evident that it would be some time before the Supreme Court could begin to serve this function adequately.

Between 1987 and 1989, the government undertook a restructuring of the Supreme Court with the intent of improving the supervision of judges and of making the administration of justice fairer and more efficient. The Supreme Court Council was responsible for overseeing the court's work relating to the registration and training of judges and lawyers. The Supreme Court Council's first annual meeting was held in August 1988, at which time it passed rules of procedure and rules and regulations for judges. Although the government reported that the courts were becoming more efficient, it admitted that there was much to be done before the heavy case burden of the courts could be relieved.

221

Chapter 15 of the constitution established the Office of the Prosecutor General, which was responsible for ensuring the uniform application and enforcement of law by all state organs, mass organizations, and other bodies. The prosecutor general was elected by the National Shengo for a five-year term and was responsible for appointing and supervising prosecutors at all levels. In carrying out their responsibilities, these officials were independent of local government offices.

Local tribunals, such as *kebele* tribunals and peasant association tribunals, were not affected by the 1987 constitution. People's courts were originally established under the jurisdiction of peasant associations and *kebeles*. All matters relating to land redistribution and expropriation were removed from the jurisdiction of the Ministry of Law and Justice and placed under the jurisdiction of the peasant association tribunals, whose members were elected by association members. In addition, such tribunals had jurisdiction over a number of minor criminal offenses, including intimidation, violation of the privacy of domicile, and infractions of peasant association regulations. The tribunals also had jurisdiction in disputes involving small sums of money and in conflicts between peasant associations, their members, and other associations. Appeals from people's tribunals could be filed with regional courts. *Kebele* tribunals had powers similar to those of their counterparts in peasant associations.

Regional and Local Government

Regional Administration

When it assumed power in 1974, the Derg only slightly reordered the imperial regime's pattern of administrative organization at the national level. By contrast, the new regime saw existing local administration as anathema to the objectives of socialist construction, and its reform efforts were initially more evident on the local level than in the central bureaucracy.

Immediately after assuming power, the Derg reorganized Ethiopia's fourteen provincial administrations and replaced all serving governors general. The fourteen provinces (*teklay ghizats*) were relabeled regions (*kifle hagers*) and were divided into 102 subregions (*awrajas*) and 556 districts (*weredas*). (By 1981 the number of administrative divisions had increased to sixteen with the addition of Addis Ababa and Aseb.) The restructuring was a major step toward dismantling feudal privilege. Moreover, all new appointees were either military men or university-educated individuals who were considered progressives.

The main charge of these new administrators initially was to promote development, and the maintenance of law and order was considered only of secondary importance. Despite the commitment to rural development and to the staffing of regional administrative positions with young, dynamic, educated people, not much could be done to accelerate the process of change. Field bureaucrats had few resources to work with, their staffs were small, and their budgets were committed almost exclusively to salaries. By the mid-1980s, the relief and rehabilitation contributions of foreign private voluntary organizations in some cases made more resources available at the local level than did the regional administrations.

After having concentrated on a gradual transformation of the state's administrative structure, with the promulgation of the 1987 constitution the Mengistu regime prepared for a further reorganization of regional administration. Hence, at its inaugural session, the National Shengo enacted a government plan for the administrative reorganization of regional government. As a result, twenty-five administrative regions and five autonomous regions were created (see fig. 1; fig. 2). The autonomous regions consisted of Eritrea (broken further into three subregions in the north, west, and south), Aseb, Tigray, Dire Dawa, and Ogaden. The change promised to alter significantly Ethiopia's traditional pattern of administrative organization.

If the plan were to be fully implemented, this reorganization would have required a dramatic expansion in the government and party bureaucracy. Relatively new institutions, like regional planning bodies, would have been eliminated and replaced with new planning agencies in the various regions. Some observers suggested that this plan was initially endorsed to pursue a Soviet-style approach to the nationalities problem. They argued that the regime was trying to organize regional administration along ethnic lines. Consequently, this reform had little positive effect on enhancing the regime's legitimacy and in fact limited its control over the general population.

The primary organs of state power at the regional level were regional *shengos*. These bodies were responsible mainly for implementing the central government's laws and decisions. Regional *shengos* could draft their own budgets and development plans, but these had to be approved by the National Shengo. Regional *shengos* also possessed some latitude in devising and enforcing local laws and regulations and in electing local judges. By the summer of 1989, however, regional *shengos* had been elected in only eleven of the twenty-five newly designated administrative regions and in only three of the five regions designated as "autonomous."

Peasant Associations

During its thirteen-year existence (1974 to 1987), the Derg worked to spread administrative reform down to the lowest echelons

223

of regional administration. To this end, it took several important steps in 1975.

With its Land Reform Proclamation in March 1975, the Derg abolished the lowest level of rural administration, the *balabat* (see Glossary), and called for the formation of peasant associations that would be responsible for the implementation and enforcement of the land reform measures. Later in the year, the Derg issued Proclamation No. 71, which gave peasant associations legal status and authorized them to create "conditions facilitating the complete destruction of the feudal order." It also empowered the associations' executive committees to draft internal regulations that would, in theory, devolve more power to local communities. These associations were to be guided initially by students in the Development Through Cooperation Campaign (commonly referred to as *zemecha*—see Glossary), who were expected to teach peasants about the revolution's goals. Students were also supposed to help local communities plan and implement development programs in their areas.

Initially, it was not clear how much power, authority, or autonomy the regime intended to devolve to local institutions. Consequently, state agents often came into conflict with local organizations under the guidance of students who were often more radical and politically astute than government functionaries. By 1976, to bring local communities under tighter central control, the Derg introduced laws spelling out the rights and obligations of peasant associations and *kebeles*.

To the extent that peasant associations maintained some of their initial autonomy, they did so almost exclusively with regard to local issues. On national issues, the regime, through the party and other agencies, manipulated peasant associations to suit its purposes. After 1978, for example, production cadres and political cadres of the National Revolutionary Development Campaign (and later the WPE) played important roles in motivating peasant production and in political indoctrination. State control of local associations was also a natural by-product of the villagization and resettlement programs of the mid- to late 1980s (see The Politics of Development, this ch.; Government Rural Programs, ch. 3).

By 1990 there were more than 20,000 peasant associations throughout the country. They represented the lowest level of government administration and, in collaboration with the local WPE office, were responsible for processing and interpreting national policies, maintaining law and order, and planning and implementing certain local development policies. State control grew further in 1975 when the Derg promoted the formation of the All-Ethiopia Peasants'

*"Cash for Work" project sponsored by United Nations Children's Fund
and Ethiopian government*
Courtesy United Nations Children's Fund (Bert Demmers)
Peasant association meeting
Courtesy Food and Agriculture Organization of the United Nations (F. Botts)

Association (AEPA), a national association having district offices responsible for overseeing the activities of local associations. Before the WPE's formation, AEPA district representatives exercised supervisory powers over the associations under their jurisdiction. The management of elections, investigations into allegations of mismanagement, changes to association boundaries, and organization of political meetings all came under the purview of the AEPA district representative. However, by 1989 WPE cadres were active in monitoring and providing guidance to local peasant associations.

Kebeles

In July 1975, the Derg issued Proclamation No. 47, which established *kebeles,* or urban dwellers' associations, in Addis Ababa and five other urban centers. Organized similarly to peasant associations, Addis Ababa's 291 *kebeles* possessed neighborhood constituencies ranging from 3,000 to 12,000 residents each. Like the peasant associations in the countryside, the *kebeles* were initially responsible only for the collection of rent, the establishment of local judicial tribunals, and the provision of basic health, education, and other social services in their neighborhoods. *Kebele* powers were expanded in late 1976 to include the collection of local taxes and the registration of houses, residents, births, deaths, and marriages.

During the height of the Red Terror (see Glossary), *kebeles* were responsible for ensuring neighborhood defense. Neighborhood defense squads patrolled their communities day and night and sometimes operated outside the control of the central authorities. Many brutal excesses were attributed to *kebele* defense squads between 1976 and 1978, but they were more closely monitored thereafter (see Political Struggles Within the Government, ch. 1; People's Protection Brigades, ch. 5).

In April 1981, the Derg issued Proclamation No. 25, which provided *kebeles* with extended powers and a more elaborate administrative structure. According to this new structure, the general assembly, composed of all *kebele* residents, was empowered to elect a policy committee, which in turn was authorized to appoint the executive committee, the revolution defense committee, and the judicial tribunal. At the time of this proclamation, there were 1,260 *kebeles* in 315 towns.

The government estimated national *kebele* membership in the late 1980s at 4.4 million. The All-Ethiopia Urban Dwellers' Association (AEUDA) linked *kebeles* throughout the country. This organization's bureaucracy extended, in layers that paralleled the central bureaucracy, down to the neighborhood level. However, as in the countryside, the WPE had become the most important political institution, capable of overriding decisions taken by *kebeles* as well as by peasant associations.

Civil Service

Upon assuming power in 1974, the Derg decided to undertake extensive reforms of the central administration. Rather than engage in immediate, wholesale reorganization, the Derg concentrated on replacing career bureaucrats in the key ministries of interior, community development, and justice. If the Derg had purged the upper echelons of the entire civil service after 1974, there would have been insufficient numbers of educated, skilled, and experienced managers to conduct the normal affairs of government.

In general, the Derg allowed most bureaucrats who had served the emperor to remain at their posts and appointed army officers to monitor their activities in every ministry. At the same time, the Derg attempted to recruit into the civil service former high school and college students who were then serving in the *zemecha*. This group tended to be committed to revolutionary change, but it often lacked the bureaucratic skills to achieve this goal. Moreover, although the campaigners generally favored the revolution, many opposed military rule, and once in positions of authority they undermined rather than promoted the regime's goals.

Eventually, the Derg required all civil servants and political appointees to undergo reeducation to acquire the proper socialist orientation. Many civil servants, as well as military personnel, traveled to the Soviet Union, Eastern Europe, and Cuba for ideological training. After the establishment in 1976 of the Yekatit '66 Ideological School and after the creation of COPWE in 1979, hundreds more could be taught Marxist-Leninist doctrine inside Ethiopia. Some became party cadres and served in various parts of the country to encourage and monitor the political education and economic productivity of both government agencies and the citizenry at large.

In the early days of the revolution, the central bureaucracy was characterized by constant bickering among the various ministries and a general lack of interministerial coordination. This situation forced the Derg to create the Ministry of National Resource Development in 1975 to promote agricultural development as a possible solution to interministerial coordination problems and to address the problem of low productivity within society at large. By 1976 this strategy had failed, and the functions of the Ministry of National Resource Development were distributed among several ministries and parastatal bodies. The creation of the Central Planning Supreme Council in 1978 represented a more concerted attempt to coordinate bureaucratic participation in development. This strategy worked for a brief time, but by the late 1980s bureaucratic inefficiency had returned.

Starting in 1978, the Mengistu regime systematically attempted to enhance its ability to control the general population, and to a certain extent it used the civil service for this purpose. The state bureaucracy expanded enormously in the first decade of the revolution, and control by the military deepened and expanded in the process. This bureaucratic expansion increased the coercive capacity of the state and laid the groundwork for the establishment of the all-embracing vanguard party. After the creation of the WPE in 1984, the regime established a wide array of government institutions that radiated from the center out to the regional and local levels. Leadership positions in these new institutions were used as patronage by the regime to reward loyal supporters or to co-opt potential adversaries in the military. Although patronage had been employed by Haile Selassie, it was different under the Mengistu regime in that it was not rooted in the traditional social order but rather in the spoils accruing to a transitional state that controlled access to wealth and power.

The inauguration of the WPE resulted in a blurring of the lines between party and state. As noted previously, party operatives tended to interject themselves freely into the areas of administration and government policy. For example, party cadres had important political and intelligence-gathering roles in the workplace. The Working People's Control Committees (WPCCs), created in 1981, had come to serve as a somewhat threatening "watchdog" over productive activities. WPCCs were supposed to be involved in the implementation, supervision, and follow-up of government policies, regulations, and directives. WPCCs also could audit the accounts of any government institution, mass organization, or private individual. By 1984 the regime was crediting WPCCs with having uncovered numerous incidents of fraud, corruption, waste, and counterrevolution. For all its authoritarianism, the Haile Selassie regime was never able to achieve such tight surveillance. The Derg's capacity in this area was an indication of the effectiveness of the training provided by security advisers from the Soviet Union and the German Democratic Republic (East Germany) (see Foreign Military Assistance, ch. 5).

Although it was difficult to calculate its actual size, the central bureaucracy evidently grew tremendously after the revolution. The dimensions of this growth can be deduced from an analysis of consumption expenditures, which include wages and salaries. Figures available in late 1989 indicated that between 1974 and 1980 such expenditure grew from about 5 billion birr (for value of the birr—see

Glossary) to almost 8 billion birr, an increase of 60 percent. Central administration and defense accounted for about 80 percent of the 1980 figures. The growth of the public bureaucracy, even when the party bureaucracy was excluded, represented a tremendous drain on the resources available for development. Moreover, it appeared that if the regional reforms announced in 1987 were to be implemented fully, the civil service would have to expand even further.

The Politics of Development

During the 1980s, the government attempted to consolidate the revolution both structurally and ideologically. When it assumed power in 1974, the Derg pledged immediate attention to the social injustices that had been perpetrated by the imperial regime. In the revolution's earliest stages, the Derg's commitment to this pledge was manifested in particular by policies such as the nationalization of rural and urban property. The first year and a half of the new order could be described as a "phase of redistribution." In the name of the "people," the "toiling masses," and the "oppressed tillers of the soil," the government confiscated property previously owned by the nobility and other persons of wealth and redistributed it to peasants, tenants, and renters.

Peasants and workers expected that the new order would bring about a fundamental change in their circumstances, and to a certain extent this did happen. They also expected to be involved in determining their own fate; this, however, did not occur. The Derg quickly declared its own preeminent role as the vanguard of the revolution, causing concern among urban workers that their role was being minimized. When labor tried to become more instrumental in the changes that were beginning to take place, the government suppressed the workers' movement. The Derg condemned the Confederation of Ethiopian Labor Unions (CELU) as reactionary and disbanded it in late 1975. In its place, in 1977 the regime created the All-Ethiopia Trade Union (AETU), a confederation of 1,700 unions whose rank and file numbered more than 300,000 in 1984 (see Labor Unions, ch. 3). The regime thus co-opted the labor movement, and after 1976 the government seemed free to devise its own social development strategy without much input from the groups that would be most affected.

The Derg tried to develop a social policy strategy to enhance its power and legitimacy. To this end, the government achieved progress in fields such as education and health care. In 1979, for example, Ethiopia launched a massive rural literacy campaign; the government also established hundreds of health stations to provide minimal health care to the citizenry. However, it proved unable to effect dramatic improvements in the quality of life among broad segments of the population. In part, this was because Ethiopia had long been one of the world's poorest countries. At the same time, two additional factors greatly affected the performance of the Mengistu regime: the interaction of natural catastrophes and civil unrest, and misguided development policies such as resettlement and villagization.

The Politics of Drought and Famine

The Derg's limited ability to lead development and to respond to crises was dramatically demonstrated by the government's reliance on foreign famine relief between 1984 and 1989. By 1983 armed conflict between the government and opposition movements in the north had combined with drought to contribute to mass starvation in Eritrea, Tigray, and Welo. Meanwhile, drought alone was having a devastating impact on an additional nine regions. This natural disaster far exceeded the drought of 1973–74, which had contributed to the demise of the Haile Selassie regime. By early 1985, some 7.7 million people were suffering from drought and food shortages. Of that number, 2.5 million were at immediate risk of starving. More than 300,000 died in 1984 alone, more than twice the number that died in the drought a decade before. Before the worst was over, 1 million Ethiopians had died from drought and famine in the 1980s (see Refugees, Drought, and Famine, ch. 2).

As it had in the past, in the mid-1980s the international community responded generously to Ethiopia's tragedy once the dimensions of the crisis became understood. Bilateral, multilateral, and private donations of food and other relief supplies poured into the country by late 1984. Contributions ranged from food to transport trucks, antibiotics, well-drilling equipment, and technical assistance. Fund raising by spontaneously created volunteer organizations in the West, such as USA for Africa, BandAid, and numerous church and humanitarian groups, was instrumental to the provision of substantial nongovernment famine relief. Most of the money and supplies sent to Ethiopia, however, were provided by Western governments, in particular those of Britain, Canada, Italy, the Scandinavian countries, and the United States. Ethiopia's Relief and Rehabilitation Commission (RRC), at the time headed by an Ethiopian official named Dawit Wolde Giorgis, coordinated delivery of this assistance. Although Mengistu and other members of the Derg were nervous about the prospect of so many

Relief camp in Kwiha, near Mekele, 1985
Courtesy International Committee of the Red Cross (D. Gignoux)

Westerners flooding into the country and having access to areas where the regime was not popular, Dawit apparently was able to develop enough trust in the international aid community to bring the catastrophe under control by late 1986 (Dawit later defected to the United States).

By 1987 the physical impact of this massive influx of aid over such a short time was noticeable not only in the abatement of famine but also in what seemed to be the permanent establishment of local offices by various donor agencies. Although many foreign relief workers had returned home by 1987, some relief agencies remained to attempt to begin the rehabilitation and development processes. These would have been difficult tasks under the best of circumstances, but in the context of a regime pursuing a specific political agenda in spite of the unprecedented humanitarian imperatives involved in the situation, those agencies that remained had difficulty engaging in effective rehabilitation and development. In the countryside, the WPE often closely regulated the activities of foreign and local nongovernment agencies. At one point in the spring of 1989, the WPE forbade the International Committee of the Red Cross to operate in areas most severely ravaged by war. Before the year was out, drought and war again threatened the lives of more than 7 million people.

Despite drought and famine of unprecedented proportions in modern Ethiopian history, the Derg persisted on its controversial political course. If the famine had a positive side for the government, it was that the flood of famine relief assistance during the period of party construction and constitution-making allowed the regime to devote more of its budget to suppression of the rebellions in Eritrea and Tigray. However, by late 1989 drought, famine, and war, combined with so-called "aid fatigue" among many donors, forced the regime to take desperate measures. The government reinstated national conscription, required workers to give one month's salary to aid in combating famine and war, and halved the development budget as funds were diverted to defense.

The Politics of Resettlement

The Derg's policies appear to have been driven more by political imperatives than by perceived economic objectives. A case in point was the controversial policy of resettling the victims of the drought and famine outside their home areas. At the height of the drought and famine in 1984, the regime set in motion a resettlement policy that was initially designed to relocate 1.5 million people from areas in the north most severely affected by drought to areas in the west and south that had experienced adequate rainfall. By 1988, despite the resettlement program's obvious failure, President Mengistu repeatedly asserted that the program would continue. He estimated that eventually 7 million of Ethiopia's approximately 48 million people would be resettled. The government claimed that it was carrying out the program for humanitarian reasons, contending that it would remove the people from exhausted and unproductive land and place them in settlements with rich agricultural potential. In addition, the government argued that the new settlements would greatly facilitate its efforts to provide social services.

Initially, settlers were chosen from feeding centers in Welo, Tigray, and northern Shewa and transported by trucks, buses, and cargo aircraft to resettlement sites in Kefa, Gojam, Gonder, Welega, and Ilubabor. The government was poorly prepared for the operation, and the first settlers experienced tremendous hardships in alien, underdeveloped, and disease-infested areas. Some peasants moved voluntarily, but many more were forced to move. Many of those forcibly resettled were able to escape. Some fled into Sudan or Somalia, and others took shelter in refugee camps or walked thousands of miles to reenter their native regions. Still others joined opposition groups dedicated to overthrowing the regime. Those who remained in resettled areas were often resented by the local residents, many of whom had been impressed into building community infrastructure and donating materials.

Some critics rejected the government's argument that resettlement was driven by humanitarian considerations. Instead, they contended that the government's motives were political. The policy led to a depopulation of areas that harbored groups that militarily opposed the regime, such as the Eritrean People's Liberation Front (EPLF), the Tigray People's Liberation Front (TPLF), and the Oromo Liberation Front (OLF).

Critics within the international community charged that the Ethiopian government's resettlement program served as an obstacle to dealing more effectively with the problems of drought and famine relief. Moving victims to settlements far from their home areas merely made them inordinately dependent on the government. In addition, they claimed that fundamental human rights were sacrificed in the name of political expediency.

Regardless of the real motive for the resettlement policy, its net effect was to increase government control over large segments of society. In each resettlement site, WPE cadres carried out political education and attempted to stimulate the population to be more productive. The government insisted that it was not trying to enforce collectivized agricultural production but rather was trying to encourage more efficient activities. However, in actual practice, cadres pressured peasants to form collectives. The main value of this policy for the regime seems to have been the political control it promised.

The Politics of Villagization

Further evidence of the Ethiopian government's desire to enhance its control over the citizenry was its villagization program. The idea of clustering villages was introduced in the Land Reform Proclamation of 1975; however, there was no immediate effort to implement such a policy on a large scale. The first area to become the object of serious government efforts was Bale, following the onset of the Ogaden War of 1977–78 (see The Somali, ch. 5). At that time, ethnic Somali and Oromo living in Bale were forced by the Ethiopian government into strategically clustered villages. The official objective of the move was to provide social services more efficiently and to stimulate voluntary self-help among villagers. By 1983 there were 519 villagized communities ranging in population from 300 to 7,000.

The government did not introduce a comprehensive villagization plan until 1985. In January of that year, the villagization process began in earnest in Harerge, and by May there were some

2,000 villagized communities there. That summer, the process was begun in Shewa and Arsi, and in 1986 small-scale villagization efforts were begun in Gojam, Welega, Kefa, Sidamo, and Ilubabor. The National Villagization Coordinating Committee of the Ministry of Agriculture, in collaboration with the WPE, organized and managed the project. By March 1987, it was estimated that there were as many as 10,000 villagized communities throughout the country. The long-term goal of the program was the movement of 33 million rural residents—approximately two-thirds of the nation's population—into villagized settlements by 1994. By late 1989, however, only about 13 million peasants had been villagized.

The WPE introduced guidelines for site selection, village layout, and related matters. At the regional level, a committee planned, coordinated, and monitored the program through a network of subcommittees (planning and programming; site selection and surveying; material procurement, transportation, and logistics; construction; propaganda and training; monitoring and evaluation; and security). This structure was replicated in successive administrative layers down to the peasant associations—the level with ultimate responsibility for implementation.

In some regions of the country, the decision to villagize was a voluntary one, but in others the process was compulsory. In either case, peasants were required to dismantle their homes and, where possible, transport the housing materials to the new village site. Campaigners were usually brought in by the party and government to help the people physically reconstruct their communities.

Like resettlement, villagization generally caused a good deal of social disruption. Families usually were required to move from their traditional locations, close to their customary farming plots, into clustered villages where the land to be cultivated often was on fragmented plots far from the homestead.

The villagization program was most successful in the central highlands and southern lowlands, regions such as central Shewa, Arsi, and highland Harerge that were firmly under government control. Government efforts to villagize parts of western Shewa, the Harerge lowlands, and Gojam met with resistance. In the case of Gojam and western Shewa, this resistance in large measure was attributed to the fact that the TPLF and the Ethiopian People's Democratic Movement (EPDM) were most active in those regions. The Harerge lowlands were populated by ethnic Somali who were not as cooperative with the government as were the highlanders, who tended to be Oromo.

But not all Oromo peasants readily supported the villagization program. Many fled from new villages in Harerge after 1986, taking refuge in camps in Somalia. By June 1986, an estimated 50,000 such refugees had fled resettlement, mainly for political reasons. Some refugees complained that they were forced to abandon their traditional patterns of cultivation and to move into villages where they had to farm collectively and to participate in "food for work" programs. Private humanitarian agencies and bilateral and multilateral development agencies were apparently aware of alleged, as well as real, violations of human rights associated with the villagization program. Nonetheless, by early 1987 many seem to have turned a blind eye to such incidents and to have concentrated on the humanitarian dimensions of their work.

On purely technical grounds, villagization, like resettlement, seemed to make sense. The official goal was to improve the access of rural residents to social services and to strengthen the ability of rural communities to defend themselves. Another motive, however, seemed to be the conversion of villagized communities into producers' cooperatives or collectives, as well as into centers for military recruitment.

Political Dynamics

Modern Ethiopian political history has been shaped and dominated by intense conflict. As the revolution unfolded in 1973 and 1974, the political environment appeared to liberalize, and political discourse became more open than at any other time in Ethiopian history. This was particularly true in urban centers, such as the capital city of Addis Ababa. In the rural areas, groups incorporated into Ethiopia in the nineteenth and twentieth centuries, such as the Oromo, Afar, Somali, and Eritreans, began to step up their demands for self-determination. Several of these groups questioned the very legitimacy of the Ethiopian state. The Derg was in essence being challenged to devise a survival strategy that would enhance its control over government and politics and create a basis for popular legitimacy. Various reorganizational and institution-building policies, such as the establishment of the Program for the National Democratic Revolution (PNDR), the creation of the WPE, and the promulgation of the 1987 constitution, were all designed to achieve these ends.

Political Participation and Repression

The period immediately following the overthrow of Haile Selassie was a time of open political debate. The new regime did not have a clearly defined ideology, but it was swept along by the growing radical discourse among members of the civilian left. Initially, the Derg tried to win the support of the Ethiopian left by declaring its socialist intentions in its program statement, Ethiopia Tikdem (Ethiopia First). The economic and social policies articulated in this document were populist in tone and did little to co-opt the civilian left.

Once it became clear that the Derg had assigned to itself the vanguard role in the revolution, elements in the civilian left began to criticize the new regime. Chief among such critics was the Ethiopian People's Revolutionary Party (EPRP). By 1976 the EPRP had become engaged in a systematic campaign to undermine and discredit the Derg. The party was successful in infiltrating the *zemecha,* the CELU, and even the Provisional Office for Mass Organizational Affairs (POMOA), the precursor to the Yekatit '66 Ideological School. At the height of its activities, the EPRP included students, intellectuals, teachers, merchants, and government bureaucrats. It even had sympathizers within the military.

During the late 1970s, apart from the military, the Derg relied for support on the All-Ethiopia Socialist Movement (whose Amharic acronym was MEISON). Rather than challenge the vanguard role of the military, MEISON entered into a strategic alliance with the Derg, accepting its hegemony at least for the short term. In the highly charged political climate of the moment, MEISON engaged in vigorous debate with the EPRP over the most appropriate strategy for reconstructing Ethiopian society. The debate between the two groups first took place in their organizations' newspapers and in pamphlets but later moved to the streets in the form of bloody assassination and counterassassination campaigns. The differences between MEISON and the EPRP were fundamental. The EPRP pressed uncompromisingly for a genuine "people's democracy," whereas MEISON favored "controlled democracy" and was prepared to give the Derg some time to return to the barracks.

The friction between the two groups inspired the Derg to become more radical in its ideology and public policies. The regime determined that to survive it would have to alter its program and co-opt or destroy its civilian opponents. It pursued both goals simultaneously by setting up three organizations: the PNDR, the Yekatit '66 Ideological School, and a political advisory body called the Politburo (not to be confused with the Political Bureau of the WPE).

The Derg seemed hesitant to permit free and open political competition, although it attempted to create the impression of openness by allowing political groups to operate in a limited fashion. Organizations resembling political parties were not allowed to organize on a mass basis, but they could participate in politics through representation on the Politburo; in fact, both the EPRP and MEISON were represented on the Politburo. Also represented were

Abyot Seded (Revolutionary Flame), founded in 1976 by members of the armed forces and led by Mengistu himself; the Waz (Labor) League, which claimed a working-class base and shared the EPRP's radical populist tendencies; and the Revolutionary Struggle of the Ethiopian Masses (whose Amharic acronym was ECHAAT), a largely Oromo political organization. The Politburo provided a forum where the differences among the various political groupings could be clarified and where the Derg could monitor the tendencies of its opponents.

By late 1976, MEISON had become the most influential civilian group on the Politburo. However, the growing power of Abyot Seded was also evident, as it challenged MEISON and the EPRP within the Politburo and in grass-roots institutions such as *kebeles* and peasant associations. To counter this threat, the Derg began to prepare Abyot Seded to assume the role of chief adviser on ideological, political, and organizational matters. The aim seems to have been the creation of a cadre of Abyot Seded members with sufficient ideological sophistication to neutralize all civilian opponents, including MEISON. Abyot Seded members received ideological training in the Soviet Union, East Germany, and Cuba. On their return, they were assigned the task of politicizing the rank and file of the military.

The EPRP's efforts to discredit and undermine the Derg and its MEISON collaborators escalated in the fall of 1976. It targeted public buildings and other symbols of state authority for bombings and assassinated numerous Abyot Seded and MEISON members, as well as public officials at all levels. The Derg, which countered with its own Red Terror campaign, labeled the EPRP's tactics the White Terror. Mengistu asserted that all "progressives" were given "freedom of action" in helping root out the revolution's enemies, and his wrath was particularly directed toward the EPRP. Peasants, workers, public officials, and even students thought to be loyal to the Mengistu regime were provided with arms to accomplish this task.

Mengistu's decision resulted in fratricidal chaos. Many civilians he armed were EPRP sympathizers rather than supporters of MEISON or the Derg. Between early 1977 and late 1978, roughly 5,000 people were killed. In the process, the Derg became estranged from civilian groups, including MEISON. By early 1979, Abyot Seded stood alone as the only officially recognized political organization; the others were branded enemies of the revolution. Growing human rights violations prompted the United States, Ethiopia's superpower patron, to counsel moderation. However, the Derg continued to use extreme measures against its real and perceived opponents to ensure its survival.

When he assumed office in early 1977, United States president Jimmy Carter curtailed arms sales to Ethiopia because of its human rights abuses. In response, Mengistu severely curtailed relations with the United States, ordering all United States military personnel and most embassy staff to leave the country. In search of an alternate source of military aid, Mengistu eventually turned to the Soviet Union. However, before the Soviet Union and its allies could establish an effective presence in Ethiopia, opposition groups stepped up their campaigns against the Derg.

In addition to the urban guerrilla warfare being waged by the EPRP, nationalist movements such as the EPLF, the OLF, the TPLF, and the Western Somali Liberation Front (WSLF) also stepped up their military campaigns in the countryside. By the end of 1976, the Eritreans had made substantial gains in rural areas, forcing Ethiopian troops into garrisons and urban centers in Eritrea. Meanwhile, armed groups such as the OLF and the TPLF were severely testing the regime, and in 1977 the WSLF, with the assistance of Somali troops, occupied most of the Ogaden. The Ethiopian government, however, with aid from the Soviet Union, Cuba, and Eastern Europe, reasserted its authority over contested areas by the following spring (see External and Internal Opponents, ch. 5).

Once it had reestablished control, the Derg resumed the creation of institutions that would enhance its political hegemony and legitimacy. After having almost met its demise, the Derg decided to form a vanguard party. In June 1978, the Derg announced that Abyot Seded would be joined with the factional remnants of the Waz League and the Marxist-Leninist Revolutionary Organization (whose Amharic acronym was MALERED), a small splinter group of MEISON, in the all-embracing Union of Ethiopian Marxist-Leninist Organizations (whose Amharic acronym was EMALEDEH). The task of the front was to identify strategies for the creation of a vanguard party. The following year, Mengistu announced that he would form a commission to develop a framework for the long-awaited vanguard party.

By 1978 all civilian opposition groups had been destroyed or forced underground. The EPRP had been driven out of the cities and into the mountains of the central highlands, where it tried unsuccessfully to develop the Ethiopian People's Revolutionary Army (EPRA). The OLF had been driven into refugee camps in Sudan and Somalia; the WSLF had sought refuge in Somalia; the TPLF and the Ethiopian Democratic Union (EDU), a group of former nobility and officials of the Haile Selassie government, had been pushed into Sudan; and the EPLF had been forced back into its strongholds along the Sudanese border. The task then facing the Derg was to establish its popular legitimacy among the various ethnic communities opposed to its rule. The most vigorous opposition came from the EPLF and the TPLF. The OLF, the EPRP, and the Afar Liberation Front (ALF) were experiencing revivals but had yet to become militarily effective.

The Eritrean Movement

Eritrea and the Imperial Regime

Eritrean separatism had its roots in World War II. In 1941, in the Battle of Keren, the Allies drove Italian forces out of Eritrea, which had been under Italy's rule since the end of the nineteenth century. Administration of the region was then entrusted to the British military until its fate could be determined by the Allies. Britain, however, sought to divide Eritrea along religious lines, giving the coast and highland areas to Ethiopia and the Muslim-inhabited northern and western lowlands to British-ruled Sudan.

In 1952 the United Nations (UN) tried to satisfy the demand for self-determination by creating an Eritrean-Ethiopian federation. In 1962, however, Haile Selassie unilaterally abolished the federation and imposed imperial rule throughout Eritrea.

Radical opposition to the incorporation of Eritrea into Ethiopia had begun in 1958 with the founding of the Eritrean Liberation Movement (ELM), an organization made up mainly of students, intellectuals, and urban wage laborers. The ELM engaged in clandestine political activities intended to cultivate resistance to the centralizing policies of the imperial state. By 1962, however, the ELM had been discovered and destroyed by imperial authorities.

Even as the ELM was being neutralized, a new organization of Eritrean nationalists was forming. In 1960 Eritrean exiles in Cairo founded the Eritrean Liberation Front (ELF). In contrast to the ELM, from the outset the ELF was bent on waging armed struggle on behalf of Eritrean independence. The ELF was composed mainly of Eritrean Muslims from the rural lowlands on the western edge of the territory. In 1961 the ELF's political character was vague, but radical Arab states such as Syria and Iraq sympathized with Eritrea as a predominantly Muslim region struggling to escape oppression and imperial domination. These two countries therefore supplied military and financial assistance to the ELF.

The ELF initiated military operations in 1961. These operations intensified in response to the 1962 dissolution of the Eritrean-Ethiopian federation. The ELF claimed that the process by which this act took place violated the Eritrean federal constitution and denied the Eritrean people their right to self-determination. By this time, the movement claimed to be multiethnic, involving individuals from Eritrea's nine major ethnic groups.

The ELF's first several years of guerrilla activity in Eritrea were characterized by poor preparation, poor leadership, and poor military performance. By 1967, however, the ELF had gained considerable support among peasants, particularly in Eritrea's north and west, and around the port city of Mitsiwa. Haile Selassie attempted to calm the growing unrest by visiting Eritrea and assuring its inhabitants that they would be treated as equals under the new arrangements. Although he doled out offices, money, and titles in early 1967 in hopes of co-opting would-be Eritrean opponents, the resistance intensified.

From the beginning, a serious problem confronting the ELF was the development of a base of popular support and a cohesive military wing. The front divided Eritrea into five military regions, giving regional commanders considerable latitude in carrying out the struggle in their respective zones. Perhaps just as debilitating were internal disputes over strategy and tactics. These disagreements eventually led to the ELF's fragmentation and the founding in 1972 of another group, the Eritrean People's Liberation Front (EPLF). The leadership of this multiethnic movement came to be dominated by leftist, Christian intellectuals who spoke Tigrinya, Eritrea's predominant language. Sporadic armed conflict ensued between the two groups from 1972 to 1974, even as they fought the Ethiopian forces. The various organizations, each waging a separate campaign against the Haile Selassie regime, had become such a serious threat that the emperor declared martial law in Eritrea and deployed half his army to contain the struggle. But the Eritrean insurgents fiercely resisted. In January 1974, the EPLF handed Haile Selassie's forces a crushing defeat at Asmera, severely affecting the army's morale and exposing the crown's ever-weakening position.

Eritrea and the Mengistu Regime

After the emperor was deposed, the Derg stated its desire to resolve the Eritrean question once and for all. There were those in the Derg's ranks who pressed for a decisive military solution, while others favored some form of negotiated settlement. Influential Derg nationalists continued to endorse, as had the imperial regime before them, the ideal of a "Greater Ethiopia," a unitary, multiethnic state. They pressed for a military solution while claiming to support the right of all Ethiopian nationalities to self-determination.

This position was first articulated in the PNDR in 1976 and clarified later that year by the Nine Point Statement on Eritrea. Subsequently, the regime made other attempts at dealing, at least rhetorically and symbolically, with the Eritrean problem.

In 1976 Osman Salah Sabbe, an Eritrean who had helped found both the ELM and the ELF, attempted to reconcile the two movements to form a united front. But after this effort failed, Osman formed a third front, the Eritrean Liberation Front-Popular Liberation Front (ELF–PLF). In later years, the Derg sought to exploit the internecine Eritrean disputes.

Disagreements among the various Eritrean factions continued throughout the 1970s and 1980s. These differences were mainly ideological. At the time, the EPLF and the ELF could best be described in ideological terms as leftist-nationalist and the ELF–PLF as moderate nationalist. Although the EPLF and the ELF–PLF consistently called for Eritrea's independence, the main ELF faction never closed the door to the possibility of an equitable federal union. As subtle as the differences among these groups appeared, they were enough to prevent the formation of a united front against Addis Ababa.

In addition to its highly disciplined combatants, the EPLF benefited from its broad base of popular support and its political organization. The EPLF became a de facto government in areas it controlled. It was a highly structured political and military institution involved not only in training its fighters militarily but also in educating them politically. The EPLF's basic units for political participation were national unions. The Eritrean national congress was the paramount political organ of the EPLF and was made up of the Central Committee, delegates elected by the national unions, and the Eritrean People's Liberation Army (EPLA). The congress defined general policy and elected the Central Committee (composed in the late 1980s of seventy-one full members and seven alternates), which in turn elected the general secretary and the Political Bureau's eight members. The EPLF charter called for national congresses to be held every three years unless circumstances dictated otherwise. Between congressional sessions, the EPLF Central Committee was the highest authority within the front. It met every nine months and was responsible for developing the EPLF political agenda and for overseeing policy implementation. The Political Bureau was the EPLF's primary executive organ. It met every three months and had broad administrative powers. When the Political Bureau was not in session, the general secretary, aided by a secretariat, possessed wide executive authority.

In March 1987, the EPLF held its second congress in areas of Eritrea that it controlled. The first congress had been held ten years earlier after Eritrean forces had captured almost all of Eritrea. At that time, the euphoric Eritreans expected that their goal of an independent Eritrea was about to be realized. However, they subsequently suffered a series of reversals from which it took the EPLF almost a decade to recover. Like that earlier meeting, the 1987 gathering was also a unity congress. It resulted in resolution of the difference between the EPLF and another splinter group, the Eritrean Liberation Front-Central Command (ELF–CC), at the time the most prominent remaining ELF faction.

Following the EPLF unity congress, the organization stepped up military pressure against the Ethiopian regime. By March 1988, the EPLF had scored some impressive battlefield successes. The EPLF broke out of entrenched positions in the Nakfa area of northern Eritrea and occupied the important garrison town of Afabet. Afabet's fall forced the Ethiopian army to evacuate the urban centers of Barca, Teseney, Barentu, and Akordat. The government also ordered all foreign relief workers out of Eritrea and Tigray, declared states of emergency in both regions, and redeployed troops from the Ogaden to Eritrea. The highly disciplined Eritrean forces faced much larger and better equipped Ethiopian units, but the Ethiopian troops, many of whom were teenagers, had become war weary and demoralized. By early 1991, the EPLF controlled most of Eritrea except for some urban centers.

The most significant attempt to address the Eritrean issue was embodied in the 1987 constitution, which allowed for the possibility of regional autonomy. At its inaugural session, the National Shengo acted on this provision and endorsed a plan for regional autonomy (see Regional and Local Government, this ch.). Among autonomous regions, the plan accorded Eritrea the greatest degree of autonomy. In particular, the plan assigned Eritrea's regional government broader powers than those assigned to the other four autonomous regions, especially in the areas of industrial development and education. Under the plan, Eritrea also was distinguished from other autonomous regions in that it was to have three administrative subregions: one in the north, made up of Akordat, Keren, and Sahel *awrajas;* one in the south-central part of historical Eritrea, consisting of Hamasen, Mitsiwa, Seraye, and Akale Guzay *awrajas;* and one encompassing the western *awraja* of Gashe na Setit. By creating Aseb Autonomous Region, the government in Addis Ababa appeared to be attempting to ensure itself a secure path to the Red Sea. Aseb Autonomous Region comprised

United Nations Commission to Eritrea, 1950. The commissioner listens to representatives of the Muslim League of Mitsiwa argue for Eritrean independence.
Courtesy United Nations

Aseb *awraja* of historical Eritrea, along with parts of eastern Welo and Tigray regions.

By 1991, however, administrative reorganization in the north-central part of the country was a reality only on paper. Since 1988 the area had been under a state of emergency. The regime had been unable to establish the necessary party and administrative infrastructure to implement the plan, mostly because of the escalation of opposition in Eritrea and Tigray since the promulgation of the 1987 constitution. The EPLF, for example, rejected the reorganization plan, terming it "old wine in new bottles." The ELF expressed particular outrage over the creation of Aseb Autonomous Region, viewing it as another WPE attempt to annex a significant part of the historical colony of Eritrea to Ethiopia. The ELF called for the Ethiopian government to agree to immediate negotiations without preconditions with a unified Eritrean delegation.

Even as the EPLF recorded its most significant battlefield success in 1988-89, a rift was developing between that organization and ELF splinter groups. This rift revolved around religion, as the ELF's conservative, primarily Islamic elements came to distrust the EPLF's predominantly Christian leadership. The EPLF also espoused a much more explicitly socialist program than did the

243

ELF factions. To encourage further divisions among the Eritreans, the Mengistu regime in late 1988 met with five former ELF members (who claimed to represent 750,000 Eritreans) to accept their proposal for the creation of an autonomous Eritrean region in the predominantly Muslim lowlands. These five men rejected the EPLF's claim that it represented all Eritreans. Mengistu forwarded the proposal to the National Shengo for consideration, but the regime collapsed before action could be taken.

The Tigrayan Movement

Tigrayan opposition to the Ethiopian government started during Emperor Menelik's reign. In 1896 Menelik, who opposed Italy's territorial designs on Ethiopia, deployed an 80,000-man army into Tigray without adequate provisions, thereby forcing the soldiers to live off the land. According to Tigrayan nationalists, the Tigray who died protecting their homes against Menelik's troops outnumbered the defeated Italians who died at the Battle of Adwa that year. Forty years later, when fascist Italy's forces invaded Ethiopia, the main battlefield was again in Tigray, and once again the inhabitants suffered. In 1943, after the Allied Powers had defeated Italy and Haile Selassie had returned to Ethiopia, Tigrayan peasants revolted against the imperial regime (see Discontent in Tigray, ch. 1). Government forces, supported by British units, suppressed the revolt. The emperor then imposed a harsh peace on Tigray.

The first sign of open resistance to the Mengistu regime in Tigray (where the rebellion became known as the Weyane, the same as the 1943 revolt) occurred in October 1974. At that time, the Derg ordered Ras Mengesha Seyoum—governor general of Tigray, member of the Tigrayan royal family, and grandson-in-law of the emperor—to relinquish his office and surrender to the authorities. Rather than submit, he fled to the bush and organized the Tigray Liberation Organization (TLO). The TLO operated in clandestine political cells and engaged in a program of systematic agitation. During the tumultuous mid-1970s, the TLO established cells in various parts of the country. In early 1975, Mengesha left Tigray and, with other aristocrats, formed the Ethiopian Democratic Union (EDU). Members of the TLO who remained in Tigray and who came under the influence of the EPLF formed the Tigray People's Liberation Front (TPLF), whose goals included the overthrow of the Mengistu regime, the establishment of a "more democratic" government, and the removal of all foreign military bases from Ethiopia (see The Tigray, ch. 5). The TPLF also condemned Mengesha, accepted Marxism-Leninism, and argued for an independent Eritrean-Tigrayan federation. Eventually, the TPLF neutralized the

TLO by killing many of its leaders and by jailing and executing others.

At the time, the TPLF shared the field with the more conservative Tigray-based EDU and the Ethiopian People's Revolutionary Party (EPRP). However, the Red Terror had decimated both of these organizations, and by 1978 they had ceased to be a factor. The TPLF was also severely weakened but, with the assistance of the EPLF, developed into an effective fighting force. Its ranks were expanded initially by the absorption of former EPRP members.

Beginning in 1980, the TPLF sought to establish local self-administration in areas under its control. The basic administrative unit was the people's council (*baito*), which was typically introduced in two stages. In the first stage, representatives from mass associations were elected to form the provisional administrative council. The second stage involved the establishment of a full-fledged people's council. Council members were elected to two-year terms. All members of a number of mass associations who were at least sixteen years of age had the right to vote and to stand for election to a people's council. People's councils were responsible for local administrative, economic, and social affairs. By late 1989, however, this structure had not grown much beyond the pilot stage in most of Tigray.

In the 1980s, the TPLF drew almost exclusively from among the Tigrayan population of north-central Ethiopia for its support, although it claimed to be dedicated toward building a united national front representing all groups and nationalities struggling against the Mengistu regime. On May 8, 1984, the TPLF issued a proposal calling for the formation of a united front based on a "minimum program," whose sole objective was the overthrow of the Mengistu regime. By 1984 the TPLF was active throughout Tigray and in parts of Welo and Gojam. Although its political program continued to have a populist orientation, the dominant ideologues within the organization claimed to be dedicated to constructing the Marxist-Leninist League of Tigray. Observers likened this group's strident rhetoric to that of Albania's Stalinist ideologues.

On the eve of its thirteenth anniversary in February 1988, the TPLF was engaged in its largest offensive against Ethiopian forces. Over the next year and a half, the TPLF captured all of Tigray, including urban centers such as Aksum, Inda Silase, and Mekele. By May 1989, the Ethiopian army had withdrawn completely from Tigray.

The TPLF's efforts to develop a united front began to bear fruit just as its major offensive was unfolding. In January 1989, it entered into an alliance with the Ethiopian People's Democratic Movement (EPDM), an organization composed mainly of Amhara from Welo, Gonder, and the northern part of Shewa, many of whom had once belonged to the EPRP. The two groups had cooperated in military activities for several years, but they had not had a formal alliance. It was estimated that by the fall of 1989, there were 2.5 million people in EPDM-controlled areas. The EPDM, like the TPLF, supported the right of all nationalities to self-determination and the formation of a democratic state once the Mengestu regime had been overthrown.

The TPLF and EPDM called their alliance the Ethiopian People's Revolutionary Democratic Front (EPRDF). The EPRDF's charter borrowed from the TPLF charter. It called for the establishment of a democratic government, the elimination of the last vestiges of feudalism and imperialism, the formation of a genuine people's government based on people's councils, the guarantee of basic human and civil rights, and self-determination for all oppressed nationalities. Subsequently, several other dissident groups, some created specifically by the EPRDF, also joined the alliance.

By the fall of 1989, the EPRDF had moved from its strongholds in Tigray, Welo, and Gonder and threatened parts of northern Shewa. At the time, the force seemed more capable of pushing back the beleaguered Ethiopian troops than of setting up any type of permanent political structures. During a six-week period beginning in August 1989, the EPRDF wounded or captured an estimated 20,000 government soldiers, seized vast stocks of military hardware, and pushed the battle line between the two sides down to northern Shewa. In part, these advances were facilitated by the demoralization of the Ethiopian military following the abortive coup of May 1989 (see Regime Stability and Peace Negotiations, this ch.). Some Ethiopian troops defected to the opposition, significantly improving the military capabilities of the EPRDF.

Other Movements and Fronts

The EPLF, the TPLF, the EPDM, and the EPRDF were the most militarily significant opposition movements challenging the Mengistu regime in 1991. In addition, several other groups, composed mainly of ethnic Oromo, Afar, and Somali, were also active.

Oromo Groups

The Oromo, representing about 40 percent of the population, occupy areas in south and central Ethiopia that only became part of modern Ethiopia during the late nineteenth and early twentieth centuries. The people in these areas largely became tenants on their own land as the empire consolidated its rule. Many Oromo resented the alien rule of Amhara and Tigray from the highland core of the empire. Haile Selassie tried to win Oromo loyalty by developing alliances with key Oromo leaders. Although this strategy enabled the emperor to co-opt many Oromo into the imperial system, it failed to end Oromo resistance. Examples of this opposition to Addis Ababa included the Azebo-Raya revolt of 1928–30; the 1936 Oromo Independence Movement; and the establishment in 1965 of the Mecha-Tulema, an Oromo self-help organization.

From 1964 to 1970, a revolt in Bale presented the most serious challenge to the Ethiopian government. During that time, separate Oromo rebel groups in Bale conducted hit-and-run raids against military garrisons and police stations. Until 1969 the Somali government provided military assistance to these rebels as part of its strategy of reestablishing a "Greater Somalia." In addition, Oromo rebels attempted to coordinate their military activities with the Western Somali Liberation Front. After Mahammad Siad Barre took over the Somali government in 1969, the Oromo rebels lost Somali support and found it impossible to sustain their campaigns in southeastern Ethiopia. In 1970 the rebels agreed to a truce with the Haile Selassie regime.

In 1973 Oromo dissidents formed the Oromo Liberation Front (OLF), an organization dedicated to the "total liberation of the entire Oromo nation from Ethiopian colonialism" (see The Oromo, ch. 5). The OLF began an offensive against the Ethiopian government in Harerge in 1974, but sustained activities did not begin until 1976. The OLF subsequently extended its sphere of activity to Welega.

Young, educated Oromo from Arsi initially composed the OLF leadership, but by 1976 the organization claimed a broad-based leadership with a following from all Oromo areas. Beyond national liberation, the OLF's program called for the establishment of an independent Democratic Republic of Oromia, which would include all of central and southern Ethiopia, excluding the Ogaden and Omo River regions.

In late 1989, the OLF had approximately 200 combatants in Harerge and about 5,000 in Welega. OLF troops were poorly armed and unable to pose a serious threat to the Ethiopian army. In addition, the OLF had been unable to mobilize popular support against the Ethiopian government. This failure resulted from the OLF's inability to organize an effective antigovernment movement, to convince the majority of Oromo people that separatism was a viable political alternative, or to sustain military operations in the geographically separated areas of Welega, Arsi, and Harerge. In spite of these difficulties, in 1989 the OLF announced several military successes against the Ethiopian armed forces, especially in Asosa, a town on the Sudanese-Ethiopian border.

On the political side, in February 1988 the OLF convened its first national congress at Begi in newly created Asosa Region. Apart from expressing support for the EPLF and the TPLF, the congress condemned the Mengistu regime and voiced opposition to the government's villagization and resettlement policies.

Afar Groups

The Afar people, numbering about 3 million in Ethiopia, reside in the area bordering Eritrea, Djibouti, and Somalia. Although there were other factions claiming to represent the Afar, the most prominent organization was the Afar Liberation Front (ALF; also called the Afar Sultanate Liberation Front), headed by Ali Mirah. The ALF was dedicated to maintaining the political, cultural, and religious autonomy of the Afar people. Ali Mirah directed his movement's sporadic activities from Saudi Arabia and Kuwait. The ALF was one of the few opposition movements to express some interest in Mengistu's plan for creating autonomous regions, primarily because most Afar inhabited the area that was to become Aseb Autonomous Region.

Somali Groups

Somali guerrilla activity in the Ogaden and in the Haud area east of Harer flared sporadically after Somalia gained its independence in 1960, but the guerrilla activity remained essentially a police concern until a border war erupted in 1964. When he seized power in Mogadishu in 1969, Siad Barre thwarted attempts at an understanding between Ethiopia and Somalia. He pledged to renew efforts to establish a "Greater Somalia" that would encompass about one-third of Ethiopia's territory. Encouraged by the breakdown of authority in Addis Ababa after the 1974 overthrow of Haile Selassie, Somalia provided matériel, moral, and organizational support to insurgent movements in the Ogaden and southern Ethiopia.

The Western Somali Liberation Front (WSLF), which operated in the Ogaden, supported the "Greater Somalia" concept. The Somali Abo Liberation Front (SALF) maintained links to the WSLF. Its sphere of operations was in Bale, Sidamo, and Arsi, where it advocated union with Somalia or the creation of an independent state. Somalia equipped both groups with Soviet arms; both also received aid and training from various Arab and communist nations, including Cuba.

After the 1977–78 Ogaden War, the WSLF was routed, and its troops flocked to camps in Somalia (see The Somali, ch. 5). The Somali government subsequently forbade the WSLF to use its territory to launch attacks into Ethiopia. By 1989 the WSLF had ceased to be an effective guerrilla organization within Ethiopia. Siad Barre's decision to restrict the WSLF led to the formation of a WSLF splinter group, the Ogaden National Liberation Front (ONLF), whose headquarters were in Kuwait. Elements of the ONLF slipped back into the Ogaden in 1988 but failed to generate a significant military capability.

Leftist Groups

Although the Ethiopian People's Revolutionary Party (EPRP) and the All-Ethiopia Socialist Movement (whose Amharic acronym was MEISON) were crippled during the Red Terror, they were not completely eliminated. In 1989 the EPRP had its main base in Sudan. It claimed to have had its ranks augmented in the late 1980s by 20,000 peasants fleeing villagization in Shewa. The EPRP and MEISON continued to exist as political organizations, but they appeared to have little military significance.

Regime Stability and Peace Negotiations

The WPE regime's attempt to create conditions for popular acceptance of its legitimacy failed. Testimony to this was the attempted coup that began on May 16, 1989. The coup was the result of months of planning by senior officers, some of whom may have been members of the Free Ethiopia Soldiers' Movement, an opposition group that involved active-duty military officers and former officers in exile. The coup began shortly after Mengistu left for a state visit to East Germany. Top generals invited colleagues to attend a meeting at the Ministry of National Defense, where they delivered an ultimatum to the defense minister, Major General Haile Giorgis Habte Mariam, to join them or be jailed. Haile Giorgis refused and was shot dead. The shots were heard by two senior officers loyal to Mengistu, who ordered army tanks to encircle the ministry and guard the road to the airport.

Officers commanding units in Eritrea and Tigray also joined in the coup. They initially seized the Asmera radio station and issued a call to the "broad masses" to join in the effort to bring down the "tyrannical and dictatorial regime of Mengistu." However, Mengistu returned to the country and, with the support of the Presidential Guard and other loyal troops, regained control three days after the coup began.

The plotters' aim had been to establish a transitional military government. Exiled supporters of the Free Ethiopia Soldiers' Movement claimed that the coup-makers planned to negotiate a settlement in Eritrea, establish a ruling council, and return the military to their barracks. Senior officers had become desperate for a political settlement of the wars raging in the north. Pamphlets expressing their discontent had been distributed to the military rank and file by junior and middle ranking officers sympathetic to their cause. The new leader reportedly was to have been Major General Seyoum Mekonnen, the former head of military intelligence.

To wipe out his enemies in the military, Mengistu purged the officer corps. At least twelve generals were executed or committed suicide rather than be captured, and 300 to 400 officers suspected of being involved in the coup were arrested. Nearly all generals, division commanders, and political commissars assigned to units stationed in the north reportedly were detained. These individuals were replaced by Mengistu loyalists, many of whom lacked experience as military leaders.

The attempted coup and continuing problems related to war, drought, and famine caused considerable instability in the WPE's upper levels. Council of State members became increasingly critical of Mengistu's policies, and some even suggested that he step down. However, Mengistu mustered enough support to retain power. At the same time, by mid-1989 the success of opposition forces, the Soviet Union's refusal to increase military assistance to Ethiopia, and pressure from Moscow had forced Mengistu to seek negotiated settlements to Ethiopia's various wars. The loss of East German military support because of the democratization movement that occurred later in the year also softened the government's stance toward negotiations.

On June 5, 1989, the National Shengo, in a special session, endorsed a proposal calling for unconditional peace talks with the EPLF. The EPLF accepted, and the two sides agreed that former United States president Jimmy Carter would mediate the negotiations. The first talks were held at the Carter Presidential Center of Emory University in Atlanta, Georgia, in early September. WPE Central Committee member Ashagre Yigletu headed the Ethiopian delegation, and Al Amin Muhammad Sayyid led the Eritrean team. The two sides agreed on several procedural issues and set the next round of talks for November 1989 in Nairobi, Kenya.

At the second meeting, additional procedural issues were resolved, and former Tanzanian president Julius K. Nyerere was asked to co-chair further talks with former President Carter. The most difficult issue resolved in the eight-day talks was determining

Commuters line up for a bus at a busy pick-up point in Addis Ababa.
Courtesy United Nations (Ray Witlin)

who would serve as international observers for the main negotiations. Seven observers were invited—each side had two unrestricted choices, and three others were chosen by mutual consent. The parties also concluded that additional observers could be invited later upon mutual agreement. At the end of the session, six observers had accepted invitations: Kenya, Senegal, Sudan, Tanzania, Zimbabwe, and the Organization of African Unity (OAU). A seventh invitation was proposed for the UN, but because Ethiopia, a UN member, refused to endorse the idea, the UN declined to participate. Subsequent meetings in Washington in October 1990 and February 1991, chaired by United States Assistant Secretary of State for African Affairs Herman Cohen, failed to resolve this issue. Even so, both sides agreed to continue their dialogue, with the next meeting tentatively scheduled for May in London.

The Ethiopian regime also agreed to peace negotiations with the TPLF, to be convened by the Italian government. Preliminary talks began in Rome on November 4, 1989. Ashagre Yigletu led the Ethiopian team, and Central Committee chairman Meles Zenawi headed the TPLF delegation. Because its troops were advancing on the battlefield, the TPLF refrained from making a cease-fire a precondition for participating in the talks. The TPLF called for the establishment of a provisional government made up of representatives

251

from all major nationality groups and political organizations. The main task of this provisional government would be to draft a democratic constitution and prepare for free elections. Before the talks began, the Ethiopian government rejected the idea of a provisional government, claiming that the Ethiopian people had approved the 1987 constitution in a fair referendum and that a popularly elected parliament had put the new government in place.

The first round of talks lasted one week and ended with agreement only on procedural points. Although the TPLF had called for a national united front, it represented only itself at the Rome talks. It suggested, however, that the main item on the agenda should be its peace proposal. The Ethiopian delegation rejected this idea but offered no counterproposal.

The second round of preliminary talks opened in Rome on December 12, 1989. The two sides reached an agreement whereby Italy and Kenya would act as mediators and Nigeria, Sweden, Sudan, and Uganda would act as observers in future peace negotiations. The Italian minister of foreign affairs announced that the third round of preliminary talks would open in Rome on March 20, 1990.

Unfortunately, the Ethiopian delegation terminated these discussions nine days after they began. According to rebel spokesmen, the talks failed because Ethiopia insisted that the TPLF deal only with questions pertaining "to the autonomous region of Tigray" rather than with Ethiopia as a whole. Moreover, Ethiopia refused to accept a joint TPLF–EPDM delegation at the main peace talks. The TPLF maintained that the EPDM, its ally in war, also should be its ally in peace. As a result of these differences, the negotiating process between the TPLF and Ethiopia ended.

On the military front, the TPLF pressed its offensive throughout the fall of 1989. By the beginning of 1990, its advances had bogged down, and the Ethiopian army had begun a counteroffensive. By mid-June 1990, however, the TPLF, operating as part of the EPRDF, had taken up positions within 160 kilometers of Addis Ababa. By contrast, the EPLF had reduced its military operations over the same period, perhaps to regroup. In February 1990, however, the EPLF mounted a major drive aimed at capturing the port city of Mitsiwa, the entry point for much of Ethiopia's food and military supplies. By mid-February the EPLF had overrun the port and severed the traffic that flowed from Mitsiwa via Asmera to the strategic garrison town of Keren. A few months later, however, Mitsiwa resumed operation in accordance with an agreement between the EPLF and government forces. By the end of the year, the EPLF had started conducting military operations in the vicinity of the Dahlak Islands and initiated an offensive toward the port of Aseb.

Mass Media

Before and after the 1974 revolution, the government controlled Ethiopia's mass communications. However, after 1974 the ideological orientation of mass media in Ethiopia underwent a substantial change insofar as they became vehicles for spreading Marxist dogma.

The Ministry of Information and National Guidance published two daily newspapers: the English-language *Ethiopian Herald,* with a circulation of 6,000, and the Amharic-language *Addis Zemen,* with a circulation of 37,000. The ministry also printed *Hibret,* a Tigrinya-language newspaper published in Asmera that had a daily circulation of 4,000. The ministry closely controlled the contents of these publications, and it used their editorial pages to analyze certain events and policies from the perspective of scientific socialism.

There were about a dozen periodicals published in Ethiopia. The WPE issued *Serto Ader,* an Amharic-language newsletter with a weekly circulation of about 100,000. Two other periodicals were the magazine *Yekatit Quarterly* and the ideological journal *Meskerem* (circulation 100,000). Both publications were printed in English as well as in Amharic. Marxist-Leninist in tone, the *Yekatit Quarterly* reported mainly on the "accomplishments of the revolution." *Meskerem* was viewed specifically as an instrument of political education.

Foreign Policy

The foreign relations of the modern Ethiopian state were driven by the government's quest to establish this multiethnic polity as a viable nation-state and to maintain its territorial integrity. In many respects, then, the foreign policy pursued by the leaders of post-revolutionary Ethiopia was consistent with the foreign policy of the old imperial regime. The aspect that changed from one era to the next was Ethiopia's ideological alignment. Whereas the regime of Emperor Haile Selassie had relied heavily on the patronage of the United States, that of President Mengistu Haile Mariam cast its fate with the Soviet Union. Both the pre- and post-1974 governments used economic and military aid from their respective superpower patrons to augment their own meager material resources, thus enhancing the ability of the regime to pursue not only certain foreign policy objectives but also specific domestic policies. Analysis of Ethiopia's foreign policy, both past and contemporary, suggests that, rather than serving as the pawns of one superpower or another, Ethiopia's leaders consistently placed their perceptions of what was best for Ethiopia before all else.

Diplomacy and State Building in Imperial Ethiopia

As one of only two African states that have never been permanently colonized (the other is Liberia), Ethiopia has a long diplomatic tradition. Tewodros II, who reigned in the mid-nineteenth century, was the first modern Ethiopian leader to try to develop a foreign policy that transcended the Horn region (see The Making of Modern Ethiopia, ch. 1). His successor, Yohannis IV, followed a less dynamic course and was greatly troubled by European expansionism in general and penetration by Italy in particular. Menelik II, who succeeded Yohannis in 1889, failed to find a peaceful solution to Italy's encroachments. He had greater success, however, in the military sphere, defeating the Italian army at Adwa in 1896.

Menelik died in 1913, and it was not until 1930 that another strong emperor, Haile Selassie I, assumed the throne. Haile Selassie quickly demonstrated that he was committed to the creation of a strong, modern, bureaucratic empire that would command unquestioned international respect. As early as 1923, while serving as regent, he negotiated Ethiopia's admission into the League of Nations. The Italian occupation of Ethiopia between 1936 and 1941 briefly halted his efforts to establish Ethiopia's position in the world community (see Italian Rule and World War II, ch. 1). However, when he reassumed the throne in 1941, he renewed his efforts to bolster Ethiopia's international standing.

After World War II, Haile Selassie achieved considerable international success primarily because of his active participation in the UN, his alignment with the West, and his vocal support for the African independence movement. As a UN member, Ethiopia committed troops to the peacekeeping mission in Korea from 1950 to 1953 and to the Congo (present-day Zaire) in 1960. Moreover, Ethiopia's military and diplomatic relationship with the United States provided it with a superpower ally (see United States, ch. 5). Finally, Haile Selassie took the lead in pressing for a resolution establishing the territorial integrity of the independent states of Africa. Over the years, he developed a reputation as a sage voice of moderation on a continent filled with militant nationalists. It was in this capacity that he offered to host the headquarters of the OAU upon its founding in the early 1960s, once again demonstrating his diplomatic acumen.

The Foreign Policy of the Derg

The foreign policy of Ethiopia did not change immediately upon the demise of the imperial regime. Initially, the country's new leaders maintained the general thrust of the foreign policy developed under Haile Selassie and concentrated mainly on consolidating their rule. Nonetheless, the Marxist ideology of the Derg and its civilian allies made conflict with Ethiopia's superpower patron, the United States, inevitable.

By the mid-1970s, Kagnew station, the communications monitoring base in Asmera granted under terms of the 1953 Mutual Defense Assistance Agreement between Ethiopia and the United States, had largely lost its value. Advances in satellite technology had rendered land-based facilities like Kagnew station less important for long-range communications monitoring. Yet the United States felt the need to maintain a presence in this strategically important part of Africa, particularly because the Soviet Union was beginning to become active in the area. The administration of President Gerald Ford (1974–77) wanted to avoid an embarrassment similar to that experienced by the United States in Angola in 1975, when covert United States aid to anticommunist combatants failed to dislodge the pro-Moscow Popular Movement for the Liberation of Angola. Even though President Ford and Secretary of State Henry Kissinger indicated uneasiness with Ethiopia's violations of human rights and growing leftist tendencies, they did no more than cautiously encourage the Derg to moderate its human rights policies.

The United States began to express concern over the Derg's human rights violations when on November 23, 1974, a day that came to be known as "Bloody Saturday," fifty-nine officials who had served in the old regime were executed. Official United States concern intensified two months later when the Derg mobilized a force consisting of regular military units and the hastily assembled People's Militia in an effort to resolve the Eritrean question through military means (see People's Militia, ch. 5). But Eritrean forces attacked first, surprising the Ethiopian forces in their base camps and scoring an impressive victory.

Whereas the administration of President Ford had been reluctant to impose sanctions on Ethiopia because of its human rights record, President Jimmy Carter made human rights a central concern of his administration (1977–81). On February 25, 1977, Carter announced that because of continued human rights violations, certain governments that were receiving Washington's military aid (including Ethiopia) would receive reduced assistance in the following fiscal year. Consequently, the Derg began to cast about for alternative sources of military assistance. Among the countries Ethiopia turned to were China and the Soviet Union. At first, the actual assistance provided by these superpowers was minimal, and the United States maintained its presence in the country. However, relations between the United States and Ethiopia deteriorated rapidly. By April 1977, Mengistu had demanded that Washington close down Kagnew station and most other installations; only a small staff was allowed to remain at the United States embassy. By then, the first supplies of Soviet military hardware had begun to arrive.

Having its military presence in Ethiopia ended, and with tensions mounting in the Middle East and Iran, the United States began to cultivate alliances in northeast Africa that could facilitate the development of a long-range military strike capability. These developments coincided with an escalation of tensions in the Horn region in general. The United States eventually began the systematic pursuit of a strategy that amounted to encircling the Arabian Peninsula. The United States asked Egypt, Sudan, Kenya, Somalia, and Oman to allow their territories to be used as staging grounds for the fledgling Rapid Deployment Force (RDF), which later became the United States Central Command. The Soviet Union's clients in the region—Ethiopia, Libya, and the People's Democratic Republic of Yemen (South Yemen)—perceiving Washington's action as a threat, signed a tripartite agreement in 1981 and pledged to repulse any effort to intervene in their respective countries. However, this alliance never played a significant role in the region.

The Derg, the Soviet Union, and the Communist World

Apparently sensing that the Mengistu regime was in desperate trouble, internal and external enemies took action to hasten its demise (see External and Internal Opponents, ch. 5). Most important, civilian opposition groups began to wage urban guerrilla campaigns to demoralize and discredit the Derg, and Somalia committed regular troops to assist ethnic Somali living in Ethiopia's Ogaden region in their efforts to separate from Ethiopia. Simultaneously, the Somali government expressed concern over the growing Soviet and Cuban presence in Ethiopia. Until then, Somalia had been an ally of the Soviet Union. After the Somali National Army (SNA) invaded the Ogaden region in July 1977, the Soviet Union withdrew its 1,000 advisers from Somalia. In November Somalia announced that it had abrogated the 1974 Treaty of Friendship and Cooperation with the Soviet Union and that it had suspended diplomatic relations with Cuba. At that point, the Soviet Union adopted Ethiopia as its main ally in the Horn of Africa. In late November, it launched a massive airlift and sealift of arms and other military equipment to Ethiopia. Over the next several months, about 17,000 Cuban and 1,000 Soviet military personnel arrived in the country and were deployed to the Ogaden front. This aid turned the tide in favor of Ethiopia by early 1978.

As had the regime of Haile Selassie, the Derg accorded its international image and territorial integrity the highest priority in its foreign policy. Opposition groups had forced the regime to rely extensively on the Soviet Union to maintain itself in power and to preserve the country's territorial integrity. From 1977 to 1990, Soviet military assistance to Ethiopia was estimated to be as much as US$13 billion. However, by 1987 there was evidence that the Soviet Union had decided to cut back military assistance to Ethiopia and to press for political solutions to that country's several civil conflicts. By that time, there were fewer than 1,800 Soviet advisers in Ethiopia and a total of about 2,000 advisers from Bulgaria, Czechoslovakia, Hungary, East Germany, and Poland. Furthermore, all Cuban troops in the Ogaden had withdrawn, and the Cuban military presence in Ethiopia had dropped to fewer than 2,000.

Although Ethiopia was dependent on the Soviet Union for military assistance and sided with it in the international diplomatic arena, Addis Ababa on numerous occasions demonstrated its independence in the area of domestic policy and international economic policy. For instance, the Derg procrastinated in setting up a vanguard party despite Soviet pressure to do so. Once the party was formed, it was dominated by former military personnel, again contrary to Soviet wishes. In the economic sphere, Addis Ababa had close aid and trade relations with the West and pursued a pragmatic investment policy.

Although Mengistu eschewed any talk of Ethiopian-style *glasnost,* Ethiopia could not escape the global impact of Soviet leader Mikhail Gorbachev's reforms. When Mengistu visited the Soviet Union in 1988, Gorbachev told him that if Moscow's support were to continue, the Soviet Union would have to see dramatic changes in Ethiopia's agricultural priorities, coupled with political liberalization. The Soviet leader also refused to continue unqualified military and economic support of the Mengistu regime. A combination of economic realities and Soviet pressure encouraged the Mengistu regime in 1989 to retreat at least partially from its dogmatically statist approach to economic development (see Role of Government, ch. 3). By late 1990, the Soviet-Ethiopian alliance had ended. As a result, Addis Ababa looked to several other nations, including Israel and China, for military assistance. None of these nations, however, was capable of replacing the amount of military equipment the Soviet Union had supplied to Ethiopia.

The Derg and the West

Although the Derg depended on the Soviet Union and its allies for military aid, it was just as reliant on the West for economic development and relief aid (see Balance of Payments and Foreign Assistance, ch. 3). For example, the European Community (EC) was Ethiopia's most significant source of economic aid. In the early 1980s, Western sources accounted for more than 90 percent of Ethiopia's economic aid, most of which came from the EC. Since then, communist countries had increased their proportion of total aid to Ethiopia to about 20 percent. Other multilateral and bilateral donors also had provided increased aid. For example, after refraining from giving aid to Addis Ababa between 1975 and 1981, the World Bank (see Glossary) pledged more than US$250 million in project aid, the European Development Fund promised about US$300 million, and the International Monetary Fund (IMF—see Glossary) agreed to a loan of almost US$100 million. The regime accepted the IMF loan even though it claimed to disagree with IMF policies. Moreover, a joint venture law in 1983 and a foreign investment policy initiated in 1988 had stimulated the gradual return of private investors, although the level of such investments remained low.

Even though Ethiopia was dependent on Western economic aid, no Western donor was able to influence day-to-day economic policy on a regular basis. For instance, the Swedish International Development Authority, the United States Agency for International Development (AID), the World Bank, and other donor agencies historically had favored the development of agricultural cooperatives if they were organized on free-market principles. However, the Ethiopian regime attempted to guide the development of cooperatives so that they might be transformed into socialist collectives compatible with a centrally planned and directed economy. Like the imperial government before it, the Derg attempted to play off a multiplicity of donors against one another and thereby maximize certain benefits without surrendering its sovereignty.

Ethiopia's Border Politics

As the Mengistu regime attempted to consolidate its rule, it had to cope with serious border problems, particularly with Somalia and Sudan. The point at issue with Somalia was the Ogaden region, an area that Mogadishu claimed as part of the historical Somali nation that had been seized by the Ethiopians during the colonial partition of the Horn of Africa. In fact, Ethiopia's only undefined boundary was the border it shared with the former Italian

Africa Hall, headquarters of the Economic Commission for Africa, Addis Ababa. The Organization of African Unity conducted its first meeting at this site.
Courtesy United Nations

Somaliland. On maps drawn after 1950, this boundary is termed "Administrative Line" (see fig. 1). Upon gaining independence from European colonial rule in 1960, the inhabitants of the Republic of Somalia nurtured the hope that all Somali eventually would be united in a modern nation-state. Somali claims to the Ogaden, Djibouti, and parts of Kenya, however, had been consistently rejected by the UN, the OAU, and most of the world's sovereign states. Still, Somalia's leadership remained unwilling to forsake these claims publicly.

In 1961, less than a year after Somalia gained independence, its troops clashed with Ethiopian soldiers along their common border. In 1964 renewed tensions erupted into a minor regional war. In both cases, Somalia was defeated. Ethnic Somali in Kenya's northeast also unsuccessfully challenged that country's new government in the early 1960s. Pan-Somalism, then, served as a basis for the continuance of cooperative relations between Nairobi and Addis Ababa, despite the change of regime in Ethiopia. The two countries first signed a mutual defense agreement in 1964 that resulted in the creation of the Ethiopia-Kenya Border Administration Commission.

The Ogaden War (1977–78) was the most serious border conflict between Ethiopia and Somalia (see The Somali, ch. 5). Beginning in the early summer of 1977, SNA units and WSLF guerrillas, a movement of ethnic Somali opposed to incorporation in Ethiopia, occupied vast tracts of the Ogaden and forced the Ethiopian army into fortresses at Jijiga, Harer, and Dire Dawa for almost eight months. The intention was to separate the Ogaden from Ethiopia to set the stage for ethnic Somali in the region to decide their own future.

It was only with Soviet and Cuban assistance that the Derg regained control over the region by early 1978. The Soviet Union not only provided massive amounts of military equipment but also advisers, who trained Ethiopian soldiers and pilots. Moreover, Cuban troops spearheaded the counteroffensive that began in March 1978. Cuban and Ethiopian troops quickly defeated the SNA and WSLF once the counteroffensive began. Many WSLF fighters returned to their villages or took refuge inside Somalia. In addition, some 650,000 Somali and Oromo fled from southeastern Ethiopia into Somalia by early 1978 to escape unsettled local conditions and repression by Ethiopian armed forces. After the defeat, Somali opposition reverted to sporadic guerrilla ambushes and occasional acts of sabotage.

On April 4, 1988, after several preparatory meetings, Ethiopia and Somalia signed a joint communiqué that supposedly ended the Ogaden conflict. According to the communiqué's terms, the two countries committed themselves to withdrawing their military forces fifteen kilometers from the border, exchanging prisoners of war, restoring diplomatic relations, and refraining from supporting each other's antigovernment guerrilla groups. Reportedly, a separate secret accord contained a Somali renunciation of all claims to the Ogaden region. From Mengistu's point of view, the joint communiqué secured Ethiopia's southeastern border, thereby enabling Addis Ababa to devote more resources to the struggle against the EPLF and TPLF in northern Ethiopia.

Nevertheless, by 1991 it had become evident that Ethiopia had failed to honor the provisions of the joint communiqué. The Mengistu regime allowed the anti-Siad Barre Somali National Movement (SNM) to maintain offices in Addis Ababa and Dire Dawa and to operate five training camps near Dire Dawa. Additionally, the Ethiopian government still provided matériel and logistical support to the SNM. Despite these violations, Somalia refrained from reinitiating hostilities with Ethiopia.

Relations between Ethiopia and Sudan were generally good until the mid-1980s, when the Sudanese People's Liberation Army (SPLA) emerged to challenge the hegemony of Khartoum. Emperor Haile Selassie had been instrumental in mediating an end to the Sudanese civil war in 1972. However, Ethiopia regularly expressed disappointment that the Sudanese government had not prevented Eritrean guerrillas from operating out of its territory. Sudan attempted to negotiate an end to the Eritrean conflict in 1975 but was unsuccessful. When Ethiopia turned to the Soviet Union and away from the United States, Sudan's government became concerned. Sudanese president Jaafar an Nimeiri had accused the Soviet Union of having inspired coup attempts against his regime in 1971 and 1976. Sudan recalled its ambassador to Ethiopia in January 1977, and for several years serious border tensions existed between the two countries.

Ethiopia's turn toward the Soviet Union caused Sudan to seek the support of new allies in preparing for the possibility of external invasions sponsored by Khartoum's regional enemies. Nimeiri decided to openly support certain Eritrean liberation movements. In addition, he supported Somalia during the Ogaden War. Nimeiri claimed that he wanted to build a "high wall against communism" in the Horn of Africa and agreed to participate with the United States, Kenya, Egypt, Somalia, and Oman in the development of the RDF. By 1980 the tensions between Sudan and Ethiopia had abated, however, with the signing of a peace treaty calling for the mutual respect of the territorial integrity and sovereignty of the two countries.

The 1981 tripartite agreement among Ethiopia, Libya, and South Yemen undermined relations between Addis Ababa and Khartoum. For some time, the Libyan government had been trying to overthrow Nimeiri. Now Ethiopia appeared to be joining the Libyan effort. Border tensions between the two countries also increased after Ethiopia started supporting the SPLA.

After Nimeiri was overthrown in 1985, Sadiq al Mahdi's regime made it clear that it wanted to improve relations with Ethiopia and Libya. Supposedly, this was the first step in the resolution of Sudan's civil war. The change in regimes in Sudan also prompted a deterioration in United States-Sudanese relations, manifested by Khartoum's cancellation of the agreement calling for the participation of Sudanese troops in the Operation Bright Star exercises. Despite Sudan's estrangement from the United States and Mahdi's growing closeness to Libya after 1985, there was no substantive improvement in Ethiopian-Sudanese relations. The problem continued to center on Sudan's support for Eritrean rebels and Mengistu's continued support of the SPLA. By 1989, following the overthrow of Sadiq al Mahdi, Khartoum and Addis Ababa had offered to negotiate their respective internal conflicts, but nothing tangible came of this.

Addis Ababa and the Middle East

To undermine regional support for the Eritrean movements, after 1987 the Ethiopian government tried to develop better relations with several Arab countries. Between 1987 and 1989, high-level Ethiopian delegations visited Egypt, Syria, Iraq, Libya, and Saudi Arabia. In the fall of 1988, Mengistu paid a two-day visit to Syria to explain to President Hafiz al Assad the various reforms the Ethiopian regime had recently made, including the creation of autonomous regions, designed to be responsive to the desires of groups like the Eritreans. Prime Minister Fikre-Selassie Wogderes made a visit to Cairo in November 1988 to seek improved relations with Egypt and to express support for Egypt's offer to negotiate a settlement of the Eritrean conflict. Despite these moves, Ethiopia's relations with the Middle East remained minimal.

By 1989 the lack of progress toward improved relations with Arab countries and the desperate need for arms appeared to have inspired Ethiopia to develop closer ties with Israel. Subsequently, diplomatic relations between the two countries, which had been broken off at the time of the October 1973 War, were restored. Approximately 10,000 Beta Israel (Ethiopian Jews; also called Falasha) had been spirited out of Ethiopia to Israel in 1984 in a secret airlift known as Operation Moses, and Israel remained committed to securing the emigration of the remaining Beta Israel. In return, Israel agreed to provide the Mengistu regime with military assistance (see Ethnic Groups, Ethnicity, and Language, ch. 2).

Israel obtained the release of an additional large number of Beta Israel in May 1991 in the midst of the collapse of the Mengistu regime. Negotiations for another Beta Israel exodus were already under way, and large numbers of them had already been brought to Addis Ababa when the military government came under intense pressure from EPRDF forces. At the behest of both Israel and the United States, the government agreed to release the Beta Israel against an Israeli payment of US$35 million. On May 24–26, in what was called Operation Solomon, some 15,000 Beta Israel were airlifted from Ethiopia to Israel, leaving an estimated 5,000 behind, mostly around Gonder.

The Demise of the Military Government

In retrospect, perhaps the two crucial factors in the fall of the Mengistu regime were the abortive coup of May 1989 and the loss of Soviet military and political support. In the aftermath of quelling the coup, disaffection spread throughout the army. Thereafter, whole military units defected, taking their arms and equipment with them as they joined insurgent groups. At the same time, Soviet military deliveries dwindled and then ceased, a source of supply that Mengistu was never able to replace, leaving government forces still further weakened and demoralized. It was these developments that led Mengistu to attempt economic reforms in 1989 and 1990 and to initiate peace talks with the EPLF and EPRDF under Italian and United States auspices.

During the early months of 1991, both the military and the political outlooks darkened considerably for the government. The EPLF pressed its sweep down the Red Sea coast with the aim of capturing Aseb (see The Eritreans, ch. 5). In February and March, EPRDF forces overran large portions of Gonder, Gojam, and Welega, threatening Addis Ababa from the northwest and west (see The Tigray, ch. 5). In mid-April the National Shengo proposed talks with all political groups that would lead to a transitional government, a cease-fire, and amnesty for all political prisoners. At the same time, the National Shengo tempered its peace initiative by calling for the mobilization of all adults over the age of eighteen and for the strengthening of the WPE. A few days later, on April 26, Mengistu, in a gesture to his opponents, reshuffled the government, dropping several hard-liners and replacing them with moderates. Among the latter were Lieutenant General Tesfaye Gebre-Kidan, one of the army's commanders in Eritrea, who was promoted to vice president, and Tesfaye Dinka, former foreign minister, who became prime minister. Both belonged to a group of advisers who had been urging Mengistu to compromise with the Eritreans and the Tigray.

The main opposition parties—the EPLF, EPRDF, and OLF—rebuffed the National Shengo's offer. During the next month, as all parties prepared for the next round of talks scheduled for London in late May, the EPLF and EPRDF pressed hard on the military front. In late April, EPRDF forces were reported to be some 100 kilometers west of Addis Ababa and still advancing; in Eritrea the EPLF made gains along the Red Sea coast and closed in on Keren and Asmera. In mid-May the last major government strongholds north of Addis Ababa—Dese and Kembolcha in southern Welo—fell to the EPRDF. With little but demoralized and fleeing troops between the capital and the EPRDF forces, Mengistu resigned the presidency and fled the country on May 21. His exit, widely regarded as essential if the upcoming negotiations were to succeed, was secured in part through the efforts of Assistant Secretary of State Herman Cohen, who pressured Mengistu to resign and arranged for his exile in Zimbabwe.

263

Lieutenant General Tesfaye, now head of state, called for a cease-fire; he also offered to share power with his opponents and went so far as to begin releasing political prisoners, but to no avail. EPRDF fighters continued their advance on the virtually defenseless capital and announced that they could enter it at will. Meanwhile, on May 24, the EPLF received the surrender of Keren and the 120,000-member garrison in Asmera, which brought the whole of Eritrea under its control except for Aseb, which fell the next day. The goal of independence from Ethiopia, for which Eritreans had fought for three decades, now seemed a virtual certainty.

Against the background of these events, the London conference opened on May 27. The main contending parties were all in attendance: the government party headed by Tesfaye Dinka, the EPLF under Issaias Afwerki, the EPRDF under TPLF leader Meles Zenawi, and the OLF under its deputy secretary general, Lencho Letta. Assistant Secretary Cohen served as a mutually acceptable mediator. Ostensibly, the conference was supposed to explore ways to set up a transitional government in Addis Ababa, but its proceedings were soon overtaken by events on the ground. The talks had hardly gotten under way when Cohen received a message to the effect that Lieutenant General Tesfaye had lost control of the government's remaining armed units and that Addis Ababa was threatened with a complete breakdown of law and order. To prevent uncontrolled destruction and looting, Cohen recommended that EPRDF forces immediately move into Addis Ababa and establish control. Tesfaye Dinka strenuously objected, but he spoke from a position of weakness and could not prevail; he subsequently withdrew from the conference. On the night of May 27–28, EPRDF forces marched into Addis Ababa and assumed control of the city and national government.

The next day, Cohen again met with leaders of the EPLF, EPRDF, and OLF, but now as an adviser and not as a mediator. The insurgent leaders committed themselves to a pluralist democratic society and government for Ethiopia and agreed that Eritreans would be free to determine their own future, including independence if they wished. They also agreed that the EPRDF should continue to exercise temporary control in Addis Ababa. The task of constructing a transitional government, however, was postponed until early July, when a national conference broadly representative of all major political groups would convene in Addis Ababa to take up the matter. With these agreements in hand, the London conference adjourned, but not before Cohen stressed the need for fundamental reforms and conditioned future United States aid upon construction of a democratic political system.

By early June, the EPRDF claimed that it had established effective control over most of the country, the last remaining government troops in Dire Dawa and Harer having surrendered along with some 300 officials and military officers of the former regime. The new rulers faced a number of daunting problems, among them famine and starvation affecting several million people, a severely dislocated economy and society, the prospect of Eritrean independence and with it the loss of direct access to the Red Sea, and the thorny and far from settled question of ethnicity. The explosive potential of these problems was immediately apparent when, only a day after having marched into Addis Ababa, EPRDF soldiers shot or wounded several demonstrators protesting the EPRDF takeover, agreements affecting Eritrea, and United States policies toward the country. Even so, there was much hope and optimism about the future among a war-weary population, as well as a palpable sense of relief that seventeen years of despised military rule had at last come to an end.

*   *   *

One of the first accounts of the Ethiopian revolution, and still a valuable book for understanding the earlier phases of the process, is Marina and David Ottaway's *Ethiopia: Empire in Revolution.* In recent years, there have been a number of outstanding scholarly works on the Ethiopian revolution. The best among these are Christopher S. Clapham's *Transformation and Continuity in Revolutionary Ethiopia,* a richly detailed institutional analysis of the revolution; Fred Halliday and Maxine Molyneux's *The Ethiopian Revolution,* a scholarly Marxian interpretation of the first five years of the revolution; John W. Harbeson's *The Ethiopian Transformation,* a study of the revolution and its military foundations; Edmond J. Keller's *Revolutionary Ethiopia: From Empire to People's Republic,* a comprehensive analysis of the underlying and precipitating causes of the revolution and its consequences; John Markakis's *National and Class Conflict in the Horn of Africa,* a critical, Marxian analysis of the regional political dimensions of the revolution; and Mulatu Wubneh and Yohannis Abate's *Ethiopia: Transition and Development in the Horn of Africa,* an overview of Ethiopian politics, economy, and society up to the late 1980s. There are few good inside accounts of the revolution, but two works stand out: Dawit Wolde Giorgis's *Red Tears,* an insightful account of the inner workings of the Mengistu regime, written by a former member of the WPE Central Committee and head of the RRC; and David A. Korn's *Ethiopia, the United States, and the Soviet Union,* which describes the revolution as seen from the perspective of a United States diplomat living in Ethiopia.

Useful accounts of the various liberation movements are scanty. Among the more notable recent works are Bereket Habte Selassie's *Conflict and Intervention in the Horn of Africa,* James Firebrace's *Never Kneel Down,* and Jordan Gebre-Medhin's *Peasants and Nationalism in Eritrea.* Each of these is best on the Eritrean struggle. The most comprehensive discussion of the TPLF can be found in Markakis's *National and Class Conflict in the Horn of Africa.* (For further information and complete citations, see Bibliography.)

Chapter 5. National Security

Lancers, adapted from an eighteenth-century religious manuscript. Traditional Ethiopian art depicts righteous warriors in full face, the enemy in profile.

FOR CENTURIES, MOST ETHIOPIANS understood that every able-bodied male might be called upon to perform military service. Despite the importance of a career as a warrior in Ethiopian society, however, it was not until 1942 that the country possessed truly national armed forces. To modernize the Ethiopian army, Emperor Haile Selassie I (reigned 1930–74) relied on foreign military assistance and advisers. From 1942 to 1952, Britain was Ethiopia's major arms supplier as a result of its role in the liberation of Ethiopia. Between 1953 and 1976, the United States provided Ethiopia with most of its weapons and training. Starting in 1977, the Soviet Union was the country's closest military partner.

In 1974 Haile Selassie's imperial regime collapsed. Eventually, a Marxist dictatorship took power in Ethiopia. Having assumed the roles of chief of state and commander in chief, Mengistu Haile Mariam consolidated his hold on the armed forces by eliminating both real and imagined political opponents. Despite the transformation of the country's military establishment from an imperial force to an instrument of Marxist policy in the "vanguard of the revolution," the Mengistu regime continued to observe Ethiopian traditions concerning the preeminent role of the soldier in state and society.

In mid-1991 Ethiopia had the largest combined military and paramilitary force in sub-Saharan Africa (438,000 personnel) and, with 150 modern combat aircraft and about 1,300 tanks, certainly one of the best equipped. Although not an integral part of the defense establishment, the Mobile Emergency Police Force participated in counterinsurgency operations. In addition, the government had transformed armed civilian People's Protection Brigades from vigilante groups into local law enforcement units.

Competing nationalisms that confront each other in the Horn of Africa have posed the most serious threat to Ethiopia's national security. Since 1961, the Ethiopian armed forces have been fighting secessionists in Eritrea and, since 1974, insurgents in Tigray. Ethiopia, aided by a large Cuban combat force and Soviet logistical support, also fought a conventional war against Somalia over the Ogaden in 1977–78.

After the Provisional Military Administrative Council seized power in 1974, Ethiopia relied almost exclusively on the Soviet Union and its allies to prosecute its various wars. By the late 1980s, however, Moscow was no longer willing to provide unlimited amounts of military assistance to Ethiopia. Instead, the Soviet Union urged the Mengistu regime to seek a negotiated settlement with Eritrean secessionists and Tigrayan rebels. Cuba, having played a vital role in Ethiopia's 1978 victory over Somalia in the Ogaden, had withdrawn all its military personnel from the country. Moreover, the dramatic events of 1989 in Eastern Europe had prompted the German Democratic Republic (East Germany), Czechoslovakia, and Romania to cancel all military agreements with the Ethiopian government. As a result, Ethiopia was seeking alternative sources of military assistance from nations such as the Democratic People's Republic of Korea (North Korea) and Israel. This strategy, however, failed to enable the Mengistu regime to defeat the Eritrean secessionists and Tigrayan rebels or even to ensure the survival of the regime in the new decade.

Military Tradition in National Life

Wars, insurrections, and rebellions have punctuated Ethiopia's history. Kings and nobles raised and maintained armies to defend the "Christian island" against Muslim invasion or to conquer neighboring territories. Even after consolidation of centralized authority under "Solomonic" emperors in the thirteenth century, subordinate *neguses* (kings) and powerful nobles, some of whom later carried the high military title of *ras* (roughly, marshal; literally, head in Amharic), ruled different regions of the kingdom and commanded their own armies as they struggled for power and position. According to a seventeenth-century European, only nature could temper the bellicosity of the Ethiopians, whom he described as "a warlike people and continually exercised in war" except during respites "caused by the winter, at which time by reason of inundation of the rivers they are forced to be quiet."

From the time of its establishment in the thirteenth century, the Christian kingdom of Ethiopia was fundamentally a warrior society. Both the Amhara and the Tigray, the two dominant peoples of the kingdom, were imbued with a military ethos that placed great value on achievement in battle and the spoils to be gained thereby. Military values influenced the political, economic, and social organization of the Christian kingdom, while senior state officers often bore military titles. Additionally, military symbolism and themes occur frequently in Amhara and Tigray art, literature, and folklore of the period. Other ethnic groups, particularly the Oromo, also had warrior traditions and admired courage in combat, although the social systems that encouraged these values differed substantially from those of the Amhara and the Tigray.

Generally, soldiering has been the surest path to social advancement and economic reward in Ethiopia. Kings and nobles traditionally awarded land, titles, and political appointments to those who proved their loyalty, competence, and courage on the battlefield. As a result, warriors traditionally gave allegiance to that commander who could assure the fruits of victory to his followers, rather than to an abstract notion of the state or to government authority.

In early times, the army's command structure, like the nation's social structure, resembled a pyramid with the emperor at its apex as supreme military leader. In the field, a hierarchy of warlords led the army. Each was subordinate to a warlord of a higher rank and commanded others at a lower rank according to a system of vertical personal loyalties that bound them all to the emperor. At each command level, the military drew troops from three sources. Each warlord, from the emperor to a minor noble, had a standing corps of armed retainers that varied in size according to the leader's importance. Many landholders also served several months each year in the local lord's retinue in lieu of paying taxes. Most troops, however, came from the mass of able-bodied adult freemen, clergy alone excepted, who could be summoned by proclamation on an ad hoc basis when and where their service was required.

Each man provided his own weapon and was expected to acquire skill in its use on his own initiative. He brought his own food for the march or foraged en route. Often a soldier brought his wife or a female servant to cook and tend mules. Indeed, the authorities recognized women as an integral part of the Ethiopian army insofar as many officers believed that their presence discouraged cowardice among the men. More important, women formed an unofficial quartermaster corps because men believed it was beneath their dignity to prepare food.

In an environment in which war was the government's regular business, the mobile army camp became the capital of its leader, whether emperor, *negus,* or *ras.* Only rarely before the late nineteenth century did a ruler maintain his court at a fixed location throughout the year. Constantly moving over his domain, a ruler took his court with him, issuing laws and decrees from the army camp, collecting and consuming taxes paid in kind, and supervising trade. So integrated was military command with government that army officers also functioned in civil capacities.

The organization of military camps remained virtually unchanged for centuries. In the royal camp, the emperor's tent, customarily pitched on an elevation, marked the center of the encampment. The tents of his immediate retinue surrounded the royal tent. The bodyguard was posted in front of the camp, thus indicating the direction of march. The highest ranking subordinate in the royal army was the *dejazmatch* (general of the door), who was in charge of the center of the battle formation. The *gannazmatch* (general of the right wing) and the *gerazmatch* (general of the left wing) and their troops camped to the right and left, respectively. At the rear of the main encampment was the rear guard, whose commander usually was a trustworthy counselor and the leader's chief minister. Subordinate warlords and their troops camped around the emperor's compound in small-scale replicas of the royal camp. The advance guard was a standard feature of this mobile army, and in times of war it might travel several days' march ahead of the main body.

Although infantrymen made up the bulk of the army, cavalry participated in most military operations. The standard attack formation was a crescent-shaped mass of foot soldiers in which both wings advanced to outflank and envelop the enemy's defenses. Once engaged, the individual soldier was the army's basic fighting unit, and a final charge to bring the enemy to hand-to-hand combat usually decided a battle. Mutilating slain enemies and abandoning the wounded and dead on the battlefield were accepted practices.

Leadership, especially among emperors and powerful nobles, was intensely personal, and commanders at all levels led their men in combat. Success or failure often depended on the leader's fate; upon his death, whole armies frequently scattered and fled.

The army lived off the ruler's subjects wherever it camped in his domain. When troops exhausted food and firewood, they struck their tents and moved on. Often, soldiers turned to brigandage. During Emperor Menelik II's reign (1889–1913), for example, many Ethiopians complained that soldiers ''eat, drink, sleep, and grow fat at the expense of what the poor have.'' Popular feeling against the military was strong in newly conquered territories, where at least a portion of the army would settle as colonists. The granting of tracts of conquered land to soldiers survived into the 1930s. Soldiers benefiting from this system became the landlords and the tax collectors in areas they had conquered. Not surprisingly, the army's demands on local populations often prompted rebellions.

The titles of rank in the traditional military system indicated position in society at large. Soldiers won promotions—and therefore enhancement of their social status—by demonstrating military ability. Titles were not inherited, and distinctions had to be earned. Even those starting at the bottom of the social scale could attain wealth and position if they could draw attention to themselves by displays of loyalty, valor, and ruthlessness. The traditional system's strength and weakness lay in the fact that every warrior strove to become great and as such saw himself the potential equal of the greatest warrior or noble.

Modernization of the Ethiopian army started during the regency of Tafari Mekonnen (who took the throne name of Haile Selassie I when crowned emperor in 1930). In 1917 he formed the Imperial Bodyguard as a regular standing force, recruiting into it some Ethiopian veterans of the British campaign in German East Africa (present-day Tanzania). The regent also hired foreign officers to develop training programs (see Training, this ch.). In the 1920s, he sent Ethiopian officers to the French military academy at Saint-Cyr and arranged for a Belgian military mission to train the Imperial Bodyguard. In January 1935, with Swedish assistance, Ethiopia established a military school at Holeta to turn out officers qualified in modern techniques. The first class, which had been scheduled to complete a sixteen-month course, never graduated because of mounting tensions with Ethiopia's nemesis, Italy, this time under the fascist leadership of Benito Mussolini.

When Mussolini's forces crossed into Ethiopia from the Italian colony of Eritrea and from Italian Somaliland in 1935 without a declaration of war, provincial armies raised by the nobility moved and fought against the mechanized Italian forces in traditional fashion. Haile Selassie's mobilization order typified the Ethiopian way of waging war: everyone would be mobilized, and all males old enough to carry a spear would be sent to Addis Ababa. Married men would bring their wives to carry food and to cook. Those without wives would take any woman without a husband. Women with small babies were not required to go. Men who were blind or who could not carry a spear were exempted.

At the time of the Italian invasion, the regular Ethiopian army had only a few units trained in European warfare and led by officers schooled in modern fighting. These included the Imperial Bodyguard and the Harer garrison. About 5,000 strong in combat against the Italians, many of these troops failed to implement tactics they had learned during training exercises. Most of the army that opposed the Italian invasion consisted of traditional warriors from the provincial militia, armed with spears and obsolete rifles and led by the provincial nobility. Even the 25,000-member regular army marched barefoot and lacked a logistical support system. By early 1936, the Italians—who used chemical weapons and air power with deadly accuracy—had inflicted a severe defeat on the Ethiopians.

After the country's liberation by allied forces in 1941, Haile Selassie started to transform Ethiopia into a centralized monarchical state. The creation of a strong national army was an important part of that transformation. The imperial regime abolished the ancient military hierarchy and abandoned the traditional method of raising armies by provincial levies. In 1942 the emperor signed a military convention with London under which the British government agreed to provide a military mission to assist in organizing and training an army that would be capable of restoring order throughout the country. Under the terms of the convention, the British assumed responsibility for policing Addis Ababa and for exercising military control over the country's principal towns (see Foreign Military Assistance, this ch.).

Another aspect of Haile Selassie's transformation strategy was the creation of the Territorial Army, whose mission was to disarm the numerous guerrilla bands that were roaming the countryside after the war and engaging in banditry. The emperor authorized the recruitment of many *shifta* (bandits) into the Territorial Army, provided they brought their weapons with them. The Territorial Army was never anything more than a loosely organized auxiliary forces; when and where it existed, it served mostly to aid in local police work and not in national defense.

In the immediate postwar period, the Ethiopian government expended about 40 percent of its annual budget on defense and internal security. Haile Selassie also diversified his sources of foreign military assistance. Over several years, he appointed Swedish officers to train Ethiopia's air force, asked Norwegian naval personnel to organize and develop a small coastal navy, signed a military assistance agreement with the United States, invited Israeli advisers to train paratroopers and counterinsurgency units, and arranged for an Indian military mission to staff the faculty of the military academy at Harer. During this period, a number of Ethiopian officers attended military schools in the United States, Britain, and Yugoslavia (see Training, this ch.).

After their modernization, Ethiopia's security forces saw action in several foreign conflicts. For example, upon the outbreak of the Korean War in June 1950, Haile Selassie raised a volunteer battalion from the Imperial Bodyguard and authorized its deployment to Korea with the United Nations (UN) forces. The Kagnew Battalion, as the unit was known, reached Korea the next year and joined the United States Seventh Division. Before the 1953 ceasefire, three Ethiopian battalions, totaling 5,000 men, had rotated to Korea, where they fought with distinction.

From 1960 to 1964, some 3,000 Imperial Bodyguard personnel—about 10 percent of the Ethiopian army's entire strength at that time—and part of an air force squadron served with the UN peacekeeping force in the Congo (present-day Zaire). In 1967 four Ethiopian air force F–86 fighter-bombers were deployed to Zaire

Haile Selassie I inspects Ethiopian troops before their departure to join a United Nations peacekeeping force in the former Belgian Congo in 1960.
Courtesy United Nations

to help dislodge a concentration of European mercenaries fighting there on behalf of secessionists in Katanga Province (present-day Shaba Region).

The reforms instituted by Haile Selassie, including the establishment of a relatively large professional standing army, separated military and civilian functions in a way that was unique in the country's history. By 1974 much of the population maintained an ambivalent attitude toward the reorganized and modernized military establishment. On the one hand, civilians, many of whom were university students, often complained that the military drained the national budget and failed to help the country develop. On the other hand, many Ethiopians expressed pride in the armed forces' ability to maintain the country's territorial integrity. Much of the civilian sector also believed that the military represented the best chance for change in Ethiopia.

After the 1974 revolution, the Provisional Military Administrative Council (PMAC; also known as the Derg—see Glossary) designated the armed forces as the "vanguard of the revolution" and apparently had expectations that military personnel would become involved in social and economic development programs. The drain on manpower and matériel caused by the wars in Eritrea, Tigray, and the Ogaden prevented the realization of this objective. However, military cadres became active in peasant associations, political organizing, drought relief, and other duties once assigned to the regular police. The army also undertook projects to improve the country's transportation infrastructure.

Despite the repressiveness of the Mengistu regime, public demonstrations of discontent with the armed forces grew in frequency in the 1980s. The army's inability to achieve victory in Eritrea and Tigray disillusioned many who had supported the 1974 revolution, and the conflicts in north-central Ethiopia caused divisions within the military itself. On May 16, 1989, a group of senior officers attempted a coup against President Mengistu. The coup failed, but it was a key factor in the fall of the military government in late May 1991.

The Armed Forces

In mid-1991 the Ethiopian armed forces, with about 438,000 personnel in uniform, constituted one of the largest and best-equipped militaries in sub-Saharan Africa. The defense establishment included the 230,000-member conscript army, supplemented by the 200,000-member People's Militia; the air force, with a personnel strength of 4,500; and the navy, with a personnel strength of 3,500, which included a marine contingent. Not included in these figures were the 9,000-member Mobile Emergency Police Force and an unknown number of border guards. In addition to its duties as protector of the country's territorial integrity, the armed forces engaged in internal security and counterinsurgency operations against the government's political opponents.

The 1987 Constitution and the Armed Forces

The constitution, which took effect on February 22, 1987, made several explicit references to the history, missions, and organization of the armed forces. The preamble took note of Ethiopia's "great victory at Adwa over [Italy's] modern colonialist army" and recalled that "the army, being an integral part of the people . . . [laid] . . . the foundations of the new people's system by eliminating the monarchy and taking various revolutionary steps." Chapter 4 of the constitution was devoted to defense issues. It called for the government, through its defense force, to defend and safeguard the revolution, and it reminded the people that these duties were their responsibilities. Accordingly, the constitution stated that the government would implement national service, and in a later chapter it stipulated that "national military service is the right and obligation of every Ethiopian. Its implementation shall be decided on by law.''

In terms of civilian control of the armed forces, the constitution stated that the highest body in the government, the National Shengo (National Assembly), was responsible for determining defense and security policy and for declaring states of war and peace. Subordinate to this body was the Council of State, charged with implementing decisions of the National Shengo. The president of the Council of State was also the president of Ethiopia and commander in chief of the armed forces. The Council of State was empowered to establish a national-level Defense Council (whose duties and responsibilities were not, however, spelled out). The president chaired the Defense Council and appointed its members. He also was entitled to ''appoint senior state, civil, and military ranks.''

Command and Force Structure

Political requirements largely determined the military's organizational structure in the first years after the 1974 revolution. Beginning in 1977, the military adopted Soviet command procedures, which reflected Moscow's influence. It should be pointed out, however, that Mengistu made all major military decisions in his capacity as commander in chief of the armed forces.

Military policy and all important decisions emanated from PMAC committees designated to deal with political and military affairs, defense, militia affairs, and security. The Council of Ministers, through the ministries of defense, interior, and public and national security, administered national security policy. The armed forces chain of command ran from the PMAC through the Ministry of Defense to the chiefs of staff of the army, air force, and navy and through the Ministry of Interior to the chief of the People's Militia. Service commanders, who operated from individual headquarters without an intermediate chairman, reported directly to Mengistu. Four regional commanders coordinated joint operations.

In August 1977, the PMAC established the National Revolutionary Operations Command (NROC) in response to unrest in the armed forces, political resistance from leftist opponents of the regime, and the deteriorating situation in Eritrea and the Ogaden. The NROC replaced the revolution and development committees founded earlier in 1977 to mobilize militia units on a regional basis and to direct regional security operations against ''reactionaries.'' Although the new command initially coordinated the recruiting, training, and equipping of the People's Militia, it eventually emerged as the central command structure and assumed sweeping civilian and military powers. Headed by a twenty-eight-member council—consisting of representatives from the PMAC, the Council of Ministers, the Provisional Office for Mass Organization Affairs (POMOA), and the official All-Ethiopia Trade Union, as well as the services' chiefs of staff—the NROC assumed command of the armed forces and responsibility for commandeering resources, public utilities, and manpower for the war effort. Mengistu served as its chairman.

In December 1977, the PMAC also created the Supreme Military Strategic Committee (SMSC) to formulate counterinsurgency strategy for Eritrea and the Ogaden and to direct military operations elsewhere in the country. Subsequently, the SMSC assumed responsibility for improving the armed forces' technical efficiency. The SMSC included eight Soviet, three Cuban, and seven Ethiopian representatives.

In April 1983, the government established the National Defense and Security Council, which was empowered to devise the country's military and civilian defense policies. This council included the head of state, the secretary general of the PMAC, and the ministers of defense, interior, and public and national security. The council's goal was to improve defense strategies and coordination among the army, the People's Militia, and the civilian population in times of war or natural disaster.

Army

Constituting about 97 percent of the uniformed services, the army was the backbone of the armed forces. In early 1991, the army was organized into five revolutionary armies, which included thirty-one infantry divisions supported by thirty-two tank battalions, forty artillery battalions, twelve air defense battalions, and eight commando brigades. The army had expanded in size from 41,000 in 1974 to 50,000 in 1977, 65,000 in 1979, and 230,000 in early 1991. Ground order of battle was difficult to ascertain because of the army's rapid increase in size, frequent reorganization and redeployment of units, and constant reshuffling within the command structure. Units from the 200,000-member People's Militia augmented army divisions, especially in Eritrea and Tigray. The First Revolutionary Army had headquarters in Harer, the Second Revolutionary Army in Asmera, the Third Revolutionary Army in Kembolcha, the Fourth Revolutionary Army in Nekemte, and the Fifth Revolutionary Army in Gonder.

Ethiopian armored and mechanized units had approximately 1,200 T–54/55 tanks and 100 T–62 tanks, all of Soviet manufacture, and about 1,100 armored personnel carriers (APCs), most of which were of Soviet origin. However, combat losses and constant resupply by the Soviet Union, East Germany, North Korea, and other communist nations reduced the reliability of these estimates. Artillery units possessed a variety of Soviet-manufactured light and medium guns and howitzers, rocket launchers, and heavy mortars. Air defense units had quick-firing antiaircraft guns and surface-to-air missiles.

Because training in maintenance techniques had failed to keep pace with the influx of new equipment, weapons maintenance by the army was poor. Moreover, Ethiopian troops often deployed new weapons systems without understanding how to operate them. During the late 1970s and early 1980s, Ethiopia relied on Soviet and Cuban technicians to maintain military equipment and to provide logistical support. However, because of the reduction in military assistance, spare parts, and Soviet military advisers, as well as the withdrawal of all Cuban troops in the late 1980s, the army's maintenance ability again deteriorated. By 1991 most army equipment was operational only about 30 percent of the time.

Air Force

Ethiopian military aviation dates from 1929, when Tafari Mekonnen (before he came to the throne as Haile Selassie) hired two French pilots and purchased four French biplanes. By the time of the Italian invasion of 1935, the air force had four pilots and thirteen aircraft. After World War II, Haile Selassie authorized the expansion of the air force. In 1947 he named a Swedish general as air force commander and contracted for a Swedish training team, equipped with eighteen Saab trainers and two squadrons of Saab-17 light bombers, to develop the air force. A Swedish officer commanded the air force until 1962, at which time Brigadier General Asefa Ayene assumed command.

The 1953 United States-Ethiopian Mutual Defense Assistance Agreement resulted in the delivery of a squadron of F-86 jet fighters in 1960. Beginning in 1966 and continuing until the early 1970s, the United States delivered Northrop F-5A/B/E fighters, which became the mainstays of the air force until the late 1970s. Beginning in 1977, the Soviet Union supplied aircraft and instructors to Ethiopia.

In early 1991, some 4,500 officers and airmen operated approximately 150 combat aircraft, most of them Soviet-manufactured fighter-bombers. A small number of the aircraft were transports and armed helicopters. The air force's tactical organization included seven fighter-ground attack squadrons, one transport squadron, and one training squadron. Approximately seventy-nine helicopters performed reconnaissance, transport, and ground support missions. Military analysts generally considered the air force competent. During the Ogaden War, the air force quickly destroyed its Somali counterpart. By the late 1980s, the air force had become vital to the Mengistu regime's war effort in northern Ethiopia. According to an Eritrean People's Liberation Front (EPLF) spokesman in the United States, the air force was almost singlehandedly preventing the EPLF from expelling the army from Eritrea (see The Eritreans, this ch.). In fact, most rebel organizations in north-central Ethiopia confined their activities to nighttime because of the daytime threat posed by the air force.

Apart from its performance as a military unit, the air force often has been involved in antigovernment activities. In May 1989, for example, several senior air force officers participated in a coup attempt against Mengistu. The purge that followed this action decimated the service's leadership ranks. Mengistu not only replaced many senior officers but also temporarily grounded the air force. Within a few weeks, the combat victories of the rebels forced Mengistu to rescind his grounding order. By 1991 it was evident that the air force was suffering from low morale and that internal divisions continued to plague its units.

The air force's command headquarters was south of Addis Ababa at Debre Zeyit, the site of the major air base, training center, and maintenance workshop. Other air bases were at Asmera, Bahir Dar, Azezo, Goba, Dire Dawa, and Jijiga. (A base at Mekele had been captured by the Tigray People's Liberation Front in 1989.)

Navy

In 1958 the Ethiopian navy became an autonomous branch of the armed forces, operating as a coast guard within the territorial waters off Eritrea. Until 1974 a small contingent of retired British naval personnel served as advisers and training supervisors. In 1974 Addis Ababa and Oslo signed an agreement whereby Norway organized and trained a modest maritime force. Starting in 1978, Soviet advisers were attached to the Ethiopian navy.

In early 1991, Ethiopia's 3,500-member navy remained modest and had seen little combat. Its inventory included two frigates, eight missile craft, six torpedo craft, six patrol boats, two amphibious craft, and two support/training craft.

Ethiopia's principal naval bases were at Mitsiwa and Aseb. The base at Aseb included a ship-repair facility. In the past, the navy had cooperated with elements of the Soviet fleet operating in the Red Sea. Soviet naval vessels also made frequent calls at Ethiopian ports to resupply and refit. Moreover, the Soviet Union maintained naval facilities in the Dahlak Islands off the coast of Eritrea. The Soviet Union had an anchorage and stationed a naval infantry detachment there; it reportedly also operated intelligence facilities there. After they were expelled from Somalia in 1977 for siding with Ethiopia, Soviet personnel moved a dry dock they had operated at Berbera in Somalia to Aseb and later positioned it off the coast in the Dahlak Islands. At one time, they also had several Il-38 maritime reconnaissance aircraft stationed at Asmera, but by 1989 these aircraft had been moved to Aden because the EPLF had destroyed one of the Soviet aircraft in a daring raid.

People's Militia

Proclamation No. 71, issued by the Derg in 1975, established the People's Militia to "safeguard the revolution." The government intended to raise a representative force on a regional basis to carry out police duties, to protect collectivized property and crops, and to enforce the decisions of peasant association tribunals. However, the militia remained largely a rural organization, despite the fact that Addis Ababa had directed urban dwellers' associations (*kebeles*—see Glossary) and workers' associations to "elect" constituents to serve in the militia.

In May 1976, the government conscripted 30,000 to 40,000 peasants into the People's Militia from the predominantly Amhara areas of Shewa, Welo, and Gojam. After only two weeks of training, Addis Ababa dispatched the militia, armed with World War II-vintage rifles, to Eritrea. There, the militia's mission was to repel the "invading Arab infidel." A month later, Eritrean guerrillas, carrying relatively modern arms, decimated this force by launching a preemptive attack on the Zela Anbesa militia camp. In the spring of 1977, Mengistu reconstituted the People's Militia as the so-called Red Army and authorized its expansion. He armed the militia with modern weapons and ordered all conscripts to undergo a twelve-week basic training and weapons familiarization course at camps in Tatek, Shashemene, Awash, Fiche, and Azezo. The government then deployed People's Militia units to Eritrea and the Ogaden to serve with the regular army. This decision proved to be disastrous because, in fighting against Eritrean guerrillas in northern Ethiopia and against the Somali National Army in the Ogaden, the People's Militia suffered heavy casualties. On occasion, antigovernment elements in the militia experienced bloody confrontations with Ethiopian army regulars (see Morale and Discipline, this ch.). In addition, captured militiamen often denounced the government's military strategy to foreign journalists.

By 1980 the People's Militia numbered 150,000 troops organized into ten divisions. Those assigned to Eritrea were known as the Northern People's Divisions; those in the Ogaden were known as the Eastern People's Divisions. Militia units were usually equipped with AK–47 rifles and rocket-propelled grenade launchers, and most units possessed mortars and antitank weapons. Cuban advisers provided infantry and artillery training.

During the early and mid-1980s, the People's Militia declined in importance, largely because of increased pressure for equal pay and survivor benefits. The May 1983 enactment of the National Military Service Proclamation required all able-bodied Ethiopian men aged eighteen to thirty to undergo six months of military training followed by two years of active duty. After their terms of active duty ended, these men would be placed on reserve status until age fifty. National military service negated the necessity for the large-scale militia call-ups that had been common in the late 1970s. Nevertheless, the government continued training militia recruits, especially from resettlement villages in frontier areas such as Asosa in Welega (see The Politics of Resettlement, ch. 4).

By 1991 the People's Militia numbered about 200,000 but no longer had to contend with a serious threat in the Ogaden. However, the deteriorating situation in Eritrea and Tigray required that militia units support the regular army's counterinsurgency operations. At the end of 1989, Addis Ababa mobilized the militia to stop the advance of the Tigray People's Liberation Front and the Ethiopian People's Democratic Movement. These and several other groups had joined forces and became known as the Ethiopian People's Revolutionary Democratic Front.

Training

Systematic military training in Ethiopia began in 1919 when, as regent, Tafari Mekonnen appointed a small group of Russian officers and some Ethiopians who had served in the British-led King's African Rifles to train Ethiopian troops. Some Ethiopian officers subsequently received instruction in France at the Saint-Cyr military academy. Between 1929 and 1935, a Belgian military mission trained the Imperial Bodyguard. In 1934 a Swedish delegation of five officers was invited to Ethiopia to open the Haile Selassie I Military Training Center at Holeta (also known as Genet Military School). Although this training helped Ethiopia field an army to resist the Italian invasion, the development of a modern army started only after liberation from Italian occupation in 1941, with British advisers primarily responsible for the training. Under a 1942 convention, Britain engaged in a ten-year military training mission to Ethiopia. In 1946, however, Addis Ababa diluted British influence somewhat by accepting a new team of Swedish military advisers. In 1953 a United States Military Assistance Advisory Group arrived in Ethiopia to train various branches of the Ethiopian security forces. Four years later, an Indian military mission came to establish and manage the Haile Selassie I Military Academy at Harer.

In 1991 there were five major military schools in Ethiopia, including the Harer Military Academy (formerly known as the Haile Selassie I Military Academy), the Holeta Military Training Center, the Air Force Training Center at Debre Zeyit, and the Naval College in Asmera.

In October 1987, the Ethiopian government announced the opening of the Armed Forces Staff Academy near Addis Ababa. According to an official statement, the academy's student body included senior officers (generals and colonels) from all branches of the armed forces. During the academy's year-long course, officers studied and conducted research on national defense issues. Initially, Soviet personnel staffed the academy's faculty; however, Addis Ababa planned to replace them eventually with Ethiopian instructors.

The Harer Military Academy provided a three-year academic and military course for officer cadets. Military instruction included tactics, political indoctrination, engineering, intelligence, and security. Academic courses included physical and social sciences, public administration, and foreign languages, such as Russian and English. Graduates received commissions as second lieutenants, and they were eligible to receive the equivalent of a bachelor's degree after completing one year of additional study at Addis Ababa University. The Holeta Military Training Center also conferred commissions as second lieutenants on students who had completed courses lasting from six to nine months that were devoted to military subjects. Holeta's officer candidates normally were promising noncommissioned officers (NCOs) or volunteers who lacked a secondary school education.

Before 1974, Harer graduates belonged to a "military aristocracy," which monopolized high-ranking army positions. By contrast, Holeta graduates were reputed to be the products of an inferior education and were considered the "poor cousins" of the officer corps. Few of them ever rose higher than the middle ranks. But after the 1974 revolution, Holeta graduates began to establish their dominance over the army and expelled many Harer graduates, including those who had been members of various armed forces committees at the beginning of the revolution.

Although the two officer training installations had maintained separate facilities and programs, they merged after 1974 and were subsequently operated as branches of the Genet Military Academy. This training complex, initially staffed by Soviet and Cuban instructors, also incorporated advanced infantry, armor, artillery, and communications schools for officers.

The Air Force Training Center at Debre Zeyit offered cadets a four-year course of study and training. Officer candidates, all of whom were volunteers, underwent four months of basic military training and, upon entering the academy, signed a ten-year service contract. Separate curricula led to degrees in aeronautical engineering, electrical engineering, and administration. Graduates received commissions as second lieutenants. Those selected as pilots attended a flight training program at Dire Dawa. In 1984 Dornier, the West German aircraft manufacturer, provided pilot training at Debre Zeyit. Pilots and mechanics also received training in Britain. The air force operated technical schools for enlisted personnel at Debre Zeyit that trained aircraft maintenance and electronics technicians, communications operators, and weapons specialists. Upon entering these courses, which lasted eighteen months to two years, recruits committed themselves to remain on active duty for ten years.

Students at the Naval College in Asmera pursued a fifty-two-month course of instruction that led to a naval science degree and a commission in the navy. The Naval College academic curriculum was broader than the army and air force programs and was supplemented by training at sea. In 1984 some forty-eight ensigns, belonging to the twenty-fourth graduating class, received diplomas; subsequent classes were of comparable size. Some naval officers received training abroad, notably at the naval academy in Leghorn, Italy, and at the Leningrad naval academy in the Soviet Union. The navy maintained training centers in the Mitsiwa area for seamen, technicians, and marines; recruits enlisted for seven years.

Officers received specialized in-service instruction at training centers throughout the country. Most of these centers' staffs included Soviet, East German, and—until Havana's 1989 decision to withdraw its forces from Ethiopia—Cuban advisers. These advanced schools emphasized preparation for the supervision of technical personnel responsible for maintaining Soviet-supplied weapons, communications equipment, and electronic gear. Senior officers attended a two-month command and leadership course, which, based on Marxist-Leninist principles, stressed the need to develop ''political consciousness'' in the ranks as well as the technical mastery of weapons and equipment. There also was instruction in international relations and public speaking.

Army recruits underwent twelve weeks of basic training before being assigned to line units or to technical schools for specialized training. The largest technical school was at Genet, where NCOs studied tactics, engineering, logistics, and communications. Genet also offered courses in technical and secondary-level academic subjects to a limited number of students prior to their assignment as NCOs to operational units. Soviet instructors at the Genet armory school taught six-month advanced courses in weapons and vehicle maintenance. The size of each class ranged from 100 to 150 students. Genet also was the training center for women's army corps recruits. The government assigned uniformed political commissars to all units for the political education of enlisted personnel.

Morale and Discipline

Before the February 1974 unrest that led to the ouster of the emperor, military morale was thought to be high. Although the demands for redress of professional grievances that precipitated the 1974 coup had created doubts about the level of military morale, the public's basic respect for the fighting man and the enduring belief that military life was an avenue of advancement helped sustain the military profession's somewhat diminished stature. Also, when the revolutionary government designated the armed forces as the "vanguard of the revolution," many officers consequently were able to assume senior military and political positions relatively early in their careers. In addition, the pay, benefits, and privileges enjoyed by Ethiopian service personnel gave them an above-average standard of living. Despite the political turmoil that accompanied the establishment of a revolutionary Marxist government, as well as the insecurity caused by purges within the military and the dangers of combat, military life still managed to attract enough volunteers to staff the uniformed services.

However, the uncertainties caused by the events of 1974 and the subsequent turnover in command personnel caused a crisis of confidence that would last until the introduction of large numbers of Soviet and Cuban advisers in training and command positions in the late 1970s. Prolonged exposure to combat and political disaffection contributed to desertion, attacks on officers, and war-zone atrocities. Incompetence among commanders in the field was also a problem. For instance, in 1975 the government tried and executed several officers for indiscipline and for a lack of military judgment resulting in the death of soldiers in battle. From 1976 to 1978, the command leadership crisis grew worse because of the army's rapid expansion. As a result of this growth, junior officers and NCOs often advanced to field-grade rank without adequate preparation. Purges and defections by officers of Eritrean origin were also factors in the poor quality of field leadership. Growing disaffection throughout the army prompted several mutinies by front-line troops, including one at Jijiga in 1977, during which officers and NCOs demanded Mengistu's resignation. Further, the disparity in pay and lack of survivor benefits embittered the People's Militia.

Although the 1978 victory over Somalia in the Ogaden War and the Soviet Union's growing support of the Ethiopian armed forces enhanced morale, troops in war zones still questioned or criticized the government's national security policy. However, a correlation existed between the quality of a unit's training and equipment and the state of its morale. The best-trained and best-equipped units—the air force and the army engineers—also had the highest morale.

During 1978 and 1979, the government reorganized units in Eritrea and the Ogaden in an effort to reduce dissatisfaction and prevent conspiracies. This strategy backfired because many soldiers resented having to leave their original units. The threat of radical land reform that affected the holdings of military personnel also caused bitterness. Additionally, combat units found it difficult to sustain high morale in a war of attrition in Eritrea that permitted few clear-cut victories. After the 1979 government defeat at Nakfa, troops in Asmera distributed antigovernment pamphlets. Western journalists also reported that large numbers of Ethiopian soldiers had switched sides, deserted, or surrendered, sometimes as units, without resistance to the Eritreans. Throughout this period, Ethiopian authorities refused to recognize the existence of the prisoners of war, who numbered about 6,000, held by Eritrean secessionist forces. To make matters worse, Mengistu told combatants who faced capture by the enemy to ''die [in battle] or kill yourselves.''

Tension between regular army and People's Militia units existed on all fighting fronts. One of the factors that led to the 1977 Jijiga mutiny concerned complaints that the government had issued better weapons, including AK–47 assault rifles, to militia units. For their part, militia personnel complained about low pay, inadequate medical attention, and inferior food. Furthermore, they charged that regulars often refused to give them supporting fire during combined operations.

During the government's large-scale 1982 Red Star campaign in Eritrea, the EPLF victory further lowered the morale of government forces and prompted many Ethiopian army units to mutiny. For example, in late October 1982 the Ninth Brigade, which was

A patrol boat at the naval base at Mitsiwa

serving on the Nakfa front, reported fighting between mutineers and loyal troops at Third Division headquarters. In February 1983, units stationed at Kudo Felasi, near Adi Ugri, also mutinied. There was also unrest among People's Militia conscripts. Throughout the 1982 Red Star campaign, thousands of government troops fled to Sudan to avoid combat.

Over the next few years, a series of battlefield reversals, coupled with the government's refusal to abandon its goal of military victory in Eritrea and Tigray, kept the armed forces demoralized. In October 1986, army officers held prisoner by the EPLF formed the Free Ethiopia Soldiers' Movement. Apart from distributing anti-Mengistu pamphlets in Ethiopia and abroad, the Free Ethiopia Soldiers' Movement sought "to organize men in uniform and prepare them for an overthrow of the government and a search for an alliance with all democratic forces." This organization also called for the creation of democracy in Ethiopia and a peaceful resolution of the Eritrean problem.

The next major mutiny occurred in mid-February 1988, when elements of the Second Revolutionary Army revolted in Asmera. Mengistu responded to this crisis by making a much-publicized sixteen-day tour of units stationed in the north and by ordering the arrest and execution of several NCOs and officers, including at least five generals. Morale fell further after the EPLF won a victory at Afabet in March. By the end of that year, veterans and discontented soldiers, many of whom had war injuries, demonstrated in Addis Ababa to pressure the Mengistu regime to end the war and increase veterans' benefits. The government suppressed the demonstration, killing several men in the process.

Continued battlefield setbacks in Eritrea and Tigray throughout early 1989 demoralized many senior officers who previously had been supporters of Mengistu's military policy in northern Ethiopia. On May 16, members of the armed forces staged a coup to oust Mengistu. With the exception of the minister of defense, Major General Haile Giorgis Habte Mariam, those directly implicated in the coup, or at least not hostile to the decision to oust Mengistu, included the entire army command structure from the chief of staff on down. The commanders of the air force and the first, second, third, and fourth revolutionary armies also supported the coup. After returning to Ethiopia, Mengistu, who had been in East Germany on an official visit, used his Presidential Guard and other loyal military personnel to reestablish his authority. Subsequently, he ordered the arrest or execution of hundreds of senior officers. Mengistu then named many of his political supporters, some of whom lacked any military experience, to replace those who had been purged. Although Mengistu succeeded in eliminating effective opposition in the armed forces (at least for the short term), morale problems continued to plague most military units, especially those assigned to war zones in northern Ethiopia, whose ranks were often filled with teenagers. In late 1989, for example, thousands of government soldiers deserted, and scores of units disintegrated after the TPLF launched a major offensive.

Manpower Considerations

Although volunteers made up a large part of the regular army, the government had to rely increasingly on conscripts to fill the lower ranks. In mid-1991 approximately 6 million Ethiopian males aged eighteen to thirty-two were eligible for military service. This number constituted an adequate source of personnel for the country's defense needs and in fact was more than the country could support logistically or train effectively.

Under the National Military Service Proclamation of May 1983, all Ethiopians aged eighteen to thirty were required to undergo six months' military training followed by two years' active service and assignment to reserve status until age fifty. In reality, the national call-up, which was administered by regional military commissars, was selective rather than universal. According to the conscription law, each peasant association or *kebele* was required to forward lists of eligible recruits to the Ministry of Internal Affairs military commissariat. The ministry then would issue call-up orders, after which the peasant associations were required to ensure that conscripts reported for duty.

The first two national call-ups occurred in May 1984 and January 1985. Each raised about 60,000 recruits. The armed forces used the first group mainly for back-up duties and the second for duty in Eritrea. The EPLF captured many soldiers belonging to the second group around the Nakfa front. The third national call-up, which sought to recruit 120,000 men, took place in December 1985. Growing public disaffection with the wars in northern Ethiopia manifested itself in popular resistance to the call-up. Many young men moved in with relatives outside the *kebeles* where they were registered. To prevent desertions, the government sent conscripts from Addis Ababa to training camps in outlying regions such as Kefa and Welega and transported Eritrean and Tigrayan recruits by air to Addis Ababa.

After the November 1986 national call-up, which also prompted widespread opposition, the Mengistu regime increasingly had to resort to force to satisfy military manpower requirements. In mid-1989, for example, armed press gangs often roamed the streets of Addis Ababa and other major cities looking for males as young as thirteen years old, or they held families at the local *kebele* office and then inducted their sons when family members went to the authorities to report their relatives missing. Parents who could afford to do so sent their sons abroad or to remote areas in Ethiopia where chances of escaping the call-up were greater.

A number of debilitating conditions, such as dietary deficiencies, endemic diseases, and illiteracy, often affected the quality of the available manpower. Despite these factors, the average soldier, with proper training and guidance, appeared capable of using modern equipment.

The ratio of officers to enlisted personnel was approximately one to twenty. Officers generally were committed to active service until they retired or were released from duty because of incapacity. Retirement benefits were modest, but officers received many perquisites, particularly in housing and transportation.

At the time of the 1974 overthrow of Haile Selassie, a generational cleavage existed between older, conservative field-grade officers and younger, better-trained, and increasingly radical officers who had joined the military in the 1950s and 1960s. Another factor in these differences was the variety of countries in which Ethiopian officers had been trained. By 1989 this problem had diminished, as an increasing number of officers had the shared experience of being trained by Soviet, East German, or Cuban military advisers. However, opposition to Mengistu and the wars in northern Ethiopia continued to cause cleavages throughout the armed forces.

The officer corps was composed largely of volunteers and included many who had risen from the enlisted ranks. Since the early 1950s, however, a significant proportion of officer candidates had been conscripted into military service for life (or until retired or physically incapacitated) from the upper levels of secondary school graduating classes and from among the most promising first-year university students. Not all of those selected in this manner were suited for military life, and many resented not being allowed to pursue civilian careers. Prior to 1974, an estimated 10 percent of all Ethiopians educated beyond secondary school level were members of the armed forces.

The officers who were among the Derg's original members came largely from the junior-grade ranks. Although many subsequently received promotions to mid-level grades, rank alone did not necessarily indicate an officer's importance. Many lieutenants and captains, for example, received assignments to important government posts. Mengistu himself became a lieutenant colonel only in 1976. In early 1977, be became chairman of the Derg. Starting with Revolution Day 1979, however, he was referred to as "commander in chief." When he appeared in uniform as commander in chief, he wore shoulder insignia identical to those worn by field marshals of the old imperial army.

Up-to-date official information on the ethnic composition of the officer corps was not available in mid-1991. However, in the early 1970s about 65 percent of officers at the rank of lieutenant colonel and above were Amhara, whereas 20 percent were Oromo, the latter proportion having nearly doubled during the previous decade. Below lieutenant colonel, the percentage who were Amhara was 60 percent, while 30 percent were Oromo. Estimates published in the late 1970s suggested that 50 percent of the officer corps was Amhara, 20 percent Tigray, and 30 percent Oromo and Eritrean (see Ethiopia's Peoples, ch. 2).

Many enlisted personnel had joined the military because it offered steady, well-paid employment, service-connected benefits, and the opportunity for advancement. Others enlisted because they could not find suitable work in the cities. Basic pay for the lowest-ranking personnel in the armed forces equaled that of an experienced skilled worker in industry. In the late 1970s, the ethnic composition of the enlisted ranks in the army was about 33 percent Amhara, 33 percent Oromo, and 25 percent Tigray, with the remainder coming from other groups. The proportion of Eritreans serving in the air force and navy was greater than in the army, the result of better access to higher education, which made Eritreans more suited for technical training.

Defense Costs

During World War II, when major military expansion programs began, the government devoted approximately 38 percent of the national budget to defense. From 1948 to 1958, the proportion of the budget dedicated to defense dropped from 27 to 17 percent of the total, not because of a decrease in military expenditures but because the size of the overall national budget had increased sharply. Throughout the 1960s and early 1970s, money for defense remained the largest single item in the budget, varying from 19 to 24 percent of the total funds appropriated for all national programs.

Beginning in the mid-1970s, defense expenditures started to rise. In 1974 Addis Ababa allocated the equivalent of US$80 million for defense, in 1976 US$103 million, and in 1979, US$526 million. By 1987–88 defense expenditures had declined to approximately US$472 million; however, it should be pointed out that between 1977 and 1990, the Soviet Union had provided approximately US$13 billion in military assistance to the Mengistu regime.

Foreign Military Assistance

The use of foreign military advisers has a long history in Ethiopia, going back to the arrival of a Portuguese military expedition in the 1530s. French, Russian, Belgian, and Swedish advisers all contributed to efforts before World War II to build a modern army (see Training, this ch.). Following the war, Britain, Sweden, Norway, Israel, and the United States assumed responsibility for training and equipping the Ethiopian armed forces.

After the 1977–78 Ogaden War, the Soviet Union became Ethiopia's major military supplier. Addis Ababa also received military assistance from a number of other communist nations, including Cuba, East Germany, and North Korea. In addition, by late 1989 Israel had resumed its military relationship with Ethiopia, which the imperial government had broken off at the time of the Arab-Israeli October 1973 War.

United States

On May 22, 1953, the United States and Ethiopia concluded an agreement that gave the United States a twenty-five-year lease on the Kagnew communications station in Asmera. At the time, Kagnew was one of the largest radio relay and communications monitoring stations in the world. The United States later developed its facilities, which were manned by 4,000 American military personnel, to monitor Soviet radio communications throughout the region. The two countries also signed a Mutual Defense Assistance Agreement, whereby the United States pledged to provide US$5 million to equip and train three 6,000-member Ethiopian divisions. A United States Military Assistance Advisory Group (MAAG) was sent to Ethiopia to administer this program. By March 31, 1954, the United States had delivered US$3.8 million worth of small arms, vehicles, and artillery to Ethiopia. In October 1954, Washington granted another US$5 million in aid to Ethiopia; and in November 1955, the United States Joint Chiefs of Staff agreed that Addis Ababa needed a minimum of US$5 million a year in military assistance supplemented by the direct sale of air force and naval equipment. Despite these increases, the Ethiopian government complained that this military aid was insufficient to satisfy its defense needs. In early 1956, Addis Ababa therefore appealed to Washington for "a combination of grants and long-term military credits to support the country's defense needs," which included the suppression of Eritrean dissenters. In October 1956, the United States National Security Council responded to this request by issuing a report that included a recommendation that United States assistance to Ethiopia be increased.

After 1960—a year in which Washington promised to provide support for a 40,000-member Ethiopian army—United States military aid to Ethiopia gradually increased. In the 1960s, at the peak of United States involvement, more than 300 American personnel were serving in the MAAG. In addition, nearly 23,000 Ethiopian service personnel, including at least twenty who subsequently became members of the Derg, received advanced training directly from United States personnel. About 4,000 of these troops were trained at facilities in the United States, Mengistu Haile Mariam among them. By 1974 Ethiopia's armed forces had become totally dependent on the United States for military hardware and spare parts.

United States assistance initially continued without interruption after the overthrow of Haile Selassie in 1974, although it was accompanied by proposals for a negotiated settlement in Eritrea. After the execution of a large number of high-ranking officals of the imperial regime in November 1974, the United States postponed the signing of a pending aid agreement, but shipments of aircraft and tanks doubled the dollar value of military assistance in 1975. Citing the "arms imbalance in the region" resulting from Soviet aid to Somalia, Washington proposed to update Ethiopia's arms inventory over a three-year period by turning over US$200 million worth of surplus matériel originally designated for the Republic of Vietnam (South Vietnam). The United States also authorized the transfer of an F-5 fighter aircraft squadron from Iran to Ethiopia. Total United States arms sales to Ethiopia in 1974 and 1975 amounted to US$35 million.

During 1976, tensions developed between Washington and Addis Ababa over the ongoing Military Assistance Program. The Derg rejected a new Foreign Military Sales (FMS) credit agreement because Washington had imposed a higher interest rate. The Ethiopian government also complained about delays in arms delivery schedules in the face of growing Soviet military assistance to Somalia. Meanwhile, the United States refused to approve a US$60 million program to replace equipment lost in Eritrea. Despite the growing rift, a United States Department of State official testifying before a congressional committee characterized the Ethiopian government as "not systematically or intrinsically anti-U.S."

The first significant shift in relations between the two countries came in December 1976, when a Derg delegation headed by Mengistu visited Moscow and concluded an arms agreement with the Soviet Union valued at US$385 million that was designed to end Washington's virtual monopoly on arms supplies to Ethiopia. Then, in testimony before a congressional committee in February 1977, United States secretary of state Cyrus Vance recommended a cessation of grant military assistance to Ethiopia because of Addis Ababa's human rights violations. (Grant military assistance represented only a small portion of the Military Assistance Program, which totaled US$26 million in United States fiscal year 1976 and was scheduled to total US$62 million in United States fiscal year 1977. These figures contrasted with an annual average of US$10 million in military assistance to the imperial regime.) The United States also informed the Derg in February that it intended to reduce the size of the United States military mission and to close the Kagnew communications station, where activities already were being phased out, by the end of September 1977.

As a result of these actions, the Ethiopian government, believing that all United States military assistance eventually would be eliminated, responded in April 1977 by closing United States military installations and giving MAAG personnel a week's notice to leave the country. A large store of equipment remained behind in the rapid American departure. Ethiopia then abrogated the 1953 United States-Ethiopian Mutual Defense Assistance Agreement and terminated the lease on Kagnew station. In the absence of a bilateral agreement, the United States had no legal basis for the delivery of aircraft, armored vehicles, ships, and a number of air-to-surface and air-to-air missiles that had been approved for delivery and on which the Derg had made partial down payment. Thus was terminated the military relationship between Washington and Addis Ababa.

Soviet Union

In 1976, after receiving Moscow's assurance of military assistance, Lieutenant Colonel Atnafu Abate, vice chairman of the Derg, announced that Ethiopia would restrict its future purchases to "socialist countries." By the time Somali forces captured Jijiga in September 1977, Moscow already had decided to supply military assistance to the Mengistu regime.

Within three months of this decision, the Soviet Union had initiated a massive arms transfer program. Approximately fifty Soviet ships had passed through the Suez Canal on the way to the port of Aseb to unload crated fighter aircraft, tanks, artillery, and munitions—an estimated 60,000 tons of hardware—for delivery to the Ogaden front. Moscow shipped additional equipment from the People's Democratic Republic of Yemen (South Yemen). At the height of the buildup, between November 1977 and February 1978, Soviet transport aircraft, including giant An-22s, landed at twenty-five-minute intervals at Ethiopian airports. An estimated 225 transports—about 15 percent of the Soviet air fleet—participated in the operation.

The 1977–78 Soviet supply operation impressed Western observers, who admitted that the display of Soviet transport capability had added a "new strategic element" to the East-West balance. The Soviet Union drew on large stockpiles of equipment created by high production levels. Soviet aid—which included eighty aircraft, 600 tanks, and 300 APCs—had an estimated value of US$1 billion, surpassing in a matter of months the total value of United States aid provided to Ethiopia between 1953 and 1977. One-fourth of the Soviet assistance was a gift; reportedly, the Libyan government financed a small portion.

In November 1978, a few months after the end of the Ogaden War, Addis Ababa and Moscow signed a twenty-year Treaty of Friendship and Cooperation. Among other things, the treaty called for close military cooperation. With the promise of future arms deliveries, the Mengistu regime continued to pursue military victory against Eritrean and Tigrayan separatists in northern Ethiopia. In July 1979, for example, the Soviet Union underwrote Ethiopia's fifth offensive against Eritrea by shipping military hardware to Ethiopian army garrisons at Mersa Teklay and Asmera.

*A United States airman trains an Ethiopian
air force technician in meteorology, 1967.
Courtesy United States Air Force*

Moreover, Soviet officers reportedly commanded Ethiopian field units. However, like the four earlier ones between 1974 and 1978, this offensive failed to bring rebel areas under government control.

By mid-1980 Ethiopia's military and economic debt to the Soviet Union had grown dramatically. The total value to be repaid was US$1.7 billion, to be spread over ten years beginning in 1984, with 2 percent interest to be paid concurrently on the principal. In addition, Ethiopia agreed to repay a US$300 million commercial debt to the Soviet Union for items such as trucks and cranes. Addis Ababa met these obligations by sending coffee to the Soviet Union and by making foreign-exchange payments from export earnings elsewhere.

Throughout the mid-1980s, the Soviet Union's military commitment to Ethiopia continued to grow, despite Moscow's purported encouragement of a political settlement of the Eritrean problem. In 1982, for example, Moscow provided about US$2 billion worth of weapons to support Ethiopia's various Red Star campaigns in Eritrea. The Red Star campaigns were planned jointly by Soviet military advisers and their Ethiopian counterparts.

Although the 1982 campaign failed to produce a military victory in Eritrea, the Soviet Union remained committed to the Mengistu regime. By 1984 Moscow had provided more than US$4 billion in military assistance to Ethiopia, with arms deliveries in 1984 (worth approximately US$1.2 billion) at their highest level since the Ogaden War. The number of Soviet and East European military advisers in Ethiopia also grew from about 1,900 in 1981 to approximately 2,600 in 1984. Additionally, by 1984 more than 1,600 Ethiopian military personnel had received training in the Soviet Union.

After Mikhail Gorbachev came to power in March 1985, Soviet policy toward Ethiopia underwent a fundamental change. The value of arms deliveries from the Soviet Union and its East European allies declined to US$774 million in 1985 and to US$292 million in 1986. The number of Soviet military advisers in Ethiopia also declined, to about 1,400 in 1988, although it returned to normal levels of approximately 1,700 in 1989.

More important, Gorbachev told Mengistu during a July 26, 1988, meeting in Moscow that the Soviet Union was unwilling to increase military assistance to Ethiopia. Instead, the Soviet leader encouraged a "just solution" to the disputes in northern Ethiopia. In subsequent meetings between Soviet and Ethiopian officials, Moscow refused Addis Ababa's request to reschedule its debt and declined to indicate whether it would conclude another arms agreement after the one in force in 1989 expired in 1991.

As further evidence of the Soviet Union's interest in a negotiated settlement of the Eritrean issue, in early July 1989 Yuri Yukalov, director of the African department at the Soviet Ministry of Foreign Affairs, met with Issaias Afwerki, secretary general of the EPLF, to discuss Ethiopia's future. Additionally, the Soviet Union expressed support for the peace talks taking place in 1989 between the Ethiopian government and the EPLF and TPLF.

Throughout 1990 Moscow continued to reduce its military commitment to Addis Ababa. In March 1990, for example, the Soviet Union announced the withdrawal of its military advisers from all combat zones. Despite Ethiopia's growing need for helicopters and other counterinsurgency equipment, Moscow refused to conclude any new weapons contracts with the Mengistu regime. It should be pointed out, however, that the Soviet Union honored all commitments set forth in the military assistance agreement, which was to expire at the beginning of 1991.

Cuba

Cuba's involvement with Ethiopia paralleled that of the Soviet Union. Prior to the outbreak of the Ogaden War, Havana, like

Moscow, had been an ally of Somalia. After a series of Somali armed incursions into the Ogaden ruptured already tense relations between Addis Ababa and Mogadishu, Cuban president Fidel Castro Ruz visited the Horn of Africa and urged the two countries to join in forming a regional federation that also would include South Yemen, an "autonomous" Ogaden, an "autonomous" Eritrea, and Djibouti. After the failure of this initiative, Cuba began moving closer to Ethiopia, abandoning its ties with Somalia in the process.

In November 1977, two months after Somali forces had captured Jijiga, Cuban military advisers started to arrive in Ethiopia. By the end of the month, the Soviet Union had also begun a six-week airlift, later supplemented by a sealift, of Cuban troops. From the end of November 1977 to February 1978, Havana deployed approximately 17,000 troops to Ethiopia, including three combat brigades. Some of these troops had previously been stationed in Angola.

The Cuban presence was crucial to Ethiopia's victory over Somalia. During the Derg's early 1978 counteroffensive in the Ogaden, Cuban troops fought alongside their Ethiopian counterparts. With Cuban support, Ethiopian units quickly scored several impressive victories. As a result, on March 9, 1978, Somali president Mahammad Siad Barre announced that his army was withdrawing from the Ogaden.

After the Ethiopian victory in the Ogaden, attention shifted to Eritrea. By early 1978, the EPLF had succeeded in gaining control of almost all of Eritrea except the city of Asmera and the ports of Mitsiwa and Aseb. After redeploying its forces from the Ogaden to northern Ethiopia, Addis Ababa launched a counteroffensive against the EPLF during late 1978.

Although there is some disagreement, most military observers believe that Cuba refused to participate in the operation in Eritrea because Castro considered the Eritrean conflict an internal war rather than a case of external aggression. However, the continued presence of Cuban troops in the Ogaden enabled the Mengistu regime to redeploy many of its troops to northern Ethiopia.

A large Cuban contingent, believed to number about 12,000, remained in Ethiopia after the Ogaden War. However, by mid-1984 Havana had reduced its troop strength in Ethiopia to approximately 3,000. In 1988 a Cuban brigade, equipped with tanks and APCs, was stationed in Dire Dawa to guard the road and railroad between Ethiopia and Djibouti, following attacks by Somali-supported rebels. A mobile battalion of various military advisers and an unknown number of Cuban instructors who were on the Harer Military Academy faculty also remained in Ethiopia.

After Ethiopia and Somalia signed an April 1988 joint communiqué intended to reduce tensions, Cuba decided to end its military presence in Ethiopia. The last Cuban troops left on September 17, 1989, thus terminating twelve years of military cooperation.

East Germany

Of all the East European nations that provided military assistance to Ethiopia, none played a more vital role than East Germany. Its importance to Addis Ababa derived not so much from its conventional military support, which at times was crucial to Ethiopian security, as from its involvement in Ethiopia's intelligence and security services.

East Germany's military relationship with the Mengistu regime started in 1977, when Socialist Unity Party of Germany leader Werner Lamberz visited Ethiopia three times (February, June, and December) to coordinate and direct the operations of the approximately 2,000 South Yemeni soldiers who were fighting against Somali forces in the Ogaden. East Germany also provided support to Soviet and Cuban pilots who flew helicopters and fighter-bombers on combat missions during the Ogaden War. Moreover, East Germany agreed to give ideological training to hundreds of Ethiopian officers. Even after the end of the Ogaden War, East Germany remained militarily active in Ethiopia. During the 1978 Ethiopian offensive against the EPLF, East German engineers, working in conjunction with their Soviet counterparts, reportedly built flanking roads, enabling Ethiopian tanks to come up behind EPLF lines. In addition, East German military advisers manned artillery and rocket units in Eritrea. Interestingly, in 1978 East Germany also sponsored unsuccessful peace talks between Ethiopia and the EPLF. When these discussions failed, the East German government abandoned diplomacy in favor of a military solution to the problem of Eritrean and Tigrayan separatism.

In May 1979, East Germany and Ethiopia signed an agreement formalizing military relations between the two countries. Then, on November 15, 1979, East German head of state Erich Honecker visited Ethiopia and signed a twenty-year Treaty of Friendship and Cooperation. In addition to calling for greater cooperation in politics, economics, trade, science, culture, and technology, the 1979 treaty also laid the groundwork for increased military assistance.

For most of the 1980s, East Germany, through its National People's Army and its State Security Service, provided Ethiopia with diverse forms of military and intelligence assistance. Apart from military aid, such as automatic rifles, ammunition, artillery, and heavy vehicles, East Germany provided up to five months' training in military and police tactics to members of the People's Protection Brigades, which concentrated on routine police duties at the local level (see People's Protection Brigades, this ch.). In 1982 East German intelligence advisers participated in that year's Red Star campaign against Eritrean separatists. East German personnel often assumed control of Ethiopian army communications sites as, for instance, they did in mid-1988 in Asmera. In addition, East German security advisers reportedly acted as Mengistu's personal bodyguard.

Even after the Soviet Union altered its policy toward Ethiopia in the late 1980s, East Germany remained Mengistu's staunch ally. In mid-1989, for example, Honecker promised Mengistu fifty to sixty T–54/55 tanks that had been scheduled to be scrapped in a force reduction. However, after Honecker's resignation and the emergence of a more broadly based government in late 1989, East German officials informed Addis Ababa that the military relationship between the two countries had been terminated and that all future arms deliveries had been canceled. In 1990 the 550 East German advisers and technicians stationed in Ethiopia were withdrawn. The end of the alliance between Ethiopia and East Germany further isolated the Mengistu regime and reduced the Ethiopian army's ability to achieve a military solution in Eritrea and Tigray.

North Korea

Given the change in Soviet policy toward Ethiopia, Addis Ababa's relations with North Korea took on added importance as the 1990s began. There was little information on the nature and scope of North Korean military assistance to Ethiopia, but most Western military observers agreed that it would be impossible for North Korea to duplicate the quantity and quality of weapons that the Soviet Union had been providing to the Mengistu regime. Nonetheless, beginning in 1985 P'yŏngyang deployed hundreds of military advisers to Ethiopia and provided an array of small arms, ammunition, and other matériel to the Mengistu regime.

In November 1985, North Korea provided Ethiopia a 6 million birr (for value of the birr—see Glossary) interest-free loan to be used to purchase equipment with which to construct a shipyard on Haleb Island, off Aseb. Planners expected the shipyard to produce wooden-hulled and steel-hulled craft ranging in size from 5,000 to 150,000 tons displacement. (As of 1991, the shipyard had not been completed.) North Korea also had paid for the training of a 20,000-man special operations force at the Tatek military camp.

Israel

Israel has been one of Ethiopia's most reliable suppliers of military assistance, largely because Tel Aviv believed that if it supported Ethiopia, hostile Arab nations would be unable to exert control over the Red Sea and the Bab el Mandeb, which forms its southern outlet. During the imperial era, Israeli advisers trained paratroops and counterinsurgency units belonging to the Fifth Division (also called the Nebelbal—or Flame—Division). In the early 1960s, Israel started helping the Ethiopian government in its campaigns against the Eritrean Liberation Front (ELF).

Even after Ethiopia broke diplomatic relations with Israel at the time of the October 1973 War, Israel quietly continued to supply military aid to Ethiopia. This assistance continued after Mengistu came to power in 1974 and included spare parts and ammunition for United States-made weapons and service for United States-made F–5 jet fighters. Israel also maintained a small group of military advisers in Addis Ababa.

In 1978, however, when former Israeli minister of foreign affairs Moshe Dayan admitted that Israel had been providing security assistance to Ethiopia, Mengistu expelled all Israelis so that he might preserve his relationship with radical Arab countries such as Libya and South Yemen. Nonetheless, although Addis Ababa claimed it had terminated its military relationship with Israel, military cooperation continued. In 1983, for example, Israel provided communications training, and in 1984 Israeli advisers trained the Presidential Guard and Israeli technical personnel served with the police. Some Western observers believed that Israel provided military assistance to Ethiopia in exchange for Mengistu's tacit cooperation during Operation Moses in 1984, in which 10,000 Beta Israel (Ethiopian Jews; also called Falasha) were evacuated to Israel (see Ethnic Groups, Ethnicity, and Language, ch. 2). In 1985 Tel Aviv reportedly sold Addis Ababa at least US$20 million in Soviet-made munitions and spare parts captured from Palestinians in Lebanon. According to the EPLF, the Mengistu regime received US$83 million worth of Israeli military aid in 1987, and Israel deployed some 300 military advisers to Ethiopia. Additionally, the EPLF claimed that thirty-eight Ethiopian pilots had gone to Israel for training.

In late 1989, Israel reportedly finalized a secret agreement to provide increased military assistance to Addis Ababa in exchange for Mengistu's promise to allow Ethiopia's remaining Beta Israel to emigrate to Israel. In addition, the two nations agreed to restore diplomatic relations (Israel opened an embassy in Addis Ababa on December 17, 1989) and to increase intelligence cooperation. Mengistu apparently believed that Israel—unlike the Soviet Union, whose military advisers emphasized conventional tactics—could provide the training and matériel needed to transform the Ethiopian army into a counterinsurgency force capable of defeating Eritrean and Tigrayan separatists.

During 1990 Israeli-Ethiopian relations continued to prosper. According to a *New York Times* report, Tel Aviv furnished an array of military assistance to Addis Ababa, including 150,000 rifles, cluster bombs, ten to twenty military advisers to train Mengistu's Presidential Guard, and an unknown number of instructors to work with Ethiopian commando units. Unconfirmed reports also suggested that Israel had provided the Ethiopian air force with surveillance cameras and had agreed to train Ethiopian pilots.

In return for this aid, Ethiopia permitted the emigration of the Beta Israel. Departures in the spring reached about 500 people a month before Ethiopian officials adopted new emigration procedures that reduced the figure by more than two-thirds. The following year, Tel Aviv and Addis Ababa negotiated another agreement whereby Israel provided agricultural, economic, and health assistance. Also, in May 1991, as the Mengistu regime neared its end, Israel paid US$35 million in cash for permission to fly nearly 15,000 Beta Israel from Ethiopia to Israel.

External and Internal Opponents

After the 1974 overthrow of Haile Selassie, the Mengistu regime confronted several internal rebellions and one major external opponent. These internal rebellions consisted of threats posed by Eritrean secessionists, Tigrayan rebels, and other, less active guerrilla movements in the center and south of the country. Whatever the political orientation or ethnic composition of these insurgent groups, the Ethiopian government characterized them variously as "traitors," "counterrevolutionaries," "feudalists," "*shifta*" (bandits), or "paid agents of the CIA." By 1991 the Eritrean People's Liberation Front (EPLF) and the Tigray People's Liberation Front (TPLF) had emerged as the strongest guerrilla groups opposed to the government.

Since the end of World War II, Somalia has posed the only serious external threat to Ethiopia. In the late 1980s, however, the nature of this threat changed, perhaps permanently, as the Somali government became more involved with maintaining its internal security and less capable of recreating a "Greater Somalia."

The Eritreans

A variety of Eritrean secessionist groups have used conventional means and guerrilla tactics to defy the forces of both the imperial and the revolutionary governments (see The Eritrean Movement, ch. 4). The Eritrean Liberation Front (ELF), a nationalist organization committed to self-rule for Eritrea, commenced a small-scale insurgency in 1961 against imperial security forces. Throughout the 1960s, the level of hostilities accelerated steadily, leading to the 1971 imposition of martial law. Ethiopian army personnel deployed to Eritrea during this period numbered about 20,000, roughly half the force's total, but much of the burden of counterinsurgency operations fell on the paramilitary mobile police.

Ideological and ethnic differences split the ELF in 1970 and resulted in the formation of the Marxist-oriented Eritrean People's Liberation Front (EPLF). From 1972 to 1974, a civil war ensued between the two groups. Eventually, the EPLF, which advocated "revolution before unity," emerged victorious. Many ELF members, and sometimes entire units, then fled into eastern Sudan, further weakening the organization in Eritrea. After establishing its dominance, the EPLF used its increased popularity to expand its personnel strength. By 1977, when secessionists controlled the countryside and most population centers, the EPLF had approximately 15,000 troops in the field. The ELF, however, still had numerical superiority, with about 20,000 troops in its ranks. Therefore, to further discredit and isolate the ELF, the EPLF and a group of former ELF cadres who had reorganized themselves as the Eritrean Liberation Front-Revolutionary Council issued a joint statement indicating that they were "the sole representatives of the Eritrean people and the only legal spokesmen on all issues concerning the Eritrean people's struggle."

In May 1978, a 100,000-member Ethiopian force was deployed in a counteroffensive whose objective was the eradication of the Eritrean revolution. Even though the EPLF and ELF succeeded in making some preemptive attacks against government units and in defending Eritrea's southern border, the ferocity of the government counteroffensive forced the rebels to undertake a "strategic withdrawal" to their base area. As a result, the Ethiopian army reoccupied most towns and cities that had been taken by the rebels. Government troops also dealt a crippling blow to the ELF, causing many of its personnel to flee into eastern Sudan, where many of them remained.

The only government setback occurred at the EPLF-held town of Nakfa, which eventually became a symbol of Eritrean determination to resist government control. After retreating EPLF units had reached Nakfa, they built heavy fortifications, including a forty-kilometer-long defensive trench in the surrounding mountains. Despite repeated attempts, the Ethiopian army was unable to dislodge the EPLF from Nakfa. Between 1978 and 1981, the Derg unleashed five large-scale military campaigns against the EPLF, none of which resulted in a government victory.

In February 1982, the Mengistu regime embarked on its sixth counteroffensive against the EPLF. Dubbed Red Star, the campaign involved 120,000 government troops. The campaign failed to drive the EPLF from Nakfa and resulted in the deaths of more than 40,000 Ethiopian troops. Although Addis Ababa managed to consolidate its hold over the Eritrean highlands, it was unable to eliminate the EPLF, which still possessed the capacity to make hit-and-run strikes against government positions.

Once the 1982 Red Star offensive ended, the EPLF regrouped its forces to seize the military initiative. In January 1984, the EPLF captured the town of Teseney in southwestern Eritrea, and two months later the rebels overran the port of Mersa Teklay, thereby establishing an EPLF presence on the northeastern coast. During this battle, the rebels also captured a significant number of weapons, which they used to take the strategic hilltop town of Barentu in early July 1985. Once again, the rebels captured an array of military equipment, including fifteen T–54/55 tanks and dozens of trucks and artillery pieces. In May 1984, EPLF commandos attacked the Asmera air base and reportedly destroyed two Soviet Il-38 maritime reconnaissance aircraft.

When news of the EPLF's victory at Barentu reached Addis Ababa, the Mengistu regime ordered the redeployment of two divisions (about 30,000 troops) from the Ogaden to northern Ethiopia and formed a new armored division to help retake the town. The Ethiopian army then made perhaps as many as thirteen attempts to recapture the town, losing 2,000 soldiers killed or wounded in the process. After the Ethiopian air force started bombing Barentu, the EPLF guerrillas withdrew from the town on August 24, 1985, taking with them at least thirteen T–55 tanks, twelve artillery pieces, and several APCs. According to the EPLF, their units killed or captured 11,250 Ethiopian soldiers during several battles fought before the withdrawal.

Within days of reoccupying Barentu, the Ethiopian army recaptured Teseney, thereby cutting off the EPLF's western territorial flank. Additional government victories forced the rebels to fall back to their Nakfa stronghold. Over the next several weeks, the Ethiopian armed forces used tanks and other armored vehicles, cluster bombs, napalm, and fighter-bombers to support the ground attack on Nakfa. By the summer of 1986, the government offensive had ended; Nakfa, however, was still in rebel hands, and the EPLF had extended its area of control southward along the Eritrean coast.

On October 10, 1985, the Derg launched another anti-EPLF offensive, whose objective was the capture of Nakfa ''within five days.'' The operation involved sixty aircraft and thirty helicopter gunships. For the first time, the Ethiopian air force dropped airborne units behind rebel lines in northeast Sahel *awraja* (subregion). When Ethiopian forces failed to capture the city, the Mengistu regime ordered two more attacks on Nakfa, each of which ended in the government's defeat.

In 1986 the EPLF relied on more traditional guerrilla tactics in its operations against the Ethiopian armed forces. On January 14, 1986, for example, a rebel commando unit, armed with rocket launchers and hand grenades, again penetrated the Asmera air base, destroying more than forty aircraft and burning the installation's ammunition and fuel depots. Apart from the impact on the Ethiopian air force, this attack caused the Soviet Union to terminate its reconnaissance flights to and from Asmera. The following May, EPLF artillery units bombarded Ethiopian positions in and around Mitsiwa, destroying fuel tanks and tankers. Regular units also overran government garrisons located about thirty kilometers south of Asmera.

Concurrent with these military operations, the EPLF continued its political offensive against the Mengistu regime. On September 23, 1986, the rebels celebrated their twenty-fifth year of resistance by calling on the Organization of African Unity (OAU), the League of Arab States (Arab League), the UN, and the Nonaligned Movement to recognize the legitimacy of their claim to nationhood. Then, on November 25, the EPLF announced that it had merged with an ELF faction that had severed ties with its parent group. The EPLF also continued efforts to reach an accommodation with another ELF faction, the Eritrean Liberation Front-Revolutionary Council, led by Ahmad Nasir.

The armed struggle in Eritrea entered 1987 with neither the EPLF nor the Ethiopian government willing to abandon the use of military force to achieve their political objectives. However, the Mengistu regime abandoned its costly strategy of launching annual major counteroffensives in Eritrea, preferring instead a policy of defensive containment while rebuilding its army, which still had not recovered from the October 1985 offensive.

The EPLF also kept its military activities to a minimum. Apart from various hit-and-run operations, one of the largest rebel engagements occurred on March 20, when the EPLF clashed with four Ethiopian army brigades in Eritrea's northern zone. In the two-day battle, the EPLF claimed government forces suffered 650 casualties.

Women veterans who have been decorated for their service to the state

The following year, the EPLF, which by then had approximately 30,000 full-time fighters plus an unknown number of part-time personnel, stepped up its military activities in Eritrea. On March 19, 1988, the rebels inflicted a defeat on Ethiopia's Second Revolutionary Army at the garrison town of Afabet. According to British historian and Africa specialist Basil Davidson, the Afabet victory was one of the biggest ever scored by any liberation movement anywhere since Dien Bien Phu in Vietnam in 1954. Rebel spokesmen indicated that the EPLF had destroyed an Ethiopian army corps, comprising three divisions totaling 18,000 to 20,000 personnel. The rebels also had captured several thousand Ethiopian soldiers, three Soviet military advisers, and an array of equipment.

The Ethiopian government, which launched an unsuccessful counteroffensive in June 1988 against the EPLF, eventually ordered the evacuation of all foreign personnel working for humanitarian and relief organizations in Eritrea. Additionally, Addis Ababa told these organizations to relinquish all food and nonfood assistance to the government's Relief and Rehabilitation Commission (RRC). Many Western governments, including that of the United States, objected to this decision because they feared Mengistu would resort to using food as a weapon against Eritrean and Tigrayan rebels and their sympathizers.

Another development associated with the Eritrean triumph at

Afabet was the EPLF's and TPLF's acknowledgment of each other's military victories, something that had not happened since a disagreement between the two groups in 1985 (see The Tigray, this ch.). In addition, the two groups issued a reconciliation statement in Damascus, Syria, and promised to coordinate future military actions to bring an end to the Mengistu regime. However, the EPLF–TPLF relationship continued to experience difficulties, largely because of disagreement over strategy and tactics, over the next several years.

Apart from further demoralizing the Ethiopian army, the Afabet victory also gave impetus to the peace process. In early July 1989, Yuri Yukalov, director of the African department at the Soviet Ministry of Foreign Affairs, met with EPLF secretary general Issaias Afwerki. The meeting was significant because it was the first serious contact between the Soviet Union and the EPLF and because it demonstrated to Mengistu that Moscow was no longer willing to provide unlimited military assistance to support his military strategy in northern Ethiopia.

The EPLF sustained its military pressure on the Mengistu regime in 1989. On January 17, rebel units launched a preemptive attack against Ethiopian troops located northwest of the Asmera-Mitsiwa road. During the two-day battle, the EPLF claimed to have killed, wounded, or captured some 2,600 Ethiopian soldiers, in the process destroying twenty-one tanks and capturing eight others, together with a variety of small- and medium-caliber weapons. On February 19, EPLF units, operating in conjunction with the TPLF, struck and captured the town of Inda Silase in Tigray. Over the next few months, the EPLF defeated an Ethiopian contingent at Adi Kwala, a town ninety kilometers south of Asmera (March 15); repulsed an Ethiopian army attempt to cut off the EPLF fortifications around Keren (March 22–29); and killed or wounded approximately 1,000 Ethiopian soldiers at Adi Goroto (March 27–29).

In mid-1989, after Mengistu had succeeded in thwarting a coup attempt, the EPLF and the Ethiopian government agreed to enter into negotiations mediated by former United States president Jimmy Carter. After a round of preliminary negotiations, which opened on September 7, 1989, at the Carter Presidential Center at Emory University in Atlanta, Georgia, the two sides agreed to hold another round of peace talks in Nairobi, Kenya, beginning on November 20, 1989. These talks failed to produce a peace agreement. Subsequent meetings in Washington, chaired by United States assistant secretary of state for African affairs Herman Cohen, also accomplished little.

Meanwhile, government forces continued to suffer battlefield defeats. On February 10, 1990, the EPLF captured the port of Mitsiwa. The fall of this strategically important port isolated Ethiopia's Second Revolutionary Army and eventually resulted in the loss of Eritrea. Additionally, the EPLF used its small fleet of armed speed boats to sink or cripple most Ethiopian navy ships anchored in Mitsiwa harbor. Then, in August, the EPLF launched an offensive along the Dekemhare front, south of Asmera. During this operation, the rebels killed or wounded more than 11,000 government soldiers and captured two tanks, many vehicles, and more than 1,000 medium and light weapons. Although government forces enjoyed a few minor victories at the end of 1990, the EPLF remained in control of most of Eritrea.

In early 1991, the rebels started their final offensive against government forces by driving south along the Red Sea coast, a movement that by early April brought them to the gates of Aseb. At the same time, they formed an alliance with other rebel groups operating as the Ethiopian People's Revolutionary Democratic Front (EPRDF) and contributed at least eight brigades to the EPRDF to aid in military operations in Gonder and Gojam. By the end of April, the EPLF controlled nearly all of Eritrea, the major exceptions being Keren, Asmera, and Aseb. In late May, the EPLF assumed control of these towns without heavy fighting and without Ethiopian government reprisals against civilians. The 120,000-member Second Revolutionary Army surrendered in Asmera on May 24, the same day that Keren capitulated, the garrison at Aseb following suit the next day. Having occupied all of Eritrea, the EPLF announced its intention to repatriate all Ethiopian soldiers, security personnel, WPE members, and ordinary citizens back to Ethiopia. Shortly thereafter, EPLF leader Issaias Afwerki indicated that as far as he was concerned, Eritrea was an independent state.

The Tigray

Formed in 1975, the Tigray People's Liberation Front (TPLF) was dedicated to the overthrow of the Mengistu regime (see The Tigrayan Movement, ch. 4). It survived during its early years only because of the money and weapons it received from the EPLF. The EPLF supported the TPLF because the latter formed a buffer between the Ethiopian army and Eritrea. Despite subsequent political and ideological rifts between the groups, the EPLF always maintained this buffer strategy.

On February 18, 1976, the TPLF convened its first congress, at Dima. The group of about 170 people in attendance elected a seven-member Central Committee. During May and June 1976, the rebels gained international attention by kidnapping a British family and a British journalist. By the end of the year, the TPLF had about 1,000 full-time fighters. It confined its military activities to attacking traffic along the main road between Mekele, the Tigrayan capital, and Asmera. Within two years, however, the TPLF had increased its strength to the point where the group controlled large parts of the countryside and threatened the Ethiopian army's supply lines.

Throughout the late 1970s and the early 1980s, Tigray, like Eritrea, suffered from the Derg's annual military counteroffensives in north-central Ethiopia. During these operations, the TPLF and the EPLF coordinated many of their military actions against government forces. However, in 1983 a rift developed between the groups after the TPLF proposed a unification of all anti-Mengistu elements, including the EPLF. Relations further deteriorated when the EPLF failed to inform the TPLF that it had started secret peace talks with Addis Ababa. As a result, the TPLF refrained from supporting the EPLF during the government's 1985 counteroffensive in northern Ethiopia. Although there was a brief reconciliation after the EPLF's victory at Afabet, the TPLF–EPLF estrangement continued for the next several years. In March 1987, for example, the TPLF refused to be represented at the EPLF's Unity Congress.

In February 1989, the TPLF, which by then included at least 20,000 full-time fighters plus an unknown number of part-time fighters, abandoned hit-and-run guerrilla tactics. The TPLF, with support from the EPLF, which wanted to open a second front against Mengistu, launched a conventional attack against the town of Inda Silase in western Tigray. The TPLF destroyed a 20,000-member Ethiopian army force. Ethiopian military units then withdrew from Mekele and the rest of Tigray without a fight. This defeat undoubtedly helped trigger the unsuccessful May 1989 coup against Mengistu.

Although government troops subsequently returned to southern Tigray and reoccupied a few towns and villages, the political and military initiative remained with the TPLF. On March 10, 1989, the TPLF opened its third congress. Apart from passing numerous antigovernment resolutions, the delegates pledged to support the EPRDF, which had been formed earlier in the year by the TPLF and a group known as the Ethiopian People's Democratic Movement (EPDM), whose members were primarily Amhara. In time, the EPRDF also included the Oromo People's Democratic Organization (OPDO) and the Ethiopian Democratic Officers' Revolutionary Movement, both of which had been created by the TPLF in May 1990. Tigrayan strategists hoped the unification of these groups eventually would enable the TPLF to widen its base of support beyond Tigray. Elements in support of the government, however, denounced the EPRDF as nothing more than a TPLF organization in Amhara clothing.

In August and September 1989, TPLF forces, operating within the framework of the EPRDF, moved south into Welo. They overran towns along the main road, routed numerous Ethiopian units, captured an array of Ethiopian army equipment, and forced the temporary evacuation of the regional capital of Dese. By the end of 1989, the EPRDF had succeeded in defeating an Ethiopian garrison at Debre Tabor. This victory enabled Tigrayan forces to cut the road between the cities of Gonder and Bahir Dar and to force their way into northern Shewa, less than 160 kilometers from Addis Ababa. Mengistu responded to these developments by persuading the National Shengo to order the mobilization of all former soldiers and police up to age seventy. Additionally, the National Shengo authorized increased military spending, assigned all transport to the war effort, and armed local populations in war zones. However, these actions failed to improve the government's battlefield performance against the EPRDF.

During 1990 the EPRDF, which controlled all of Tigray with the exception of one small government outpost, concentrated on consolidating the gains it had made the previous year, although in June the insurgents repulsed a major offensive by the Ethiopian army. The year 1991, however, saw the EPRDF launch three offensives in rapid succession that destroyed the Ethiopian army and the Mengistu regime. On February 23, the rebels began Operation Tewodros to drive the government out of Gonder and Gojam, and they succeeded after only two weeks of fighting. The inhabitants of both regions supported the operation largely because of their opposition to the heavy conscription campaign of the previous year and because of their hatred of the villagization program.

In March the EPRDF launched Operation Dula Billisuma Welkita into Welega, which resulted in the capture of the regional military headquarters in Nekemte. Insurgent units then advanced south and east and soon occupied Fincha, site of an electric power station that served Addis Ababa. In mid-May Operation Wallelign was begun along the Welo front. Within hours the rebels had overrun Dese and Kembolcha. By May 20, the EPRDF had captured all government positions in southern Welo and northern Shewa and were advancing on Addis Ababa from the west. The next morning, Mengistu fled the country.

In the aftermath of these three campaigns, the Ethiopian armed forces disintegrated. Tens of thousands of soldiers crowded into Addis Ababa and sold their weapons or used them to rob civilians. Countless other soldiers went home, while many senior army and air force officers fled to Djibouti, Kenya, or Sudan. Ethiopian naval personnel and vessels dispersed to Saudi Arabia, Yemen, and Djibouti.

During the final week of the war, the EPRDF slowly advanced toward Addis Ababa, capturing the air force base at Debre Zeyit along the way. The final battle for the capital occurred on the morning of May 28, when the EPRDF entered the city. Resistance to the takeover consisted largely of street fighting and a low-level clash at the Grand (Menelik's) Palace. About 600 to 800 people, both civilians and combatants, reportedly died during the operation. For the TPLF, the long road from the hills of Tigray had finally ended in victory.

The Oromo

Created in July 1973, the Oromo Liberation Front (OLF) set forth as its goals Oromo liberation from "Ethiopian colonialism" and the establishment of an independent Democratic Republic of Oromia in southern Ethiopia (see Other Movements and Fronts, ch. 4). The following year, the OLF began an offensive against the Ethiopian army in Harerge. After the collapse of the imperial regime in 1974, the OLF increased its military activities after it became evident that the Mengistu regime would not allow the Oromo to elect their own representatives to run peasant associations or to use their own language in schools and newspapers. However, the OLF had little success in mobilizing support in the late 1970s and early 1980s.

Beginning in the mid-1980s, the OLF experienced a resurgence. According to spokesmen, the organization had 5,000 fighters and more than 10,000 militia personnel; most other sources, however, suggested that the OLF's personnel strength was much lower. In 1985 the OLF overran the gold-mining town of Agubela and "freed" about 1,000 mine workers. The rebels also confiscated coffee valued at approximately US$2 million from the Ethiopian Coffee Marketing Board.

In early 1988, the Ethiopian army attacked OLF forces in Welega. Fierce fighting occurred around the garrison towns in Kelem and Gimbi *awraja*. Shortly after these battles, the OLF acknowledged that it had received support from the EPLF and the TPLF. Despite this activity, however, some Western observers believed that the OLF was still in the fledgling stage of its growth. Its chief weakness remained its inability to mobilize and coordinate the activities of its eastern wing in Harerge, Bale, Sidamo, and Arsi. As a result, another organization, the Ogaden National Liberation Front (ONLF), competed with the OLF for the loyalty and support of the peoples living in the east (see The Somali, this ch.).

On June 10, 1989, the OLF reported that it had "disarmed" an unspecified number of Ethiopian soldiers and freed more than 2,000 Oromo prisoners by destroying five "concentration camps" in Gara Muleta *awraja* in Harerge. The following October, the OLF also engaged the Ethiopian army in Welega and Harerge. From November 10 to November 17, 1989, the OLF held its second congress in Golelola in Harerge. Besides adopting many antigovernment resolutions, the congress promised increased military activities against the Mengistu regime. A few weeks later, in December, OLF units, with EPLF support, launched an offensive that eventually resulted in the capture of the town of Asosa along the Ethiopian-Sudanese border. The OLF also escalated activities in Harerge after many Ethiopian army units redeployed to other locations in Ethiopia.

After occupying Asosa in January 1990, the OLF launched no further offensives against Mengistu's army until the end of the year, when OLF units saw action at several locations in western parts of the country. In 1991 the OLF remained largely in the background as the EPRDF and the EPLF fought their final battles against government forces. The OLF's last military action before the demise of the Mengistu regime occurred at Dembi Dolo in southerwestern Welega, when some of its units reportedly killed more than 700 government soldiers.

Relations between the OLF and the EPRDF seem to have been ambivalent even at the best of times because the Oromo were deeply suspicious of the ultimate designs of the Tigrayan leadership. These relations hardly improved during 1990 when the OLF was confronted by a rival group, the Oromo People's Democratic Organization (OPDO), sponsored by the TPLF as a member of the EPRDF umbrella organization. OLF spokesmen also repeatedly denounced EPRDF claims that it was the EPRDF that had freed the Oromo from the regime's domination. Actions such as these further alienated the OLF and helped account for the rift that developed shortly after the occupation of Addis Ababa between the OLF and the EPRDF over the composition of a new government—a disagreement that did not augur well for the future.

The Somali

The most significant antigovernment force operating in the Ogaden was the Western Somali Liberation Front (WSLF; see

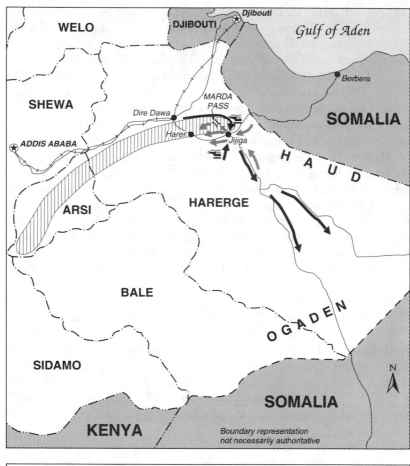

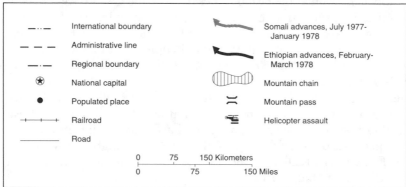

Figure 11. The Ogaden War, 1977–78

Other Movements and Fronts, ch. 4). WSLF guerrillas first engaged Ethiopian troops in combat in 1975, systematically attacking police posts and army garrisons from base camps across the border in Somalia. In June 1977, the WSLF, supported by the Somali government and joined by Somali National Army (SNA) "volunteers," succeeded in cutting the railroad bridges between Addis Ababa and Djibouti, which carried about a third of Ethiopia's external trade, and in establishing control over 60 percent of the Ogaden. At that time, the WSLF numbered about 6,000 troops. As the tempo of the conflict increased, the WSLF relied more and more on Somalia's armored and artillery capabilities.

In July 1977, mechanized units of the SNA army invaded Ethiopia in a preemptive thrust at Harer—the Ogaden region's military command center—that was intended to decide the Ogaden issue before promised Soviet military equipment arrived in Ethiopia (see fig. 11). Jijiga fell to Somali forces in September, when the Ethiopian mechanized unit defending it mutinied and fled in panic. The Somali forces then focused their efforts on the strategic Marda (also known as Karamarda) Pass, carrying the attack into the unfamiliar highlands to block Ethiopian reinforcements coming into Harerge. The move diverted Ethiopian forces from the main offensive aimed at Harer and Dire Dawa, site of the air base from which strikes were flown against targets inside Somalia.

After weeks of being bogged down by bad weather, in January 1978 the SNA pressed a three-pronged attack on Harer, where nearly 50,000 Ethiopian troops had regrouped, backed by Soviet-supplied heavy artillery and reinforced by 10,000 Cuban troops from units hurriedly flown in from Angola. Early in February 1978, the Ethiopians launched a two-stage counterattack toward Jijiga that had been planned and directed by Soviet advisers and backed by Cuban troops. Moving east and south from Dire Dawa, an Ethiopian column crossed the highlands between Jijiga and the Somali border, bypassing Somali troops dug in around the Marda Pass. In the second offensive strike, joined by Cuban troops, the Ethiopian army trapped the Somali forces around Jijiga between helicopter-borne tanks that had landed to their rear and a determined frontal assault from Harer. On March 5, the Ethiopians retook Jijiga after two days of fierce fighting in which they defeated four Somali brigades and killed 3,000 Somali troops. Within a week, the Ethiopian army had reestablished control over all the region's major towns. Meanwhile, the Ethiopian air force's F–5 fighters had won air superiority in engagements against Soviet-made Somali jets. On March 9, Siad Barre ended the undeclared war by announcing that he had recalled all SNA troops from the Ogaden.

The introduction of Soviet equipment and 17,000 Cuban troops had decisively altered the balance of power in the Horn of Africa.

After the withdrawal of the Somali regulars, the WSLF reverted to classic guerrilla tactics against the Ethiopian army, whose soldiers they characterized as black colonialist troops. Western journalists visiting the region in early 1980 confirmed that the WSLF once again controlled the countryside and many of the main roads. Also, "volunteers," believed by many to have been troops of the SNA, reportedly had rejoined the WSLF. Renewed fighting occurred in June and July 1980, when, according to an official spokesman in Addis Ababa, Ethiopian troops repelled an incursion by a mechanized Somali force. Meanwhile, Ethiopia had started training and equipping the Somali Salvation Democratic Front (SSDF) and later the Somali National Movement (SNM), both of which began launching raids inside Somalia against the Siad Barre regime. The renewed conflict forced Mogadishu to declare a state of emergency in October 1980.

Another major incident occurred on June 30, 1983, when Ethiopian troops staged a two-pronged operation against Somalia. Part of the invading Ethiopian force intended to capture high ground in Hiiraan Region near Feerfeer on the Ethiopia-Somalia frontier. However, the SNA garrison at Beledweyne repulsed the Ethiopian attack. Farther north, an Ethiopian armored column overran a Somali settlement in Galguduud Region. On July 17, Ethiopian warplanes bombed and strafed the airstrip and other parts of Galcaio, the capital of Mudug Region. Ethiopian armored columns also crossed the border to the north and west of Galcaio and occupied the village of Galdogob. Until late 1983, there were numerous clashes between Ethiopian and Somali units, especially near Balumbale and in the northwest around Hargeysa. However, the Somali forces were unable to dislodge the Ethiopians from Balumbale and Galdogob.

For two more years, Ethiopian-Somali relations remained tense. In July 1985, Mengistu and Siad Barre held discussions at the OAU summit in Addis Ababa in order to lay the groundwork for a peaceful resolution of the Ogaden problem. Although Ethiopian and Somali officials held several more meetings, they were unable to reach a settlement. In mid-January 1986, a meeting between Mengistu and Siad Barre in Djibouti resulted in a "general understanding" on the Ogaden issue. This "understanding" was undermined on February 12, 1987, when Ethiopia launched ground and air raids on areas of western Somalia three weeks after protests and mass arrests cut off Hargeysa from the rest of the country. Although an agreement to end hostilities was signed in April 1988, the dispute remained unresolved because of Addis Ababa's continued support of the SNM. After the downfall of the Siad Barre regime in January 1991, tens of thousands of Somali refugees fled to the Ogaden. This exodus only added to eastern Ethiopia's increasing instability during the final months of the Mengistu regime.

Public Order and Internal Security

As a result of insurgencies affecting a large part of the country in the 1970s and after, questions of internal security and public order became inseparable from the general problem of national security. Revisions made to the penal code in 1976 helped blur the distinction between political opposition to the government (defined as criminal activity) and categories of crime against persons and property. Army security services and counterinsurgency units assumed many functions formerly assigned to the national police's paramilitary and constabulary units, and local law enforcement was delegated largely to the civilian paramilitary People's Protection Brigades, drawn from peasant association and *kebele* defense squads. Although criminal investigation remained an important part of the mission of the national police, units of its heavily armed Mobile Emergency Police Force were employed in pursuing insurgents and rooting out political dissidents. The gradual isolation of the Mengistu regime during the 1980s meant that these and other measures designed to suppress internal dissent remained in force until the military government collapsed.

The National Police

In traditional Ethiopian society, customary law resolved conflicts, and families usually avenged wrongs committed against their members. The private armies of the nobility enforced law in the countryside according to the will of their leaders. In 1916 the imperial government formed a civilian municipal guard in Addis Ababa to ensure obedience to legal proclamations. The general public despised the municipal guard, nearly all of whose members were inefficient at preserving public order or investigating criminal activities.

In 1935 the emperor authorized the establishment of formal, British-trained police forces in Addis Ababa and four other cities. Seven years later, he organized the Imperial Ethiopian Police under British tutelage as a centralized national force with paramilitary and constabulary units. In 1946 the authorities opened the Ethiopian Police College at Sendafa. In 1956 the imperial government amalgamated the separate city police forces with the national police force. Initially administered as a department of the Ministry of

315

Interior, the national police had evolved, by the early 1970s, into an independent agency commanded by a police commissioner responsible to the emperor.

Local control over police was minimal, despite imperial proclamations that granted police authority to governors general of the provinces. Assistant police commissioners in each of the fourteen provinces worked in conjunction with the governors general, but for the most part Addis Ababa directed administration. The Territorial Army's provincial units, commanded by the governor general and by an unpaid civilian auxiliary in areas where police were scarce, assisted the national police force. Police posts were found in all cities and larger towns and at strategic points along the main roads in the countryside. The police usually recruited local men who were familiar with the social values of the areas in which they served; however, the populace rarely looked upon such individuals with affection. Police operations generally emphasized punishment rather than prevention.

In 1974 the national police numbered approximately 28,000 in all branches, including 6,000 in the Mobile Emergency Police Force; 1,200 frontier guards; and a 3,200-member commando unit with rapid reaction capability. The Federal Republic of Germany (West Germany) supplied the paramilitary police with weapons and vehicles and installed a nationwide teleprinter system, while Israeli counterinsurgency specialists trained commandos and frontier guards. About 5,000 constabulary police, mostly recruited locally, served in Eritrea, as did 2,500 commandos.

After the 1974 overthrow of Haile Selassie, the new Marxist government severely circumscribed the authority of the national police, which had been identified with the old regime and regional interests. The authorities accused constables of protecting landowners against peasants in the countryside, of arresting supporters of the military regime in Addis Ababa, and of being members of the "rightist opposition." In Eritrea, however, the army already had taken over police functions in January 1975 from local police units suspected of being sympathetic to the secessionists. The Asmera police voluntarily stayed at their posts for some time after their dismissal to protect civilians from attack by unruly soldiers.

In 1977 the Mengistu regime reorganized the national police, placing a politically reliable commissioner in command. A security committee formulated policy, which then was implemented by the Ministry of Interior. The army assumed a larger role in criminal investigation and in maintaining public order. People's Protection Brigades took over local law enforcement duties previously assigned to the constabulary. As a result of these changes, by 1982 the strength of the national police had declined to about 17,000. Mengistu also created the army's new Eighth Division from police commando units. Other special units joined the augmented 9,000-member paramilitary Mobile Emergency Police Force for employment in counterinsurgency operations.

The Directorate of Police, which reported to the commissioner, included the special Criminal Investigation Branch, which had the role in directing police counterinsurgency activities through regional branch offices. Another branch of the directorate investigated economic crimes, particularly smuggling and other forms of illicit commerce. The Revolutionary Operations Coordinating Committee, organized at the subregion level, cooperated with the police in battling smuggling and economic sabotage.

The Marxist regime stressed that the mission of the national police was essentially political—more involved with suppressing political dissent as the local law enforcement role shifted to People's Protection Brigades. Mengistu described the police mission as contributing to the "intensification of the class struggle."

The government adopted a policy whereby police constables were recruited at an early age and trained in their native regions. Training was designed to allow police stationed in remote areas to be self-sufficient in building and maintaining their posts. Training standards were not uniform, and, unless it took place in Addis Ababa, in-service or specialized training was limited. In politically stable rural areas where duty requirements and supervision were less exacting, the police were less efficient than their urban counterparts. A high percentage of rural constables could neither read nor write and therefore did not keep records of their activities. Many crimes were considered to be matters concerning only the persons involved and were often ignored by the police unless one of the interested parties filed a complaint.

The Addis Ababa police, by contrast, were organized into uniformed, detective, and traffic units; a riot squad, or "flying column"; and a police laboratory—organizational refinements not found in regional police units. A small number of women served in police units in large cities. Generally, they were employed in administrative positions or as guards for female prisoners. National police officers were paid according to the same standardized wage scale that applied to members of the armed forces.

As a rule, police in constabulary units were armed only with batons. Small arms usually were kept in designated armories and were issued for specific duties. Matériel used by paramilitary units included heavy machine guns, submachine guns, automatic rifles, side arms, mortars, grenades, tear gas, light armored vehicles, and other equipment adaptable to riot control and counterinsurgency operations. Larger police units, such as the one in Addis Ababa, were also equipped with modern military vehicles, which were used as patrol cars and police vans. In many rural areas, however, horses and mules were often the sole means of transportation for constables.

Officers usually were commissioned after completion of a cadet course at the Ethiopian Police College at Sendafa, near Addis Ababa. Staffed by Swedish instructors, the school opened in 1946, but since 1960 the faculty had consisted entirely of Ethiopians who were police college graduates. Candidates for the two-year course had to have a secondary school education or its equivalent. After the Derg took power, the government increased enrollment to bring new blood into the national police; from 1974 to 1979, about 800 graduates received commissions as second lieutenants.

Instruction at the college included general courses in police science, criminal law, tactics, traffic control, sociology, criminology, physical education, and first aid, as well as political indoctrination. Practical training was offered midway in the program and sometimes entailed field service in troubled areas. Those few cadets who had passed their final examinations with distinction were selected for further specialized training. The police college also offered short-term courses and refresher training for service officers. It cooperated with the army in training military police in traffic control and criminal investigation techniques. By the end of 1990, the police college had graduated a total of 3,951 officer cadets in the years since its establishment in 1946.

People's Protection Brigades

Soon after the overthrow of the imperial regime, the Derg moved to consolidate the revolution at the grass-roots level by promoting the creation of peasant associations and *kebeles* (see Peasant Associations; *Kebeles*, ch. 4). These associations had tribunals that permitted them to exercise criminal and civil jurisdiction over legal matters (see The Legal System, this ch.). More important, the government also legitimized local defense squads, granting them police powers within designated areas. Defense squads also protected public property and enforced land reform measures, but their original function was the essentially political one of rounding up— and often disposing of—suspected government opponents. During the Red Terror (see Glossary) campaign of 1977–78, the power of the *kebeles* was virtually unrestricted, and the defense squads emerged as the regime's chief instruments of coercion within the capital. However, in reaction to the defense squads' excessive use of violence, Mengistu curbed their powers in April 1978.

In 1978 the People's Protection Brigades were created from an estimated 10,000 defense squad vigilantes. Their function was to act as local law enforcement agencies within the jurisdiction of each peasant association and *kebele*. Although promoted as instruments of decentralization, the brigades answered to the security chief of the Central Committee of the Commission to Organize the Party of the Workers of Ethiopia (COPWE; see Toward Party Formation, ch. 4). Although the People's Protection Brigades retained a political role, after 1980 these paramilitary units concentrated on local police duties. Brigade members received up to five months' training in police and military tactics from East German instructors. Some brigade personnel had served on active duty in Eritrea, Tigray, and the Ogaden.

Crime and Punishment

The Legal System

Although Ethiopians have long depended on written laws, the criminal legal system observed at the time of the 1974 revolution was of relatively recent origin. The first integrated legal code, the *Fetha Nagast* (Law of Kings), was translated from Arabic in the mid-fifteenth century. Attributed to a thirteenth-century Egyptian Coptic scholar, it was inspired by the Pentateuch (the first five books of the Old Testament), the New Testament, canons of the Christians' early church councils, Roman civil law, and tenets of Quranic law. However, the *Fetha Nagast* applied only to Christians. Muslims who became subject to Ethiopian rule through conquest continued to be judged in their own courts according to sharia law (see Islam, ch. 2). Also, outside the ordinary judicial system, clan and tribal courts exercised unofficial but effective coercive powers, and people rarely appealed their decisions to regular courts.

The *Fetha Nagast* and customary laws remained the basis of criminal judicial procedure until 1930, when Haile Selassie introduced a penal code, which, although primitive in its application, strove for modernity in its articulation. Unlike the old system, the 1930 penal code set down specific punishments for precisely defined offenses. It was a legal principle that a person who performed an act not prohibited by law committed no crime; nor were acts of omission punishable by law. The code made distinctions among preparatory acts, attempted crimes, and completed offenses. Preparation in itself was not considered criminal, nor were unsuccessful attempts, especially ones in which commission of the offense was judged to be "absolutely impossible." Courts did not inflict punishment if the accused acted out of superstition or "simplicity of mind."

319

The penal code was strong on retribution, but the courts determined penalties according to the degree of individual guilt. In addition, the courts took into consideration an offender's background, education, and motives, as well as the offense's gravity and the circumstances of its commission. In theory, the courts meted out the most severe punishments to persons of title and wealth on the premise that such offenders had less reasonable motives for criminal action than did persons of lower station. Among the complaints of ethnic dissidents, however, was the allegation that any offense against an Amhara resulted in more severe punishment than an Amhara's offense against a non-Amhara. The new code abolished mutilation but retained capital punishment and permitted flogging. Although more sophisticated than the *Fetha Nagast,* from which it ostensibly was derived, the 1930 penal code lacked a comprehensive approach to the disposition and treatment of offenders.

In 1958 a Swiss legal expert drafted a revised penal code to meet the needs of a developing nation. A 1961 criminal procedures code, drafted by a British jurist, augmented the 1930 penal code. The former was based on the Swiss penal code and many secondary sources; the latter reflected the influence of English common law.

For virtually every offense listed in the revised penal code, there were upper and lower limits of punishment. The effect was to stress acceptance of the concept of degrees of culpability, as well as the concept of extenuating and aggravating circumstances. Separate provisions existed for juveniles. Nevertheless, the commission appointed to approve the revision repeatedly expressed the traditional view that "punishment should remain the pillar of Ethiopian criminal law."

Following the 1974 revolution, a normal legal process theoretically was in effect for dealing with criminal offenses. Existing parallel to it was a "revolutionary" system of neighborhood justice. In practice, it was impossible to distinguish between criminal acts and political offenses according to the definitions adopted in post-1974 revisions of the penal code.

A November 1974 decree introduced martial law, which set up a system of military tribunals empowered to impose the death penalty or long prison terms for a wide range of political offenses. The decree applied the law retroactively to the old regime's officials who had been accused of responsibility for famine deaths, corruption, and maladministration and who had been held without formal charges since earlier in the year. Special three-member military tribunals sat in Addis Ababa and in each of the country's fourteen administrative regions.

In July 1976, the government amended the penal code to institute the death penalty for "antirevolutionary activities" and economic crimes. Investigation of political crimes came under the overall direction of the Revolutionary Operations Coordinating Committee in each *awraja*. In political cases, the courts waived search warrants required by the criminal procedures code. The government transferred jurisdiction from the military tribunals, which had been inactive for some time, to *kebele* and peasant association tribunals. Political trials constituted the main business of these tribunals well into 1978.

More generally, the 1976 revision of the penal code empowered association tribunals to deal with criminal offenses but limited their jurisdiction to their urban neighborhood or rural area. Elected magistrates, without formal legal training, conducted criminal trials. Procedures, precedents, and punishments varied widely from tribunal to tribunal, depending on the imperatives of the association involved. Peasant association tribunals accepted appeals at the *wereda* (district) level. Appellate decisions were final, but decisions disputed between associations could be brought before peasant association courts at the *awraja* level. In cities, *kebele* tribunals were similarly organized in a three-tier system. Change of venue was arranged if a defendant committed an offense in another jurisdiction.

The judicial system was designed to be flexible. Magistrates could decide not to hear a case if the defendant pleaded guilty to minor charges and made a public apology. Nonetheless, torture was sometimes used to compel suspects and witnesses to testify. Penalties imposed at the local association level included fines of up to 300 birr, compensation to victims in amounts determined by the tribunal, imprisonment for up to three months, and hard labor for up to fifteen days. Serious criminal cases were held over, depending on their gravity, for association tribunals sitting at the *awraja* or *wereda* level, which were qualified to hand down stiffer sentences. In theory, death sentences were reviewed by government officials, but little effort was made to interfere with the administration of local justice. Tribunal decisions were implemented through an association's public safety committee and were enforced by the local People's Protection Brigade. Without effective review of their actions, tribunals were known to order indefinite jailings, during which their suspects sometimes disappeared, as well as summary executions. On rare occasions, the government would condemn association officials for murder and torture committed in the course of dispensing "revolutionary justice."

The 1976 revision of the penal code also created new categories of so-called economic crimes. The list included hoarding, overcharging, and interfering with the distribution of consumer commodities. More serious offenses concerned engaging in sabotage at the work place or of agricultural production, conspiring to confuse work force members, and destroying vehicles and public property. Security sections of the Revolutionary Operations Coordinating Committee investigated economic crimes at the *awraja* level and enforced land reform provisions through the peasant associations. These committees were empowered to indict suspects and hold them for trial before local tribunals. Penalties could entail confiscation of property, a long prison term, or a death sentence.

In 1981 the Amended Special Penal Code replaced the Special Penal Code. This amended code included offenses against the government and the head of state, such as crimes against the state's independence and territorial integrity, armed uprising, and commission of "counterrevolutionary" acts (these provisions also were in the earlier Special Penal Code); breach of trust by public officials and economic offenses, including grain hoarding, illegal currency transactions, and corruption; and abuse of authority, including "improper or brutal" treatment of a prisoner, unlawful detention of a prisoner, and creating or failing to control famine.

The Amended Special Penal Code also abolished the Special Military Courts and created new Special Courts to try offenses under the Amended Special Penal Code. Special Courts consisted of three civilian judges and applied the existing criminal and civil procedure codes. Defendants had the right to legal representation and to appeal to a Special Appeal Court.

Prisons

Detailed information on Ethiopia's prison system was limited. Only generalized data were available on prison installations.

Although the imperial regime achieved some progress in the field of prison reform, most prisons failed to adopt modern penological methods. Government-published figures on prison populations since 1974 were considered incomplete and misleading. Amnesty International, the London-based human rights organization, and a few individuals who survived detention and escaped from the country have described prison conditions in a critical light.

The administrator of prisons managed the national penal system. Each administrative unit—including *kifle hager* (region), *awraja* (subregion), and *wereda* (district)—had at least one prison. Addis Ababa's Akaki (or Central) Prison, considered Ethiopia's most modern penal facility in 1974, was the central prison for Shewa.

Somali troops in the Ogaden

Akaki had separate facilities for female political prisoners. The largest number of political prisoners, approximately 1,500 in 1989, was housed in Akaki's maximum security section. Reportedly, the government had jailed political dissidents at numerous other prisons in Addis Ababa, including Fourth Division headquarters; the Third Police Station, which also served as national police headquarters and an interrogation center; and the Grand (Menelik's) Palace. Asmera, another center for political prisoners, had penal facilities at three locations. Most police stations and army garrisons also had jails. Each *kebele* and peasant association operated a jail in its jurisdiction. Association headquarters in each *wereda* and *awraja* also had prisons.

A prison farm at Robi in Arsi provided facilities for about 850 prisoners. In 1978 the government proposed a plan for deploying large numbers of inmates imprisoned for minor offenses to work on minimum-security state farms as part of the agricultural development plan. A single institution oversaw the rehabilitation of male juvenile criminal offenders. There was no comparable facility for female juvenile offenders, who usually were placed in the custody of their parents or guardians. In exceptional pre-1974 cases, the authorities jailed juveniles in larger prisons. After the emergence of the Marxist regime, a large but unspecified number of youthful political detainees of both genders were held in prisons and association jails. Many were released after a period of "political rehabilitation."

Historically, prison life in Ethiopia was gloomy and for political prisoners extremely brutal. The so-called process of rehabilitation often consisted of severe beatings, exhausting work and calisthenics, and political indoctrination. A public confession normally was proof of rehabilitation; in some cases, a political detainee's willingness to torture fellow prisoners was regarded as an indication of his penitence. Recreational facilities were rare, and no program existed to assist prisoners after their release. Punishment was the major concern of prison officials. Conditions in smaller, more remote prisons were worse than in the prisons of Addis Ababa, and peasant association jails were worse yet. As part of a program in the late 1970s to expand and improve the Ethiopian prison system, the Cuban government reportedly constructed new prisons that included facilities for solitary confinement.

In its 1978 report on human rights violations in Ethiopia, Amnesty International stated that Ethiopian prisons had failed to abide by UN regulations for the treatment of prisoners. A large number of prisoners might share a common cell. In the Central Prison's maximum security section, for example, Amnesty International reported that as many as fifty prisoners shared cells measuring four meters by four meters. Ad hoc committees—organized in each cell for self-imposed discipline, food distribution, care of the sick and aged, and orientation of new inmates—often communalized food and luxuries, such as tea and tobacco, donated by relatives. Complaints reached Amnesty International that cells were infested with pests and were unventilated and lacking the most basic sanitary facilities. Medical attention was generally inadequate and not even available at all facilities. Even seriously ill prisoners rarely received hospital treatment, and many died of natural causes aggravated by their imprisonment. Cell mates viewed death as a means of relieving the gross overcrowding typical of facilities housing political prisoners during the late 1970s. The authorities usually informed families of the death of their relatives by telling them "food is no longer necessary."

Although conditions in Addis Ababa's Central Prison improved somewhat by the late 1980s, most prison facilities remained substandard. In 1989 Amnesty International reported that individuals incarcerated in government-operated prisons were held in poor and sometimes harsh conditions. However, the report noted that prisons were subject to formal regulations, and there were few reports of torture.

The human rights organization also indicated that conditions in the Central Prison, which Menelik II had built in the nineteenth century, had improved in the 1980s. The prison's 4,500 inmates were allowed regular family visits, and relatives were permitted to send food, laundry, books, medicine, and other "comfort" items to jailed family members. Although the Central Prison provided basic medical treatment, the authorities authorized prisoners to see an independent physician or to seek treatment at local hospitals. During daylight hours, prisoners were free to associate with each other. The Central Prison opened a shop where small items were sold; a nursery and a primary school were established for children who stayed with their imprisoned mothers; and a secondary school was created where prisoners taught or studied. Additionally, prisoners were free to open their own recreational and educational facilities. Despite these findings, however, Amnesty International concluded that the Central Prison suffered from "inadequate medical care, poor hygiene, delays in obtaining professional medical or hospital treatment, overcrowding of cells . . . [and] . . . epidemics of cholera and meningitis." In addition, conditions at other special detention centers were substandard.

In regional prisons, Amnesty International found prison conditions to be much worse than those in Addis Ababa because of greater overcrowding and poorer hygiene and medical facilities. Prison authorities in Asmera, Mekele, and Harer subjected inmates to harsher restrictions than did authorities in the capital. In Harer and other unstable areas, civilian political prisoners often were held in military custody at military facilities under more severe conditions than were found in other prisons.

Emphasis·in larger prisons was placed on work during confinement for criminal offenders, but these activities generally were limited to individuals serving long sentences. Priority was given to production, and there was little effort to provide vocational training. The largest prison industry was weaving, which was usually done on primitive looms. The prison weavers produced cotton material used for making clothes and rugs. Carpentry was a highly developed prison industry, and inmates produced articles of relatively good quality. Other prison industries included blacksmithing, metalworking, jewelry making, basket weaving, flour milling, and baking. Those short-term prisoners not absorbed into established prison industries worked in gardens that provided food for some of the penal institutions.

Income from materials produced by prison labor was applied to the upkeep of penal facilities. Prisoners received about 10 percent of the proceeds derived from the sale of items, but typically most of these funds were dedicated to communal projects intended to improve prison amenities. Although prison industries were not geared to rehabilitation, some inmates acquired useful skills. In certain cases, the government permitted work furloughs for some classes of political prisoners.

Most prison guards were military veterans who had received small plots of land in exchange for temporary duty at a prison. Under this system, the guards changed frequently as the duty rotated among a number of such persons living in the vicinity of a penal institution.

Human Rights

Despite much rhetoric on the part of the Mengistu government to the contrary and an entire chapter of the 1987 constitution devoted to "basic freedoms and rights," Ethiopia under Mengistu had one of the worst human rights records in the world. Haile Selassie's modernization of the penal code and the introduction of legal guarantees in the 1955 constitution indicated at least a recognition of the human rights problem. But Amnesty International described subsequent improvements in human rights conditions as "severely qualified." Human rights violations after 1974 increased dramatically, despite the regime's assurances to the UN that political prisoners received "fair trials" and obtained adequate food and clothing from their families. According to reports issued by Amnesty International, the International Committee of the Red Cross, and the testimony of refugees, the human rights situation deteriorated still further from 1976 to 1978. Although human rights organizations often lacked verification of the exact extent of violations, many observers made repeated charges that Ethiopian troops had massacred civilians and committed atrocities in Eritrea and that the Ethiopian government had perpetrated human rights violations throughout the country, including arbitrary arrests, imprisonment without due process, torture, summary executions, and mass killings during the Red Terror.

In a report based on the observations of a 1976 fact-finding visit to Ethiopia, Amnesty International stated that, since 1974, "there has developed a consistent pattern of widespread gross human rights violations," and it singled out the association tribunals for the most egregious disregard of basic human values. Addis Ababa responded to this charge by labeling the evidence presented by Amnesty International as "imperialist propaganda [against] authentic socialist revolution" and claimed that actions taken against political dissidents during the Red Terror were "justified" for the elimination of "counterrevolutionaries." Official sources subsequently added that the human rights enjoyed by the "broad masses" were greater than they had been before the revolution and dismissed the "individual human rights" concept that was the premise of Western criticism of the regime as being irrelevant to a revolutionary government building a Marxist society.

The enormity of government-sponsored operations against suspected political opponents during the Red Terror has defied accurate analysis and has made attempts at quantification of casualties irrelevant. Amnesty International, for example, concluded that "this campaign resulted in several thousand to perhaps tens of thousands of men, women, and children, killed, tortured, and imprisoned." Other sources estimated that, during 1977–78, about 30,000 people had perished as a result of the Red Terror and harsh conditions in prisons, *kebele* jails, and concentration camps. Ethiopian sources opposed to the Marxist regime claimed that the security forces had killed 2,000 teachers and students in a pre-May Day 1978 massacre in Addis Ababa. The authorities also executed hundreds of unarmed Eritrean civilians in Asmera while the city was under siege by secessionists in December 1977. In a single sweep in Addis Ababa the same month, troops killed about 1,000 students for distributing antigovernment leaflets.

During the Red Terror in Addis Ababa, security forces frequently mutilated the bodies of political dissidents, dumping them along roads or stacking them on street corners. They also forced some victims to dig their own graves before being executed. The government required families to pay a "bullet fee" of about 125 birr to retrieve bodies of relatives, when they could be found and identified. Sweden's Save the Children Fund lodged a protest in early 1978 alleging the execution of about 1,000 children, many below the age of thirteen, whom the government had labeled "liaison agents of the counterrevolutionaries." Based on its assessment of the human rights situation in Ethiopia in 1979, the United States Department of State reported to congressional committees in February 1980 that "serious violations of individual rights and civil and political liberties take place in Ethiopia amidst a restructed economic and social system that is aimed at improving the basic living conditions of the great majority of the country's poor."

During the 1984–85 famine in northern Ethiopia, the Mengistu regime devised a scheme to resettle 1.5 million people onto so-called virgin lands in southern Ethiopia. The government forcibly moved people who resisted the plan, and many of those who were resettled fled to Sudan and took refuge in camps or tried to walk back to their northern homelands (see Resettlement and Villagization, ch. 2; The Politics of Resettlement, ch. 4). According to a report

327

issued by an international medical group, 100,000 people died as a result of Mengistu's resettlement policy; Cultural Survival, another humanitarian organization, estimated that 50,000 to 100,000 died. To make matters worse, Mengistu refused to allow food to be distributed in areas where inhabitants were sympathetic to the EPLF, TPLF, or other antigovernment groups, a strategy that resulted in the deaths of tens of thousands.

When a new famine emerged in late 1989, threatening the lives of 2 million to 5 million people, Mengistu again used food as a weapon by banning the movement of relief supplies along the main road north from Addis Ababa to Tigray and also along the road from Mitsiwa into Eritrea and south into Tigray. As a result, food relief vehicles had to travel overland from Port Sudan, the major Red Sea port of Sudan, through guerrilla territory into northern Ethiopia. After an international outcry against his policy, Mengistu reversed his decision, but international relief agencies were unable to move significant amounts of food aid into Eritrea and Tigray via Ethiopian ports. By 1990 there also were many reports that the Ethiopian air force had bombed relief convoys and that the Ethiopian armed forces had used napalm and cluster bombs against separatists in Eritrea and Tigray. The EPLF, too, attacked food convoys, claiming that the regime was using them to ship weapons to its troops.

Due process of law and legal guarantees prohibiting abuse of power basically did not exist in revolutionary Ethiopia. After revision of the penal code and the criminal procedures code in 1976, judicial warrants were no longer required for house searches or for the arbitrary off-the-street arrests that became the norm in the late 1970s. Specific charges were not necessarily brought against detainees after politically motivated arrests, and those held had no right to counsel. The bulk of noncriminal arrests involved suspects seized at the discretion of authorities on charges of nonparticipation in mandatory political activities, curfew violations, and participation in unauthorized meetings. In most cases, those arrested or summoned to association tribunals for questioning would be released after a scare or a roughing up, but many would disappear without a trace. Whole families—including young children—would be taken into custody and held for indefinite periods in lieu of a missing relative who was a suspect.

In Addis Ababa, special security force squads, assisted by *kebele* defense squads, would arrest political suspects, who would then be taken to police headquarters for interrogation by officials. After questioning, often accompanied by torture, the authorities would assign suspects to a prison to await trial or hold them in detention camps without charges. Under these circumstances, many detainees welcomed sentencing, even if it was for a long period. The government confiscated a suspect's possessions after arrest and required families to search prisons to locate their relatives.

According to a variety of estimates, there were 6,000 to 10,000 political prisoners, including surviving officials of the former imperial regime, in Ethiopian prisons in 1976. During the Red Terror, as many as 100,000 persons may have passed through Ethiopian jails. Appeals by Amnesty International in support of approximately 3,000 known political detainees in 1978 had no effect, and most of these individuals were believed to have been killed while in custody. Other sources put the number of political prisoners at 8,000, of whom half eventually were released.

Categories of political prisoners still held in 1991 included former government officials; prominent civil servants and businessmen; armed forces officers, including those implicated in the May 1989 coup attempt against Mengistu; students and teachers; members of ethnic, regional, and separatist groups; leaders of professional and women's groups and trade unionists who resisted government takeover of their organizations; churchmen; suspected members of the EPLF, TPLF, or other guerrilla movements; and others arrested on various pretexts on orders from the government or from *kebeles* or peasant associations. Political prisoners generally included a large number of young persons and educated professionals, a high proportion of them Eritrean or Oromo.

Censorship, openly imposed under the old regime, became even harsher after 1974. The press, radio, and television were controlled by the state and were considered instruments of government policy (see Mass Media, ch. 4). Independent media outlets, such as the Lutheran broadcasting station in Addis Ababa, were seized by the Mengistu government. Censorship guidelines for the press were vague, but many Ethiopian journalists were imprisoned for less than enthusiastic cooperation with the Mengistu regime. All reports to the foreign press had to be transmitted through the Ethiopian News Agency. After 1975 government authorities expelled many Western journalists for "mischief and distortion" in their reporting. The Mengistu government also banned songs, books, and periodicals that were judged to be contrary to the spirit of the revolution.

* * *

Because of the limited access to Ethiopia afforded Western observers and the secrecy surrounding almost all of the Mengistu government's activities, accurate and consistent information and statistics pertaining to the Mengistu regime are difficult to obtain. In 1991 there still were no definitive studies describing in sufficient detail the entire scope of national security problems in contemporary Ethiopia. Those interested in Ethiopian national security affairs therefore must rely on a variety of periodicals, including *Africa Research Bulletin, Keesing's Contemporary Archives, Third World Reports,* and *Africa Confidential.* The International Institute for Strategic Studies' annuals, *The Military Balance* and *Strategic Survey,* also are essential for anyone who wishes to understand the evolution of Ethiopia's security forces. The same is true of the annuals *Africa Contemporary Record* and *World Armaments and Disarmament,* the latter published by the Stockholm International Peace Research Institute.

Harold G. Marcus's *Ethiopia, Great Britain, and the United States, 1941–1974* provides an excellent analysis of the historical evolution of the Ethiopian armed forces. Other useful historical sources include Donald N. Levine's "The Military in Ethiopian Politics"; Richard A. Caulk's "The Army and Society in Ethiopia"; and Yohannis Abate's "Civil-Military Relations in Ethiopia." Marina and David Ottaway's *Ethiopia: Empire in Revolution* also is essential for an understanding of the military's role in contemporary Ethiopia.

Material on human rights practices in Ethiopia can be found in the annual *Amnesty International Report* and in other Amnesty International publications, such as *Ethiopia: Human Rights Violations, Ethiopia: Political Imprisonment and Torture,* and *Ethiopia: Political Imprisonment.* Although dated (1979), Bekele Mesfin's "Prison Conditions in Ethiopia" remains a valuable first-hand account of the life of a political prisoner in Mengistu's Ethiopia. For an analysis of the human costs of Mengistu's resettlement policy, Jason W. Clay and Bonnie K. Holcomb's *Politics and the Ethiopian Famine, 1984–1985* is fundamental. (For further information and complete citations, see Bibliography.)

Appendix

Table 1. Metric Conversion Coefficients and Factors

When you know	Multiply by	To find
Millimeters	0.04	inches
Centimeters	0.39	inches
Meters	3.3	feet
Kilometers	0.62	miles
Hectares (10,000 m²)	2.47	acres
Square kilometers	0.39	square miles
Cubic meters	35.3	cubic feet
Liters	0.26	gallons
Kilograms	2.2	pounds
Metric tons	0.98	long tons
....	1.1	short tons
....	2,204	pounds
Degrees Celsius	1.8	degrees Fahrenheit
(Centigrade)	and add 32	

Table 2. Population by Urban-Rural Breakdown and by Region and Addis Ababa, May 1988

Region	Urban	Rural	Total
Arsi	127,547	1,733,059	1,860,606
Bale	79,159	1,047,538	1,126,697
Eritrea	440,875	2,497,238	2,938,113
Gamo Gofa	61,015	1,334,316	1,395,331
Gojam	252,042	3,380,234	3,632,276
Gonder	239,010	3,031,430	3,270,440
Harerge	321,202	4,336,657	4,657,859
Ilubabor	59,454	1,018,854	1,078,308
Kefa	145,205	2,595,568	2,740,773
Shewa	701,294	8,358,623	9,059,917
Sidamo	267,093	3,974,734	4,241,827
Tigray	261,890	2,439,031	2,700,921
Welega	141,043	2,629,555	2,770,598
Welo	264,697	3,811,262	4,075,959
Aseb Administration *	36,348	65,004	101,352
Addis Ababa *	1,654,327	n.a.	1,654,327
TOTAL	5,052,201	42,253,103	47,305,304

n.a.—not applicable.

* In 1988 Aseb and Addis Ababa were both separate administrative divisions.

Source: Based on information from Ethiopia, Central Statistical Authority, *Census Supplement,* I, Addis Ababa, 1989, Table 1-2.

Table 3. *Area, Population, and Population Density by Region and Addis Ababa, 1975 and 1987*

Region	Area (in thousands of square kilometers)	Population (in thousands)		Population Density (persons per square kilometer)	
		1975	1987	1975	1987
Arsi	23.7	1,337.8	1,808.5	56.4	76.3
Bale	127.1	810.7	1,095.1	6.4	8.6
Eritrea	93.7	2,107.9	2,852.9	22.5	30.4
Gamo Gofa	40.3	1,005.3	1,356.7	24.9	33.7
Gojam	61.2	2,612.4	3,530.5	42.7	57.7
Gonder	79.6	2,350.1	3,178.7	29.5	39.9
Harerge	272.6	3,348.5	4,527.4	12.3	16.6
Ilubabor	46.5	775.6	1,048.3	16.7	22.5
Kefa	56.6	1,971.5	2,664.6	34.8	47.1
Shewa	85.1	6,512.0	8,805.3	76.5	103.5
Sidamo	119.7	3,052.4	4,123.3	25.5	34.4
Tigray	64.9	1,938.9	2,624.4	29.9	40.4
Welega	70.5	1,993.1	2,693.6	28.3	38.2
Welo	82.1	2,931.7	3,962.0	35.7	48.3
Aseb Administration [1] .	27.5	73.8	98.2	2.7	3.6
Addis Ababa [2]	0.2	1,136.6	1,589.2	5,683.6	7,946.0
ETHIOPIA	1,251.3	33,958.3	45,958.7	27.1	36.7

[1] Aseb Administration was carved out of southern Eritrea and made into a separate administrative division in 1981.

[2] Addis Ababa was part of Shewa in 1975 but is listed separately for comparative purposes. By 1981 Addis Ababa had become an administrative division of its own.

Source: Based on information from Ethiopia, Central Statistical Authority, *Facts and Figures,* Addis Ababa, 1987, Table 7-1, 22.

Table 4. Population of Largest Cities and Towns, 1967, 1975, and 1987

City or Town	1967	1975	1987
Addis Ababa	644,190	1,136,600	1,589,176
Asmera	178,537	221,801	309,807
Dire Dawa	50,733	76,639	107,150
Harer	42,771	48,559	67,892
Dese	40,619	56,849	79,458
Gonder	36,309	64,562	90,220
Jima	30,580	49,044	68,618
Nazret	27,812	59,176	82,725
Mekele	23,105	47,157	65,581
Debre Zeyit	22,055	39,675	55,461
Debre Markos	21,536	31,842	44,410
Asela	13,886	29,637	41,313
Nekemte	12,691	23,342	32,637
Bahir Dar	12,463	43,826	61,121
Dila	11,287	18,898	26,392
Aseb	10,945	25,000	39,917
Akaki	10,924	42,002	58,717
Sodo	10,842	19,414	27,116
Debre Birhan	9,188	19,978	27,929
Agaro	8,995	15,090	21,107
Shashemene	7,837	24,459	34,193
Goba	7,304	18,515	25,835
Awasa	5,575	27,517	39,827
Metu	4,060	10,057	14,042
Jijiga	4,031	18,111	25,320
Arba Minch	2,890	14,261	26,711
Wonji	n.a.	n.a.	38,408
Keren	n.a.	n.a.	29,416

n.a.—not available.

Source: Based on information from Ethiopia, Central Statistical Authority, *Ethiopia: Statistical Abstract, 1967 and 1968,* Addis Ababa, 1969, 30–36; and Ethiopia, Central Statistical Authority, *Facts and Figures,* Addis Ababa, 1987, 25–28.

Table 5. *Number of Schools by Grade Level*
and by Region and Addis Ababa, Ethiopian
Calendar Years 1974/75 and 1985/86 [1]

	1974/75			1985/86		
Region	Grades 1-6	Grades 7-8	Grades 9-12	Grades 1-6	Grades 7-8	Grades 9-12
Arsi	135	19	3	333	43	14
Bale	83	8	1	310	18	5
Eritrea	428	66	14	225	55	18
Gamo Gofa	77	8	3	323	18	5
Gojam	135	14	4	676	58	17
Gonder	184	21	4	578	33	18
Harerge	214	47	7	659	65	13
Ilubabor	137	14	4	405	35	10
Kefa	93	11	3	499	40	9
Shewa	538	100	25	1,443	246	50
Sidamo	148	31	6	786	56	13
Tigray	178	19	7	82	24	11
Welega	463	28	10	723	100	15
Welo	158	23	3	649	45	15
Aseb Administration [2]	n.a.	n.a.	n.a.	12	1	1
Addis Ababa [3]	225	98	30	197	127	31
TOTAL	3,196	507	124	7,900	964	245

n.a.—not available.

[1] For explanation of the Ethiopian calendar year—see Glossary.

[2] Aseb Administration was carved out of southern Eritrea and made into a separate administrative division in 1981.

[3] Addis Ababa was part of Shewa in 1974/75 but is listed separately for comparative purposes. By 1981 Addis Ababa had become an administrative division of its own.

Source: Based on information from Ethiopia, Central Statistical Authority, *Facts and Figures*, Addis Ababa, 1987, Table 16-3, 107.

Table 6. *Number of Students by Grade Level*
and Sex, Ethiopian Calendar Years
1974/75 and 1985/86 *

	1974/75			1985/86		
Grade Level	Male	Female	Total	Male	Female	Total
Grades 1-6	651,893	305,408	957,301	1,491,015	957,763	2,448,778
Grades 7-8	85,286	39,298	124,584	221,102	142,030	363,132
Grades 9-12	47,439	16,774	64,213	178,699	113,686	292,385
University	523	72	595	16,438	1,998	18,436
TOTAL	785,141	361,552	1,146,693	1,907,254	1,215,477	3,122,731

* For explanation of the Ethiopian calendar year—see Glossary.

Source: Based on information from Ethiopia, Central Statistical Authority, *Facts and Figures*, Addis Ababa, 1987, Table 61-1, 105.

Table 7. *Number of Teachers by Grade Level*
and by Region and Addis Ababa, Ethiopian
Calendar Years 1974/75 and 1985/86 [1]

Region	1974/75			1985/86		
	Grades 1–6	Grades 7–8	Grades 9–12	Grades 1–6	Grades 7–8	Grades 9–12
Arsi	874	126	66	2,864	373	311
Bale	514	53	24	2,050	210	191
Eritrea	2,307	480	355	2,471	561	604
Gamo Gofa	605	64	39	2,155	167	197
Gojam	1,124	167	100	3,415	430	413
Gonder	1,104	148	71	2,919	321	367
Harerge	1,384	242	153	3,444	411	362
Ilubabor	739	92	32	2,463	207	182
Kefa	678	109	55	3,190	172	265
Shewa	3,094	613	357	6,856	1,309	1,277
Sidamo	1,341	238	110	5,234	641	578
Tigray	3,105	175	152	1,879	280	302
Welega	1,709	177	148	4,238	526	508
Welo	1,187	172	96	3,542	371	487
Aseb Administration [2]	n.a.	n.a.	n.a.	128	14	22
Addis Ababa [3]	3,086	852	770	4,074	1,322	1,837
TOTAL	22,851	3,708	2,528	50,922	7,315	7,903

n.a.—not available.

[1] For explanation of the Ethiopian calendar year—see Glossary.

[2] Aseb Administration was carved out of southern Eritrea and made into a separate administrative division in 1981.

[3] Addis Ababa was part of Shewa in 1974/75 but is listed separately for comparative purposes. By 1981 Addis Ababa had become an administrative division of its own.

Source: Based on information from Ethiopia, Central Statistical Authority, *Facts and Figures,* Addis Ababa, 1987, Table 16–2, 108.

*Table 8. Medical Facilities by Region
and Addis Ababa, Ethiopian Calendar Years
1975/76 and 1983/84* [1]

Region	Hospitals		Hospital Beds [2]		Clinics		Health Centers	
	1975/76	1983/84	1975/76	1983/84	1975/76	1983/84	1975/76	1983/84
Arsi	2	2	121	176	45	96	4	6
Bale	1	1	95	140	34	79	4	5
Eritrea [3]	17	16	2,324	2,895	121	163	3	5
Gamo Gofa	3	3	137	151	49	75	4	7
Gojam	3	3	242	285	47	104	7	8
Gonder	10	3	191	438	51	112	12	13
Harerge	2	10	828	887	111	150	10	13
Ilubabor	2	2	163	140	51	79	5	7
Kefa	3	3	230	226	61	102	6	9
Shewa	11	10	590	882	122	265	15	18
Sidamo	5	5	419	469	89	145	8	10
Tigray	4	4	298	570	64	102	9	9
Welega	4	4	297	337	78	164	7	10
Welo	4	5	189	454	70	144	12	14
Addis Ababa [4] ..	13	14	2,499	3,257	16	129	n.a.	7
TOTAL	84	8	8,623	11,307	1,009	1,909	106	141

n.a.—not available.

[1] For explanation of the Ethiopian calendar year—see Glossary. Table does not include police and armed forces facilities.

[2] Does not include number of beds in three hospitals.

[3] Includes Aseb Administration, which was carved out of southern Eritrea and made into a separate administrative division in 1981.

[4] Addis Ababa was part of Shewa in 1975/76 but is listed separately for comparative purposes. By 1981 Addis Ababa had become an administrative division of its own.

Source: Based on information from Ethiopia, Central Statistical Authority, *Facts and Figures,* Addis Ababa, 1987, Table 17-1, 110.

Table 9. *Medical Personnel by Region and Addis Ababa,*
Ethiopian Calendar Years
1974/75 and 1983/84 [1]

Region	Physicians		Nurses		Health Assistants	
	1974/75	1983/84	1974/75	1983/84	1974/75	1983/84
Arsi	5	12	24	40	149	269
Bale	7	13	74	6	34	158
Eritrea	30	50	129	199	486	654
Gamo Gofa	4	4	18	46	107	200
Gojam	10	15	38	81	173	337
Gonder	8	30	36	87	172	367
Harerge	25	38	63	109	314	470
Ilubabor	6	8	22	34	101	190
Kefa	17	15	31	81	120	341
Shewa	20	35	95	196	562	985
Sidamo	9	23	47	112	247	522
Tigray	7	13	42	65	212	286
Welega	10	20	54	101	210	495
Welo	5	22	31	78	193	426
Aseb Administration [2] ...	22	4	44	16	111	66
Addis Ababa [3]	165	244	523	652	1,083	1,114
TOTAL	350	546	1,271	1,903	4,274	6,880

[1] For explanation of the Ethiopian calendar year—see Glossary. Table does not include police and armed forces personnel.

[2] Aseb Administration was carved out of southern Eritrea and made into a separate administrative division in 1981.

[3] Addis Ababa was part of Shewa in 1974/75 but is listed separately for comparative purposes. By 1981 Addis Ababa had become an administrative division of its own.

Source: Based on information from Ethiopia, Central Statistical Authority, *Facts and Figures,* Addis Ababa, 1987, Table 17-4, 114–15.

339

Table 10. *Key Economic Indicators, Ethiopian Fiscal Years 1974/75 to 1988/89* [1]

Phase and Year	GDP [2]	Agriculture [3]	Manufacturing [3]	Current Account Deficit [4]	Overall Fiscal Deficit [4]	Retail Price Index [5]	Debt Service Ratio [6]
Phase I—Revolution							
1974/75	0.0	-1.8	-1.6	3.0	4.1	6.5	7.3
1975/76	1.7	3.0	0.8	0.3	5.4	28.6	7.2
1976/77	1.1	0.1	2.3	2.7	3.9	16.6	6.4
1977/78	-1.3	-1.5	-3.9	5.1	6.8	14.3	6.7
Average	0.4	0.4	-0.3	2.8	5.1	16.5	6.9
Phase II—Economic *zemecha* [7]							
1978/79	5.7	2.4	27.3	4.2	3.4	16.0	11.0
1979/80	5.7	4.8	10.5	5.7	5.1	4.5	7.6
Average	5.7	3.6	18.9	4.6	3.8	10.3	9.3
Phase III—Decline							
1980/81	3.1	2.6	5.6	6.8	4.5	6.1	7.5
1981/82	1.2	-1.3	4.6	8.8	8.2	5.6	13.7
1982/83	5.3	4.7	7.3	7.0	16.1	-0.4	17.8
1983/84	-3.6	-9.9	3.8	8.6	8.9	8.4	19.9
1984/85	-7.0	-16.3	1.6	8.1	15.8	19.1	19.2
Average	-0.2	-4.1	5.2	7.9	10.7	7.8	15.6

Table 10—Continued

Phase and Year	GDP [2]	Agriculture [3]	Manufacturing [3]	Current Account Deficit [4]	Overall Fiscal Deficit [4]	Retail Price Index [5]	Debt Service Ratio [6]
Phase IV—Stagnation							
1985/86	6.7	9.2	5.3	8.9	11.6	-9.8	23.4
1986/87	9.0	14.4	5.9	10.9	9.9	-2.4	29.5
1987/88	3.6	-0.2	2.2	11.6	9.6	7.1	38.6
1988/89 [8]	2.9	2.7	1.7	11.1	22.7	n.a.	33.8
1989/90 [8]	2.9	-1.9	-2.1	n.a.	n.a.	n.a.	51.6 [8]
Average	5.0	4.8	3.3	10.6	13.5	-1.7	35.4

n.a.—not available.

[1] For explanation of the Ethiopian fiscal year—see Glossary.
[2] GDP—gross domestic product; percentage growth per annum.
[3] Contribution to GDP; percentage growth per annum.
[4] As a percentage of GDP.
[5] Percentage increase.
[6] As a percentage of exports.
[7] For definition of *zemecha*—see Glossary.
[8] Estimated.

Source: Based on information from Ethiopia, Office of the National Council for Central Planning, National Accounts Division, Addis Ababa, various publications; Ethiopia, Central Statistical Authority, *Ethiopia: Statistical Abstract*, Addis Ababa, various issues; and World Bank, Washington, various publications.

Table 11. *Average Annual Income, Retail Price Index,*
and Real Income, Selected Ethiopian Calendar
Years, 1970/71 to 1987/88 [1]

		Retail Price Index		Real Income	
	Average		Percentage		Percentage
	Annual		Change over		Change over
Year	Income [2]	Index [3]	Previous Year	Income	Previous Year
1970/71	1,125	143.7	n.a.	783	n.a.
1974/75	1,577	170.1	18.4	927	18.4
1980/81	2,298	375.2	120.6	612	-34.0
1981/82	2,352	396.1	5.6	594	-2.9
1982/83	2,530	394.5	-0.4	641	7.9
1983/84	2,540	427.8	8.4	594	-7.3
1984/85	2,745	509.4	19.1	537	-9.3
1985/86	2,793	459.4	-9.8	608	12.8
1986/87	2,990	448.3	-2.4	667	8.8
1987/88	3,107	480.0	7.1	647	-3.0

[1] For explanation of the Ethiopian calendar year—see Glossary.
[2] Wages and salaries of industrial workers; in birr (for value of the birr—see Glossary).
[3] 1963 = 100.

Source: Based on information from Ethiopia, Central Statistical Authority, *Ethiopia: Statistical Abstract,* Addis Ababa, various issues; and Ethiopia, Central Statistical Authority, *Annual Survey of Manufacturing Industries,* Addis Ababa, various issues.

Table 12. *Retail Price Index for Addis Ababa,*
Selected Ethiopian Calendar Years,
1970/71 to 1987/88 [1]

Year	General Index [2]	Food	Household Items	Clothing	Transportation
1970/71	143.7	155.4	133.5	141.3	100.0
1974/75	170.1	175.1	179.8	190.6	104.8
1980/81	375.2	441.2	366.1	281.3	140.6
1981/82	396.1	467.6	379.3	279.3	153.5
1982/83	394.5	470.7	352.6	273.5	156.4
1983/84	427.8	522.8	376.1	272.8	154.9
1984/85	509.4	654.7	406.8	268.2	156.4
1985/86	459.4	553.1	436.9	273.2	156.9
1986/87	448.3	521.3	479.4	271.4	162.7
1987/88	480.0	562.4	506.9	275.1	164.8

[1] For explanation of the Ethiopian calendar year—see Glossary.
[2] 1963 = 100.

Source: Based on information from Ethiopia, Central Statistical Authority, *Ethiopia: Statistical Abstract,* Addis Ababa, various issues.

Table 13. Production of Major Crops, Selected Ethiopian Calendar Years, 1974/75 to 1988/89 [1]
(in thousands of tons)

Crop	1974/75	1980/81	1984/85	1985/86	1986/87	1987/88	1988/89
Cereals							
Barley	624.9	1,075.2	842.1	913.9	993.2	995.3	1,075.0
Corn	840.8	948.2	1,087.8	1,037.0	1,715.4	1,819.5	2,001.5
Millet	156.7	204.4	187.4	189.9	119.8	n.a.	n.a.
Oats	n.a.	46.4	27.4	31.5	36.4	n.a.	n.a.
Sorghum	630.5	1,410.8	507.2	904.5	963.2	993.3	1,112.6
Teff [2]	847.9	1,312.1	912.2	968.7	1,033.2	1,049.6	1,182.0
Wheat	698.9	613.2	675.6	774.4	775.3	835.8	894.3
Total cereals [3] .	3,799.7	5,610.4	4,239.8	4,820.0	5,636.4	5,949.5	6,544.5
Pulses							
Broad beans	282.1	469.3	265.9	233.3	293.5	259.2	n.a.
Chick-peas	93.4	118.3	92.3	84.4	72.2	n.a.	n.a.
Field peas	44.7	147.7	84.4	69.3	83.5	n.a.	n.a.
Haricot	32.8	19.7	26.9	23.3	33.3	n.a.	n.a.
Lentils	46.6	59.9	18.9	25.9	26.9	n.a.	n.a.
Soybeans	n.a.	1.9	0.5	0.3	0.6	n.a.	n.a.
Vetch	12.6	31.3	41.7	30.9	n.a.	n.a.	n.a.
Total pulses [3] .	512.2	848.0	530.6	467.4	540.8	562.9	619.2
Other							
Fenugreek	n.a.	2.5	4.7	0.1	2.4	n.a.	n.a.
Flaxseed	18.9	27.2	33.9	38.3	31.1	27.2	n.a.
Groundnuts							
(peanuts)	n.a.	n.a.	0.2	0.4	0.6	n.a.	n.a.
Niger seed (*neug*) .	26.6	64.1	61.8	59.5	45.5	43.9	n.a.
Rapeseed	n.a.	1.5	1.6	2.0	4.1	n.a.	n.a.
Sesame	n.a.	6.5	0.1	0.2	0.1	0.4	n.a.
Sunflower seed ..	n.a.	0.2	1.3	0.9	0.6	n.a.	n.a.
Total other [3] ..	58.1	102.1	102.6	101.4	84.5	87.3	96.0
Total [3]	4,370.0	6,560.6	4,873.0	5,388.8	6,261.7	6,599.7	7,259.7

n.a.—not available.

[1] For explanation of the Ethiopian calender year—see Glossary.

[2] For definition of teff—see Glossary.

[3] Figures may not add to totals because of rounding.

Source: Based on information from Ethiopia, Central Statistical Authority, *Area, Production, and Yield of Major Crops: Estimates,* Addis Ababa, various issues.

Table 14. Value of Principal Exports,
Selected Ethiopian Fiscal Years,
1974/75 to 1988/89 [1]
(in millions of birr) [2]

Product	1974/75	1980/81	1984/85	1985/86	1986/87	1987/88	1988/89 [3]
Coffee	117.5	524.3	466.3	664.8	524.3	439.2	525.4
Oilseeds	89.1	28.4	15.6	7.9	9.8	22.0	12.8
Pulses	73.5	23.7	16.9	12.6	8.5	16.1	17.0
Hides and skins	37.2	92.7	95.4	119.5	108.3	133.0	140.0
Live animals	16.9	9.8	19.7	18.2	15.6	32.4	30.0
Meat, canned and							
frozen	9.9	6.3	3.9	3.9	5.4	5.1	5.4
Fruits and vegetables ...	9.8	3.6	5.9	6.0	12.8	11.8	15.6
Raw cotton	8.0	28.2	1.8	0.0	1.6	1.1	1.0
Petroleum products	7.4	76.1	67.3	44.2	27.3	36.0	30.6
Oilseed cake	7.2	8.8	1.0	2.0	1.7	1.1	1.0
Sugar [4]	6.8	9.8	9.3	10.4	12.6	16.4	16.5
Other [5]	62.0	39.4	40.2	33.8	66.9	59.4	106.8
Reexports	30.9	0.4	0.0	0.5	0.0	0.0	n.a.
TOTAL	476.2	851.5	743.3	923.8	794.8	773.6	902.1

n.a.—not available.
[1] For explanation of the Ethiopian fiscal year—see Glossary.
[2] For value of the birr—see Glossary.
[3] Estimated.
[4] Primarily molasses.
[5] Includes 26.7 million birr of nonmonetary gold in 1979/80.

Source: Based on information from National Bank of Ethiopia, Addis Ababa, various pub-
        lications.

Table 15. Balance of Payments, Selected Ethiopian
Fiscal Years, 1980/81 to 1988/89 [1]
(in millions of United States dollars)

	1980/81	1984/85	1985/86	1986/87	1987/88	1988/89
Exports	554.1	548.9	662.2	616.1	629.2	735.0
Imports	770.5	962.2	1,192.0	1,217.0	1,259.0	1,345.5
Trade balance	−216.4	−413.3	−529.8	−600.9	−629.8	−610.5
Factor services (net)	−7.1	−33.0	−28.8	−37.0	−63.0	−94.2
Private transfers (net)	24.7	144.9	209.4	162.5	182.6	195.6
Official transfers (net) [2]	59.8	298.3	293.2	211.8	121.7	132.0
Current account balance ..	−139.0	−3.1	−56.0	−263.6	−388.5	−377.1
Private loans (net) [3]	0.0	0.0	0.0	0.0	0.0	0.0
Public loans (net) [3]	161.6	162.3	277.2	181.3	260.4	280.7
Short-term capital (net)	−6.0	42.3	−12.8	9.7	9.7	0.0
Capital account balance ..	16.6	201.5	208.4	−72.6	−118.4	−96.4
Errors and omissions	108.9	153.9	43.3	−52.7	71.3	−123.6
Overall balance	125.5	355.4	251.7	−125.3	−47.1	−220.0
Change in net reserves						
(− means increase)	59.2	−47.6	−165.2	19.9	189.7	−27.2

[1] For explanation of the Ethiopian fiscal year—see Glossary.

[2] Excludes technical assistance and similar transfers recorded in government budget.

[3] Includes medium- and long-term loans.

Source: Based on information from National Bank of Ethiopia, Addis Ababa, various publications.

Bibliography

Chapter 1

Abir, Mordechai. *Ethiopia: The Era of the Princes. The Challenge of Islam and Re-unification of the Christian Empire, 1769–1855.* New York: Praeger, 1968.

———. *Ethiopia and the Red Sea.* London: Frank Cass, 1980.

Akpan, M.B. "Ethiopia and Liberia, 1914–35: Two Independent African States in the Colonial Era." Pages 712–45 in A. Adu Boahen (ed.), *General History of Africa, 7: Africa under Colonial Domination.* Berkeley: University of California Press, 1985.

Alvarez, Francisco. *The Prester John of the Indies.* (Trans., C.F. Beckingham and G.W.B. Huntingford.) Cambridge: Cambridge University Press, 1961.

Baer, George W. *The Coming of the Italian-Ethiopian War.* Cambridge: Harvard University Press, 1967.

Bahru Zewde. *A History of Modern Ethiopia, 1855–1974.* Athens: Ohio University Press, 1991.

Bates, Darrell. *The Abyssinian Difficulty: The Emperor Theodorus and the Magdala Campaign, 1867–68.* Oxford: Oxford University Press, 1979.

Bender, M. Lionel (ed.). *Peoples and Cultures of the Ethio-Sudan Borderlands.* East Lansing: African Studies Center, Michigan State University, 1981.

Brietzke, Paul. "Land Reform in Revolutionary Ethiopia," *Journal of Modern African Studies* [London], 14, No. 4, December 1976, 637–60.

Bruce, James. *Travels to Discover the Source of the Nile in the Years 1768, 1769, 1770, 1771, 1772, and 1773.* (5 vols.) London: G.G.J. and J. Robinson, 1790.

Caraman, Philip. *The Lost Empire: The Story of the Jesuits in Ethiopia, 1555–1634.* Notre Dame, Indiana: University of Notre Dame Press, 1985.

Caulk, Richard A. "Menelik II and the Diplomacy of Commerce: Prelude to an Imperial Foreign Policy," *Journal of Ethiopian Studies* [Addis Ababa], 17, 1984, 62–87.

Cerulli, Enrico. "Ethiopia's Relations with the Muslim World." Pages 575–85 in Ivan Hrbek (ed.), *General History of Africa, 3: Africa from the Seventh to the Eleventh Century.* Berkeley: University of California Press, 1988.

Chege, Michael. "The Revolution Betrayed: Ethiopia, 1974–79," *Journal of Modern African Studies* [London], 17, No. 3, 1979, 359–80.

Clapham, Christopher S. *Haile Selassie's Government.* New York: Praeger, 1969.

_____. *Transformation and Continuity in Revolutionary Ethiopia.* Cambridge: Cambridge University Press, 1988.

_____. "The Workers' Party of Ethiopia," *Journal of Communist Studies* [London], 1, No. 1, 1985, 76–77.

Clarke, John. *Resettlement and Rehabilitation: Ethiopia's Campaign Against Famine.* London: Harney and Jones, n.d.

Cohen, John M. "Ethiopia after Haile Selassie: The Government Land Factor," *African Affairs* [London], 72, No. 289, October 1973, 365–82.

Darkwah, R.H. Kofi. *Shewa, Menelik, and the Ethiopian Empire, 1813–1880.* London: Heinemann, 1975.

Donham, Donald L. *Work and Power in Maale, Ethiopia.* Ames: Iowa State University Press, 1985.

Donham, Donald L., and Wendy James. *The Southern Marches of Imperial Ethiopia: Essays in History and Social Anthropology.* New York: Cambridge University Press, 1986.

Dow, Thomas E., Jr., and Peter Schwab. "Imperial Leadership in Contemporary Ethiopia," *Genève-Afrique* [Geneva], 12, No. 1, 1973, 53–62.

Drysdale, John. *The Somali Dispute.* New York: Praeger, 1964.

Dugan, James, and Laurence Lafore. *Days of Emperor and Clown: The Italo-Ethiopian War, 1935–1936.* Garden City, New York: Doubleday, 1973.

Ehret, Christopher. "On the Antiquity of Agriculture in Ethiopia," *Journal of African History* [Cambridge], 20, 1979, 161–77.

Ellingson, Lloyd. "The Emergence of Political Parties in Eritrea, 1941–1950," *Journal of African History* [Cambridge], 18, No. 2, 1977, 261–81.

Erlich, Haggai. *Ethiopia and the Challenge of Independence.* Boulder, Colorado: Rienner, 1986.

Ethiopia's Bitter Medicine, Settling for Disaster: An Evaluation of the Ethiopian Government's Resettlement Programme. London: Survival International for the Rights of Threatened Tribal Peoples, 1986.

Fage, J.D., and Roland Oliver (eds.). *The Cambridge History of Africa.* (8 vols.) Cambridge: Cambridge University Press, 1975–86.

Farer, Tom J. *War Clouds on the Horn of Africa: The Widening Storm.* New York: Carnegie Endowment for International Peace, 1979.

FitzGibbon, Louis. *The Evaded Duty.* London: Rex Collings, 1985.

Gebru Tareke. *Ethiopia: Power and Protest. Peasant Revolts in the Twentieth Century.* Cambridge: Cambridge University Press, 1991.

Ghose, Ajit Kumar. "Transforming Feudal Agriculture: Agrarian Change in Ethiopia since 1974," *Journal of Development Studies* [London], 22, No. 1, October 1985, 127–49.

Gilkes, Patrick. *The Dying Lion: Feudalism and Modernization in Ethiopia.* New York: St. Martin's Press, 1975.

Greenfield, Richard. *Ethiopia: A New Political History.* New York: Praeger, 1965.

Haile Selassie. *My Life and Ethiopia's Progress, 1892–1937.* (Trans. and annotated by Edward Ullendorff.) Oxford: Oxford University Press, 1976.

Harbeson, John W. *The Ethiopian Transformation: The Quest for the Post-Imperial State.* Boulder, Colorado: Westview Press, 1988.

Henze, Paul B. *Communist Ethiopia: Is It Succeeding?* Santa Monica, California: Rand, 1985.

Hess, Robert L. *Ethiopia: The Modernization of Autocracy.* Ithaca: Cornell University Press, 1970.

Hoben, Allan. *Land Tenure among the Amhara of Ethiopia: The Dynamics of Cognatic Descent.* Chicago: University of Chicago Press, 1973.

Huntingford, G.W.B. *The Galla of Ethiopia: The Kingdoms of Kafa and Janjero.* London: International African Institute, 1955.

Kaplan, Steven. *The Beta Israel (Falasha) in Ethiopia: From Earliest Times to the Twentieth Century.* New York: New York University Press, 1992.

Keller, Edmond J. *Revolutionary Ethiopia: From Empire to People's Republic.* Bloomington: Indiana University Press, 1988.

Kobishchanov, Yuri M. *Axum.* University Park: Pennsylvania State University Press, 1979.

Lang, Werner J. *History of the Southern Gonga.* Wiesbaden: Steiner, 1982.

Legum, Colin. "Realities of the Ethiopian Revolution," *World Today* [London], 33, No. 8, August 1977, 305–12.

Levine, Donald N. *Greater Ethiopia: The Evolution of a Multi-Ethnic Society.* Chicago: University of Chicago Press, 1974.

_____. *Wax and Gold: Tradition and Innovation in Ethiopian Culture.* Chicago: University of Chicago Press, 1965.

Lewis, Herbert S. *A Galla Monarchy: Jimma Abba Jifar, Ethiopia, 1830–1932.* Madison: University of Wisconsin Press, 1965.

Lipsky, G.A. *Ethiopia: Its People, Its Society, Its Culture.* New Haven: Human Relations Area Files, 1962.

Lockot, Hans Wilhelm. *The Mission: The Life, Reign, and Character of Haile Selassie I.* London: Hurst, 1989.

McCann, James. *From Poverty to Famine in Northeast Ethiopia: A Rural History, 1900–1935.* Philadelphia: University of Pennsylvania Press, 1987.

_____. *The Political Economy of Rural Rebellion in Ethiopia: Northern Resistance to Imperial Expansion, 1928–1935.* Boston: African Studies Center, Boston University, 1984.

McClellan, Charles W. *State Transformation and National Integration: Gedeo and the Ethiopian Empire, 1895-1935.* East Lansing: African Studies Center, Michigan State University, 1988.

Marcus, Harold G. *Ethiopia, Great Britain, and the United States, 1941-1974: The Politics of Empire.* Berkeley: University of California Press, 1983.

———. *Haile Selassie I: The Formative Years, 1892-1936.* Berkeley: University of California Press, 1987.

———. *The Life and Times of Menelik II.* Oxford: Clarendon Press, 1974.

Markakis, John. *Ethiopia: Anatomy of a Traditional Polity.* New York: Oxford University Press, 1974.

———. *National and Class Conflict in the Horn of Africa.* Cambridge: Cambridge University Press, 1987.

Markakis, John, and Nega Ayele. *Class and Revolution in Ethiopia.* Nottingham, United Kingdom: Spokesman Books, 1978.

Mathew, David. *Ethiopia: The Study of a Polity, 1540-1935.* London: Eyre and Spottiswoode, 1947.

Mesfin Wolde-Mariam. "The Ethio-Somalian Boundary Dispute," *Journal of Modern African Studies* [London], 2, No. 2, July 1964, 189-219.

Mockler, Anthony. *Haile Selassie's War: The Italian-Ethiopian Campaign, 1935-1941.* New York: Oxford University Press, 1984.

Mohammed Hassen. *The Oromo of Ethiopia: A History, 1570-1850.* Cambridge: Cambridge University Press, 1990.

Mulatu Wubneh and Yohannis Abate. *Ethiopia: Transition and Development in the Horn of Africa.* Boulder, Colorado: Westview Press, 1988.

Munro-Hay, Stuart. *Aksum: An African Civilisation of Late Antiquity.* Edinburgh: Edinburgh University Press, 1991.

Ottaway, Marina. "Democracy and New Democracy: The Ideological Debate in the Ethiopian Revolution," *African Studies Review,* 21, No. 1, April 1978, 19-31.

———. "Social Classes and Corporate Interests in the Ethiopian Revolution," *Journal of Modern African Studies* [London], 14, No. 3, September 1976, 469-86.

———. *Soviet and American Influence in the Horn of Africa.* New York: Praeger, 1982.

Ottaway, Marina (ed.). *The Political Economy of Ethiopia.* New York: Praeger, 1990.

Ottaway, Marina, and David Ottaway. *Ethiopia: Empire in Revolution.* New York: Africana, 1978.

Pankhurst, Richard K. *Economic History of Ethiopia, 1800-1935.* Addis Ababa: Haile Selassie I University Press, 1968.

———. *History of Ethiopian Towns: From the Mid-Nineteenth Century to 1935.* Wiesbaden: Steiner, 1985.

_____. *The History of Famine and Epidemics in Ethiopia prior to the Twentieth Century.* Addis Ababa: Relief and Rehabilitation Commission, 1986.

_____. *A Social History of Ethiopia.* Addis Ababa: Institute of Ethiopian Studies, 1990.

Pankhurst, Richard K., and L.V. Cassanelli. "Ethiopia and Somalia." Pages 376–411 in J.F. Ade Ajayi (ed.), *General History of Africa, 6: Africa in the Nineteenth Century until the 1880s.* Berkeley: University of California Press, 1989.

Perham, Margery F. *The Government of Ethiopia.* Evanston: Northwestern University Press, 1969.

Prouty, Chris. *Empress Taytu and Menelik II: Ethiopia, 1883–1910.* Trenton: Red Sea Press, 1986.

Prouty, Chris, and Eugene Rosenfeld. *Historical Dictionary of Ethiopia.* Metuchen, New Jersey: Scarecrow Press, 1981.

Quirin, James Arthur. *The Evolution of the Ethiopian Jews: A History of the Beta Israel (Falasha) to 1920.* Philadelphia: University of Pennsylvania Press, 1992

Ram, K.V. *The Barren Relationship: Britain and Ethiopia, 1805–1868.* New Delhi: Concept, 1985.

Rubenson, Sven. "Ethiopia and the Horn." Pages 51–98 in John E. Flint (ed.), *The Cambridge History of Africa, 5: From ca. 1790 to ca. 1870.* Cambridge: Cambridge University Press, 1976.

_____. *King of Kings: Tewodros of Ethiopia.* Addis Ababa: Haile Selassie I University, 1966.

Sbacchi, Alberto. *Ethiopia under Mussolini: Fascism and the Colonial Experience.* London: Zed Press, 1985.

Schwab, Peter. *Ethiopia: Politics, Economics, and Society.* Boulder, Colorado: Rienner, 1985.

Sergew Habte Selassie. *Ancient and Medieval Ethiopian History to 1270.* Addis Ababa: United Printers, 1972.

Shehim, K. "Ethiopia, Revolution, and the Question of Nationalities: The Case of the Afar," *Journal of Modern African Studies* [London], 23, No. 2, 1985, 331–48.

Shinnie, Peter L. "The Nilotic Sudan and Ethiopia." Pages 210–71 in J.D. Fage (ed.), *The Cambridge History of Africa, 2: From ca. 500 B.C. to ca. A.D. 1050.* Cambridge: Cambridge University Press, 1978.

Spencer, John H. *Ethiopia at Bay: A Personal Account of the Haile Sellassie Years.* Algonac, Michigan: Reference Publications, 1984.

Taddesse Tamrat. *Church and State in Ethiopia, 1270–1527.* Oxford: Clarendon Press, 1972.

_____. "Ethiopia, the Red Sea, and the Horn." Pages 98–182 in Roland Oliver (ed.), *The Cambridge History of Africa, 3: From ca. 1050 to ca. 1600.* Cambridge: Cambridge University Press, 1977.

Tekeste Negash. *Italian Colonialism in Eritrea, 1882-1941: Policies, Praxis, and Impact.* Stockholm: Almqvist and Wiksell International, 1987.

Thesiger, Wilfred. *The Life of My Choice.* New York: Norton, 1987.

Trimingham, John Spencer. *Islam in Ethiopia.* London: Oxford University Press, 1952.

Tubiana, Joseph (ed.). *Modern Ethiopia from the Accession of Menelik II to the Present.* Rotterdam: Balkema, 1980.

Ullendorff, Edward. *Ethiopia and the Bible.* London: Oxford University Press, 1968.

————. *The Ethiopians: An Introduction to Country and People.* (3d ed.) London: Oxford University Press, 1973.

Zewde Gabre-Sellassie. *Yohannes IV of Ethiopia: A Political Biography.* London: Oxford University Press, 1975.

(Various issues of the following publications were also used in the preparation of this chapter: *Africa Contemporary Record; Africa Research Bulletin* (Political, Social, and Cultural Series) [Exeter, United Kingdom]; *Annales d'Ethiopie* [Paris]; *Ethiopia Observer* [London and Addis Ababa]; *Journal of Ethiopian Studies* [Addis Ababa]; and *Northeast African Studies,* formerly *Ethiopianist Notes.*)

Chapter 2

Almagor, Uri. *Pastoral Partners: Affinity and Bond Partnership among the Dassanetch of South-West Ethiopia.* New York: Africana, 1978.

Ambaye Zekarias. *Land Tenure in Eritrea (Ethiopia).* Addis Ababa: n. pub., 1966.

Bauer, Dan Franz. "For Want of an Ox . . . : Land, Capital, and Social Stratification in Tigre." Pages 235-48 in Harold G. Marcus and John Hinnant (eds.), *Proceedings of the First United States Conference on Ethiopian Studies, 1973.* East Lansing: African Studies Center, Michigan State University, 1975.

————. *Household and Society in Ethiopia.* (Committee on Ethiopian Studies, Occasional Papers Series, Monograph No. 6.) East Lansing: African Studies Center, Michigan State University, 1977.

————. "Politics and Social Change in Tigre." Pages 201-13 in W. Arens (ed.), *A Century of Change in East Africa.* The Hague: Mouton, 1976.

Baxter, P.T.W. "*Atete* in a Highland Arssi Neighborhood," *Northeast African Studies,* 1, No. 2, 1979, 1-22.

_____. "Boran Age-Sets: *Gada,* a Puzzle or a Maze." Pages 151–82 in P.T.W. Baxter and Uri Almagor (eds.), *Age, Generation, and Time: Some Features of East African Age Organizations.* New York: St. Martin's Press, 1978.

_____. "Ethiopia's Unacknowledged Problem: The Oromo," *African Affairs* [London], 77, July 1978, 283–96.

Bekure W. Semait. "Ecological Stress and Political Conflict in Africa: The Case of Ethiopia." Pages 37–50 in Anders Hjort af Ornas and M.A. Mohamed Salih (eds.), *Ecology and Politics: Environmental Stress and Security in Africa.* Uppsala: Scandinavian Institute of African Studies, 1989.

Bender, M. Lionel. "The Eastern Edge of the Sahel: Ethiopian Nilo-Sahelians." Pages 15–23 in Robert L. Hess (ed.), *Proceedings of the Fifth International Conference on Ethiopian Studies.* Chicago: University of Illinois at Chicago Circle, 1979.

Bender, M. Lionel (ed.). *The Non-Semitic Languages of Ethiopia.* (Committee on Ethiopian Studies, Occasional Papers Series, Monograph No. 5.) East Lansing: African Studies Center, Michigan State University, 1976.

Bender, M. Lionel, J. Donald Bowen, Robert L. Cooper, and Charles A. Ferguson (eds.), *Language in Ethiopia.* London: Oxford University Press, 1976.

Black, Paul. "Linguistic Evidence on the Origins of the Konsoid Peoples." Pages 291–302 in Harold G. Marcus and John Hinnant (eds.), *Proceedings of the First United States Conference on Ethiopian Studies, 1973.* East Lansing: African Studies Center, Michigan State University, 1975.

Blackhurst, Hector. "Continuity and Change in the Shoa Galla *Gada* System." Pages 245–67 in P.T.W. Baxter and Uri Almagor (eds.), *Age, Generation, and Time: Some Features of East African Age Organizations.* New York: St. Martin's Press, 1978.

_____. "Ethnicity in Southern Ethiopia: The General and the Particular," *Africa* [London], 50, No. 1, 1980, 55–65.

Brietzke, Paul. *Law, Development, and the Ethiopian Revolution.* Lewisburg, Pennsylvania: Bucknell University Press, 1988.

Burley, Dexter. "The Despised Weavers of Addis Ababa." Pages 145–49 in Robert L. Hess (ed.), *Proceedings of the Fifth International Conference on Ethiopian Studies.* Chicago: University of Illinois at Chicago Circle, 1979.

Carr, Claudia J. *Pastoralism in Crisis: The Desanetch and Their Ethiopian Lands.* (Research Paper No. 180.) Chicago: Department of Geography, University of Chicago, 1977.

Caulk, Richard A. "The Army and Society in Ethiopia," *Ethiopianist Notes,* 1, No. 3, Spring 1978, 17–24.

353

Ethiopia: A Country Study

Clarke, John. *Resettlement and Rehabilitation: Ethiopia's Campaign Against Famine.* London: Speediprinters, 1986.

Clay, Jason W., and Bonnie K. Holcomb. *Politics and the Ethiopian Famine, 1984–1985.* Cambridge: Cultural Survival, 1986.

Clay, Jason W., Sandra Steingraber, and Peter Niggli. *The Spoils of Famine: Ethiopian Famine Policy and Peasant Agriculture.* Cambridge: Cultural Survival, 1988.

Cohen, John M. *Integrated Rural Development: The Ethiopian Experience and the Debate.* Uppsala: Scandinavian Institute of African Studies, 1987.

Cohen, John M., and Peter H. Koehn. *Ethiopian Provincial and Municipal Government: Imperial Patterns and Postrevolutionary Changes.* (Committee on Northeast African Studies, Ethiopian Series, Monograph No. 9.) East Lansing: African Studies Center, Michigan State University, 1980.

Cohen, John M., and Dov Weintraub. *Land and Peasants in Imperial Ethiopia: The Social Background to a Revolution.* Assen, Netherlands: Van Gorcum, 1975.

Connell, Dan. "Eritrea: The Politics of Refugees," *Horn of Africa,* 2, No. 4, October–December 1979, 4–7.

Desta Asayehegn. *Socio-Economic and Educational Reforms in Ethiopia, 1942–1974: Correspondence and Contradiction.* Paris: International Institute for Educational Planning, United Nations Educational, Scientific, and Cultural Organization, 1979.

Ellis, Gene. "The Feudal Paradigm as a Hindrance to Understanding Ethiopia," *Journal of Modern African Studies* [London], 14, No. 2, June 1976, 275–95.

Eritrea and Tigray. London: Minority Rights Group, 1983.

Erlich, Haggai. "Ethiopia and Islam in Postrevolution Perspective," *Ethiopianist Notes,* 1, No. 1, Spring 1977, 9–16.

Ethiopia. Central Statistical Authority. *Census Supplement,* I. Addis Ababa: 1989.

_____. Central Statistical Authority. *Ethiopia: Statistical Abstract, 1967 and 1968.* Addis Ababa: 1969.

_____. Central Statistical Authority. *Facts and Figures.* Addis Ababa: 1987.

_____. Ministry of Education. *New Educational Objectives and Directions for Ethiopia.* Addis Ababa: 1980.

_____. Ministry of Education. *Ten-Year Perspective Plan of General Education, 1984/85–1993/94.* Addis Ababa: 1980.

_____. Relief and Rehabilitation Commission. *The Challenges of Drought: Ethiopia's Decade of Struggle in Relief and Rehabilitation.* Addis Ababa: 1985.

_____. Relief and Rehabilitation Commission. *Guidelines for Resettlement.* Addis Ababa: 1983.

_____. Relief and Rehabilitation Commission. *The New Approach.* Addis Ababa: 1984.

_____. Relief and Rehabilitation Commission. *Review of Drought Relief and Rehabilitation Activities for the Period of December 1984–August 1985, and 1986 Assistance Requirements.* Addis Ababa: 1985.

_____. Relief and Rehabilitation Commission. *Review of the Current Drought Situation in Ethiopia.* Addis Ababa: 1984.

Ethiopia: The Politics of Famine. New York: Freedom House, 1990.

Fassil R. Kiros. *Implementing Educational Policies in Ethiopia.* Washington: World Bank, 1990.

Fleming, Harold C. "Sociology, Ethnology, and History in Ethiopia." (Review of D.N. Levine's *Greater Ethiopia: The Revolution of a Multi-Ethnic Society.*) *International Journal of African Historical Studies,* 9, No. 2, 1976, 248–78.

Fleming, Harold C., and M. Lionel Bender. "Non-Semitic Languages." Pages 34–62 in M. Lionel Bender, J. Donald Bowen, Robert L. Cooper, and Charles A. Ferguson (eds.), *Language in Ethiopia.* London: Oxford University Press, 1976.

For Their Own Good: Ethiopia's Villagisation Programme. London: Survival International, 1988.

Gaim Kibreab. *Refugees and Development in Africa: The Case of Eritrea.* Trenton: Red Sea Press, 1987.

Gamst, Frederick C. *The Qemant: A Pagan-Hebraic Peasantry of Ethiopia.* New York: Holt-Rinehart-Winston, 1969.

_____. "Wayto Ways: Change from Hunting to Peasant Life." Pages 233–38 in Robert L. Hess (ed.), *Proceedings of the Fifth International Conference on Ethiopian Studies.* Chicago: University of Illinois at Chicago Circle, 1979.

Getachew Woldemeskel. "The Consequences of Resettlement in Ethiopia," *African Affairs* [London], 88, No. 352, July 1989, 359–74.

Greenfield, Richard. "An Historical Introduction to Refugee Problems in the Horn," *Horn of Africa,* 2, No. 4, October–December 1979, 14–26.

Hallpike, C.R. *The Konso of Ethiopia: A Study of the Values of a Cushitic People.* Oxford: Clarendon Press, 1972.

_____. "The Origins of the Borana *Gada* Systems," *Africa* [London], 46, No. 1, 1976, 48–56.

Halperin, R., and J. Olmstead. "To Catch a Feastgiver: Redistribution among the Dorze of Ethiopia," *Africa* [London], 46, No. 2, 1976, 146–65.

Hamer, John. "Dispute Settlement and Sanctity: An Ethiopian Example," *Anthropological Quarterly,* 45, No. 4, 1972, 232–47.

————. "Myth, Ritual, and the Authority of the Elders in an Ethiopian Society," *Africa* [London], 46, No. 4, 1976, 327–39.

————. "Sidamo Generational Class Cycles: A Political Gerontocracy," *Africa* [London], 40, No. 1, 1970, 50–70.

Hance, William A. *The Geography of Modern Africa.* New York: Columbia University Press, 1975.

Harbeson, John W. "Afar Pastoralists and Ethiopian Rural Development," *Rural Africana,* No. 28, Fall 1975, 1–5.

Harris, Myles F. *Breakfast in Hell.* New York: Poseidon Press, 1987.

Hetzron, Robert, and M. Lionel Bender. "The Ethio-Semitic Languages." Pages 23–33 in M. Lionel Bender, J. Donald Bowen, Robert L. Cooper, and Charles A. Ferguson (eds.), *Language in Ethiopia.* London: Oxford University Press, 1976.

Hinnant, John. "The Guji: *Gada* as a Ritual System." Pages 207–43 in P.T.W. Baxter and Uri Almagor (eds.), *Age, Generation, and Time: Some Features of East African Age Organizations.* New York: St. Martin's Press, 1978.

Hoben, Allan. *Land Tenure among the Amhara of Ethiopia: The Dynamics of Cognatic Descent.* Chicago: University of Chicago Press, 1973.

————. "Perspectives on Land Reform in Ethiopia: The Political Role of the Peasantry," *Rural Africana,* No. 28, Fall 1975, 55–69.

————. "Social Stratification in Traditional Amhara Society." Pages 187–224 in Arthur Tuden and Leonard Plotnicov (eds.), *Social Stratification in Africa.* New York: Free Press, 1970.

Hultin, J. "Social Structure, Ideology, and Expansion: The Case of the Oromo of Ethiopia," *Ethnos* [Stockholm], 1, No. 4, 1975, 273–84.

Karadawi, Ahmed. "The Smuggling of the Ethiopian Falasha to Israel Through Sudan," *African Affairs* [London], 90, No. 358, January 1991, 23–49.

Kessler, David. *The Falashas: The Forgotten Jews of Ethiopia.* New York: Africana, 1982.

Kessler, David, and Tudor Parfitt. *The Falashas: The Jews of Ethiopia.* London: Minority Rights Group, 1985.

Knutsson, Karl Eric. *Authority and Change: A Study of the Kallu Institution among the Macha Galla of Ethiopia.* (Ethnologiska Studier, No. 29.) Gothenburg, Sweden: Etnografiska Museet, 1967.

————. "Dichotomization and Integration: Aspects of Interethnic Relations in Southern Ethiopia." Pages 86–100 in Fredrik Barth (ed.), *Ethnic Groups and Boundaries.* Boston: Little, Brown, 1969.

Levine, Donald N. *Greater Ethiopia: The Evolution of a Multi-Ethnic Society.* Chicago: University of Chicago Press, 1974.

———. *Wax and Gold: Tradition and Innovation in Ethiopian Culture.* Chicago: University of Chicago Press, 1965.

Lewis, Herbert S. *A Galla Monarchy: Jimma Abba Jifar, Ethiopia, 1830–1932.* Madison: University of Wisconsin Press, 1965.

———. "Wealth, Influence, and Prestige among the Shoa Galla." Pages 163–85 in Arthur Tuden and Leonard Plotnicov (eds.), *Social Stratification in Africa.* New York: Free Press, 1970.

Lewis, I.M. *Peoples of the Horn of Africa: Somali, Afar, and Saho.* (Ethnographic Survey of Africa: North Eastern Africa, Pt. 1.) London: International African Institute, 1955.

Markakis, John. *Ethiopia: Anatomy of a Traditional Polity.* New York: Oxford University Press, 1974.

Markakis, John, and Nega Ayele. *Class and Revolution in Ethiopia.* Nottingham, United Kingdom: Spokesman Books, 1978.

Mekuria Bulcha. *Flight and Integration: Causes of Mass Exodus from Ethiopia and Problems of Integration in the Sudan.* Uppsala: Scandinavian Institute of African Studies, 1988.

Mesfin Wolde-Mariam. *An Atlas of Ethiopia.* Addis Ababa: n. pub., 1970.

———. *An Introductory Geography of Ethiopia.* Addis Ababa: Haile Selassie I University, 1972.

———. *Rural Vulnerability to Famine in Ethiopia, 1958–1977.* Addis Ababa: Vikas and Addis Ababa University Press, 1984.

Messing, S.D. "Traditional Healing and the New Health Centers," *Conch,* 8, Nos. 1–2, 1976, 52–64.

Mulatu Wubneh and Yohannis Abate. *Ethiopia: Transition and Development in the Horn of Africa.* Boulder, Colorado: Westview Press, 1988.

Ottaway, Marina. "Land Reform and Peasant Associations: A Preliminary Analysis," *Rural Africana,* No. 28, Fall 1975, 39–54.

———. "Social Classes and Corporate Interests in the Ethiopian Revolution," *Journal of Modern African Studies* [London], 14, No. 3, September 1976, 469–86.

Ottaway, Marina, and David Ottaway. *Ethiopia: Empire in Revolution.* New York: Africana, 1978.

Pankhurst, Richard K. *An Introduction to the Medical History of Ethiopia.* Trenton: Red Sea Press, 1990.

Parfitt, Tudor. *Operation Moses: The Untold Story of the Exodus of the Falasha Jews from Ethiopia.* London: Weidenfeld and Nicholson, 1985.

"Plight of Refugees in the Horn," *Horn of Africa,* 2, No. 4, October–December 1979, 3.

Rapoport, Louis. *The Lost Jews: The Last of the Ethiopian Falashas.* New York: Stein and Day, 1980.

Ruiz, Hiram A. *Beyond the Headlines: Refugees in the Horn of Africa.* Washington: U.S. Committee for Refugees, 1988.

_____. *Detained in Exile: Ethiopians in Somalia's Shelembod Camp.* Washington: U.S. Committee for Refugees, 1987.

Salole, Gerry. "Who're the Shoans?" *Horn of Africa,* 2, No. 3, July–September 1979, 20–29.

Shack, William A. *The Central Ethiopians: Amhara, Tigrina, and Related Peoples.* (Ethnographic Survey of Africa Series.) London: International African Institute, 1974.

_____. "Guilt and Innocence: Oathing, Evidence, and the Judicial Process among the Gurage," *Journal of African Studies,* 3, No. 3, Fall 1976, 297–309.

_____. *The Gurage: A People of the Ensete Culture.* London: Oxford University Press, 1966.

_____. "Notes on Voluntary Associations and Urbanization in Africa with Special Reference to Addis Ababa, Ethiopia," *African Urban Notes* (Series B.), No. 1, Winter 1974–75, 5–10.

_____. "Occupational Prestige, Status, and Social Change in Modern Ethiopia," *Africa* [London], 46, No. 2, 1976, 166–81.

_____. "Politics of the Free Spirit: The Sacred and the Secular in the Gurage Polity." Pages 169–89 in William A. Shack and Percy S. Cohens (eds.), *Politics in Leadership: A Comparative Perspective.* Oxford: Oxford University Press, 1979.

Shepherd, Jack. *The Politics of Starvation.* New York: Carnegie Endowment for International Peace, 1975.

Stahl, Michael. "Environmental Degradation and Political Constraints in Ethiopia." Pages 181–96 in Anders Hjort af Ornas and M.A. Mohamed Salih (eds.), *Ecology and Politics: Environmental Stress and Security in Africa.* Uppsala: Scandinavian Institute of African Studies, 1989.

Stauder, Jack. *The Majangir: Ecology and Society of a Southwest Ethiopian People.* London: Cambridge University Press, 1971.

Stommes, Eileen, and Seleshi Sisaye. "The Development and Distribution of Health Care Services in Ethiopia: A Preliminary Review," *Canadian Journal of African Studies* [Ottawa], 13, No. 3, 1980, 487–95.

Super, Susan. "Earth, Water, and Air: Casualties of Development?" *Agenda,* 3, No. 4, May 1980, 2–9.

Taddesse Tamrat. *Church and State in Ethiopia, 1270–1527.* Oxford: Clarendon Press, 1972.

Teshome G. Wagaw. *The Development of Higher Education and Social Change: An Ethiopian Experience.* East Lansing: Michigan State University Press, 1990.

————. *Education in Ethiopia: Prospect and Retrospect.* Ann Arbor: University of Michigan Press, 1979.

Trimingham, John Spencer. *Islam in Ethiopia.* London: Oxford University Press, 1952.

————. *The Sufi Orders in Islam.* London: Oxford University Press, 1971.

Turton, David. "Territorial Organisation and Ages among the Mursi." Pages 95–131 in P.T.W. Baxter and Uri Almagor (eds.), *Age, Generation, and Time: Some Features of East African Age Organizations.* New York: St. Martin's Press, 1978.

United Nations. *Demographic Yearbook, 1989.* New York: 1991.

United States. Department of State. Bureau of Intelligence and Research. *Ethiopia-French Territory of the Afars and Issas Boundary.* (International Boundary Study No. 154.) Washington: February 20, 1976.

————. Department of State. Bureau of Intelligence and Research. *Ethiopia-Kenya Boundary.* (International Boundary Study No. 152.) Washington: October 15, 1975.

————. Department of State. Bureau of Intelligence and Research. *Ethiopia-Somalia Boundary.* (International Boundary Study No. 153.) Washington: November 5, 1975.

(Various issues of the following publications were also used in the preparation of this chapter: *Africa Confidential* [London]; *Africa Events* [London]; *Africa News; Africa Now* [London]; *Africa Report; Africa Research Bulletin* (Political, Social, and Cultural Series) [Exeter, United Kingdom]; *Christian Science Monitor;* Ethiopia, Central Statistical Authority, *Ethiopia: Statistical Abstract* [Addis Ababa]; Ethiopia, Ministry of Education, *Educational Statistics* [Addis Ababa]; *Ethiopian Herald* [Addis Ababa]; Foreign Broadcast Information Service, *Daily Report: Sub-Saharan Africa; Keesing's Contemporary Archives* [London]; *New York Times; Times* [London]; and *Washington Post.*)

Chapter 3

Alemneh Dejene. *Environment, Famine, and Politics in Ethiopia: A View from the Village.* Boulder, Colorado: Rienner, 1990.

————. *Peasants, Agrarian Socialism, and Rural Development in Ethiopia.* Boulder, Colorado: Westview Press, 1987.

Alemseged Tesfai. *Communal Land Ownership in Northern Ethiopia and Its Implications for Government Development Politics.* Madison: Land Tenure Center, University of Wisconsin, 1973.

Assefa Bequele and Eshetu Chole. *A Profile of the Ethiopian Economy*. Addis Ababa: Oxford University Press, 1969.

Assefa Kuru. "The Environmental Impact of Agriculture in Ethiopia," *Environmental Conservation* [Lausanne], 5, No. 3, Autumn 1978, 213–21.

Baker, J. "Developments in Ethiopia's Road System," *Geography* [Sheffield, United Kingdom], 59, No. 263, April 1974, 150–54.

Barinov, M. "Socialist Ethiopia Moves Confidently Ahead," *International Affairs* [Moscow], November 1980, 22–28.

Berhanu Abegaz. "A Brief Note on Recent Ethiopian Economic Statistics," *Northeast African Studies,* 8, No. 1, 1986, 31–34.

Blase, Melvin G., and Marcus L. Winter. *Assessment of Ethiopian Agricultural Sector*. Addis Ababa: n. pub., December 1973.

Bondestam, Lars. "Notes on Multinational Corporations in Ethiopia," *African Review* [Dar es Salaam], 5, No. 4, 1975, 535–49.

———. "People and Capitalism in the North Eastern Lowlands of Ethiopia," *Journal of Modern African Studies* [London], 12, No. 3, September 1974, 432–39.

Bottomley, Anthony. "Garment Making in a Low-Wage Nation: The Case of Ethiopia," *Economic Bulletin for Africa,* 11, No. 1, 1975, 1–11.

Brietzke, Paul. "Land Reform in Revolutionary Ethiopia," *Journal of Modern African Studies* [London], 14, No. 4, December 1976, 637–60.

Bringing Africa Together: The Story of Ethiopian Airlines. Addis Ababa: Ethiopian Airlines, 1988.

Burley, Dexter. "The Despised Weavers of Addis Ababa." Pages 145–49 in Robert L. Hess (ed.), *Proceedings of the Fifth International Conference on Ethiopian Studies*. Chicago: University of Illinois at Chicago Circle, 1979.

Cassiers, Anne. "Handicrafts and Technical Innovation in Ethiopia," *Cultures* [Paris], 2, No. 3, 1975, 103–18.

Clark, Ronald J. "The Ethiopian Land Reform: Scope, Accomplishments, and Future Objectives," *Land Reform, Land Settlement, and Cooperatives* [Rome], No. 2, 1975, 65–68.

Clay, Jason W., Sandra Steingraber, and Peter Niggli. *The Spoils of Famine: Ethiopian Famine Policy and Peasant Agriculture*. Cambridge: Cultural Survival, 1988.

Cohen, John M. "Ethiopia after Haile Selassie: The Government Land Factor," *African Affairs* [London], 72, No. 289, October 1973, 365–82.

———. *Integrated Rural Development: The Ethiopian Experience and the Debate*. Uppsala: Scandinavian Institute of African Studies, 1987.

———. "Rural Change in Ethiopia: The Chilalo Agricultural Development Unit," *Economic Development and Cultural Change,* 22, No. 4, July 1974, 580–614.

Cohen, John M., and Peter H. Koehn. "Rural and Urban Land Reform in Ethiopia," *African Law Studies,* No. 14, 1977, 3–61.

Cohen, John M., and Dov Weintraub. *Land and Peasants in Imperial Ethiopia: The Social Background to a Revolution.* Assen, Netherlands: Van Gorcum, 1975.

Cohen, John M., J.W. Mellor, and Arthur A. Goldsmith. "Rural Development Issues Following Ethiopia's Land Reform," *Africa Today,* 23, No. 2, 1976, 7–28.

Daniel Teferra. "The Lack of Development in Ethiopia," *Northeast African Studies,* 6, Nos. 1–2, 1984, 13–22.

Dessalegn Rahmato. *Agrarian Reform in Ethiopia.* Trenton: Red Sea Press, 1985.

———. *Famine and Survival Strategies: A Case Study from Northeast Ethiopia.* Addis Ababa: Institute of Development Research, Addis Ababa University, 1987.

Disney, Richard. "Some Measures of Rural Income Distribution in Ethiopia," *Development and Change* [The Hague], 7, 1976, 35–44.

Dunning, Harrison C. "Land Reform in Ethiopia: A Case Study in Non-Development," *UCLA Law Review,* 18, No. 2, December 1970, 271–307.

Ethiopia. Central Statistical Authority. *Results on Area, Production, and Yield of Major Crops.* (Bulletin No. 74.) Addis Ababa: 1989.

———. Central Statistical Authority. *Time Series Data on Area, Production, and Yield of Major Crops, 1979–80/1985–86.* (Bulletin No. 56.) Addis Ababa: October 1987.

———. Ministry of Agriculture. Planning and Programming Department. *Area, Production, and Yield of Major Crops.* Addis Ababa: July 1979.

Ethiopian Revolution Information Center. *Ethiopia in Revolution.* Addis Ababa: July 1977.

"Foreign Economic Relations and Our Path of Development," *Meskerem* [Addis Ababa], 3, No. 12, March 1982, 88–104.

Getahun Amare. "Agricultural Systems in Ethiopia," *Agricultural Systems* [Barking, United Kingdom], 3, October 1978, 281–93.

Ghose, Ajit Kumar. "Transforming Feudal Agriculture: Agrarian Change in Ethiopia since 1974," *Journal of Development Studies* [London], 22, No. 1, October 1985, 127–49.

Gilkes, Patrick. *The Dying Lion: Feudalism and Modernization in Ethiopia.* New York: St. Martin's Press, 1975.

Gill, Gerard J. "Bottlenecks in a Single-Cropping System in Chilalo, Ethiopia: The Acceptance and Relevance of Improved Farming Equipment," *World Development* [Oxford], 5, Nos. 9–10, 1977, 867–78.

Gill, Gerard J. (ed.). *Reading on the Ethiopian Economy.* Addis Ababa: Institute of Development Research, Haile Selassie I University, November 1974.

Gill, Peter. *A Year in the Death of Africa.* London: Paladin Grafton Books, 1986.

Griffin, Keith, and Roger Hay. "Problems of Agricultural Development in Socialist Ethiopia: An Overview and a Suggested Strategy," *Journal of Peasant Studies* [London], 13, No. 1, October 1985, 37–66.

Gyenge, Zoltán. *Ethiopia on the Road of Non-Capitalist Development.* (Studies on Developing Countries, No. 90.) Budapest: Institute for World Economics, Hungarian Academy of Sciences, 1976.

Haile Yesus Abegaz. *The Organization of State Farms in Ethiopia after the Land Reform of 1975: Planning, Realization, Potential, and Problems.* (Socioeconomic Studies on Rural Development, No. 46.) Saarbrücken: Breitenbach, 1982.

Harbeson, John W., and Paul H. Brietzke (eds.). "Rural Development in Ethiopia," *Rural Africana,* No. 28, Fall 1975, 1–155.

Henze, Paul B. *Ethiopia: Crisis of a Marxist Economy.* Santa Monica, California: Rand, 1989.

———. *Ethiopia's Economic Prospects for the 1990s.* Santa Monica, California: Rand, 1989.

Hess, Robert L. (ed.). *Proceedings of the Fifth International Conference on Ethiopian Studies.* Chicago: University of Illinois at Chicago Circle, 1979.

Holmberg, Johan. *Grain Marketing and Land Reform in Ethiopia.* (Research Report No. 41.) Uppsala: Scandinavian Institute of African Studies, 1977.

Imperial Ethiopian Government and Swedish International Development Authority. Evaluation Team. *Final Report on the Appraisal of CADU and EPID.* n. pl.: May 1974.

Kidane Mengisteab. *Ethiopia: Failure of Land Reform and Agriculture Crisis.* New York: Greenwood Press, 1990.

Koehn, Peter. "Ethiopia: Famine, Food Production, and Changes in the Legal Order," *African Studies Review,* 22, No. 1, April 1979, 51–71.

Legum, Colin, and Bill Lee. *The Horn of Africa in Continuing Crisis.* New York: Africana, 1979.

M. Fisseha-Tsion. "A Short Review of the Ethiopian Income Tax System," *Bulletin of International Fiscal Documentation* [Amsterdam], 34, No. 1, January 1980, 4–16.

McBain, N.S. "Developing Country Product Choice: Footwear in Ethiopia," *World Development* [Oxford], 5, Nos. 9–10, 1977, 829–38.

McCann, James. *From Poverty to Famine in Northeast Ethiopia: A Rural History, 1900–1935.* Philadelphia: University of Pennsylvania Press, 1987.

Makin, M.J., et al. *Development Prospects in the Southern Rift Valley, Ethiopia.* Surbiton, United Kingdom: Land Resources Division, Ministry of Overseas Development, 1975.

Manig, Winfried. *Socio-Economic Conditions of Peasant Holdings in Ethiopia.* Saarbrücken: Verlag der SSIP-Schriften, 1976.

Markakis, John. *Ethiopia: Anatomy of a Traditional Polity.* New York: Oxford University Press, 1974.

Markie, John. "Some Recent Developments Affecting Agricultural Cooperatives, Marketing, and Credit in Ethiopia," *Land Reform, Land Settlement, and Cooperatives* [Rome], No. 1, 1975, 54–61.

Mesfin Wolde-Mariam. *An Atlas of Ethiopia.* Addis Ababa: n. pub., 1970.

_____. *An Introductory Geography of Ethiopia.* Addis Ababa: Haile Selassie I University, 1972.

Mulatu Wubneh. *A Spatial Analysis of Urban-Industrial Development in Ethiopia.* Syracuse: Maxwell School of Citizenship and Public Affairs, University of Syracuse, 1982.

Mulatu Wubneh and Yohannis Abate. *Ethiopia: Transition and Development in the Horn of Africa.* Boulder, Colorado: Westview Press, 1988.

Nair, K.N.N.S. *Ethiopia: Economic Analysis of Land Use.* Rome: Food and Agriculture Organization of the United Nations, 1986.

National Bank of Ethiopia. *Annual Report, 1987–88.* Addis Ababa: 1988.

Newcombe, Kenneth. *An Economic Justification for Rural Afforestation: The Case of Ethiopia.* Washington: World Bank, 1984.

Ottaway, Marina. "Land Reform in Ethiopia, 1974–1977," *African Studies Review,* 20, No. 3, December 1977, 79–90.

_____. "Social Classes and Corporate Interests in the Ethiopian Revolution," *Journal of Modern African Studies* [London], 14, No. 3, September 1976, 469–86.

Ottaway, Marina (ed.). *The Political Economy of Ethiopia.* New York: Praeger, 1990.

Ottaway, Marina, and David Ottaway. *Ethiopia: Empire in Revolution.* New York: Africana, 1978.

Pankhurst, Richard K. *Economic History of Ethiopia, 1800–1935.* Addis Ababa: Haile Selassie I University Press, 1968.

Pausewang, Siegfried. "Land, Market, and Rural Society (Rural Ethiopia, 1840–1976)." Pages 701–12 in Robert L. Hess (ed.), *Proceedings of the Fifth International Conference on Ethiopian Studies.* Chicago: University of Illinois at Chicago Circle, 1979.

_____. *Peasants, Land, and Society: A Social History of Land Reform in Ethiopia.* Munich: Ifo-Institut für Wirtschaftsforschung, 1983.

"Reconstruction of the Economy," *Yekatit* [Addis Ababa], 8, No. 1, September 1984, 15–19.

Royal Swedish Embassy. *Ethio-Swedish Development Co-Operation.* Addis Ababa: March 1976.

Sadler, Peter G. *Regional Development in Ethiopia.* (Bangor Occasional Papers in Economics, No. 8.) Bangor: University of Wales Press, 1976.

Schulz, Manfred. *Organizing Extension Services in Ethiopia Before and After Revolution.* Saarbrücken: Verlag der SSIP-Schriften, 1976.

Seleshi Sisaye. "Agricultural Systems in Ethiopia: A Review Article," *Agricultural Systems* [Barking, United Kingdom], 5, 1980, 29–38.

"Spotlight on Ethiopia," *Africa: An International Business, Economic and Political Magazine* [London], No. 21, May 1973, 73–82.

Stahl, Michael. *New Seeds in Old Soil: A Study of the Land Reform Process in Western Wollega, Ethiopia, 1975–76.* (Research Report No. 40.) Uppsala: Scandinavian Institute of African Studies, 1977.

Teketel Haile-Mariam. "The Impact of Coffee on the Economy of Ethiopia." Pages 117–34 in Scott R. Pearson et al. (eds.), *Commodity, Exports, and African Economic Development.* Lexington, Massachusetts: Lexington Books, 1974.

Teshome Mulat. "The Revenue Effectiveness of the Ethiopian Coffee Export Taxation," *Public Finance* [The Hague], 34, No. 3, 1979, 375–83.

United States. Agency for International Development. Food and Agricultural Division. *Ethiopia: A Review of the Agricultural Sector.* Washington: GPO, 1970.

_____. Department of Agriculture. *A Survey of Agriculture in Ethiopia.* Washington: GPO, 1969.

Wood, A.P. "Rural Development and National Integration in Ethiopia," *African Affairs* [London], 82, No. 329, 1983, 509–39.

World Bank. *Economic Memorandum on Ethiopia.* Washington: 1981.

_____. *Ethiopia: An Export Action Program.* Washington: 1986.

_____. *Ethiopia: Forestry Project.* Washington: 1986.

_____. *Ethiopia: Industrial Sector Review.* Washington: 1985.

_____. *Ethiopia: Policy Agenda for Economic Revival.* Washington: 1989.

_____. *Ethiopia: Recent Economic Developments and Prospects for Recovery and Growth.* Washington: 1987.

(Various issues of the following publications were also used in the preparation of this chapter: *Africa Contemporary Record; Africa Events* [London]; *African Business* [London]; *Africa Research Bulletin* (Economic, Financial, and Technical Series) [Exeter, United Kingdom]; Economist Intelligence Unit, *Country Profile: Uganda, Ethiopia, Somalia, Djibouti* [London]; Ethiopia, Central Statistical Authority, *Annual Survey of Manufacturing Industries* [Addis Ababa], *Area, Production, and Yield of Major Crops: Estimates* [Addis Ababa], and *Ethiopia: Statistical Abstract* [Addis Ababa]; *Ethiopian Herald* [Addis Ababa]; Foreign Broadcast Information Service, *Daily Report: Sub-Saharan Africa;* National Bank of Ethiopia, *Annual Report* and *Quarterly Bulletin* [Addis Ababa]; and *New African* [London].)

Chapter 4

Andargachew Tiruneh. *The Ethiopian Revolution, 1974–87: A Transformation from an Aristocratic to a Totalitarian Autocracy.* Cambridge: Cambridge Unitversity Press, 1993.

Babile Tola. *To Kill a Generation: The Red Terror in Ethiopia.* Washington: Free Ethiopia Press, 1989.

Beauchamp, Kay. *Ethiopia: An African Giant Awakens.* London: Liberation, 1983.

Bereket Habte Selassie. *Conflict and Intervention in the Horn of Africa.* London: Monthly Review Press, 1980.

_____. "Political Leadership in Crisis: The Ethiopian Case," *Horn of Africa,* 3, No. 1, January–March 1980, 3–13.

Brietzke, Paul H. "Law, Revolution, and the Ethiopian Peasant," *Rural Africana,* No. 28, Fall 1975, 7–37.

Chaliland, Gérard. "The Horn of Africa's Dilemma," *Foreign Policy,* No. 10, Spring 1978, 116–31.

Clapham, Christopher S. *Transformation and Continuity in Revolutionary Ethiopia.* Cambridge: Cambridge University Press, 1988.

Cohen, John M., and Nils-Ivar Isaksson. *Villagization in the Arsi Region of Ethiopia.* Uppsala: Swedish University of Agricultural Sciences, 1987.

Cohen, John M., and Peter H. Koehn. *Ethiopian Provincial and Municipal Government: Imperial Patterns and Postrevolutionary Changes.* (Committee on Northeast African Studies, Ethiopian Series, Monograph No. 9.) East Lansing: African Studies Center, Michigan State University, 1980.

David, Steven. "Realignment in the Horn: The Soviet Advantage," *International Security*, 4, No. 2, Fall 1979, 69–90.

Dawit Wolde Giorgis. *Red Tears: War, Famine, and Revolution in Ethiopia*. Trenton: Red Sea Press, 1989.

Dessalegn Rahmato. *Agrarian Reform in Ethiopia*. Uppsala: Scandinavian Institute of African Studies, 1984.

Erlich, Haggai. *Ethiopia and the Challenge of Independence*. Boulder, Colorado: Rienner, 1986.

"Ethiopia: Five Years Later," *Africa* [London], No. 97, September 1979, 29–33.

"Ethiopia: Revolutions in the Revolution," *Africa* [London], No. 92, April 1979, 42–43.

Ethiopian Revolution Information Center. *The Ethiopian Revolution and the Problem in Eritrea*. Addis Ababa: July 1977.

Firebrace, James, with Stuart Holland. *Never Kneel Down: Drought, Development, and Liberation in Eritrea*. Trenton: Red Sea Press, 1985.

Fitzgerald, James F. "Gunboat Diplomacy and the Horn," *Horn of Africa*, 2, No. 2, April–June 1979, 49–54.

Hall, Marilyn Ann. "The Ethiopian Revolution: Group Interaction and Civil-Military Relations." (Ph.D. dissertation.) Washington: George Washington University, 1977.

Halliday, Fred, and Maxine Molyneux. *The Ethiopian Revolution*. London: Verso, 1981.

Harbeson, John W. "Ethiopia and the Horn of Africa," *Northeast African Studies*, 1, No. 1, 1979, 27–40.

_____. *The Ethiopian Transformation: The Quest for the Post-Imperial State*. Boulder, Colorado: Westview Press, 1988.

_____. "Revolution and Rural Development in Ethiopia," *Rural Africana*, No. 28, Fall 1975, 1–7.

_____. "Socialism, Traditions, and Revolutionary Politics in Contemporary Ethiopia," *Canadian Journal of African Studies* [Ottawa], 11, No. 2, 1977, 217–35.

_____. "Socialist Politics in Revolutionary Ethiopia." Pages 345–417 in Carl G. Rosberg and Thomas M. Callaghy (eds.), *Socialism in Sub-Saharan Africa: A New Assessment*. Berkeley: Institute of International Studies, University of California, 1979.

Henze, Paul B. *Communist Ethiopia: Is It Succeeding?* Santa Monica, California: Rand, 1985.

_____. *Ethiopia in 1990: The Revolution Unraveling*. (Rand Paper No. P-7707.) Santa Monica, California: Rand, 1991.

_____. *The Ethiopian Revolution: Mythology and History*. Santa Monica, California: Rand, 1989.

Jansson, Kurt. *The Ethiopian Famine*. London: Zed Books, 1987.

Jordan Gebre-Medhin. *Peasants and Nationalism in Eritrea.* Trenton: Red Sea Press, 1989.

Kaplan, Robert D. *Surrender or Starve: The Wars Behind the Famine.* Boulder, Colorado: Westview Press, 1988.

Katz, Donald R. "Children's Revolution: A Bloodbath in Ethiopia," *Horn of Africa,* 1, No. 3, July–September 1978, 3–11.

Keller, Edmond J. "The Ethiopian Revolution at the Crossroads," *Current History,* 83, March 1984, 117–21.

_____. *Revolutionary Ethiopia: From Empire to People's Republic.* Bloomington: Indiana University Press, 1988.

_____. "State, Party, and Revolution in Ethiopia," *African Studies Review,* 28, No. 1, March 1986, 1–17.

Keller, Edmond J., and Donald Rothchild (eds.). *Afro-Marxist Regimes: Ideology and Public Policy.* Boulder, Colorado: Rienner, 1987.

Koehn, Peter. "Ethiopia: Famine, Food Production, and Changes in the Legal Order," *African Studies Review,* 22, No. 1, April 1979, 51–71.

Korn, David A. *Ethiopia, the United States, and the Soviet Union.* Carbondale: Southern Illinois University Press, 1986.

Lefort, Rene. *Ethiopia: An Heretical Revolution?* London: Zed Press, 1983.

Legum, Colin. "Ethiopia in Turmoil," *New African* [London], 262, July 1989, 9–14.

Legum, Colin, and Bill Lee. *The Horn of Africa in Continuing Crisis.* New York: Africana, 1979.

Makinda, Samuel. *Superpower Diplomacy in the Horn of Africa.* London: Croom Helm, 1987.

Markakis, John. *Class and Revolution in Ethiopia.* Trenton: Red Sea Press, 1986.

_____. "Garrison Socialism: The Case of Ethiopia," *MERIP Reports, No. 79,* 9, No. 5, June 1979, 3–17.

_____. *National and Class Conflict in the Horn of Africa.* Cambridge: Cambridge University Press, 1987.

_____. "Nationalities and the State in Ethiopia," *Third World Quarterly* [London], 10, No. 4, October 1989, 118–47.

Markakis, John, and Nega Ayele. *Class and Revolution in Ethiopia.* Nottingham, United Kingdom: Spokesman Books, 1978.

Matatu, Godwin. "Ethiopia's Finest Hour," *Africa* [London], No. 79, March 1978, 17–20, 25–26.

Mekasha Getachew. "An Inside View of the Ethiopian Revolution," *Munger Africana Library Notes,* No. 39, July 1977, 3–39.

Mulatu Wubneh and Yohannis Abate. *Ethiopia: Transition and Development in the Horn of Africa.* Boulder, Colorado: Westview Press, 1988.

Ethiopia: A Country Study

Okbazghi Yohannes. *Eritrea: A Pawn in World Politics.* Gainesville: University of Florida Press, 1991.

Ottaway, David. "Africa: U.S. Policy Eclipse," *Foreign Affairs (Special Edition, America and the World, 1979)*, 58, No. 3, 1980, 637–58.

Ottaway, Marina. "Democracy and New Democracy: The Ideological Debate in the Ethiopian Revolution," *African Studies Review,* 21, No. 1, April 1978, 19–31.

_____. "Land Reform and Peasant Associations: A Preliminary Analysis," *Rural Africana,* No. 28, Fall 1975, 39–54.

_____. *Soviet and American Influence in the Horn of Africa.* New York: Praeger, 1982.

Ottaway, Marina (ed.). *The Political Economy of Ethiopia.* New York: Praeger, 1990.

Ottaway, Marina, and David Ottaway. *Ethiopia: Empire in Revolution.* New York: Africana, 1978.

Parent, Marc. "Ethiopia after the Empire: A Nation Torn Asunder," *International Perspectives* [Ottawa], July–August 1978, 35–42.

Peberdy, Max. *Tigray: Ethiopia's Untold Story.* London: Relief Society of Tigray UK Support Committee, 1985.

Pliny the Middle-Aged (pseud.). "The PMAC: Origins and Structure," Pt. 1, *Ethiopianist Notes,* 2, No. 3, 1978–79, 1–18.

_____. "The PMAC: Origins and Structure," Pt. 2, *Northeast African Studies,* 1, No. 1, 1979, 1–20.

Pool, David. *Eritrea: Africa's Longest War.* London: Anti-Slavery Society, 1982.

Ruiz, Hiram A. *Beyond the Headlines: Refugees in the Horn of Africa.* Washington: U.S. Committee for Refugees, 1988.

Sherman, Richard. "Center-Periphery Relations in Ethiopia," *Horn of Africa,* 2, No. 2, April–June 1979, 36–48.

Singer, Norman J. "Legal Development in Post-Revolutionary Ethiopia," *Horn of Africa,* 1, No. 2, April–June 1978, 21–26.

Spencer, John H. *Ethiopia at Bay: A Personal Account of the Haile Sellassie Years.* Algonac, Michigan: Reference Publications, 1984.

Testfatsion Medhanie. *Eritrea: Dynamics of a National Question.* Amsterdam: Gruner, 1986.

Woodward, Peter. "Ethiopia and the Sudan: The Inter-State Outcome of Domestic Conflict," *Contemporary Review* [London], No. 230, May 1977, 231–34.

Yodfat, Aryeh Y. "The Soviet Union and the Horn of Africa," *Northeast African Studies,* 1, No. 3, 1979–80, 1–17.

(The following publications were also used in the preparation of this chapter: *Africa Confidential* [London]; *Africa Contemporary Record; Africa Events* [London]; *Africa News; Africa Report; Africa*

Research Bulletin (Political, Social, and Cultural Series) [Exeter, United Kingdom]; *Christian Science Monitor; Ethiopian Herald* [Addis Ababa]; Foreign Broadcast Information Service, *Daily Report: Sub-Saharan Africa; Keesing's Contemporary Archives* [London]; *New African* [London]; *New York Times; Times* [London]; and *Washington Post.*)

Chapter 5

Abbati, A.H. *Italy and the Abyssinian War.* London: London General Press, 1936.

Agyeman-Duah, Baffour. "The U.S. and Ethiopia: The Politics of Military Assistance," *Armed Forces and Society,* 12, No. 2, Winter 1986, 287–306.

Amnesty International. *Amnesty International Report, 1977.* London: 1977.

_____. *Ethiopia: Human Rights Violations.* London: 1977.

_____. *Ethiopia: Political Imprisonment.* London: 1989.

_____. *Ethiopia: Political Imprisonment and Torture.* London: 1986.

_____. *Ethiopia: Violation of Rights of Man.* London: 1978.

Asante, S.K.B. *Pan-African Protest: West Africa and the Italo-Ethiopian Crisis, 1934–1941.* London: Longman, 1977.

Babazade, Eduard. "Fraternal Relations: Ten Years of Soviet-Ethiopian Treaty of Friendship," *Soviet Military Review* [Moscow], 11, November 1988, 55–56.

_____. "Strength in Unity: Revitalised Ethiopian Army," *Soviet Military Review* [Moscow], 6, June 1987, 53–54.

Babile Tola. *To Kill a Generation: The Red Terror in Ethiopia.* Washington: Free Ethiopia Press, 1989.

Badoglio, Pietro. *The War in Abyssinia.* London: Methuen, 1937.

Baissa, Marilyn Hall. "Civil-Military Elite Interaction in the Ethiopian Revolution: The Role of Students." Pages 771–82 in Robert L. Hess (ed.), *Proceedings of the Fifth International Conference on Ethiopian Studies.* Chicago: University of Illinois at Chicago Circle, 1979.

Bates, Darrell. *The Abyssinian Difficulty: The Emperor Theodorus and the Magdala Campaign, 1867–68.* Oxford: Oxford University Press, 1979.

Baynham, Simon, and Richard Snailham. "Ethiopia." Pages 206–11 in John Keegan (ed.), *World Armies.* New York: Facts on File, 1979.

Bekele Mesfin. "Prison Conditions in Ethiopia," *Horn of Africa,* 2, No. 2, April–June 1979, 4–11.

Bell, John B. "Endemic Insurgency and International Order: The Eritrean Experience," *Orbis,* 18, No. 2, 1974, 427–50.

Bereket Habte Selassie. *Conflict and Intervention in the Horn of Africa.* London: Monthly Review Press, 1980.

_____. "Eritrea: A Colonial Question," *Africa Currents* [London], 11, Summer 1978, 28–29.

Berger, Carol. "Eritrea: The Longest War," *Africa Report,* 32, No. 2, 1987, 30–32.

Berhane Woldemichael. "Ethiopian Military in Disarray," *Review of African Political Economy* [Sheffield, United Kingdom], 44, 1989, 60–63.

Berkeley, G.F.H. *The Campaign of Adowa and the Rise of Menelik.* New York: Negro Universities Press, 1969.

Brown, James Ambrose. *The War of a Hundred Days: Springboks in Somalia and Abyssinia, 1940–41.* Johannesburg: Ashanti, 1990.

Campbell, John Franklin. "Rumblings along the Red Sea: The Eritrean Question," *Foreign Affairs,* 48, No. 4, April, 1970, 537–48.

Caulk, Richard A. "Armies as Predators: Soldiers and Peasants in Ethiopia, c. 1850–1935," *International Journal of African Historical Studies,* 1, No. 3, 1978, 475–93.

_____. "The Army and Society in Ethiopia," *Ethiopianist Notes,* 1, No. 3, Spring 1978, 17–24.

Christides, Vassilios. "The Himyarite-Ethiopian War and the Ethiopian Occupation of South Arabia in the Acts of Gregentius (ca. 530 A.D.)," *Annales d'Ethiopie* [Paris], 9, No. 2, 1972, 115–46.

Clapham, Christopher S. "Ethiopia and Somalia." Pages 1–23 in *Conflicts in Africa.* London: International Institute of Strategic Studies, 1972.

_____. "The Ethiopian Coup d'Etat of December 1960," *Journal of Modern African Studies* [London], 6, No. 4, 1968, 495–507.

_____. *Transformation and Continuity in Revolutionary Ethiopia.* Cambridge: Cambridge University Press, 1988.

Clay, Jason W., and Bonnie K. Holcomb. *Politics and the Ethiopian Famine, 1984–1985.* Cambridge: Cultural Survival, 1986.

Cliffe, Lionel, and Basil Davidson. *The Long Struggle of Eritrea for Independence and Constructive Peace.* Trenton: Red Sea Press, 1988.

Cliffe, Lionel, Basil Davidson, and Bereket Habte Selassie (eds.). *Behind the War in Eritrea.* Nottingham, United Kingdom: Spokesman Books, 1980.

Cole, Ernest. *Ethiopia: Political Power and the Military.* Paris: Banque d'information et de documentation de l'océan Indien, 1985.

David, Steven. "Realignment in the Horn: The Soviet Advantage," *International Security*, 4, No. 2, Fall 1979, 69–90.

Dawit Wolde Giorgis. *Red Tears: War, Famine, and Revolution in Ethiopia*. Trenton: Red Sea Press, 1989.

Diamond, Robert A., and David Fouquet. "American Military Aid to Ethiopia and Eritrean Insurgency," *Africa Today*, 19, No. 1, 1972, 37–43.

Dugan, James, and Laurence Lafore. *Days of Emperor and Clown: The Italo-Ethiopian War, 1935–1936*. Garden City, New York: Doubleday, 1973.

Ellingson, Lloyd. "The Origin and Development of the Eritrea Liberation Movement." Pages 613–28 in Robert L. Hess (ed.), *Proceedings of the Fifth International Conference on Ethiopian Studies*. Chicago: University of Illinois at Chicago Circle, 1979.

Enahoro, Peter. "Ethiopia: Army Tightens Grip," *Africa* [London], No. 68, April 1977, 16–18.

_____. "Ethiopia-Sudan-Somalia: War of Nerves," *Africa* [London], No. 66, February 1977, 16–17.

Eritrean Liberation Front. *The Eritrean Revolution*. Beirut: ELF Information Centre, 1977.

_____. *The Struggle of Eritrea*. Damascus: n.d.

Eritrean Relief Association. *Health Service Delivery in Eritrea*. Khartoum: 1983.

Eritreans for Liberation in North America. *Revolution in Eritrea: The Ethiopian Military Dictatorship and Imperialism*. New York: 1975.

Erlich, Haggai. *The Struggle over Eritrea, 1962–1978*. Stanford, California: Hoover Institute, 1982.

Farer, Tom J. *War Clouds on the Horn of Africa: The Widening Storm*. New York: Carnegie Endowment for International Peace, 1979.

Firebrace, James, with Stuart Holland. *Never Kneel Down: Drought, Development, and Liberation in Eritrea*. Trenton: Red Sea Press, 1985.

Fuller, J.F.C. *The First of the League Wars: Its Lessons and Omens*. London: Eyre and Spottiswode, 1936.

Garthoff, Raymond L. *Détente and Confrontation*. Washington: Brookings Institution, 1985.

Glover, Michael. *An Improvised War: The Abyssinian Campaign of 1940–1941*. London: Leo Cooper, 1987.

Gorman, Robert. *Conflict in the Horn of Africa*. New York: Praeger, 1981.

Great Britain. Ministry of Information. *The Abyssinian Campaigns*. London: HMSO, 1942.

Grilz, Almerigo. "Ethiopia Fights a War of Confusion," *Jane's Defence Weekly* [London], April 25, 1987, 762–64.

Haile Semere. "The Roots of the Ethiopia-Eritrea Conflict: The Erosion of the Federal Act," *Journal of Eritrean Studies,* 1, No. 1, 1986, 1–18.

Hall, Marilyn Ann. "The Ethiopian Revolution: Group Interaction and Civil-Military Relations." (Ph.D. dissertation.) Washington: George Washington University, 1977.

Heiden, Lynda. "The Eritrean Struggle," *Monthly Review,* 30, No. 2, 1978, 13–29.

Henze, Paul B. "Arming the Horn, 1960–1980: Military Expenditures, Arms Imports, and Military Aid in Ethiopia, Kenya, Somalia, and Sudan with Statistics on Economic Growth and Government." Pages 637–56 in Sven Rubenson (ed.), *Proceedings of the Seventh International Conference on Ethiopian Studies.* Uppsala: Scandinavian Institute of African Studies, 1984.

_____. *Eritrea: The Dilemmas of Marxism.* Philadelphia: Foreign Policy Research Institute, 1988.

_____. "Eritrea: The Endless War," *Washington Quarterly,* 9, No. 2, Spring 1986, 23–36.

_____. *Mengistu's Ethiopian Marxist State in Terminal Crisis: How Long Can It Survive? What Will Be Its Legacy?* Washington: Rand, 1990.

_____. *Rebels and Separatists in Ethiopia: Regional Resistance to a Marxist Regime.* Santa Monica, California: Rand, 1985.

_____. *Russians and the Horn: Opportunism and the Long View.* Marina del Rey, California: European American Institute for Security Research, 1983.

Johnson, Michael, and Trish Johnson. "Eritrea: The National Question and the Logic of Protracted Struggle," *African Affairs* [London], 80, No. 319, April 1981, 181–95.

Jordan Gebre-Medhin. "Nationalism, Peasant Politics, and the Emergence of a Vanguard Front in Eritrea," *Review of African Political Economy* [Sheffield, United Kingdom], 30, 1984, 48–57.

_____. *Peasants and Nationalism in Eritrea.* Trenton: Red Sea Press, 1989.

Kaplan, Robert D. *Surrender or Starve: The Wars Behind the Famine.* Boulder, Colorado: Westview Press, 1988.

Kaufman, Michael T. "A Reign of War in the Land of Sheba," *New York Times Magazine,* January 8, 1978, 16–19, 22–28, 48–49.

Kinnock, Glenys. *Eritrea: Images of War and Peace.* London: Chatto and Windus, 1988.

Korn, David A. *Ethiopia, the United States, and the Soviet Union.* Carbondale: Southern Illinois University Press, 1986.

Legum, Colin, and Bill Lee. *The Horn of Africa in Continuing Crisis.* New York: Africana, 1979.

Levine, Donald N. "The Military in Ethiopian Politics: Capabilities and Constraints." Pages 5–34 in Henry Bienen (ed.), *The Military Intervenes: Case Studies in Political Development.* New York: Russell Sage Foundation, 1968.

Lobban, Richard. *Eritrean Liberation Front: A Close-Up View.* (Munger Africana Library Notes, No. 13.) Pasadena: Munger Africana Library, 1972.

_____. "The Eritrean War: Issues and Implications," *Canadian Journal of African Studies* [Ottawa], 10, No. 2, 1976, 335–46.

Machida, Robert. *Eritrea: The Struggle for Independence.* Trenton: Red Sea Press, 1987.

Marcus, Harold G. *Ethiopia, Great Britain, and the United States, 1941–1974: The Politics of Empire.* Berkeley: University of California Press, 1983.

Markakis, John. *National and Class Conflict in the Horn of Africa.* Cambridge: Cambridge University Press, 1987.

_____. "Nationalities and the State in Ethiopia," *Third World Quarterly* [London], 10, No. 4, October 1989, 118–47.

Markakis, John, and Nega Ayele. *Class and Revolution in Ethiopia.* Nottingham, United Kingdom: Spokesman Books, 1978.

Markakis, John, and M. Waller (eds.). *Military Marxist Regimes in Africa.* London: Frank Cass, 1986.

"Mengistu Unleashes People's Militia," *Africa* [London], 72, August 1977, 29–30.

Merriam, John G. "Military Rule in Ethiopia," *Current History,* 60–71, No. 421, November 1976, 170–73, 183–84.

Milivojević, Marko. "The Ethiopian Armed Forces," *Armed Forces* [London], 7, March 1988, 134–39.

Mockler, Anthony. *Haile Selassie's War: The Italian-Ethiopian Campaign, 1935–1941.* New York: Oxford University Press, 1984.

Morison, Geoffrey. *Eritrea and the Southern Sudan: Aspects of Some Wider African Problems.* London: Minority Rights Group, 1976.

Myatt, Frederick. *The March to Magdala: The Abyssinian War of 1868.* London: Leo Cooper, 1970.

Orpen, Neil. *South African Forces in World War II: East Africa and Abyssinia.* Cape Town: Purnell, 1968.

Ottaway, Marina. *Soviet and American Influence in the Horn of Africa.* New York: Praeger, 1982.

Ottaway, Marina, and David Ottaway. *Ethiopia: Empire in Revolution.* New York: Africana, 1978.

Pankhurst, Richard K. "The Effects of War in Ethiopian History," *Ethiopia Observer* [London and Addis Ababa], 7, No. 2, 1963, 143–64.

_____. "The Ethiopian Army of Former Times," *Ethiopia Observer* [London and Addis Ababa], 7, No. 2, 1963, 118–43.

_____. "Fire-Arms in Ethiopian History (1800–1935)," *Ethiopia Observer* [London and Addis Ababa], 6, No. 2, 1962, 135–80.

_____. "The History of Fire-Arms in Ethiopia prior to the Nineteenth Century," *Ethiopia Observer* [London and Addis Ababa], 11, No. 3, 1976, 202–25.

_____. *A History of the Ethiopian Army.* Addis Ababa: Artistic Printers, 1967.

_____. "An Inquiry into the Penetration of Fire-Arms into Southern Ethiopia in the 19th Century prior to the Reign of Menelik," *Ethiopia Observer* [London and Addis Ababa], 12, No. 2, 1968, 128–36.

_____. *An Introduction to the History of the Ethiopian Army.* Genbot, Ethiopia: Imperial Ethiopian Air Force, 101st Training Centre, 1959.

Parfitt, Tudor. *Operation Moses: The Untold Story of the Exodus of the Falasha Jews from Ethiopia.* London: Weidenfeld and Nicholson, 1985.

Pateman, Roy. *Eritrea: Even the Stones Are Burning.* Trenton: Red Sea Press, 1990.

_____. "The Eritrean War," *Armed Forces and Society,* 17, No. 1, Fall 1990, 81–98.

_____. "Eritrea's Struggle for Independence," *Current Affairs Bulletin,* 60, No. 11, 1984, 25–31.

Patman, Robert G. *The Soviet Union in the Horn of Africa.* Cambridge: Cambridge University Press, 1990.

Peninou, Jean Louis. *Eritrea: The Guerrillas of the Red Sea.* New York: Eritrean People's Liberation Forces, 1976.

Perham, Margery F. *The Government of Ethiopia.* Evanston: Northwestern University Press, 1969.

Petterson, Donald. "Ethiopia Abandoned? An American Perspective," *International Affairs* [London], 62, No. 4, Autumn 1986, 627–45.

Pool, David. *Eritrea: Africa's Longest War.* London: Anti-Slavery Society, 1982.

Porter, Bruce D. *The USSR in Third World Conflicts.* Cambridge: Cambridge University Press, 1984.

Redden, Kenneth R. *The Legal System of Ethiopia.* Charlottesville, Virginia: Mitchie, 1968.

Rennell, Francis James. *British Military Administration of Occupied Territories in Africa During the Years 1941–1947.* Westport, Connecticut: Greenwood Press, 1970.

Research and Information Centre on Eritrea. *Revolution in Eritrea: Eyewitness Reports.* Rome: 1979.

Schwab, Peter. "Human Rights in Ethiopia," *Journal of Modern African Studies* [London], 14, No. 1, March 1976, 155-60.

Sherman, Richard. *Eritrea: The Unfinished Revolution.* New York: Praeger, 1980.

Singer, Norman J. "Ethiopia: Human Rights, 1948-1978." Pages 663-78 in Robert L. Hess (ed.), *Proceedings of the Fifth International Conference on Ethiopian Studies.* Chicago: University of Illinois at Chicago Circle, 1979.

Sisaye Seleshi. "Human Rights and U.S. Aid to Ethiopia: A Policy Dilemma," *Africa Quarterly* [New Delhi], 18, No. 4, April 1979, 17-30.

Skordiles, Kimon. *Kagnew: The Story of the Ethiopian Fighters in Korea.* Tokyo: Radiopress, 1954.

Spencer, John H. *Ethiopia, the Horn of Africa, and U.S. Policy.* Cambridge, Massachusetts: Institute for Foreign Policy Analysis, 1977.

Tekeste Negash. *No Medicine for the Bite of a White Snake: Notes on Nationalism and Resistance in Eritrea, 1890-1940.* Uppsala: Uppsala University Press, 1987.

Tesfatsion Medhanie. *Eritrea: Dynamics of a National Question.* Amsterdam: Gruner, 1986.

With, Peter. *Politics and Liberation: The Eritrean Struggle, 1961-86.* Aarhus, Denmark: University of Aarhus, 1987.

_____. "The Radicalisation of the Eritrean Liberation Struggle." (Research paper.) Aarhus, Denmark: University of Aarhus, 1987.

Woodward, Peter. "Ethiopia and the Sudan: The Inter-State Outcome of Domestic Conflict," *Contemporary Review* [London], No. 230, May 1977, 231-34.

_____. *War—or Peace—in North-East Africa?* London: Centre for Security and Conflict Studies, 1989.

Yohannis Abate. "Civil-Military Relations in Ethiopia," *Armed Forces and Society,* 10, No. 3, Spring 1984, 380-400.

_____. "The Legacy of Imperial Rule: Military Intervention and the Struggle for Leadership in Ethiopia, 1974-78," *Middle Eastern Studies* [London], January 1983, 28-42.

(Various issues of the following publications were also used in the preparation of this chapter: *Africa Confidential* [London]; *Africa Contemporary Record; Africa Events* [London]; *African Defense Journal* [London]; *Africa Research Bulletin* (Political, Social, and Cultural Series) [Exeter, United Kingdom]; *Christian Science Monitor; Ethiopian*

Herald [Addis Ababa]; Foreign Broadcast Information Service, *Daily Report: Sub-Saharan Africa;* International Institute for Strategic Studies, *The Military Balance* [London] and *Strategic Survey* [London]; *Keesing's Contemporary Archives* [London]; *New African* [London]; *New York Times;* Stockholm International Peace Research Institute, *World Armaments and Disarmament; Third World Reports* [West Sussex, United Kingdom]; *Times* [London]; and *Washington Post.*)

age-set system—A system comprising several named sets (or groups) of men, each of which consists of those initiated in a given period. Each set passes through a series of age-grades, taking on the rights, duties, and activities specific to the grade. In Ethiopia such a system coexists with a generation-set system in some ethnic groups, e.g., the *gada* system (*q.v.*) among the Oromo.

balabat—An Amharic term originally referring to any person with a claim to *rist* (*q.v.*) land by virtue of membership in a cognatic descent group (*q.v.*). Commonly used since the establishment of present-day Ethiopia by Menelik II in the late nineteenth century for those local chiefs and other non-Amhara who were assigned low-level administrative positions among their own people and who were allocated substantial landholdings.

birr (pl., birr; no symbol used)—The Ethiopian monetary unit, composed of 100 cents. Introduced officially in 1976, replacing the Ethiopian dollar at par. Through mid-1991, US$1 equaled 2.07 birr, or 1 birr was worth about US$0.48.

clan—A group whose members are descended in the male line from a putative common male ancestor (patriclan) or in the female line from a putative common female ancestor (matriclan—not reported in Ethiopia). Clans may be divided into subclans organized on the same principle or into lineages (*q.v.*) believed to be linked by descent from a remote common ancestor.

clan-family—Among the Somali, a group of clans (*q.v.*) believed to be linked by descent from a remote common ancestor.

cognatic descent group—A group comprising those persons tracing descent from a common ancestor through both males and females, thereby differing from unilineal descent groups (*q.v.*), such as clans (*q.v.*) and lineages (*q.v.*). This entity is important among the Amhara and the Tigray as the one holding the block of land in which its members claim *rist* (*q.v.*) rights. The group has no other function.

Derg—Formed in June 1974 and composed of a substantial body of young military officers, none above the rank of major, drawn from the main units of the army, air force, navy, and police. The Derg's membership ranged from perhaps 106 to 120 or more. New officers were never admitted, whereas original members were continuously eliminated, especially during the Derg's early years. Its inner workings were almost never disclosed. Known at first as the Coordinating Committee of the Armed

Forces, Police, and Territorial Army, after September 1974
it was known as the Provisional Military Administrative Council
(PMAC), or simply as the Derg (Amharic for "committee"
or "council"), a term derived from Gi'iz and little used before the 1974 revolution. The Derg lasted officially from June
1974 to September 1987, when the People's Democratic Republic of Ethiopia came into being.

descent group—A group having political, economic, or social functions. Formation of the group is based on actual or putative
descent through persons of one sex from a common ancestor
of the same sex, and therefore called unilineal descent groups
(clans or lineages—*q.v.*), or through persons of both sexes from
a common ancestor of either sex (cognatic descent groups—
q.v.).

Ethiopian calendar year—The Ethiopian year consists of 365 days,
divided into twelve months of thirty days each plus one additional month of five days (six in leap years). Ethiopian New
Year's falls on September 11 and ends the following September 10, according to the Gregorian (Western) calendar. From
September 11 to December 31, the Ethiopian year runs seven
years behind the Gregorian year; thereafter, the difference is
eight years. Hence, the Ethiopian year 1983 began on September 11, 1990, according to the Gregorian calendar, and ended
on September 10, 1991. This discrepancy results from differences between the Ethiopian Orthodox Church and the Roman
Catholic Church as to the date of the creation of the world.

Ethiopian fiscal year (EFY)—Based on the Ethiopian calendar year
(*q.v.*). Corresponds to July 8 to July 7, seven years behind the
Gregorian (Western) calendar through December 31, and eight
years behind thereafter.

gada system—An Oromo term used to refer to a system that groups
persons (invariably males) of the same generation (rather than
age) into sets. The sets are ordered hierarchically and assigned
a range of social, military, political, and ritual rights and responsibilities. Generation-set systems are found in varying forms
among the Oromo and other groups, e.g., the Konso and
Sidama.

gross domestic product (GDP)—A measure of the total value of
goods and services produced by a domestic national economy
during a given period, usually one year. Obtained by adding
the value contributed by each sector of the economy in the form
of profits, compensation to employees, and depreciation (consumption of capital). Only domestic production is included,
not income arising from investments and possessions owned

abroad, hence the use of the word "domestic" to distinguish GDP from the gross national product (GNP—*q.v.*). Real GDP is the value of GDP when inflation has been taken into account. In this book, subsistence production is included and consists of the imputed value of production by the farm family for its own use and the imputed rental value of owner-occupied dwellings. In countries lacking sophisticated data-gathering techniques, such as Ethiopia, the total value of GDP is often estimated.

gross national product (GNP)—The total market value of all final goods and services produced by an economy during a year. Obtained by adding the gross domestic product (GDP—*q.v.*) and the income received from abroad by residents and then subtracting payments remitted abroad to nonresidents. Real GNP is the value of GNP when inflation has been taken into account.

gult—A principle of land tenure among the Amhara, Tigray, and, with modifications, elsewhere. Abolished by the military government in 1975. *Gult* rights were rights granted by the emperor or his designated representative either to members of the ruling group as a reward for service or to Ethiopian Orthodox churches or monasteries as endowments. The holder of *gult* rights, often but not always an official, was entitled to collect tribute and demand labor from those on the land over which he held rights. Some of the tribute was kept, and the remainder was passed upward.

International Monetary Fund (IMF)—Established along with the World Bank (*q.v.*) in 1945, the IMF is a specialized agency affiliated with the United Nations that is responsible for stabilizing international exchange rates and payments. The main business of the IMF is the provision of loans to its members (including industrialized and developing countries) when they experience balance of payments difficulties. These loans frequently carry conditions that require substantial internal economic adjustments by the recipients, most of which are developing countries.

kebele—Popular term used to describe a cooperative urban neighborhood association. *Kebeles* were formed after the nationalization of all urban land and rentable dwellings in July 1975. These cooperatives became the counterpart of the peasant associations developed under the military government's Land Reform Proclamation of March 1975. After their introduction, *kebeles* became the basic unit of urban government and served as instruments of sociopolitical control in urban areas.

lineage—A group whose members are descended through males from a common male ancestor (patrilineage) or through females from a common female ancestor (matrilineage—not reported in Ethiopia). Such descent can in principle be traced. Lineages vary in genealogical depth from the ancestor to living generations; the more extensive ones often are internally segmented.

Lomé Convention—A series of agreements between the European Community (EC) and a group of African, Caribbean, and Pacific (ACP) states, mainly former European colonies, that provide duty-free or preferential access to the EC market for almost all ACP exports. The Stabilization of Export Earnings (Stabex) scheme, a mechanism set up by the Lomé Convention, provides for compensation for ACP export earnings lost through fluctuations in the world prices of agricultural commodities. The Lomé Convention also provides for limited EC development aid and investment funds to be disbursed to ACP recipients through the European Development Fund and the European Investment Bank. The Lomé Convention is updated every five years. Lomé I took effect on April 1, 1976; Lomé II, on January 1, 1981; Lomé III, on March 1, 1985; and Lomé IV, on December 15, 1989.

Red Terror—The campaign of terror unleashed by the Derg (*q.v.*) in response to the urban guerrilla warfare—the so-called White Terror—of the Ethiopian People's Revolutionary Party and later of other leftist civilian opponents of the Derg, such as the All-Ethiopia Socialist Movement. Beginning in February 1977, untold thousands of mostly young people were jailed, tortured, and killed before the Red Terror had run its course by early 1978.

rist—A principle of land tenure among the Amhara and, with some variations, among the Tigray. *Rist* rights are land-use rights that any Amhara or Tigray, peasant or noble, can claim by virtue of descent through males and females from the original holder of such rights. Claims must be recognized by the cognatic descent group (*q.v.*). Once held, such rights cannot be withdrawn except in favor of one who presumably holds a better claim or, in extreme cases, by the emperor.

sublineage—A segment of a lineage (*q.v.*) and organized on the same principles.

teff (*eragrostis abyssinica*)—A cereal indigenous to Ethiopia, to which its consumption is almost entirely confined. It is the most widely grown grain in the highlands, where its flour is preferred in

the making of the unleavened bread *injera,* the traditional form
of cereal intake.

World Bank—Informal name used to designate a group of four
affiliated international institutions that provide advice and assistance on long-term finance and policy issues to developing
countries: the International Bank for Reconstruction and Development (IBRD), the International Development Association (IDA), the International Finance Corporation (IFC), and
the Multilateral Investment Guarantee Agency (MIGA). The
IBRD, established in 1945, has as its primary purpose the provision of loans at market-related rates of interest to developing countries at more advanced stages of development. The
IDA, a legally separate loan fund but administered by the staff
of the IBRD, was set up in 1960 to furnish credits to the poorest
developing countries on much easier terms than those of conventional IBRD loans. The IFC, founded in 1956, supplements
the activities of the IBRD through loans and assistance designed
specifically to encourage the growth of productive private enterprises in the less developed countries. The president and certain senior officers of the IBRD hold the same positions in the
IFC. The MIGA, which began operating in June 1988, insures
private foreign investment in developing countries against such
noncommercial risks as expropriation, civil strife, and incon-
vertibility of currency. The four institutions are owned by the
governments of the countries that subscribe their capital. To
participate in the World Bank Group, member states must first
belong to the International Monetary Fund (IMF—*q.v.*).

zemecha—Amharic for "campaign," in the military sense; popular term used to denote the military government's Development Through Cooperation Campaign, which was launched
as part of the initial land reform in 1975. Early implementation included forced mobilization of university and secondary
school students to explain the socialist revolution, including land
reform, to peasants and to improve their traditionally low literacy rate. The term "green" *zemecha* was used to describe the
agricultural aspects of the National Revolutionary Development
Campaign in 1979.

Contributors

LaVerle Berry is a Research Analyst in African Affairs with the Federal Research Division of the Library of Congress.

Edmond J. Keller is Professor of Political Science and Director of the James S. Coleman African Studies Center at the University of California at Los Angeles.

Mulatu Wubneh is Associate Professor of Planning at East Carolina University.

Thomas P. Ofcansky is a Senior African Analyst with the Department of Defense.

John W. Turner is an African Analyst with the Department of Defense.

Yohannis Abate is a Geographer and African Analyst with the Department of Defense.

Index

ELM. *See* Eritrean Liberation Movement
ELPA. *See* Ethiopian Light and Power Authority
EMALEDEH. *See* Union of Ethiopian Marxist-Leninist Organizations
emigration: of educated people, 88
emperor(s): armed forces under, 271; battle under, 271–72; court, 272
Endalkatchew Mekonnen, 52, 54; executed, 56
energy resources, 190–92; imports of, 202; potential, 190; traditional, 192
English: as language of broadcasting, 200
ensete (false banana), 93; cultivation of, 97, 98
environment: damage to, 86
EPDM. *See* Ethiopian People's Democratic Movement
EPLA. *See* Eritrean People's Liberation Army
EPLF. *See* Eritrean People's Liberation Front
EPRA. *See* Ethiopian People's Revolutionary Army
EPRDF. *See* Ethiopian People's Revolutionary Democratic Front
EPRP. *See* Ethiopian People's Revolutionary Party
Era of the Princes. *See* Zemene Mesafint
ERESA. *See* Eritrean Region Electricity Supply Agency
Eritrea, 8, 38, 45, 86; administrative subregions in, 242; annexed by Ethiopia, 5; attempts to secede, 90; constitution referendum in (1987), 216; demands for self-determination, 235, 255; drought in, 89; earthquakes in, 77; etymology of, 36; European attempts to colonize, 4; famine relief in, 230; government defeated in, 64–65; granted autonomy, 65, 102, 223, 242; independence of, xxxiii–xxxiv, 264, 307; as Italian colony, 31, 36, 273; labor union in, 161; land tenure in, 167, 168; martial law in, 240; membership of, in Lomé Convention, xxxiv; membership of, in Organization of African Unity, xxxiv; membership of, in United Nations, xxxiv; Muslims in, 103; population of, xxxvi; postwar disposition of, 46; as province of Ethiopia, 47; requests to annex, 41, 44; schools in, xxxiii, 130, 131; soil erosion in, 166; state of emer-
gency declared in, 242; United Nations plan to join with Ethiopia, 46
Eritrea, Government of, xxxiv
Eritrean Assembly, 46, 47
Eritrean insurgency, xxvi, 5, 46–48, 60–62, 87, 90, 101, 239–44, 269, 297, 301–7; Arab support for, 103; disagreements within, 241; government defeats in, 302–3, 304, 305–6, 307; government victories in, 302, 303; under Haile Selassie, 240; under Mengistu, 240–44; military campaign against, 87, 88, 276; Sudanese support for, 261
Eritrean Liberation Front (ELF), 60, 241, 300; attempts to co-opt, 240; founded, 47, 239–40, 302; goals of, 239; growth of, 47; guerrilla activities of, 240; internal disputes, 240; split of, with Eritrean People's Liberation Front, 243–44, 302; support for, 47, 240; troop strength of, 302
Eritrean Liberation Front-Central Command, 242
Eritrean Liberation Front-Popular Liberation Front, 48, 241
Eritrean Liberation Front-Revolutionary Council 302, 304
Eritrean Liberation Movement (ELM), 241; founded, 239
Eritrean People's Liberation Army (EPLA), 241
Eritrean People's Liberation Front (EPLF), xxvi, 60, 210, 233, 239, 241–44, 280, 301, 302, 307; call by, for recognition of independence, 304; Central Committee, xxxiv, 241; congresses of, 241, 242; cooperation of, with Tigray People's Liberation Front, 60; defeats of, 302, 303; image of, 48; members of, 47, 48, 239; matériel captured by, 303, 306; military assistance by, to Tigray People's Liberation Front, 245, 306; military campaigns against, 302–4; military campaigns of, 238; military training of, 300; organization of, 241; peace talks, 250–52, 263; Political Bureau, 241; relief services attacked by, 89; rift of, with Eritrean Liberation Front groups, 243–44, 302; successes of, xxvii, 89, 197–98, 242, 303, 304, 305–6, 307; support for, 239, 241; territory controlled by, 216; troop strength of, 302, 305

Eritrean Region Electricity Supply Agency (ERESA), 191

Eritrean Relief Association, 89; food convoys of, 89

ESR. *See* Education Sector Review

Ethio-Nippon Mining Share Company, 193

Ethiopia: etymology of, 9

Ethiopia, People's Democratic Republic of (PDRE) (*see also* Derg): 209, 214, 216; collapse of, 263; constitution of, 214, 216–18; Council of Ministers, 220–21; Council of State, 218–19; foreign policy toward Israel, 292; judicial system, 221–22; National Shengo (National Assembly), 218; presidency, 219–20; proclaimed, 65, 216; referendum for, 215–16

Ethiopia-Kenya Border Administration Commission, 259–60

Ethiopian Air Lines (EAL), 198–99, 204; aircraft of, 199; plans to expand, 199; reputation of, 198–99; service to, 198

Ethiopian Democratic Officers' Revolutionary Movement, 308

Ethiopian Democratic Union (EDU), 238–39, 244, 245

Ethiopian Evangelical Church Mekane Yesus, 125–26

Ethiopian Forestry Action Plan (EFAP), 184–85

Ethiopian Herald (newspaper), 253

Ethiopian Insurance Corporation, 155–56

Ethiopian Investment Corporation, 188

Ethiopian Light and Power Authority (ELPA), 191

Ethiopian News Agency, 329

Ethiopian Orthodox Church, 116–20; attempts to reform, 27–28; bishoprics created in, 42–43; Church Council of, 117; community in Jerusalem, 21; conversion of, 93, 94; disestablished, 103, 115–16, 217; doctrinal quarrel of, with Jesuits, 23, 24; doctrine of, 119; education by, 126; emphasis on Judaic roots, 13; Episcopal Synod of, 117; established, 3, 9–10; ethnic groups in, 116; faith and practice, 119–20; fast days, 119, 179; under Haile Selassie, 43, 103; headquarters of, 117; holy days, 119; isolation of, 11, 12; land held by, 31, 108, 167, 168; land tax on, 43; Lij Iyasu excommunicated by, 33;

members of, 96, 98; monastic orders of, 23; organization of, 117–19, 120; patriarch of, 11, 21, 42, 56, 117; percentage of population practicing, 72, 116; reform in, 42; reorganized, 15, 22; rituals of, 119; saint's days, 119; spirits in, 119–20; as state religion, 72, 103, 115, 124

Ethiopian People's Democratic Movement (EPDM), 234, 282, 308; alliance of, with Tigray People's Liberation Front, 246, 252; members of, 246

Ethiopian People's Revolutionary Army (EPRA), 238

Ethiopian People's Revolutionary Democratic Front (EPRDF), 210, 282; formed, 308; goals of, 246; members of, 308; military actions of, 246, 252–53; peace talks with, 263; relations of, with Oromo Liberation Front, 311; role in National Conference, xxvii

Ethiopian People's Revolutionary Party (EPRP), xxxii–xxxiii, 56, 239, 245, 249; agitation by, 58, 236, 238; debate with MEISON, 236; members of, 236; victims of Red Terror, 58–59, 237

Ethiopian Plateau. *See* highlands

Ethiopian Police College, 315, 318

Ethiopian Pulses and Oilseeds Corporation, 177

Ethiopian Road Authority, 194

Ethiopian Workers Commission, 161

Ethiopia Soldiers' Movement, 287

Ethiopia Tikdem, 54, 236

Ethiopia Trade Union (ETU), 161

Ethio-Semitic language family, 91–94

ethnic groups (*see also under individual groups*): diversity in, 105; geographic distribution of, 100–101; marriage between, 100; relations among, 100–105; and religion, 71; in Transitional Government, xxviii: in Workers' Party of Ethiopia, 214

ETU. *See* Ethiopia Trade Union

Europe, Eastern: medical assistance from, 140; military aid from, 238

European Development Fund, 258

European Community (EC): agricultural assistance from, 183; educational assistance from, 135; financial assistance from, xxx, 203, 258; technical assistance from, 194

European Investment Bank, 198

of, 104, 152, 169, 229; use, 165–66
landholdings: by Amhara, 71, 110; by
cognatic descent group, 106; distribution, 107, 108; by Ethiopian Orthodox
Church, 31, 108, 167, 168; individual,
170; by kin group, 106; as marker of
social status, 104, 110; redistribution,
111, 168, 170; by state, 106; taxes, 42,
50, 128; tenancy, 71, 168
landlord class, 104; eliminated, 111
land reform, 145, 163, 166–70; desire for,
51, 110; impact of, 111, 169, 170; opposition to, 58, 169; proposals, 57;
reactions to, 31; women under, 114
Land Reform Proclamation (1975), 57,
170, 224; implementation of, 57; resettlement under, 174; villagization under,
233
land rights system (*see also gult* rights; *rist*
rights), 124; consequences of, 107–8;
established, 31; under imperial government, 106; in south, 107–8; usufruct
rights, 167
land tenure: of Amhara, 106; under imperial government, 35, 166; security of,
170; types of, 167
language policy, 103
languages (*see also under individual languages*), 6–7, 91; distribution of, 91,
103; of radiobroadcasts, 200
Lasta, 8; Aksumite influence in, 12; ethnic groups in, 100; and Zagwe kings,
12–13
law: customary, 123–24, 315, 319; martial, 320; sharia, 122, 319
League of Nations, 5, 37; arms embargo
by, 37; Haile Selassie's speech to,
37–38; membership in, 34, 254
Lebna Dengel, 19, 28; Portuguese military assistance to, 19
legal system, 319–22
Lege Dimbi gold mine, 192
Lencho Letta, 264
Libya, 256; aid from, 294; relations with,
262
literacy, 134–35; classes, 135; among
women, 115
literacy campaign, 72, 134, 229; books
for, 135; languages of, 134; women in,
134
literacy rate, 44, 126, 134
livestock, 7, 98, 146, 147, 165, 180–82,
201; cattle, 7, 181–82; distribution of,

181; economic potential of, 181;
equines, 7, 182; goats, 7, 182; as percentage of gross domestic product, 180;
population, 181; poultry, 182; production, 181; role of, 181; sheep, 182
living standards, 107; in agriculture, 147,
149; urban, 162; under villagization, 85
Lomé Convention, xxxiv, 203
London peace talks, 251, 264
Lowland East Cushitic languages, 95
lowlanders: languages spoken by, 91;
rivalry of, with highlanders, 3
lowlands, 72, 76, 102; climate in, 77; land
reform in, 169; land tenure in, 168; life-
styles in, 79; population density in, 79;
soil types in, 165–66

MAAG. *See* United States Military Assistance Advisory Group
maderia rights, 167–68
Mahdi, Sadiq al, 261
Mahdists, 29
malaria, 165, 168
MALERED. *See* Marxist-Leninist Revolutionary Organization
manufacturing, 111–12, 185–87; capacity utilization of, 186–87; decline in,
150; government involvement in, 188–
89; growth in, 148, 150, 186; of handicrafts, 185; investment in, 188; labor
union in, 161; nationalization in, 149;
as percentage of gross domestic product, 186; production, 186; productivity, 187
Marda Pass. *See* Karamarda Pass
maritime trade: ancient, 8, 10; effect of
Islam on, 11
Markakis, John, 106, 113–14, 116
Marxist-Leninist League of Tigray, 145
Marxist-Leninist Revolutionary Organization (MALERED), 238
Mecha-Tulema, 247
media, 253; censorship of, 329
MEISON. *See* All-Ethiopia Socialist Move-
ment
Mekele: airport, 89; fall of, 48
Mekonnen (*ras*), 32
Meles Zenawi, xxv, xxvi, xxviii, 251, 264
Mendebo Mountains, 76
Menelik II (king, 1889–1913), xxv–xxvi,
4, 25, 27, 28, 91, 101, 194; accession
of, 29, 71; conquest of Harer by, 49;

members of, killed, 245; organized, 244

Tigray people, 4, 25, 71, 91, 101; education of, 126; influences on, 4; landholdings of, 110; Muslim attack on, 4; political power of, 214; religion of, 72, 92, 115, 116; as ruling class, 71; semipastoralists, 48; slaves held by, 34; social organization of, 93

Tigray People's Liberation Front (TPLF), xxvi, 60, 84, 210, 233, 234, 239, 244–45, 280, 282, 301, 307–10; administration, 245; alliance with Ethiopian People's Democratic Movement, 246; Central Committee, 307; congresses of, 307, 308; efforts to form Ethiopian People's Revolutionary Democratic Front, 245–46; formed, 307; goals of, 244; matériel captured by, 309; military assistance by Eritrean People's Liberation Front to, 60, 245, 306, 308; military campaigns of, 238, 252–53, 308; peace talks, 251–52, 308; relief services attacked by, 89; successes of, xxvii, 245; support for, 245; territory controlled by, 216; terrorism by, 308

Tigrinya language, 47, 92, 103; literacy training in, 134

TLO. *See* Tigray Liberation Organization

TPLF. *See* Tigray People's Liberation Front

trade (*see also* balance of trade; exports; imports): ancient, 146; attempts to improve, 200; by barter, 201; deficit, 202; under Derg, 58; growth in, 148; under Haile Selassie, 47; impact of, 26; investment in, 153; as occupation, 104, 111, 112; as percentage of gross domestic product, 200; routes, 146

traders, 112, 146; fate of, 112–13; role of, 112–13

Trade Unions' Organization Proclamation (1982), 161

Transitional Government of Ethiopia (TGE), xxv; established, xxvii, 264; problems faced by, xxvii, xxxvi, 265

transportation, 193–99; airports, 193, 198–99; development of, 193; growth in, 148; under Haile Selassie, 47; imports of, 202; labor union in, 161; loans for, 193; railroads, 193, 194–97; roads, 34, 39, 146, 193–94, 197; under villagization, 86

Travels to Discover the Source of the Nile (Bruce), 24

Treaty of Wuchale (1889), 31; annuled, 32

Tripartite Treaty, 32, 256, 261

UNDP. *See* United Nations Development Programme

unemployment, 83, 145, 157–60

UNFPA. *See* United Nations Population Fund

UNHCR. *See* United Nations High Commissioner for Refugees

UNICEF. *See* United Nations Children's Fund

Union of Ethiopian Marxist-Leninist Organizations (EMALEDEH), 59, 238

United Nations, 46, 73, 89, 304; Eritrea in, xxxiv; membership in, 43, 254; peacekeeping forces, 274; plan to associate Eritrea and Ethiopia, 46

United Nations, Food and Agriculture Organization of the (FAO): agricultural assistance from, 183; technical assistance from, 147

United Nations Children's Fund (UNICEF): medical assistance from, 136, 140

United Nations Development Programme (UNDP), 192; agricultural assistance from, 183

United Nations High Commissioner for Refugees (UNHCR), 89; repatriation program, 90

United Nations Population Fund (UNFPA): medical assistance from, 140

United Nations Universal Declaration of Human Rights, xxviii

United States, 305; aid from, 253; compensation to, after nationalization, 189; economic assistance from, 43; economic mission, 40; exports to, 201; imports from, 202; Kagnew station leased by, 255, 256, 291–92; matériel acquired from, 238, 279, 292–93; military assistance from, 43, 274, 292; military training in, 274, 292; refusal by, to recognize Italian occupation, 38; relations with, 238, 253, 254, 256, 293–94; relief from, 230; technical assistance from, 147, 194

United States Agency for International

Published Country Studies

(Area Handbook Series)

550-65	Afghanistan		550-87	Greece
550-98	Albania		550-78	Guatemala
550-44	Algeria		550-174	Guinea
550-59	Angola		550-82	Guyana and Belize
550-73	Argentina		550-151	Honduras
550-169	Australia		550-165	Hungary
550-176	Austria		550-21	India
550-175	Bangladesh		550-154	Indian Ocean
550-170	Belgium		550-39	Indonesia
550-66	Bolivia		550-68	Iran
550-20	Brazil		550-31	Iraq
550-168	Bulgaria		550-25	Israel
550-61	Burma		550-182	Italy
550-50	Cambodia		550-30	Japan
550-166	Cameroon		550-34	Jordan
550-159	Chad		550-56	Kenya
550-77	Chile		550-81	Korea, North
550-60	China		550-41	Korea, South
550-26	Colombia		550-58	Laos
550-33	Commonwealth Caribbean, Islands of the		550-24	Lebanon
550-91	Congo		550-38	Liberia
550-90	Costa Rica		550-85	Libya
550-69	Côte d'Ivoire (Ivory Coast)		550-172	Malawi
550-152	Cuba		550-45	Malaysia
550-22	Cyprus		550-161	Mauritania
550-158	Czechoslovakia		550-79	Mexico
550-36	Dominican Republic and Haiti		550-76	Mongolia
550-52	Ecuador		550-49	Morocco
550-43	Egypt		550-64	Mozambique
550-150	El Salvador		550-35	Nepal and Bhutan
550-28	Ethiopia		550-88˙	Nicaragua
550-167	Finland		550-157	Nigeria
550-155	Germany, East		550-94	Oceania
550-173	Germany, Fed. Rep. of		550-48	Pakistan
550-153	Ghana		550-46	Panama

411